Our dear friend John writes with both head and heart! Like his other books—and like himself—this one is full of both thought and passion. Anne and I laughed for joy, devouring the great truths of *Desiring God*, but the new edition, including a chapter on suffering, is right. It's true. It's important.

Give it thinking time when you read.

Ray Ortlund
Renewal Ministries

Arresting, stirring, never faltering, paragraph by paragraph, this book is one of the most serious but yet engaging books I have ever known. Here is the pastors' pastor not necessarily speaking to pastors but demonstrating dynamically how penetrating a pastor can be.

Dr. Ralph D. Winter
William Carey International University

The charged spirituality and often shimmering prose of my well-thumbed copy of *Desiring God* is all here in the new edition along with a joyous, lyrical new chapter on suffering.

R. Kent Hughes
Pastor, College Church
Wheaton, Illinois

DESIRING
GOD

MEDITATIONS OF A CHRISTIAN HEDONIST

JOHN PIPER

MULTNOMAH BOOKS
SISTERS, OREGON

DESIRING GOD
published by Multnomah Publishers, Inc.
© 1986 by Multnomah Press
© 1996 by John Piper

International Standard Book Number: 0-88070-869-7
(previously 0-88070-169-2, hdbk.)
(previously 0-88070-221-4, pbk.)

Edited by Steve Halliday
Cover design by David Carlson
Cover illustration by Tivador Boté

Unless otherwise indicated, Scripture references are the
author's own translation.

Printed in the United States of America

For information:
MULTNOMAH PUBLISHERS, INC.
POST OFFICE BOX 1720
SISTERS, OREGON 97759

00 01 02 03 04 - 29 28 27 26 25

To
WILLIAM SOLOMON HOTTLE PIPER
my Father
in whom
I have seen
the holiness and happiness
of God

CONTENTS

What's New in the 1996 Edition? 8

Preface 9

Introduction: How I Became a Christian Hedonist 14

What Is Christian Hedonism? Lessons from a Love Poem 25

   1. The Happiness of God: Foundation for Christian Hedonism .32
   2. Conversion: The Creation of a Christian Hedonist 52
   3. Worship: The Feast of Christian Hedonism 72
   4. Love: The Labor of Christian Hedonism 96
   5. Scripture: Kindling for Christian Hedonism 122
   6. Prayer: The Power of Christian Hedonism 136
   7. Money: The Currency of Christian Hedonism 158
   8. Marriage: A Matrix for Christian Hedonism 174
   9. Missions: The Battle Cry of Christian Hedonism 188
  10. Suffering: The Sacrifice of Christian Hedonism 212

Epilogue: Why I Have Written This Book: Seven Reasons 239

Appendix 1: The Goal of God in Redemptive History 255
Appendix 2: Is the Bible a Reliable Guide to Lasting Joy? 267
Appendix 3: What Does It Mean to Love Your Neighbor
              as You Love Yourself? 277
Appendix 4: Why Call It Christian Hedonism? 287

A Note on the Resources of Desiring God Ministries 291
Other Books by the Author 292

Notes 293
Scripture Index 309
Subject and Person Index 321
Study Guide 332

WHAT'S NEW IN THE 1996 EDITION?

A new preface
"After Ten Years"

An expansion of the Introduction
"How I Became a Christian Hedonist"

"What Is Christian Hedonism?
Lessons from a Love Poem"

An updating of Chapter 9
"Missions: The Battle Cry of Christian Hedonism"

An additional chapter
Chapter 10
"Suffering: The Sacrifice of Christian Hedonism"

An expansion of Appendix 3
"What Does It Mean to Love Your Neighbor
As You Love Yourself?"

A Study Guide prepared by the author

Some wording improvements and new subheadings

PREFACE

After Ten Years

There is a kind of happiness and wonder that makes you serious.

C. S. LEWIS
The Last Battle

This is a serious book about being happy in God. It's about happiness because that is what our Creator commands: "Delight yourself in the LORD!" (Psalm 37:4). And it is serious because, as Jeremy Taylor said, "God threatens terrible things if we will not be happy."

The heroes of this book are *Jesus Christ*, who "endured the cross for the joy that was set before him"; and *St. Paul*, who was "sorrowful, yet always rejoicing"; and *Jonathan Edwards*, who deeply savored the sweet sovereignty of God; and *C. S. Lewis*, who knew that the Lord "finds our desires not too strong but too weak"; and all the *missionaries* who have left everything for Christ and in the end said, "I never made a sacrifice."

Ten years have passed since *Desiring God* first appeared in 1986. The significance of a truth is judged in part by whether over time it has transforming power in very different circumstances. What about the message of this book? Since its first edition, my body has passed from a forty-year-old body to a fifty-year-old body. My marriage advanced from a seventeen-year-old marriage to a twenty-seven-year-old marriage. My pastorate at Bethlehem Baptist Church has persisted from six years to sixteen years. My oldest son grew from thirteen and single to twenty-three and married. Noël and I have nurtured Karsten and Benjamin through the teen years, and Abraham and Barnabas are still in this critical season. In 1986 there were no daughters. Now there is Talitha Ruth whom we adopted at nine weeks in December of 1995.

In other words, things have changed. But not my commitment to the message of this book. It is my life. That *God is most glorified in me when I am most satisfied in him* continues to be a spectacular and precious truth in my mind and heart. It has sustained me into my second half-century, and I do not doubt that it will carry me Home.

I have added a chapter called "Suffering: The Sacrifice of Christian

Hedonism." The reason is partly biographical and partly biblical. These have been the hardest ten years of my life. Marriage, we found, passes through deep water as husband and wife pass through mid-life. We made it. But we will not diminish the disquietude of those years. We were not ashamed to seek help. God was good to us. Entering our sixth decade of life and nearing our fourth decade of marriage, the roots are deep, the covenant is solid, the love is sweet.

The other "marriage" in my life (with Bethlehem Baptist Church) has been a mingling of heartache and happiness. Can so much devastation and so much delight coexist in one community and one soul? It can. The apostle Paul spoke a deep pastoral reality when he said that he was "sorrowful yet *always rejoicing*" (2 Corinthians 6:10). There is a joy without which pastors cannot profit their people (Hebrews 13:17). Mercifully, God has preserved it for sixteen years. And the truth of this book has been his means.

Biblically, I have not been able to escape, in these passing years, that we are appointed to suffer for the advancement of the kingdom in the world. "Through many tribulations *we* must enter the kingdom of God" (Acts 14:22). Yes, but also *others* must enter the kingdom through our tribulations. "I endure all things for the sake of the elect, that they also may obtain salvation" (2 Timothy 2:10). "I am being poured out as a drink offering on the sacrifice and service of your faith" (Philippians 2:17). "If we are afflicted, it is for your comfort and salvation" (2 Corinthians 1:6). It is clearer to me now than ever, as the third millennium dawns, that the final saving purposes of God in the world will triumph only through the loving sacrifice of suffering. Chapter ten has been added as a passionate call to join Jesus on the Calvary road of suffering "for the joy set before us."

During these ten years since *Desiring God* first appeared, I have been testing it and applying its vision in connection with more of life and ministry and God. The more I do so, the more persuaded I become that it will bear all the weight I can put on it. You can test this for yourself in relation to the nature of God (*The Pleasures of God*, Multnomah, 1991), the gravity and gladness of preaching (*The Supremacy of God in Preaching*, Baker Book House, 1990), the power and the price of world evangelization (*Let the Nations Be Glad*, Baker Book House, 1993), the meaning of marriage (*What's the Difference*, Crossway Books, 1990), and the daily battle against unbelief and sin (*The Purifying Power of Living by Faith in FUTURE GRACE*, Multnomah, 1995). The more I reflect and the more I minister and the more I live, the more all-encompassing the vision of God and life in this book becomes.

The older I get, the more I am persuaded that Nehemiah 8:10 is crucial for living and dying well: "The joy of the LORD is your strength." As we grow older and our bodies weaken, we must learn from the Puritan pastor

Richard Baxter (who died in 1691) to redouble our efforts to find strength from spiritual joy, not natural supplies. He prayed, "May the Living God, who is the portion and rest of the saints, make these our carnal minds so spiritual, and our earthly hearts so heavenly, that loving him, and *delighting in him, may be the work of our lives.*"[1] When delighting in God is the work of our lives (which I call Christian Hedonism), there will be an inner strength for ministries of love to the very end.

J. I. Packer described this dynamic in Baxter's life: "The hope of heaven brought him joy, and joy brought him strength, and so, like John Calvin before him and George Whitefield after him (two verifiable examples) and, it would seem, like the apostle Paul himself . . . he was astoundingly enabled to labor on, accomplishing more than would ever have seemed possible in a single lifetime."[2]

But not only does the pursuit of joy in God give strength to endure, it is the key to breaking the power of sin on our way to heaven. Matthew Henry, another Puritan pastor, put it like this: "The joy of the Lord will arm us against the assaults of our spiritual enemies and put our mouths out of taste for those pleasures with which the tempter baits his hooks."[3]

This is the great business of life — to "put our mouths out of taste for those pleasures with which the tempter baits his hooks." I know of no other way to triumph over sin long-term, than to gain a distaste for it, because of a superior satisfaction in God. One of the reasons this book is still "working" after ten years is that this truth simply does not and will not change. God remains gloriously all-satisfying. The human heart remains a ceaseless factory of desires. Sin remains powerfully and suicidally appealing. The battle remains: where will we drink? Where will we feast? Therefore *Desiring God* is still a compelling and urgent message. Feast on God.

If God would be pleased to use this book to raise up one man or woman in this line of serious and happy saints who inspired it, then those of us who have rejoiced in the making of this book would delight all the more in the display of God's grace. It has indeed been a happy work. And my heart overflows to many:

Steve Halliday believed in the book from the beginning and has remained a faithful friend and helpful editor also through this new edition.

As with almost everything I do, the influence of Daniel P. Fuller pervades. It was his class in 1968 where the seminal discoveries were made. I would be happy to view this book as explanation and application of his great book, *Unity of the Bible* (Zondervan, 1992). He remains a treasured friend and mentor.

My friend and assistant and partner in the Great Work, Jon Bloom, made the revision possible in the middle of our busy Advent season of 1995. Jon's passion for the supremacy of God expressed in this book is a precious source of energy for me.

Carol Steinbach, after ten years, was willing again to tackle the indexes and give the book her sharp editorial attention. I do not take the constancy of friendships for granted.

Chapter eight is the tribute to my wife Noël. Our first seventeen years together coincided exactly with the gestation period of this book. Our next ten years together have proved its value. The marriage has been indeed a "Matrix for Christian Hedonism." The mystery of mirroring Christ and the Church is an inexhaustible spring of hope that finding our joy in the holy joy of the other will make us one until the departure of death.

The church that I love and serve heard the chapters in sermon form back in 1983. Of course the length has quadrupled since then. And they have not begrudged my labor! The partnership that I enjoy with the elders and staff is priceless. There is a chapter yet to be written. It is called "The Camaraderie of Christian Hedonism." May the Spirit himself write it on the tablets of our hearts!

Finally, a word to my father. The dedicatory words I wrote in 1986 are still true ten years later. I can recall mother laughing so hard at the dinner table that the tears ran down her face. She was a very happy woman. But especially when you came home on Monday. You had been gone two weeks. Or sometimes three or four. She would glow on Monday mornings when you were coming home.

At the dinner table that night (these were the happiest of times in my memory) we would hear about the victories of the gospel. Surely it is more exciting to be the son of an evangelist than to sit with knights and warriors. As I grew older I saw more of the wounds. But you spared me most of that until I was mature enough to "count it all joy." Holy and happy were those Monday meals. O, how good it was to have you home!

John Piper
December, 1995
Minneapolis, Minnesota

"It was good of you to look for Quentin."

"Good!" she exclaimed. "Good! O Anthony!"

"Well, so it was," he answered. "Or good in you. How accurate one has to be with one's prepositions! Perhaps it was a preposition wrong that set the whole world awry."

CHARLES WILLIAMS
The Place of the Lion

INTRODUCTION

How I Became a Christian Hedonist

You might turn the world on its head by changing one word in your creed. The old tradition says,

The chief end of man is to glorify God
AND
enjoy him forever.

"And"? Like ham *and* eggs? Sometimes you glorify God *and* sometimes you enjoy him? Sometimes he gets glory, sometimes you get joy? "And" is a very ambiguous word! Just how do these two things relate to each other?

Evidently the old theologians didn't think they were talking about two things. They said "chief end," not "chief ends." Glorifying God and enjoying him were one end in their minds, not two. How can that be?

That's what this book is about.

Not that I care too much about the intention of seventeenth century theologians. But I care tremendously about the intention of God in Scripture. What does God have to say about the chief end of man? How does God teach us to give him glory? Does he command us to enjoy him? If so, how does this quest for joy in God relate to everything else? Yes, everything! "Whether you eat or drink, or whatever you do, do all to the glory of God."

The overriding concern of this book is that in all of life God be glorified the way he himself has appointed. To that end this book aims to persuade you that

The chief end of man is to glorify God
BY
enjoying him forever.

How I Became a Christian Hedonist

When I was in college I had a vague, pervasive notion that if I did something good because it would make me happy, I would ruin its goodness.

I figured that the goodness of my moral action was lessened to the degree I was motivated by a desire for my own pleasure. At the time, buying ice cream in the Student Center just for pleasure didn't bother me, because

the moral consequences of that action seemed so insignificant. But to be motivated by a desire for happiness or pleasure when I volunteered for Christian
service or went to church — that seemed selfish, utilitarian, mercenary.

This was a problem for me because I couldn't formulate an alternative
motive that worked. I found in me an overwhelming longing to be happy, a
tremendously powerful impulse to seek pleasure, yet at every point of moral
decision I said to myself that this impulse should have no influence.

One of the most frustrating areas was that of worship and praise. My
vague notion that the higher the activity, the less there must be of self-interest
in it, caused me to think of worship almost solely in terms of duty. And that
cuts the heart out of it.

Then I was converted to Christian Hedonism. In a matter of weeks I
came to see that it is unbiblical and arrogant to try to worship God for any
other reason than the pleasure to be had in him. (Don't miss those last two
words: IN HIM. Not his gifts, but him. Not ourselves, but him.) Let me
describe the series of insights that made me into a Christian Hedonist. Along
the way I hope it will become clear what I mean by this strange phrase.

1. During my first quarter in seminary I was introduced to the argument for Christian Hedonism and one of its great exponents, Blaise Pascal. He
wrote,

> All men seek happiness. This is without exception. Whatever
> different means they employ, they all tend to this end. The cause
> of some going to war, and of others avoiding it, is the same
> desire in both, attended with different views. The will never
> takes the least step but to this object. This is the motive of every
> action of every man, even of those who hang themselves.[1]

This statement so fit with my own deep longings and all that I had ever
seen in others that I accepted it and have never found any reason to doubt it.
What struck me especially here was that Pascal was not making any moral
judgment about this fact. As far as he was concerned, seeking one's own happiness is not a sin; it is a simple given in human nature. It is a law of the
human heart as gravity is a law of nature.

This thought made great sense to me and opened the way for the second discovery.

2. I had grown to love the work of C. S. Lewis in college. But not until
later did I buy the sermon called "The Weight of Glory." The first page of that
sermon is one of the most influential pages of literature I have ever read. It
goes like this:

If you asked twenty good men today what they thought the highest of the virtues, nineteen of them would reply, Unselfishness. But if you asked almost any of the great Christians of old he would have replied, Love. You see what has happened? A negative term has been substituted for a positive, and this is of more than philological importance. The negative ideal of Unselfishness carries with it the suggestion not primarily of securing good things for others, but of going without them ourselves, as if our abstinence and not their happiness was the important point. I do not think this is the Christian virtue of Love. The New Testament has lots to say about self-denial, but not about self-denial as an end in itself. We are told to deny ourselves and to take up our crosses in order that we may follow Christ; and nearly every description of what we shall ultimately find if we do so contains an appeal to desire.

If there lurks in most modern minds the notion that to desire our own good and earnestly to hope for the enjoyment of it is a bad thing, I submit that this notion has crept in from Kant and the Stoics and is no part of the Christian faith. Indeed, if we consider the unblushing promises of reward and the staggering nature of the rewards promised in the Gospels, it would seem that Our Lord finds our desires not too strong, but too weak. We are half-hearted creatures, fooling about with drink and sex and ambition when infinite joy is offered us, like an ignorant child who wants to go on making mud pies in a slum because he cannot imagine what is meant by the offer of a holiday at the sea. We are far too easily pleased.[2]

There it was in black and white, and to my mind it was totally compelling: It is not a bad thing to desire our own good. In fact the great problem of human beings is that they are far too easily pleased. They don't seek pleasure with nearly the resolve and passion that they should. And so they settle for mud pies of appetite instead of infinite delight.

I had never in my whole life heard any Christian, let alone a Christian of Lewis's stature, say that all of us not only seek (as Pascal said) but also *ought* to seek our own happiness. Our mistake lies not in the intensity of our desire for happiness, but in the weakness of it.

3. The third insight was there in Lewis's sermon, but Pascal made it more explicit. He goes on to say,

> There once was in man a true happiness of which now remain
> to him only the mark and empty trace, which he in vain tries to
> fill from all his surroundings, seeking from things absent the
> help he does not obtain in things present. But these are all in-
> adequate, because the infinite abyss can only be filled by an
> infinite and immutable object, that is to say, only by God Him-
> self.[3]

As I look back on it now it seems so patently obvious, I don't know
how I could have missed it. All those years I had been trying to suppress my
tremendous longing for happiness so I could honestly praise God out of some
"higher," less selfish motive. But now it started to dawn that this persistent and
undeniable yearning for happiness was not to be suppressed but was to be
glutted — on God! The growing conviction that praise should be motivated
solely by this happiness we find in God seemed less and less strange.

4. The next insight came again from C. S. Lewis, but this time from his
Reflections on the Psalms. Chapter nine of this book bears the modest title "A
Word about Praise." In my experience it has been *the* word about praise —
the best word on the nature of praise I have ever read.

Lewis says that as he was beginning to believe in God, a great stumbling block was the presence of demands scattered through the Psalms that
he should praise God. He did not see the point in all this; besides, it seemed
to picture God as craving "for our worship like a vain woman who wants
compliments." He goes on to show why he was wrong.

> But the most obvious fact about praise — whether of God or
> anything — strangely escaped me. I thought of it in terms of
> compliment, approval, or the giving of honor. I had never
> noticed that all enjoyment spontaneously overflows into
> praise. . . . The world rings with praise — lovers praising their
> mistresses, readers their favorite poet, walkers praising the
> countryside, players praising their favorite game. . . .
>
> My whole, more general, difficulty about the praise of God
> depended on my absurdly denying to us, as regards the
> supremely Valuable, what we delight to do, what indeed we
> can't help doing, about everything else we value.
>
> I think we delight to praise what we enjoy because the praise
> not merely expresses but completes the enjoyment; it is its
> appointed consummation.[4]

This was the capstone of my emerging hedonism. Praising God, the highest calling of humanity and our eternal vocation, did not involve the renunciation but rather the consummation of the joy I so desired. My old effort to achieve worship with no self-interest in it proved to be a contradiction in terms. Worship is basically adoration, and we adore only what delights us. There is no such thing as sad adoration or unhappy praise.

We have a name for those who try to praise when they have no pleasure in the object. We call them hypocrites. This fact — that praise means consummate pleasure and that the highest end of man is to drink deeply of this pleasure — was perhaps the most liberating discovery I ever made.

5. Then I turned to the Psalms for myself and found the language of hedonism everywhere. The quest for pleasure was not even optional, but commanded: "Delight yourself in the LORD; and he will give you the desires of your heart" (Psalm 37:4).

The psalmists sought to do just this: "As the deer pants for the water brooks, so my soul pants for thee, O God, for the living God" (Psalm 42:1-2). "My soul thirsts for thee, my flesh yearns for thee, in a dry and weary land where there is no water" (Psalm 63:1). The motif of thirsting has its satisfying counterpart when the psalmist says that men "drink their fill of the abundance of thy house; and thou dost give them to drink of the river of thy delights" (Psalm 36:8).

I found that the goodness of God, the very foundation of worship, is not a thing you pay your respects to out of some kind of disinterested reverence. No, it is something to be enjoyed: "O taste and see that the LORD is good" (Psalm 34:8). "How sweet are thy words to my taste! Yes, sweeter than honey to my mouth!" (Psalm 119:103).

As C. S. Lewis says, God in the Psalms is the "all-satisfying Object." His people adore him unashamedly for the "exceeding joy" they find in him (Psalm 43:4). He is the source of complete and unending pleasure: "In thy presence is fullness of joy; in thy right hand there are pleasures forever" (Psalm 16:11).

That is the short story of how I became a Christian Hedonist. I have now been brooding over these things for some twenty-eight years, and there has emerged a philosophy that touches virtually every area of my life. I believe it is biblical, that it fulfills the deepest longings of my heart, and that it honors the God and Father of our Lord Jesus Christ. I have written this book to commend these things to all who will listen.

Many objections rise in people's minds when they hear me talk this way. I hope the book will answer the most serious problems. But perhaps I can defuse some of the resistance in advance by making a few brief clarifying comments.

First, Christian Hedonism as I use the term does not mean God becomes a means to help us get worldly pleasures. The pleasure Christian Hedonism seeks is the pleasure which is in God himself. He is the end of our search, not the means to some further end. Our exceeding joy is he, the Lord — not the streets of gold, or the reunion with relatives or any blessing of heaven. Christian Hedonism does not reduce God to a key that unlocks a treasure chest of gold and silver. Rather it seeks to transform the heart so that "the Almighty will be your gold and choice silver to you" (Job 22:25).

Second, Christian Hedonism does not make a god out of pleasure. It says that one has already made a god out of whatever he finds most pleasure in. The goal of Christian Hedonism is to find most pleasure in the one and only God and thus avoid the sin of covetousness, that is, idolatry (Colossians 3:5).

Third, Christian Hedonism does not put us above God when we seek him out of self-interest. A patient is not greater than his physician. I will say more about this in chapter three.

Fourth, Christian Hedonism is not a "general theory of *moral justification*."[5] In other words, nowhere do I say: an act is right because it brings pleasure. My aim is not to decide what is right by using joy as a moral criterion. My aim is to own up to the amazing, and largely neglected, fact that some dimension of joy is a moral duty in all true worship and all virtuous acts. I do not say that loving God is good because it brings joy. I say God commands that we find joy in loving God. ("Delight yourself in the LORD," Psalm 37:4). I do not say that loving people is good because it brings joy. I say that God commands that we find joy in loving people. ("Let the one who shows mercy do so with cheerfulness," Romans 12:8.)[6]

I do not come to the Bible with a hedonistic theory of moral justification. On the contrary, I find in the Bible a divine command to be a pleasure-seeker — that is, to forsake the two-bit, low-yield, short-term, never-satisfying, person-destroying, God-belittling pleasures of the world and to sell everything "with joy" (Matthew 13:44) in order to have the kingdom of heaven, and thus "enter into the joy of your Master" (Matthew 25:21,23). In short, I am a Christian Hedonist not for any philosophical, or theoretical reason, but because God commands it (though he doesn't command that you use these labels!).

Fifth, I do not say that the relationship between love and happiness is this: "true happiness requires love." This is an oversimplification that misses the crucial and defining point. The distinguishing feature of Christian

Hedonism is not that pleasure-seeking demands virtue, but that virtue consists essentially, though not only, in pleasure-seeking.

The reason I come to this conclusion is that I am operating here not as a philosophical hedonist but as a biblical theologian and pastor who must come to terms with divine commands

- to "*love* mercy" (not just *do* it, Micah 6:8),

- to "show mercy *with cheerfulness*" (Romans 12:8),

- to suffer loss "*with joy*" in the service of prisoners (Hebrews 10:34),

- to be a *cheerful* giver (2 Corinthians 9:7),

- to make *our joy* the joy of others (2 Corinthians 2:3),

- to tend the flock of God willingly and *eagerly* (1 Peter 5:2), and

- to keep watch over souls "*with joy*" (Hebrews 13:17).

When you reflect long and hard on such amazing commands, the moral implications are stunning. Christian Hedonism attempts to take these divine commands with blood-earnestness. The upshot is piercing and radically life-changing: the pursuit of true virtue includes the pursuit of the joy, because joy is an essential component of true virtue. This is vastly different from saying, let's all be good because it will make us happy.

Sixth, Christian Hedonism is not a distortion of historic Reformed Catechisms of faith. This was one of the criticisms of Richard Mouw in his book, *The God Who Commands.* He said,

> Piper might be able to alter the first answer in the Westminster Shorter Catechism — so that glorifying *and* enjoying God becomes glorifying *by* enjoying the deity — to suit his hedonistic purposes, but it is a little more difficult to alter the opening lines of the Heidelberg Catechism: That I, with body and soul, both in life and death, am not my own but belong unto my faithful Savior Jesus Christ.[7]

The remarkable thing about the beginning of the Heidelberg Catechism is not that I can't change it for hedonistic purposes but that I don't have to. It already places the entire catechism under the human longing for

21

"comfort." Question One: "What is your only *comfort* in life and death?" The pressing question for critics of Christian Hedonism is: Why did the original framers of the four-hundred-year-old catechism structure all 129 questions so that they are an exposition of the question, "What is my only comfort"?

Even more remarkable is to see the concern with "happiness" emerge explicitly in the second question of the catechism, which provides the outline for the rest of the catechism. The second question is, "How many things are necessary for thee to know, that thou in this *comfort (Troste)* mayest live and die *happily (seliglich)*?" Thus the overarching theme of "comfort" is clarified as essentially "happiness," and the entire catechism is an answer to the concern for how to live and die *happily*.

The answer to this the second question of the catechism is: "Three things: First, the greatness of my sin and misery. Second, how I am redeemed from all my sins and misery. Third, how I am to be thankful to God for such redemption." Then the rest of the entire catechism is divided into three sections to deal with these three things: "The First Part: Of Man's Misery" (questions 3-11), "The Second Part: Of Man's Redemption" (questions 12-85), and "The Third Part: Of Thankfulness" (questions 86-129). What this means is that *the entire Heidelberg Catechism is written to answer the question: What must I know to live happily?*

I am puzzled that anyone would think that Christian Hedonism needs to "alter the opening lines to the Heidelberg Catechism." The fact is, the entire catechism is structured the way Christian Hedonism would structure it. Therefore Christian Hedonism does not distort the historic Reformed Catechisms. Both the Westminster Catechism and the Heidelberg Catechism begin with a concern for man's enjoyment of God, or his quest to "live and die happily." I have no desire to be doctrinally novel. I am glad that the Heidelberg Catechism was written four hundred years ago.

Toward a Definition of Christian Hedonism

Fresh ways of looking at the world (even when they are centuries old) do not lend themselves to simple definitions. A whole book is needed so people can begin to catch on. Quick and superficial judgments will almost certainly be wrong. Beware of conjecture about what lies in the pages of this book! The surmise that here we have another spinoff from modern man's enslavement to the centrality of himself will be very wide of the mark. Ah, what surprises lie ahead!

For many the term "Christian Hedonism" will be new. Therefore I have included Appendix 4: "Why Call It Christian Hedonism?" If this is a strange or troubling term, you may want to read those pages before plunging into the main chapters.

I would prefer to reserve a definition of Christian Hedonism until the end of the book, when misunderstandings would have been swept away. A writer often wishes his first sentence could be read in light of his last, and vice versa! But, alas, one must begin somewhere. So I offer the following advance definition in hope that it will be interpreted sympathetically in light of the rest of the book.

Christian Hedonism is a philosophy of life built on the following five convictions:

1. The longing to be happy is a universal human experience, and it is good, not sinful.

2. We should never try to deny or resist our longing to be happy, as though it were a bad impulse. Instead we should seek to intensify this longing and nourish it with whatever will provide the deepest and most enduring satisfaction.

3. The deepest and most enduring happiness is found only in God. Not from God, but in God.

4. The happiness we find in God reaches its consummation when it is shared with others in the manifold ways of love.

5. To the extent we try to abandon the pursuit of our own pleasure, we fail to honor God and love people. Or, to put it positively: the pursuit of pleasure is a necessary part of all worship and virtue. That is,

The chief end of man is to glorify God
BY
enjoying him forever.

The Root of the Matter

This book will be predominantly a meditation on Scripture. It will be expository rather than speculative. If I cannot show that Christian Hedonism comes from the Bible, I do not expect anyone to be interested, let alone persuaded. There are a thousand man-made philosophies of life. If this is another, let it pass. There is only one rock: the Word of God. Only one thing ultimately matters: glorifying God the way he has appointed. That is why I am a Christian Hedonist. That is why I wrote this book.

WHAT IS CHRISTIAN HEDONISM?

Lessons from a Love Poem

Then Let Me All My Pleasures Tell *

For Noël on Our Twenty-Fifth Wedding Anniversary

> I am a Christian Hedonist,
> Though there are some who still insist
> I drop the name. I do not bid,
> Much less demand, nor ever did,
> That anyone should follow me
> In wearing this strange badge. The key
> To joy and holiness is not
> In names or labels we have got,
> Nor is much truth or love assured
> By ranks and titles we've secured.
>
> But I do bid that all will come
> And drink with me the waters from
> The Fountain of delights whom we
> Call Christ, and that we taste and see
> The fullness of his Father's joy
> Which none can make and none destroy;
> And that we take from his right hand
> Eternal pleasures he has planned
> For those who love him more than all
> His gifts, and gladly leave the small
> And fleeting pleasures of this earth
> To savor God and all he's worth.
> I bid the world and everyone
> Who's ever wanted joy to shun
> With me the ease of wealth, the chill

And rush of faithless sex, the thrill
Of fame, and pride of power and all
The thousand pleasures that enthrall
Us with their godless innocence,
And pay instead a tribute whence
All great and lasting pleasures come:
To show by our pursuit that from
His holy Fountain flows far more
Than earth could ever hold in store.

Call this whatever name you may,
It is the truth. Shall God display
His great all-satisfying grace
In joyless souls? And shall he trace
The outlines of his majesty
In hearts that neither taste nor see
Enough in him to comprehend
That here their quest is at an end?
No, God has made another way
To put his glory on display.

His goodness shines with brightest rays
When we delight in all his ways.
His glory overflows its rim
When we are satisfied in him.
His radiance will fill the earth
When people revel in his worth.
The beauty of God's holy fire
Burns brightest in the heart's desire.

Now I have taught these things for years
And found that sometimes there are fears
In people's minds that even though
This may be true, it is not so
For them, or seems remote without
Some story they might think about
Relating to their daily life.
And so I tell one of my wife.

I say, Suppose it is today
Our anniversary, let's say
The twenty-fifth; and I go down
To some small florist in our town
And buy a rose for every year
That we've been married, then appear
At our front door and ring the bell.
And then you picture that Noël
Swings wide the door and hears me say,
As I hold out the rose display,
"A happy anniversary,
Noël!" And she responds, "For me?
O these are beautiful, but why
So much?" To which I then reply,
While holding up my hand, "You know
It is my duty that I go
Each year and buy what husbands ought
To buy. I think I was well-taught
That there are proper ways to do
These things, and I just wanted you
To know that I am duty bound
And that my character is sound."

Well, at this point the story stops
Because they laugh, unless it flops,
And then they groan. But I inquire,
"What's wrong with duty? I admire
This virtue very much. Do you
Not think that she was given due
Esteem, the object of such high
And noble sentiments, that I
Should do what's right because it's right
And not debase myself with vain delight?
It's odd that you should laugh, or groan,
When so much rectitude was shown.
Is not she honored as the goal
Of all my work and self-control
By which all hedonistic thirst
Was held in check with no outburst?"

A question that I hope will show,
"The answer, folks, is clearly NO."
How then shall she be honored more
If not by duty at the door?
To answer this let us return
Now to the scene and watch and learn.
Noël swings wide the door. I say,
While holding out the rose display,
"A happy anniversary,
Noël!" And she responds, "For me?
O these are beautiful, but why
So much?" To which I then reply,
"It makes me glad to bring you things.
In fact, Noël, I think it brings
Me more delight to spend this night
With you than anyone I might.
Why don't you go dress for a date
And tell the boys it may be late.
I cannot think of any way
I'd rather celebrate this day
Than satisfying my desire
With one that I so much admire."

Now at this point the story ends,
And I inquire to all my friends,
Does anyone believe that my
Good wife would angrily reply,
"You selfish Christian Hedonist!
Next thing you know I might be kissed!
It makes YOU glad to bring me things,
And I suppose your heart has wings
And next you'll prob'ly write some verse
About how nothing could be worse
For YOU than living without me.
Well, I suggest that you should see
What duty, discipline and strain
Might make you do for me through pain."

And then I ask, why doesn't she
Take such offense when I'm so free

To say, "It gladdens me to be
With you"? The answer all can see:
The pleasure that I take in her
Is but the measure I infer
That all her excellence conveys.
Delight does not indict but praise.
It fills the longing of my life
And glorifies my worthy wife.

I am a Christian Hedonist
Because I know that if I kissed
My wife simply because it's right
And not because it's my delight
It would not honor her so well.
With pleasures I will praise Noël,
And I will magnify my wife
By making her my joy in life.

Her courage and her fearless grace
To venture well beyond the place
That people call secure, and serve
With even pace and steady nerve
The cause of Christ, and call it good
To live in Phillips neighborhood;

Her patience, living with five men,
Named Karsten, Aber, Barna, Ben
And me, who lack a woman's touch,
And maybe make a bit too much
At mealtime of a cat's defeat,
And which roadkills are fit to eat;

Her sharp and penetrating mind
That is not duped, but sees behind
The ruse of advertising schemes
And is not snared with empty dreams
But pierces through the polished skin
And sees the heart and truth within;

Her love for simple home decor,
To keep things modest during war,
To put no stock in passing fads,
Nor be intrigued with glossy ads,
Nor join the mass through empty miles
Spent chasing ever-changing styles;

Her busy hands that never harm
But fill a room with Christmas charm
Or Lenten lights, that make and mend,
And weave an afghan for a friend;

Her faith and hope and love to Christ,
Her confidence that it sufficed
For him to die and rise again
To cover all our daily sin;

Her fortitude and strength of will
When warmth and tenderness were nil,
To do what one must do, and walk
In hope when we could scarcely talk.

Her kneeling by me at the bed
Day in day out as we have spread
Our hope and pain before the throne
And watched God make his mercies known.

Her grace that never holds a grudge
And lays aside the right to judge,
Nor seeks revenge or to revile
But always comes to reconcile;

Her faithfulness and love to me
As solid as a great oak tree,
But soft to touch and warm to feel,
I've often called it velvet steel.

These are a few of my delights,
A taste of what my wife ignites.

Now answer this: when I indulge
My joy this way does it divulge
A miserly, self-centered bent
Or that my wife is excellent?
My answer does in this consist:
I am a Christian Hedonist.
When I would magnify Noël
Then let me all my pleasures tell.

I hope that now it is not odd
When I say, So it is with God.
His goodness shines with brightest rays
When we delight in all his ways.
His glory overflows its rim
When we are satisfied in him.
His radiance will fill the earth
When people revel in his worth.
The beauty of God's holy fire
Burns brightest in the heart's desire.

And if you ask, Do my delights
In wife and sons compete with heights
Of joy in God, here's what I've seen,
A prayer from wise Saint Augustine:

Our love for Thee is far too small
Who love another thing at all,
Unless from Thy pure hand we take
And love it for Thine own name's sake.

So may the Spirit's holy flame
Ignite in us for God's great name
A holy passion, zeal and fire
That magnify him with desire.
I hail him as my joy in life,
And take from his pure hand my wife.

                                    Johnny

Our God is in the heavens;
he does whatever he pleases.

There has been a wonderful alteration in my mind,
in respect to the doctrine of God's sovereignty. . . . The doctrine
has very often appeared exceeding pleasant, bright and sweet.
Absolute sovereignty is what I love to ascribe to God.

JONATHAN EDWARDS

The climax of God's happiness
is the delight he takes
in the echoes of his excellence
in the praises of his people.

JOHN PIPER

CHAPTER 1

THE HAPPINESS OF GOD

Foundation for Christian Hedonism

The ultimate ground of Christian Hedonism is the fact that God is uppermost in his own affections:

> *The chief end of God is to glorify God*
> *and enjoy himself forever.*

The reason this may sound strange is that we are more accustomed to think about our duty than God's design. And when we do ask about God's design we are too prone to describe it with ourselves at the center of God's affections. We may say, for example, his design is to redeem the world. Or to save sinners. Or to restore creation. Or the like.

But God's saving designs are penultimate, not ultimate. Redemption, salvation, and restoration are not God's ultimate goal. These he performs for the sake of something greater: namely, the enjoyment he has in glorifying himself. The bedrock foundation of Christian Hedonism is not God's allegiance to us, but to himself.

If God were not infinitely devoted to the preservation, display, and enjoyment of his own glory, we could have no hope of finding happiness in him. But if he does in fact employ all his sovereign power and infinite wisdom to maximize the enjoyment of his own glory, then we have a foundation on which to stand and rejoice.

I know this is perplexing at first glance. So I will try to take it apart a piece at a time, and then put it back together at the end of the chapter.

God's Sovereignty: The Foundation of His Happiness and Ours

> God has the right and power and wisdom to do whatever makes him happy.
>
> None of his purposes can be frustrated.
>
> Therefore, he is never deficient or needy. He is never gloomy or discouraged.
>
> He is always full and overflowingly energetic for the sake of his people who seek their happiness in him.

"Our God is in the heavens; he does whatever he pleases" (Psalm 115:3). The implication of this text is that God has the right and power to do whatever makes him happy. That is what it means to say God is sovereign.

Think about it for a moment: If God is sovereign and can do anything he pleases, then none of his purposes can be frustrated.

The LORD brings the counsel of the nations to nought; he frustrates the plans of the peoples. The counsel of the LORD stands forever, the thoughts of his heart to all generations. (Psalm 33:10-11)

And if none of his purposes can be frustrated, then he must be the happiest of all beings. This infinite, divine happiness is the fountain from which the Christian Hedonist drinks and longs to drink more deeply.

Can you imagine what it would be like if the God who ruled the world were not happy? What if God were given to grumbling and pouting and depression like some Jack-and-the-beanstalk giant in the sky? What if God were frustrated and despondent and gloomy and dismal and discontented and dejected? Could we join David and say, "O God, thou art my God, I seek thee; my soul thirsts for thee; my flesh faints for thee, as in a dry and weary land where no water is" (Psalm 63:1)?

I don't think so. We would all relate to God like little children who have a frustrated, gloomy, dismal, discontented father. They can't enjoy him. They can only try not to bother him, and maybe try to work for him to earn some little favor.

Therefore if God is not a happy God, Christian Hedonism has no foundation. For the aim of the Christian Hedonist is to be happy in God to delight in God, to cherish and enjoy his fellowship and favor. But children cannot enjoy the fellowship of their father if he is unhappy. Therefore the foundation of Christian Hedonism is the happiness of God.

But the foundation of the happiness of God is the sovereignty of God: "Our God is in the heavens; he does whatever he pleases." If God were not sovereign if the world he made were out of control, frustrating his design again and again — God would not be happy.

Just as our joy is based on the promise that God is strong enough and wise enough to make all things work together for our good, so God's joy is based on that same sovereign control: He makes all things work together for his glory.

If so much hangs on God's sovereignty we should make sure the biblical basis for it is secure.

The Biblical Basis of God's Sovereign Happiness[1]

> God says,
> "My counsel will stand and I will accomplish all my purpose."
>
> Therefore Job says,
> "No purpose of yours can be thwarted."
>
> His purposes encompass all things, including sin.
> Thus the crucifixion of Christ was the will of God,
> even though it was the greatest sin ever committed.
>
> "The lot is cast in the lap,
> but every decision is from the Lord."[2]

The sheer fact that God is God implies that his purposes cannot be thwarted — so says the prophet Isaiah:

> "I am God and there is no other; I am God and there is none like me declaring the end from the beginning and from ancient times things not yet done, saying, 'My counsel shall stand, and I will accomplish all my purpose.'" (Isaiah 46:9-10)

The purposes of God cannot be frustrated; there is none like God. If a purpose of God came to nought it would imply that there is a power greater than God's. It would imply that someone could stay his hand when he designs to do a thing. But "none can stay his hand" — as Nebuchadnezzar says:

> His dominion is an everlasting dominion, and his kingdom endures from generation to generation; all the inhabitants of the

earth are accounted as nothing; and he does according to his will in the host of heaven and among the inhabitants of the earth, and none can stay his hand or say to him, "What are you doing?" (Daniel 4:34-35)

His Sovereignty Covers Calamities

This was also Job's final confession after God had spoken to him out of the whirlwind: "I know that you can do all things, and that no purpose of yours can be thwarted" (Job 42:2). "Our God is in the heavens; he does whatever he pleases."

This raises the question whether the evil and calamitous events in the world are also part of God's sovereign design. Jeremiah looks over the carnage of Jerusalem after its destruction and cries,

> My eyes are spent with weeping; my soul is in tumult; my heart is poured out in grief because of the destruction of the daughter of my people, because infants and babes faint in the streets of the city. (Lamentations 2:11)

But when he looked to God he could not deny the truth:

> Who has commanded and it came to pass, unless the LORD has ordained it? Is it not from the mouth of the Most High that good and evil come? (Lamentations 3:37-38)

"Shall We Receive Good at the Hand of the Lord and Not Evil?"

If God reigns as sovereign over the world, then the evil of the world is not outside his design. "Does evil befall a city, unless the LORD has done it?" (Amos 3:6).

This was the reverent saying of God's servant Job when he was afflicted with boils: "Shall we receive good at the hand of God, and shall we not receive evil?" (Job 2:10). He said this even though the text says plainly that "Satan went forth from the presence of the LORD, and afflicted Job with loathsome sores" (Job 2:7). Was Job wrong to attribute to God what came from Satan? No, because the writer tells us immediately after Job's words, "In all this Job did not sin with his lips" (Job 2:10).

The evil Satan causes is only by the permission of God. Therefore Job is not wrong to see it as ultimately from the hand of God. It would be unbiblical and irreverent to attribute to Satan (or to sinful man) the power to frustrate the designs of God.

Who Planned the Murder of Christ?

The clearest example that even moral evil fits into the designs of God is the crucifixion of Christ. Who would deny that the betrayal of Jesus by Judas was a morally evil act?

Yet in Acts 2:23, Peter says, "This, Jesus, delivered up according to the definite plan and foreknowledge of God, you crucified and killed by the hands of lawless men." The betrayal was sin, but it was part of God's ordained plan. Sin did not thwart his plan or stay his hand.

Or who would say that Herod's contempt (Luke 23:11) or Pilate's spineless expediency (Luke 23:24) or the Jews' "Crucify! Crucify him!" (Luke 23:21) or the Gentile soldiers' mockery (Luke 23:36) — who would say that these were not sin? Yet Luke in Acts 4:27-28 records the prayer of the saints:

> "Truly in this city there were gathered together against thy holy servant Jesus, whom thou didst anoint, both Herod and Pontius Pilate, with the Gentiles and the peoples of Israel to do whatever thy hand and thy plan had predestined to take place."

People lift their hand to rebel against the Most High only to find that their rebellion is unwitting service in the wonderful designs of God. Even sin cannot frustrate the purposes of the Almighty. He himself does not commit sin, but he has decreed that there be acts which are sin — for the acts of Pilate and Herod were predestined by God's plan.

God Turns It Wherever He Will

Similarly, when we come to the end of the New Testament and to the end of history in the Revelation of John, we find God in complete control of all the evil kings who wage war. In Revelation 17, John speaks of a harlot sitting on a beast with ten horns. The harlot is Rome, drunk with the blood of the saints; the beast is the antichrist and the ten horns are ten kings "who give over their power and authority to the beast . . . [and] make war on the Lamb."

But are these evil kings outside God's control? Are they frustrating God's designs? Far from it. They are unwittingly doing his bidding. "For God has put it in their hearts to carry out his purpose by being of one mind and giving over their royal power to the beast, until the words of God shall be fulfilled" (Revelation 17:17). No one on earth can escape the sovereign control of God: "The king's heart is a stream of water in the hand of the LORD; he turns it wherever he will" (Proverbs 21:1; cf. Ezra 6:22).

The evil intentions of men cannot frustrate the decrees of God. This is the point of the story of Joseph's fall and rise in Egypt. His brothers sold him into slavery. Potiphar's wife slandered him into the dungeon. Pharaoh's butler forgot him in prison for two years. Where was God in all this sin and misery? Joseph answers in Genesis 50:20. He says to his guilty brothers, "As for you, you meant evil against me; but God meant it for good, to bring it about that many people should be kept alive, as they are today."

The hardened disobedience of men's hearts leads not to the frustration of God's plans, but to their fruition.

Consider the hardness of heart in Romans 11:25-26. "Lest you be wise in your own conceits, I want you to understand this mystery, brethren: A hardening has come upon part of Israel, until the full number of the Gentiles come in, and so all Israel will be saved." Who is governing the coming and going of this hardness of heart so that it has a particular limit and then gives way at the appointed time to the certain salvation of "all Israel"?

Or consider the disobedience in Romans 11:31. Paul speaks to his Gentile readers about Israel's disobedience in rejecting their Messiah: "So they [Israel] have now been disobedient in order that by the mercy shown to you [Gentiles] they also may receive mercy." When Paul says Israel was disobedient in order that Gentiles might get the benefits of the gospel, whose purpose does he have in mind?

It could only be God's. For Israel certainly did not conceive of their disobedience as a way of blessing the Gentiles or winning mercy for themselves in such a roundabout fashion! Is not then the point of Romans 11:31 that God rules over the disobedience of Israel and turns it precisely to the purposes he has planned?

There Is No Such Thing As Mere Coincidence

God's sovereignty over men's affairs is not compromised even by the reality of sin and evil in the world. It is not limited to the good acts of men or the pleasant events of nature. The wind belongs to God whether it comforts or whether it kills.

> For I know that the LORD is great, and that our Lord is above all gods. Whatever the LORD pleases he does, in heaven and on earth, in the seas and all deeps. He it is who makes the clouds rise at the end of the earth, who makes lightnings for the rain and brings forth the wind from his storehouses. (Psalm 135:5-7)

In the end, one must finally come to see that if there is a God in heaven, there is no such thing as mere coincidence, not even in the smallest affairs of life: "The lot is cast into the lap, but the decision is wholly from the LORD"

(Proverbs 16:33). Not one sparrow "will fall to the ground without your Father's will" (Matthew 10:29).

The Struggle and Solution of Jonathan Edwards

> How can God be happy and decree calamity?
>
> Consider that he has the capacity to view the world through two lenses.
>
> Through the narrow one
> he is grieved and angered at sin and pain.
>
> Through the wide one
> he sees evil in relation to its eternal purposes.
>
> Reality is like a mosaic.
> The parts may be ugly in themselves,
> But the whole is beautiful.

Many of us have gone through a period of deep struggle with the doctrine of God's sovereignty. If we take our doctrines into our hearts where they belong, they can cause upheavals of emotion and sleepless nights. This is far better than toying with academic ideas that never touch real life. The possibility at least exists that out of the upheavals will come a new era of calm and confidence.

It has happened for many of us the way it did for Jonathan Edwards. Edwards was a pastor and a profound theologian in New England in the early 1700s. He was a leader in the First Great Awakening. His major works still challenge great minds of our day. His extraordinary combination of logic and love make him a deeply moving writer. Again and again when I am dry and weak, I pull down my collection of Edwards's works and stir myself up with one of his sermons.

He recounts the struggle he had with the doctrine of God's sovereignty:

> From my childhood up, my mind had been full of objections against the doctrine of God's sovereignty. . . . It used to appear like a horrible doctrine to me. But I remember the time very well, when I seemed to be convinced, and fully satisfied, as to this sovereignty of God. . . .
>
> But never could I give an account, how, or by what means, I was thus convinced, not in the least imagining at the time, nor a

long time after, that there was any extraordinary influence of God's Spirit in it; but only that now I saw further, and my reason apprehended the justice and reasonableness of it. However, my mind rested in it; and it put an end to all those cavils and objections.

And there has been a wonderful alteration in my mind, in respect to the doctrine of God's sovereignty, from that day to this; so that I scarce ever have found so much as the rising of an objection against it, in the most absolute sense. . . . I have often since had not only a conviction but a delightful conviction. The doctrine has very often appeared exceeding pleasant, bright, and sweet. Absolute sovereignty is what I love to ascribe to God. But my first conviction was not so.[3]

It is not surprising, then, that Jonathan Edwards struggled earnestly and deeply with a problem that stands before us now. How can we affirm the happiness of God on the basis of his sovereignty when much of what God permits in the world is contrary to his own commands in Scripture? How can we say God is happy when there is so much sin and misery in the world?

Edwards did not claim to exhaust the mystery here. But he does help us find a possible way of avoiding outright contradiction while being faithful to the Scriptures. Putting it in my own words, he said that the infinite complexity of the divine mind is such that God has the capacity to look at the world through two lenses. He can look through a narrow lens or through a wide-angle lens.

When God looks at a painful or wicked event through his narrow lens, he sees the tragedy or the sin for what it is in itself and he is angered and grieved. "I have no pleasure in the death of anyone, says the LORD God" (Ezekiel 18:32).

But when God looks at a painful or wicked event through his wide-angle lens, he sees the tragedy or the sin in relation to everything leading up to it and everything flowing out from it. He sees it in relation to all the connections and effects that form a pattern or mosaic stretching into eternity. This mosaic in all its parts — good and evil — brings him delight.[4]

"It Was the Will of the Lord to Bruise Him"

> God willed the crucifixion of his Son.
>
> The sin and pain
> he abhorred
> (through the narrow lens).
>
> The sin-covering, death-conquering obedience
> he delighted in
> (through the wide lens).
>
> So it is with all pain and sin:
> Grievous in itself, it does not thwart his plans,
> or diminish his deepest delight.

For example, the death of Christ was the will and work of God the Father. Isaiah writes, "We esteemed him stricken, smitten by God. . . . It was the will of the LORD to bruise him; he has put him to grief" (53:4,10). Yet surely, as God the Father saw the agony of his beloved Son and the wickedness that brought him to the cross, he did not delight in those things in themselves (viewed through the narrow lens). Sin in itself, and the suffering of the innocent, are abhorrent to God.

Nevertheless, according to Hebrews 2:10, God the Father thought it was fitting to perfect the Pioneer of our salvation through suffering. God willed what he abhorred. He abhorred it in the narrow-lens view, but not in the wide-angle view of eternity. When the universality of things was considered, the death of the Son of God was seen by the Father as a magnificent way to demonstrate his righteousness (Romans 3:25-26) and bring his people to glory (Hebrews 2:10) and keep the angels praising forever and ever (Revelation 5:9-13).

Therefore when I say the sovereignty of God is the foundation of his happiness, I do not ignore or minimize the anger and grief God can express against evil. But neither do I infer from this wrath and sorrow that God is a frustrated God who cannot keep his creation under control. He has designed from all eternity, and is infallibly forming with every event, a magnificent mosaic of redemptive history.[5] The contemplation of this mosaic (with both its dark and bright tiles) fills his heart with joy.

And if our Father's heart is full of deep and unshakable happiness, we may be sure that when we seek our happiness in him we will not find him "out of sorts" when we come. We will not find a frustrated, gloomy, irritable

Father who wants to be left alone, but instead a Father whose heart is so full of joy it spills over onto all those (Christian Hedonists) who are thirsty.

God's Happiness Is in Himself

> God employs his sovereignty to display
> the great object of his delight,
> his GLORY,
> the beauty of his manifold perfections.
>
> He does all that he does to magnify the worth of his glory.
>
> He would be unrighteous if he valued anything more
> than what is supremely valuable,
> namely, himself.

I began this chapter by saying the ultimate ground of Christian Hedonism is the fact that God is uppermost in his own affections:

> *The chief end of God is to glorify God
> and enjoy himself forever.*

What we have seen so far is that God is absolutely sovereign over the world and that he can therefore do anything he pleases, and is therefore not a frustrated God, but a deeply happy God, rejoicing in all his works (Psalm 104:31), when he considers them in relation to redemptive history.

What we have not yet seen is how this unshakable happiness of God is indeed a happiness in *himself*. We have seen that God has the sovereign power to do whatever he pleases, but we have not yet seen specifically what it is that pleases him. Why is it that contemplating the mosaic of redemptive history delights the heart of God? Is this not idolatry — for God to delight in something other than himself?

So now we must ask: What does make God happy? What is it about redemptive history that delights the heart of God? The way to answer this question is to survey what God pursues in all his works. If we could discover what one thing God pursues in everything he does, we would know what he delights in most. We would know what was uppermost in his affections.

God Delights in His Glory

In Appendix 1, I present a brief survey of the high points of redemptive history in order to discover God's ultimate goal in all he does. If what follows seems out of sync with Scripture, I urge you to examine the supporting evidence of that appendix.

My conclusion there is that God's own glory is uppermost in his own affections. In everything he does, his purpose is to preserve and display that glory. To say his glory is uppermost in his own affections means that he puts a greater value on it than on anything else. He delights in his glory above all things.

Glory is not easy to define. It is like beauty. How would you define beauty? Some things we have to point at rather than define. But let me try. God's glory is the beauty of his manifold perfections. It can refer to the bright and awesome radiance that sometimes breaks forth in visible manifestations. Or it can refer to the infinite moral excellence of his character. In either case it signifies a reality of infinite greatness and worth. C. S. Lewis helps us with his own effort to point at it:

> Nature never taught me that there exists a God of glory and of infinite majesty. I had to learn that in other ways. But nature gave the word glory a meaning for me. I still do not know where else I could have found one. I do not see how the "fear" of God could have ever meant to me anything but the lowest prudential efforts to be safe, if I had never seen certain ominous ravines and unapproachable crags.[6]

God's ultimate goal therefore is to preserve and display his infinite and awesome greatness and worth, that is, his glory.

God has many other goals in what he does. But none of them is more ultimate than this. They are all subordinate. God's overwhelming passion is to exalt the value of his glory. To that end he seeks to display it, to oppose those who belittle it, and to vindicate it from all contempt. It is clearly the uppermost reality in his affections. He loves his glory infinitely.

This is the same as saying: he loves himself infinitely. Or: he himself is uppermost in his own affections. A moment's reflection reveals the inexorable justice of this fact. God would be unrighteous (just as we would) if he valued anything more than what is supremely valuable. But he himself is supremely valuable. If he did not take infinite delight in the worth of his own glory he would be unrighteous. For it is right to take delight in a person in proportion to the excellence of that person's glory.

God Delights in the Glory of His Son

> "Christ reflects the glory of God
> and bears the very stamp of his nature."[7]
> Therefore the Father delights infinitely in the Son.
>
> "The heavens are telling the glory of God."[8]
> Therefore God delights in creation
> as the spillover of the exuberance
> he has for his own excellence.

Another moment's reflection reminds us that this is exactly what we affirm when we affirm the eternal divinity of God's Son. We stand at the foothills of mystery in all these things. But the Scriptures have given us some glimpses of the heights. They teach us that the Son of God is himself God: "In the beginning was the Word, and the Word was with God, and the Word was God" (John 1:1). "In him the whole fullness of deity dwells bodily" (Colossians 2:9).

Therefore when the Father beheld the Son from all eternity, he was beholding the exact representation of himself. As Hebrews 1:3 says, the Son "reflects the glory of God and bears the very stamp of his nature." And 2 Corinthians 4:4 speaks of "the glory of Christ, who is the likeness of God."

From these texts we learn that through all eternity God the Father has beheld the image of his own glory perfectly represented in the person of his Son. Therefore one of the best ways to think about God's infinite enjoyment of his own glory is to think of it as the delight he has in his Son who is the perfect reflection of that glory (see John 17:24-26).

When Christ entered the world, God the Father said, "This is my beloved Son with whom I am well pleased" (Matthew 3:17). As God the Father contemplates the image of his own glory in the person of his Son, he is infinitely happy. "Behold my servant, whom I uphold, my chosen, in whom my soul delights" (Isaiah 42:1).

Within the triune Godhead (Father, Son, and Holy Spirit), God has been uppermost in his own affections for all eternity. This belongs to his very nature, for he has begotten and loved the Son from all eternity. Therefore God has been supremely and eternally happy in the fellowship of the Trinity.[9]

God Delights in the Glory of His Work

In creation God "went public"[10] with the glory that reverberates joyfully between the Father and the Son! There is something about the fullness of

God's joy that inclines it to overflow. There is an expansive quality to his joy. It wants to share itself. The impulse to create the world was not from weakness, as though God were lacking in some perfection which creation could supply. "It is no argument of the emptiness or deficiency of a fountain, that it is inclined to overflow."[11]

God loves to behold his glory reflected in his works. So the eternal happiness of the triune God spilled over in the work of creation and redemption. And since this original happiness was God's delight in his own glory, therefore the happiness that he has in all his works of creation and redemption is nothing other than a delight in his own glory. This is why God has done all things, from creation to consummation, for the preservation and display of his glory. All his works are simply the spillover of his infinite exuberance for his own excellence.

Is God for Us or for Himself?

> God does all things for his own sake.
> "For my own sake, for my own sake, I do it. . . .
> My glory I will not give to another."[12]
>
> This is love,
> because in pursuing the praise of his name
> in the hearts of his people,
> he commands the very thing
> that completes our joy.
>
> God is the one being in the universe
> for whom self-exaltation
> is the highest virtue
> and the most loving act.

But now the question arises: If God is so utterly enamored of his own glory, how can he be a God of love? If he unwaveringly does all things for his own sake, how then can we have any hope that he will do anything for our sake? Does not the apostle say, "Love seeks not its own" (1 Corinthians 13: 5)?

Now we begin to see how the issue of God's happiness can make or break the philosophy of Christian Hedonism. If God were so self-centered that he had no inclination to love his creatures, then Christian Hedonism would be dead. Christian Hedonism depends on the open arms of God. It depends on the readiness of God to accept and save and satisfy the heart of all who seek their joy in him. But if God is on an ego trip and out of reach, then it is in vain that we pursue our happiness in him.

Is God for us or for himself? Precisely in answering this question we will discover the great foundation for Christian Hedonism.

Is He Vain or Loving to Command Our Praise?

The Bible is replete with commands to praise God. God commands it because this is the ultimate goal of all he does — "to be glorified in his saints, and to be marveled at in all who have believed" (2 Thessalonians 1:10). Three times in Ephesians 1 this great aim is proclaimed: God "predestined us in love to be his sons . . . to the praise of the glory of his grace!" (1:5-6); "We . . . have been predestined and appointed to live for the praise of his glory" (1:12); the Holy Spirit "is the guarantee of our inheritance until we acquire possession of it, to the praise of his glory" (1:14).

All the different ways God has chosen to display his glory in creation and redemption seem to reach their culmination in the praises of his redeemed people. God governs the world with glory precisely that he might be admired, marveled at, exalted, and praised. The climax of his happiness is the delight he takes in the echoes of his excellence in the praises of the saints.

But again and again I have found that people stumble over this truth. People do not like to hear that God is uppermost in his own affections, or that he does all things for his own glory, or that he exalts himself and seeks the praise of men.

Why? There are at least two reasons. One is that we just don't like people who are like that. The other is that the Bible teaches us not to be like that. Let's examine these objections and see if they can apply to God.

Is God a Second-Hander?

First, we just don't like people who seem to be enamored by their own intelligence or strength or skill or good looks or wealth. We don't like scholars who try to show off their specialized knowledge, or who recite for us all their recent publications. We don't like businessmen who talk about how shrewdly they have invested their money and how they stayed right on top of the market to get in low and out high. We don't like children to play one-upmanship (Mine's bigger! Mine's faster! Mine's prettier!). And unless we are one of them, we disapprove of men and women who dress not functionally and simply, but to attract attention with the latest style.

Why don't we like all that? I think at root it's because those people are inauthentic. They are what Ayn Rand calls "second-handers." They don't live from the joy that comes through achieving what they value for its own sake. Instead, they live secondhand from the compliments of others. They have one eye on their action and one on their audience. We simply do not admire second-handers. We admire people who are secure and composed enough that they don't need to shore up their weaknesses and compensate for their deficiencies by trying to get compliments.

It stands to reason, then, that any teaching that puts God in the category of a second-hander will be unacceptable to Christians. And for many the teaching that God seeks to show off his glory and get the praise of men does in fact put him in the category of a second-hander. But should it?

One thing is certain: God is not weak and has no deficiencies. "All things are from him and through him and to him" (Romans 11:36). "He is not served by human hands as though he needed anything, since he himself gives to all men life and breath and everything" (Acts 17:25). Everything that exists owes its existence to him, and no one can add anything to him which is not already flowing from him. Therefore God's zeal to seek his own glory and to be praised by men cannot be owing to his need to shore up some weakness or compensate for some deficiency. He may look, at first glance, like one of the second-handers, but he is not like them, and the superficial similarity must be explained another way.

"Love Seeks Not Its Own" — Except in the Joy of Others

The rules of humility that belong to a creature
cannot apply in the same way to its Creator.

Ultimate self-denial would be idolatry in God.

By upholding his own glory
he upholds the ground of our joy.
And that is love.

The second reason people stumble over the teaching that God exalts his own glory and seeks to be praised by his people is that the Bible teaches us not to be like that. For example, the Bible says that "Love seeks not its own" (1 Corinthians 13:5). How can God be loving and yet be utterly devoted to "seeking his own" glory and praise and joy? How can God be for us if he is so utterly for himself?

The answer I propose is this: Because God is unique as an all-glorious, totally self-sufficient Being, he must be for himself if he is to be for us. The rules of humility that belong to a creature cannot apply in the same way to its Creator. If God should turn away from himself as the Source of infinite joy, he would cease to be God. He would deny the infinite worth of his own glory.

He would imply that there is something more valuable outside himself. He would commit idolatry.

This would be no gain for us. For where can we go when our God has become unrighteous? Where will we find a Rock of integrity in the universe when the heart of God has ceased to value supremely the supremely valuable? Where shall we turn with our adoration when God himself has forsaken the claims of infinite worth and beauty?

No, we do not turn God's self-exaltation into love by demanding that God cease to be God. Instead we must come to see that God is love precisely because he relentlessly pursues the praises of his name in the hearts of his people.

Delight Is Incomplete Until It Is Expressed

Consider this question: In view of God's infinite power and wisdom and beauty, what would his love to a human being involve? Or to put it another way: What could God give us to enjoy that would prove him most loving? There is only one possible answer: *himself!* If he withholds himself from our contemplation and companionship, no matter what else he gives us, he is not loving.

Now we are on the brink of what for me was a life-changing discovery. What do we all do when we are given or shown something beautiful or excellent? We *praise* it! We praise new little babies: "Oh, look at that nice round head! And all that hair! And her hands, aren't they perfect!" We praise a lover after a long absence: "Your eyes are like a cloudless sky! Your hair like forest silk!" We praise a grand slam in the bottom of the ninth when we are down by three. We praise the October trees along the banks of the St. Croix.

But the great discovery for me, as I said, came when reading "A Word about Praise" in C. S. Lewis's *Reflections on the Psalms*. His recorded thoughts — born from wrestling with the idea that God not only wants our praise but commands it — bear looking at again, in fuller form:

> But the most obvious fact about praise — whether of God or any thing — strangely escaped me. I thought of it in terms of compliment, approval, or the giving of honor. I had never noticed that all enjoyment spontaneously overflows into praise unless (sometimes even if) shyness or the fear of boring others is deliberately brought in to check it. The world rings with praise — lovers praising their mistresses, readers their favorite poet, walkers praising the countryside, players praising their favorite game — praise of weather, wines, dishes, actors, motors, horses,

colleges, countries, historical personages, children, flowers, mountains, rare stamps, rare beetles, even sometimes politicians or scholars. I had not noticed how the humblest, and at the same time most balanced and capacious, minds, praised most, while the cranks, misfits and malcontents praised least. . . .

I had not noticed either that just as men spontaneously praise whatever they value, so they spontaneously urge us to join them in praising it: "Isn't she lovely? Wasn't it glorious? Don't you think that magnificent?" The Psalmists in telling everyone to praise God are doing what all men do when they speak of what they care about. My whole, more general, difficulty about the praise of God depended on my absurdly denying to us, as regards the supremely Valuable, what we delight to do, what indeed we can't help doing, about everything else we value.

I think we delight to praise what we enjoy because the praise not merely expresses but completes the enjoyment; it is its appointed consummation. It is not out of compliment that lovers keep on telling one another how beautiful they are; the delight is incomplete till it is expressed.[13]

There is the solution! We praise what we enjoy because the delight is incomplete until it is expressed in praise. If we were not allowed to speak of what we value, and celebrate what we love, and praise what we admire, our joy would not be full. So if God loves us enough to make our joy full, he must not only give us himself; he must also win from us the praise of our hearts — not because he needs to shore up some weakness in himself or compensate for some deficiency, but because he loves us and seeks the fullness of our joy that can be found only in knowing and praising him, the most magnificent of all Beings. If he is truly for us he must be for himself!

God is the one Being in all the universe for whom seeking his own praise is the ultimately loving act. For him, self-exaltation is the highest virtue. When he does all things "for the praise of his glory," he preserves for us and offers to us the only thing in all the world which can satisfy our longings. God is for us! And the foundation of this love is that God has been, is now, and always will be, for himself.

Summary

> The happiness of *God* in God
> is the foundation of *our* happiness in God.
>
> If God did not joyfully uphold and display his glory,
> the ground of our joy would be gone.
>
> God's pursuit of praise from us
> and our pursuit of pleasure in him
> are in perfect harmony.
>
> For God is most glorified in us
> when we are most satisfied in him.

God is absolutely sovereign. "Our God is in the heavens; he does whatever he pleases!" (Psalm 115:3). Therefore he is not frustrated. He rejoices in all his works when he contemplates them as colors of the magnificent mosaic of redemptive history. He is an unshakably happy God.

His happiness is the delight he has in himself. Before creation he rejoiced in the image of his glory in the person of his Son. Then the joy of God "went public" in the works of creation and redemption. These works delight the heart of God because they reflect his glory. He does everything he does to preserve and display that glory, for in this his soul rejoices.

All the works of God culminate in the praises of his redeemed people. The climax of his happiness is the delight he takes in the echoes of his excellence in the praises of the saints. This praise is the consummation of our own joy in God. Therefore God's pursuit of praise from us and our pursuit of pleasure in him are the same pursuit. This is the great gospel! This is the foundation of Christian Hedonism.

"Not every one who says to me 'Lord, Lord,'
shall enter into the kingdom of heaven."

MATTHEW 7:21

"The kingdom of heaven is like treasure hidden in a field,
which a man found and covered up;
then in his joy he goes and sells all that he has
and buys that field."

MATTHEW 13:44

CHAPTER 2

CONVERSION

The Creation of a Christian Hedonist

"The Gate Is Narrow"

If everyone were bound to enter the kingdom of heaven we might not have to speak of conversion. But not everyone is bound to enter. "For the gate is narrow and the way is hard that leads to life, and those who find it are few" (Matthew 7:14).

Chapter one ended with the discovery that God's pursuit of praise from us and our pursuit of pleasure in him are one and the same pursuit. God's quest to be glorified and our quest to be satisfied reach their goal in this one experience: our delight in God which overflows in praise. For God, praise is the sweet echo of his own excellence in the hearts of his people. For us, praise is the summit of satisfaction that comes from living in fellowship with God.

> With the very zeal that God has for his own glory
> he pursues us with goodness and mercy.
>
> But who is "us"?
>
> "Those who love him
> and are called according to his purpose."[1]
>
> To belong to this group
> one must be converted.
>
> Which is the creation of a Christian Hedonist.

The stunning implication of this discovery is that all the omnipotent energy that drives the heart of God to pursue his own glory, also drives him to satisfy the hearts of those who seek their joy in him. The good news of the Bible is that God is not at all disinclined to satisfy the hearts of those who hope in him. Just the opposite: The very thing that can make us most happy is what God delights in with all his heart and with all his soul.

"I will make with them an everlasting covenant, that I will not turn away from doing good to them. . . . I will rejoice in doing them good . . . with all my heart and all my soul." (Jeremiah 32:40-41)

With all his heart and with all his soul God joins us in the pursuit of our everlasting joy, because the consummation of that joy in him redounds to the glory of his own infinite worth. All who cast themselves on God find that they are carried into endless joy by God's omnipotent commitment to his own glory:

> "For my own sake, for my own sake, I do it, for how should my name be profaned? My glory I will not give to another!" (Isaiah 48:11)

Yes, Omnipotent Joy pursues the good of all who cast themselves on God! "The LORD takes pleasure in those who . . . hope in him" (Psalm 147:11). But this is not everyone.

"All things work together for good for *those who love God* and are called according to his purpose" (Romans 8:28) — but not for everyone. There are sheep and there are goats (Matthew 25:32). There are wise and there are foolish (Matthew 25:2). There are those who are being saved and those who are perishing (1 Corinthians 1:18). And the difference is that one group has been converted and the other hasn't.

The aim of this chapter is to show the necessity of conversion and to argue that it is nothing less than the creation of a Christian Hedonist.

Why Not Just Say "Believe"?

Someone may ask, "If your aim is conversion, why don't you just use the straightforward, biblical command, 'Believe in the Lord Jesus, and you will be saved'? Why bring in this new terminology of Christian Hedonism?"

My answer has two parts. First, we are surrounded by unconverted people who think they *do* believe in Jesus. Drunks on the street say they believe. Unmarried couples sleeping together say they believe. Elderly people who haven't sought worship or fellowship for forty years say they believe. All kinds of lukewarm, world-loving church attenders say they believe. The world abounds with millions of unconverted people who say they believe in Jesus.

It does no good to tell these people to believe in the Lord Jesus. The phrase is empty. My responsibility as a preacher of the gospel and a teacher in the church is not to preserve and repeat cherished biblical sentences, but to pierce the heart with biblical truth.

This leads to the second part of my answer. There are other straightforward biblical commands besides "Believe in the Lord Jesus, and you will

be saved." The reason for introducing the idea of Christian He
force these commands to our attention.

Could it be that today the most straightforward biblical command for
conversion is not, "Believe in the Lord," but, "Delight yourself in the LORD"?
And might not many slumbering hearts be stabbed broad awake by the
words, "Unless a man be born again into a Christian Hedonist he cannot see
the Kingdom of God"?

Six Crucial Truths to Summarize Our Need and God's Provision[2]

Why is conversion so crucial? What is there about God and man that makes
it necessary? And what has God done to meet our desperate need? And what
must we do to enjoy the benefits of his provision? These are huge questions.
I attempt a summary answer with the following six truths from Scripture.

How Have We Failed?

> 1. God created us for his glory.
>
> 2. Therefore it is our duty to live for his glory.

1. *God created us for his glory.*

"Bring my sons from afar and my daughters from the end of the
earth, everyone who is called by my name, whom I created for
my glory." (Isaiah 43:6-7)

The proper understanding of everything in life begins with God. No
one will ever understand the necessity of conversion who does not know why
God created us. He created us "in his image" so that we would image forth his
glory in the world. We were made to be prisms refracting the light of God's
glory into all of life. Why God should want to give us a share in shining with
his glory is a great mystery. Call it grace or mercy or love — it is an unspeakable wonder. Once we were not. Then we existed — for the glory of God!

2. *Therefore it is the duty of every person to live for the glory of God.*

So, whether you eat or drink or whatever you do, do all to the
glory of God. (1 Corinthians 10:31)

If God made us for his glory, it is clear that we should live for his glory.
Our duty comes from God's design.

What does it mean to glorify God?

It does not mean to make him more glorious. It means to acknowledge his glory, and to value it above all things, and to make it known. It implies heartfelt gratitude: "He who brings thanksgiving as his sacrifice glorifies me" (Psalm 50:23). It also implies trust: Abraham "grew strong in his faith, giving glory to God" (Romans 4:20).

Glorifying God is the duty not only of those who have heard the preaching of the gospel, but also of peoples who have only the witness of nature and their own conscience:

> Ever since the creation of the world his invisible nature, namely, his eternal power and deity, has been clearly perceived in the things that have been made. So they are without excuse; for although they knew God they did not glorify him and thank him as God. (Romans 1:20-21)

God will not judge anyone for failing to perform a duty if the person had no access to the knowledge of that duty. But even without the Bible, all people have access to the knowledge that we are created by God and therefore depend on him for everything, thus owing him the gratitude and trust of our hearts. Deep within us we all know that it is our duty to glorify our Maker by thanking him for all we have, trusting him for all we need, and obeying all his revealed will.

How Desperate Is Our Condition?

> 3. We have all failed to glorify God.
>
> 4. We are all subject to eternal condemnation.

3. Yet all of us have failed to glorify God as we ought.

> All have sinned and fall short of the glory of God. (Romans 3:23)

What does it mean to "fall short" of the glory of God? It does not mean we were supposed to be as glorious as God is and have fallen short. We ought to fall short in that sense! The best explanation of Romans 3:23 is Romans 1:23. It says that those who did not glorify or thank God "became fools, and exchanged the glory of the immortal God for images." This is the way we "fall short" of the glory of God: we exchange it for something of lesser value. All sin comes from not putting supreme value on the glory of God — this is the very essence of sin.

And we have all sinned. "None is righteous, no, not one" (Romans 3:10). None of us has trusted God the way we should. None of us has felt the depth and consistency of gratitude we owe him. None of us has obeyed him according to his wisdom and right. We have exchanged and dishonored his glory again and again. We have trusted ourselves. We have taken credit for his gifts. We have turned away from the path of his commandments because we thought we knew better.

In all this we have held the glory of the Lord in contempt. The exceeding evil of sin is not the harm it does to us or to others (though that is great!). The wickedness of sin is owing to the implicit disdain for God. When David committed adultery with Bathsheba and even had her husband killed, what did God say to him through the prophet Nathan? He did not remind the king that marriage is inviolable or that human life is sacred. He said, "You have despised *me*" (2 Samuel 12:10).

But this is not the whole account of our condition. We not only choose to sin, we *are* sinful. The Bible describes our heart as blind (2 Corinthians 4:4) and hard (Ezekiel 11:19; 36:26) and dead (Ephesians 2:1,5) and unable to submit to the law of God (Romans 8:7-8). By nature we are "children of wrath" (Ephesians 2:3).

4. *Therefore, all of us are subject to eternal condemnation by God.*

The wages of sin is death. (Romans 6:23)

They shall suffer the punishment of eternal destruction and exclusion from the presence of the Lord and from the glory of his might. (2 Thessalonians 1:9)

Having held the glory of God in contempt through ingratitude and distrust and disobedience, we are sentenced to be excluded from the enjoyment of that glory forever and ever in the eternal misery of hell.

The word "hell" (*gehenna*) occurs in the New Testament twelve times — eleven on the lips of Jesus. It is not a myth created by dismal and angry preachers. It is the solemn warning of the Son of God who died to deliver sinners from its curse. We ignore it at great risk.

Hell is a place of torment. It is not merely the absence of pleasure. It is not annihilation.[3] Jesus repeatedly describes it as an experience of fire. "Whoever says, 'You fool!' shall be liable to the hell of fire" (Matthew 5:22). "It is better for you to enter life with one eye than with two eyes to be thrown into the hell of fire" (Matthew 18:9). "It is better for you to enter the kingdom of God with one eye than with two eyes to be thrown into hell, where their worm does not die, and the fire is not quenched" (Mark 9:47-48). He warned often that there would be "weeping and gnashing of teeth" (Matthew 8:12; 22:13; 24:51; 25:30).

Not only is it a place of torment, it is also everlasting. Hell is not remedial, contrary to what many popular writers are saying these days.[4] Jesus closes the parable of the last judgment with these words: " 'Depart from me, you cursed, into the eternal fire prepared for the devil and his angels.' . . . And they will go away into eternal punishment, but the righteous into eternal life" (Matthew 25:41,46). The "punishment" is eternal the same way the "life" is eternal.

Another evidence that hell is everlasting is the teaching of Jesus that there is sin which will not be forgiven in the age to come. "Whoever says a word against the Holy Spirit will not be forgiven, either in this age or in the age to come" (Matthew 12:32). If hell is remedial and will some day be emptied of all sinners, then they would have to be forgiven. But Jesus says there is sin that will never be forgiven.

John sums up the terrible realities of torment and endlessness in Revelation 14:11 — "And the smoke of their torment goes up forever and ever: and they have no rest, day or night."

Therefore hell is just. Some have objected that an everlasting punishment is out of proportion to the seriousness of the sin committed. But this is not true, because the seriousness of our sin is infinite. Consider the explanation of Jonathan Edwards:

> The crime of one being despising and casting contempt on another, is proportionably more or less heinous, as he was under greater or less obligations to obey him. And therefore if there be any being that we are under infinite obligations to love, and honor, and obey, the contrary towards him must be infinitely faulty.

> Our obligation to love, honor, and obey any being is in proportion to his loveliness, honorableness, and authority. . . . But God is a being infinitely lovely, because he hath infinite excellency and beauty. . . .

> So sin against God, being a violation of infinite obligations, must be a crime infinitely heinous, and so deserving infinite punishment. . . . The eternity of the punishment of ungodly men

renders it infinite . . . and therefore renders no more than pro-
portionate to the heinousness of what they are guilty of.[5]

When every human being stands before God on the day of judgment,
God would not have to use one sentence of Scripture to show us our guilt and
the appropriateness of our condemnation. He would need only to ask three
questions: 1) Was it not plain in nature that everything you had was a gift, and
that you were dependent on your Maker for life and breath and everything?
2) Did not the judicial sentiment[6] in your own heart always hold other people
guilty when they lacked the gratitude they should have had in response to a
kindness you performed? 3) Has your life been filled with gratitude and trust
toward me in proportion to my generosity and authority? Case closed.

What Has God Done to Save Us from His Wrath?

---

5. "Jesus Christ came into the world to save sinners."

---

*5. Nevertheless, in his great mercy, God sent forth his Son, Jesus
Christ, to save sinners by dying in their place on the cross and rising
bodily from the dead.*

The saying is sure and worthy of full acceptance, that Christ
Jesus came into the world to save sinners. (1 Timothy 1:15)

[Jesus] was put to death on account of our trespasses, and raised
on account of our justification. (Romans 4:25)

Over against the terrifying news that we have fallen under the condemnation of our Creator and that he is bound by his own righteous character
to preserve the worth of his glory by pouring out eternal wrath on our sin,
there is the wonderful news of the gospel. This is a truth no one can ever learn
from nature. It has to be told to neighbors and preached in churches and carried by missionaries.

The good news is that God himself has decreed a way to satisfy the
demands of his justice without condemning the whole human race. Hell is
one way to settle accounts with sinners and uphold his justice. But there is
another way. The wisdom of God has ordained a way for the love of God to
deliver us from the wrath of God without compromising the justice of God.

And what is this wisdom?

The death of the Son of God for sinners! "We preach Christ crucified, a stumbling block to the Jews and folly to the Gentiles, but to those who are called, both Jews and Greeks, Christ the power of God and the wisdom of God" (1 Corinthians 1:23-24).

The death of Christ is the wisdom of God by which the love of God saves sinners from the wrath of God, and all the while upholds and demonstrates the righteousness of God. Romans 3:25-26 may be the most important verses in the Bible:

> God put Christ forward as a propitiation[7] by his blood, to be received by faith. This was to show God's righteousness because in his divine forbearance he had passed over former sins. It was to prove at the present time that he himself is just and that he justifies him who has faith in Jesus.

Not either/or! Both! God is wholly just! *And* he justifies the ungodly! He acquits the guilty, but is not guilty in doing so. This is the greatest news in the world!

> God made Christ to be sin, who knew no sin, so that in him we might become the righteousness of God. (2 Corinthians 5:21)

> Sending his own Son in the likeness of sinful flesh and for sin, he condemned sin in the flesh. (Romans 8:3)

> Christ bore our sins in his body on the tree. (1 Peter 2:24)

> He died for sins once for all, the righteous for the unrighteous, to bring us to God. (1 Peter 3:18)

> If we have been united with him in a death like his, we shall certainly be united with him in a resurrection like his. (Romans 6:5)

If the most terrifying news in the world is that we have fallen under the condemnation of our Creator and that he is bound by his own righteous character to preserve the worth of his glory by pouring out his wrath on our sin, then the best news in all the world (the gospel!) is that God has decreed a way of salvation which also upholds the worth of his glory. He has given his Son to die for sinners and to conquer their death by his own resurrection.

What Must We Do to Be Saved?

---

6. Turn from sin and trust the Savior.

---

6. *The benefits purchased by the death of Christ belong to those who repent and trust in him.*

"Repent, and be converted, that your sins may be blotted out." (Acts 3:19)

"Believe in the Lord Jesus and you will be saved." (Acts 16:31)

Not everybody is saved from God's wrath just because Christ died for sinners. There is a condition we must meet in order to be saved. I want to try to show that the condition, summed up here as repentance and faith, is conversion and that conversion is nothing less than the creation of a Christian Hedonist.

What Is Conversion?

"Conversion"[8] is used in the Authorized Version of the Bible only once, in Acts 15:3. Paul and Barnabas "passed through Phoenicia and Samaria, declaring the conversion of the Gentiles: and they caused great joy unto all the brethren." This conversion involved repentance and faith, as the other reports in Acts show.

For example, in Acts 11:18 the apostles respond to Peter's testimony about Gentile conversions like this: "Then to the Gentiles also God has granted *repentance* unto life." And in Acts 14:27 Paul and Barnabas report the conversion of the Gentiles by saying that "God . . . had opened a door of *faith* to the Gentiles."

Conversion, then, is repentance (turning from sin and unbelief) and faith (trusting in Christ alone for salvation). They are really two sides of the same coin. One side is tails — turn tail on the fruits of unbelief. The other side is heads — head straight for Jesus and trust his promises. You can't have the one without the other any more than you can face two ways at once, or serve two masters.

This means that saving faith in Christ always involves a profound change of heart. It is not merely agreement with the truth of a doctrine. *Satan* agrees with true doctrine (James 2:19). Saving faith is far deeper and more pervasive than that.

Conversion Is a Gift of God

> The native hardness of our hearts makes us
> unwilling and unable
> to turn from sin and trust the Savior.
>
> Therefore conversion involves a miracle of new birth.
> Thus new birth precedes and enables faith and repentance.
>
> Nevertheless, faith and repentance are *our* acts.
> We are accountable to do them.
>
> By the miracle of new birth,
> by pure grace,
> God grants us the inclination we need.

We get an inkling of something awesome behind repentance and faith when we see hints in the book of Acts that conversion is the gift of God. "God has granted repentance unto life" (11:18). "God exalted Christ at his right hand . . . to give repentance to Israel" (5:31). "God opened a door of faith to the Gentiles" (14:27). "The Lord opened [Lydia's] heart to give heed to what was said by Paul" (16:14).

We will never fully appreciate what a deep and awesome thing conversion is until we own up to the fact that it is a miracle. It is a gift of God. Recall again the point that we not only sin, but we also *are* sinful. The Bible describes our heart as blind (2 Corinthians 4:4) and hard (Ezekiel 11:19; 36:26) and dead (Ephesians 2:1,5) and unable to submit to the law of God (Romans 8:7-8). By *nature* we are "children of wrath" (Ephesians 2:3). And so when we hear the gospel we will never respond positively unless God performs the miracle of regeneration.[9]

Faith Is Our Act, but Is Possible Because of God's Act

Repentance and faith are our work. But we will not repent and believe unless God does his work to overcome our hard and rebellious hearts. This divine work is called *regeneration*. Our work is called *conversion*.[10]

Conversion does indeed include an act of will by which we renounce sin and submit ourselves to the authority of Christ and put our hope and trust in him. We are responsible to do this, and will be condemned if we don't. But just as clearly the Bible teaches that, owing to our hard heart and willful blindness and spiritual insensitivity, we cannot do this.[11]

We must first experience the regenerating work of the Holy Spirit. The

Scriptures promised long ago that God would devote himself to this work in order to create for himself a faithful people:

> And the LORD your God will circumcise your heart and the heart of your offspring, so that you will love the LORD your God with all your heart and with all your soul, that you may live. (Deuteronomy 30:6)

> "I will give them a heart to know that I am the LORD; and they shall be my people and I will be their God, for they shall return to me with their whole heart." (Jeremiah 24:7)

> "And I will give them one heart, and put a new spirit within them; I will take the stony heart out of their flesh and give them a heart of flesh, that they may walk in my statutes and keep my ordinances and obey them; and they shall be my people, and I will be their God." (Ezekiel 11:19-20)

> "A new heart I will give you, and a new spirit I will put within you; and I will take out of your flesh the heart of stone and give you a heart of flesh. And I will put my spirit within you, and cause you to walk in my statutes and be careful to observe my ordinances." (Ezekiel 36:26-27)

These great promises from the Old Testament describe a work of God that changes a heart of stone into a heart of flesh and causes people to "know" and "love" and "obey" God. Without this spiritual heart transplant, people will not know and love and obey God. This prior work of God is what we mean by regeneration.

We Are "Called" the Way Jesus Called Lazarus: Death to Life
In the New Testament, God is clearly active, creating a people for himself by calling[12] them out of darkness and enabling them to believe the gospel and walk in the light. John teaches most clearly that regeneration precedes and enables faith.

> Everyone who believes that Jesus is the Christ *has been* born of God. (1 John 5:1)

The verb tenses make John's intention unmistakable: "Everyone who goes on believing [present, continuous action] that Jesus is the Christ has been born of God [perfect, completed action with abiding effects]." Faith is the evidence of new birth, not the cause of it. This is consistent with John's whole book (cf. 1 John 2:29; 3:9; 4:2-3; 4:7).

Since faith and repentance are possible only because of the regenerating work of God, both are called the gift of God:

> Even when we were dead through our trespasses, [God] made us alive together with Christ (by grace you have been saved). . . . By grace are you saved through faith; and this[13] is not your own doing, it is the gift of God. (Ephesians 2:5,8)

> The Lord's servant must not be quarrelsome, but kindly to everyone, an apt teacher, forbearing, correcting his opponents with gentleness. *God may, perhaps, grant that they will repent* and come to know the truth, and they may escape from the snare of the devil, after being captured by him to do his will. (2 Timothy 2:24-26)

Conversion Is a Condition of Salvation and a Miracle of God

> New birth is *not* conditional.
> No act of ours brings it about.
> It is supernatural.
>
> Final salvation from future judgment is conditional.
> It will not happen apart from our persevering faith.
>
> The supernatural act of God in new birth
> and the utterly crucial human act of persevering faith
> show how momentous is the change
> which we need in order to be saved.

This meditation on the nature and origin of conversion clarifies two things. One is the sense in which conversion is a condition for salvation. Continuous confusion is caused at this point by failing to define salvation precisely.

If "salvation" refers to new birth, conversion is *not* a condition of it. New birth comes first and enables the repentance and faith of conversion. Before new birth we are dead, and dead men don't meet conditions. Regeneration is totally unconditional. It is owing solely to the free grace of God. "It does not depend on the one who wills or runs, but on God who has mercy" (Romans 9:16).[14] We get no credit. He gets all the glory.

But if "salvation" refers to our future deliverance from the wrath of God at the judgment and entrance into eternal life, then yes, conversion is a condition of salvation. When we cry, "What must I do to be saved?" we are asking how to be forgiven for sin, and have fellowship with God and escape from the wrath to come. The answer is always, Meet the condition: Be converted!

Which brings us to the second thing that has become clear from our discussion. Conversion is no mere human decision. It is a human decision. But oh, so much more! Repentant faith (or believing repentance) is based on an awesome miracle performed by the sovereign God. It is the breath of a new creature in Christ.

Saving faith is no simple thing. It has many dimensions. "Believe on the Lord Jesus" is a massive command. It contains a hundred other things. Unless we see this, the array of conditions for salvation in the New Testament will be utterly perplexing. Consider the following partial list.

What must I do to be saved?

The answer in Acts 16:31 is, "Believe on the Lord Jesus and you will be saved."

The answer in John 1:12 is that we must receive Christ: "To all who receive him . . . he gave power to become children of God."

The answer in Acts 3:19 is, "Repent therefore, and turn again, that your sins may be blotted out."

The answer in Hebrews 5:9 is obedience to Christ. Christ "became the source of eternal salvation to all who obey him." So also in John 3:36, "He who does not obey the Son shall not see life."

Jesus himself answered the question in a variety of ways. For example, he said in Matthew 18:3 that childlikeness is the condition for salvation: "Truly, I say to you, unless you turn and become like children, you will never see the kingdom of heaven."

In Mark 8:34-35 the condition is self-denial: "If any man would come after me, let him deny himself and take up his cross and follow me. For whoever would save his life will lose it; and whoever loses his life for my sake and the gospel's will save it."

In Matthew 10:37 Jesus lays down the condition of loving him more than anyone else: "He who loves father or mother more than me is not worthy of me; and he who loves son or daughter more than me is not worthy of me." The same thing is expressed in 1 Corinthians 16:22 — "If anyone has no love for the Lord, let him be accursed."

And in Luke 14:33 the condition for salvation is that we be free from the love of our possessions: "Whoever does not renounce all that he has cannot be my disciple."

These are just some of the conditions that the New Testament says we must meet in order to inherit final salvation. We must believe on Jesus and receive him and turn from our sin and obey him and humble ourselves like little children and love him more than we love our family, our possessions, or our own life. This is what it means to be converted to Christ. This alone is the way of life everlasting.

But what is it that holds all these conditions together and gives them unity?[15] And what keeps them from becoming a way of earning salvation by works? One answer is the awesome reality of saving faith — trusting in the pardon of God, the promises of Christ, and the power of the Holy Spirit, not ourselves.

Yes, but what is it about saving faith that unites and changes so much of our lives?

The Creation of a Christian Hedonist

> Conversion is what happens to the heart
> when Christ becomes for us
> a Treasure Chest of holy joy.
>
> Saving faith is the heartfelt conviction that
> Christ is both
> solidly reliable
> and supremely desirable.
>
> The newness of a Christian convert
> is a new spiritual taste for the glory of Christ.

Jesus pointed to the answer in the little parable of Matthew 13:44.

"The kingdom of heaven is like treasure hidden in a field, which a man found and covered up; then in [literally, *from*] his joy he goes and sells all that he has and buys that field."

This parable describes how someone is converted and brought into the kingdom of heaven.[16] A person discovers a treasure and is impelled by joy to sell all he has in order to have this treasure. The kingdom of heaven is the abode of the King. The longing to be there is not the longing for heavenly real estate, but for camaraderie with the King. The treasure in the field is the fellowship of God in Christ.

I conclude from this parable that we must be deeply converted in order to enter the kingdom of heaven, and we are converted when Christ becomes for us a Treasure Chest of holy joy.

The Creation of a New Taste

How then does this arrival of joy relate to saving faith? The usual answer is that joy is the fruit of faith. And in one sense it is. "May the God of hope fill you with all joy and peace *in believing*" (Romans 15:13). It is "in believing" that we are filled with joy. Confidence in the promises of God overcomes anxiety and fills us with peace and joy. Paul even calls it the "joy of faith" (Philippians 1:25).

But there is a different way of looking at the relationship of joy and faith. In Hebrews 11:6 the writer says, "Without faith it is impossible to please God. For whoever would draw near to God must believe that he exists and that he is the rewarder of those who seek him." In other words, the faith which pleases God is a confidence that God will reward us when we come to him. But surely this does not mean that we are to be motivated by material things. Surely the reward we long for is the glory of God himself and the perfected companionship of Christ (Hebrews 2:10; 3:6; 10:34; 11:26; 12:22-24; 13:5). We will sell everything to have the treasure of Christ himself.

So the faith which pleases God is the assurance that when we turn to him we will find the all-satisfying Treasure. We will find our heart's eternal delight. But do you see what this implies? It implies that something has happened in our hearts *before* the act of faith. It implies that beneath and behind the act of faith which pleases God, a new taste has been created. A taste for the glory of God and the beauty of Christ. Behold, a joy has been born!

Once we had no delight in God, and Christ was just a vague historical figure. What we enjoyed was food and friendships and productivity and investments and vacations and hobbies and games and reading and shopping and sex and sports and art and TV and travel . . . but not God. He was an idea — even a good one — and a topic for discussion; but he was not a treasure of delight.

Then something miraculous happened. It was like the opening of the eyes of the blind during the golden dawn. First the stunned silence before the unspeakable beauty of holiness. Then a shock and terror that we had actually loved the darkness. Then the settling stillness of joy that this is the soul's end. The quest is over. We would give anything if we might be granted to live in the presence of this glory forever and ever.

And then, faith — the confidence that Christ has made a way for me, a sinner, to live in his glorious fellowship forever, the confidence that if I come to God through Christ, he will give me the desire of my heart to share his holiness and behold his glory.

But before the confidence comes the craving. Before decision comes delight. Before trust comes the discovery of treasure.

We Come to Christ When We Love the Light

Is not this the teaching of John 3:18-20?

> "He who believes in [the Son of God] is not condemned; he who does not believe is condemned already, because he has not believed in the name of the only Son of God. And this is the judgment, that light has come into the world, and men loved darkness rather than light, because their deeds were evil. For everyone who does evil hates the light and does not come to the light, lest his deeds should be exposed."

The reason people do not come to the light is because they do not love it. Love for the light is not caused by coming to the light. We come because we love it. Otherwise our coming is no honor to the light. Could there be any holy motivation to believe in Christ where there is no taste for the beauty of Christ? To be sure we could be motivated by the desire to escape hell, or the desire to have material riches, or the desire to rejoin a departed loved one. But how does it honor the light when the only reason we come to the light is to find those things that we loved in the dark?

Is this saving faith?

Christ Died to Give Us Our Heart's Desire: God

Saving faith is the cry of a new creature in Christ. And the newness of the new creature is that it has a new taste. What was once distasteful or bland is now craved. Christ himself has become a Treasure Chest of holy joy. The tree of faith grows only in the heart that craves the supreme gift that Christ died to give: not health, not wealth, not prestige, but God![17]

"Christ died for sins once for all . . . that he might bring us to *God*" (1 Peter 3:18). "Through him we have access in one Spirit to *the Father*" (Ephesians 2:18). "Through him we have obtained access to grace . . . and we rejoice in our hope of sharing the glory of *God*. . . . We rejoice in *God* through our Lord Jesus Christ" (Romans 5:2,11).

A New Passion for the Pleasure of God's Presence

> The awakening of an irresistible thirst for Christ
> is the creation of a Christian Hedonist.
>
> The pursuit of joy in God is
> not only innocent,
> it is essential.
>
> The birth of that pursuit is the birth of Christian life.

The pursuit of joy in God is not optional. It is not an "extra" that a person might grow into after he comes to faith. Until your heart has hit upon this pursuit, your "faith" cannot please God. It is not saving faith.

Saving faith is the confidence that if you sell all you have, and forsake all sinful pleasures, the hidden treasure of holy joy will satisfy your deepest desires. Saving faith is the heartfelt conviction not only that Christ is reliable, but also that he is desirable. It is the confidence that he will come through with his promises *and* that what he promises is more to be desired than all the world.

We may speak of the "joy of faith" at three levels. First, there is the new spiritual taste created by the Spirit of God for the glory of God. This new taste is the seed and root of joy. Thus it is the "joy of faith" in embryo, as it were. Second, there is the shoot, the stem, of faith itself reaching out actively for all that God is for us in Christ. The pith of this stem is joy in God. It is not possible for vital, genuine faith in the Fountain of Joy not to partake of that joy. Joyless embracing of the God of hope, for who he really is, is impossible. Third, there is the fruit of daily gladness that Paul speaks of in Romans 15:13, "May the God of hope fill you with *joy* and peace *in believing*." Here joy and peace flow out *from* faith into the whole of life.

In conversion we find the hidden Treasure of the kingdom of God. We venture all on it. And year after year in the struggles of life we prove the value of the treasure again and again, and we discover new depths of riches we had never known. And so the joy of faith grows. When Christ calls us to a new act of obedience that will cost us some temporal pleasure, we call to mind the surpassing value of following him, and by faith in his proven worth we forsake the worldly pleasure. The result? More joy! More faith! Deeper than before. And so we go on from joy to joy, and faith to faith.

Behind the repentance that turns away from sin and behind the faith that embraces Christ is the birth of a new taste, a new longing, a new passion for the pleasure of God's presence. This is the root of conversion. This is the creation of a Christian Hedonist.

"The hour is coming, and now is, when the true worshipers
will worship the Father in spirit and truth, for such the Father
seeks to worship him. God is spirit, and those who worship him
must worship him in spirit and in truth."

JOHN 4:23-24

WORSHIP

The Feast of Christian Hedonism

Soul-Hunter

Sometimes spiritual sleepers need to be shocked. If you want them to hear what you have to say, you might even need to scandalize them. Jesus is especially good at this. When he wants to teach us something about worship, he uses a whore!

"Go call your husband," he says to the Samaritan woman.

"I don't have a husband," she answers.

"That's right," Jesus says. "But you've had five, and the man you sleep with now is not your husband."

She is shocked. We're shocked! But Jesus simply sits there on the edge of the well with his hands folded, looking at the woman with razors in his eyes, ready to teach us about worship.

The first thing we learn is that worship has to do with real life. It is not a mythical interlude in a week of reality. Worship has to do with adultery and hunger and racial conflict.

Jesus is bone-weary from the journey. He is hot and thirsty. He decides: "Yes, even now, just now, I will seek someone to worship the Father — a Samaritan adultress. I will show my disciples how my Father seeks worship in the midst of real life from the least likely. She is a Samaritan. She is a woman. She is a harlot. Yes, I will even show them a thing or two about how to make true worshipers out of the white harvest of harlots in Samaria."

Lifting the Level of Amazement

Let's back up to the beginning of the story. "Jesus had to pass through Samaria" on his way to Galilee. "So he came to a city of Samaria called Sychar . . . Jacob's well was there and so Jesus, wearied as he was with his journey, sat down beside the well. It was about noon" (John 4:4-6).

The Samaritans were leftovers from the northern Jewish kingdom who had intermarried with foreigners after the chiefs and nobles were taken into exile in 722 B.C. They had once built a separate worship place on their own Mount Gerizim. They rejected all of the Old Testament except their own version of the first five books of Moses. Their animosity toward Jews (such as Jesus) was centuries old.

Jesus walks right into this hostility, sits down, and asks for a drink. The woman is stunned that Jesus would even speak to her: "How is it that you, a Jew, ask a drink of me, a woman of Samaria?"

Instead of answering her directly, Jesus shifts the focus of her amazement up a level. He says, "If you knew the gift of God and who it is that says to you 'Give me a drink,' you would have asked him and he would have given you living water." The really amazing thing is not that he asked her for a drink, but that she didn't ask him! He has "living water" and he calls it the "gift of God."

But the woman doesn't rise very high. She simply says, "How can you give me water when you don't have a bucket?" She is not on Jesus' wavelength yet.

So Jesus again lifts the level of amazement. "Every one who drinks of this water will thirst again, but whoever drinks of the water that I shall give him will never thirst; the water that I shall give him will become in him a spring of water welling up to eternal life." The amazing thing is not that he can give her water without a bucket, but that his water satisfies forever. Even more: when you drink it your soul becomes a spring. It is miracle water: it buries itself in a sandy soul and bubbles up a spring of life.

What does this mean?

The Water That Becomes a Well

"The teaching of the wise is a fountain of life," says Proverbs 13:14. Perhaps, then, Jesus means that his teaching is a fountain of life. When thirsty people drink it, they revive and then give it to others. Did he not say, "The words that I have spoken to you are spirit and life" (John 6:63)?

But the closest parallel to the image of a soul becoming a spring is in John 7:37-39: "Jesus stood up and proclaimed, 'If anyone thirsts, let him come to me and drink. He who believes in me, as the Scripture has said, out of his heart shall flow rivers of living water.' Now this he said about the Spirit which those who believed in him were to receive."

So the water Jesus gives is the Holy Spirit. The presence of God's Spirit in your life takes away the frustrated soul-thirst and turns you into a fountain where others can find life.

But probably both these meanings are true. Both the teaching of Jesus and the Holy Spirit satisfy the longing of our souls and make us into fountains for others. Jesus held the Word and the Spirit together.

For example, in John 14:26 he said, "The Spirit whom the Father will send in my name, he will teach you all things and bring to your remembrance all that I have said." The work of the Spirit of Christ is to make the Word of Christ clear and satisfying to the soul.

The water offered to the Samaritan adultress was the Word of truth and the power of the Spirit. When we come to Christ to drink, what we drink is truth — not dry, lifeless, powerless truth, but truth soaked with the life-giving Spirit of God! The Word of promise and the power of the Spirit are the living water held out to the Samaritan harlot.

To the Heart through a Wound

But again the woman misses the point. She cannot rise above her five senses. "Sir, give me this water that I may not thirst, nor come here to draw." Beware of giving up on people too soon, though. Jesus has set his saving sights on this woman. He aims to create a worshiper of God "in spirit and truth."

So now he touches the most sensitive and vulnerable spot in her life. "Go call your husband." The quickest way to the heart is through a wound.

Why does Jesus strip open the woman's inner life like this? Because he had said in John 3:20, "Everyone who does evil hates the light and does not come to the light lest his deeds should be exposed." Concealed sin keeps us from seeing the light of Christ.

Sin is like spiritual leprosy. It deadens your spiritual senses so that you rip your soul to shreds and don't even feel it. But Christ lays bare her spiritual leprosy. "You have had five husbands and the man you are sleeping with now is not your husband."

A Trapped Animal Will Chew Off Its Leg

Now watch the universal reflex of a person trying to avoid conviction. She has to admit that he has extraordinary insight: "Sir, I perceive that you are a prophet." But instead of going the direction he pointed, she tries to switch over to an academic controversy: "Our fathers worshiped on this mountain; but you Jews say that in Jerusalem is the place where people ought to worship. What's your position on this issue?"

A trapped animal will chew off its own leg to escape. A trapped sinner will mangle her own mind and rip up the rules of logic. "Why, yes, as long as we are talking about my adultery, what is your stance on the issue of where people should worship?" This is standard evasive double-talk for trapped sinners.

But the great Soul-Hunter is not so easily eluded. He does not insist she stay on his path. He will follow her into the bush. Or could it be that he circled around and is waiting there for her as she brings up the subject of worship? He never goes back to the issue of adultery. It was a thrust against the sealed door of her heart. But now his foot is in and he is willing to deal with the issue of worship.

The How and Whom of Worship

She raised the issue of *where* people ought to worship. Jesus responds by saying, "That controversy can't compare in importance with the issue of *how* and *whom* you worship."

First he draws her attention to the *how*. "Jesus said to her, 'Woman, believe me, the hour is coming when neither on this mountain nor in Jerusalem will you worship the Father.'" In other words, don't get bogged down in unessential controversies. It is possible to worship God in vain both in your place and in ours! Did not God say, "This people honor me with their lips, while their hearts are far from me" (Isaiah 29:13)? The issue is not where, but how.

Then he rivets her attention on *whom*. "You worship what you do not know; we worship what we know, for salvation is from the Jews." These are harsh words. But when life and death are at stake there comes a point when you put the matter bluntly — like telling a person with lung disease to stop smoking.

The Samaritans rejected all the Old Testament except their own version of the first five books. Their knowledge of God was deficient. Therefore Jesus tells her that Samaritan worship is deficient. It matters whether you know the One you worship!

How and *whom* are crucial, not *where*. Worship must be vital and real in the heart, and worship must rest on a true perception of God. There must be spirit and there must be truth. So Jesus says, "The hour is coming, and now is, when the true worshipers will worship the Father in spirit and truth." The two words, "spirit and truth," correspond to the *how* and *whom* of worship.

Worshiping in spirit is the opposite of worshiping in merely external ways. It is the opposite of empty formalism and traditionalism. Worshiping in truth is the opposite of worship based on an inadequate view of God. Worship must have heart and head. Worship must engage emotions and thought.

Truth without emotion produces dead orthodoxy and a church full (or half-full) of artificial admirers (like people who write generic anniversary cards for a living). On the other hand, emotion without truth produces empty frenzy and cultivates shallow people who refuse the discipline of rigorous thought. But true worship comes from people who are deeply emotional and who love deep and sound doctrine. Strong affections for God rooted in truth are the bone and marrow of biblical worship.

Fuel, Furnace, and Heat

Perhaps we can tie things together with this picture: The fuel of worship is the truth of God, the furnace of worship is the spirit of man, and the heat of worship is the vital affections of reverence, contrition, trust, gratitude, and joy.

But there is something missing from this picture. There is furnace, fuel, and heat, but no *fire*. The fuel of truth in the furnace of our spirit does not automatically produce the heat of worship. There must be ignition and fire. This is the Holy Spirit.

When Jesus says, "True worshipers will worship the Father in spirit and truth," some interpreters take this to refer to the Holy Spirit. I have taken it to mean our spirit. But maybe these two interpretations are not far apart in Jesus' mind. In John 3:6 Jesus connects God's Spirit and our spirit in a remarkable way.

He says, "That which is born of the Spirit is spirit." In other words, until the Holy Spirit quickens our spirit with the flame of life, our spirit is so dead and unresponsive it does not even qualify as spirit. Only that which is born of the Spirit is spirit. So when Jesus says that true worshipers worship the Father "in spirit" he must mean that true worship comes only from spirits made alive and sensitive by the quickening of the Spirit of God.

Now we can complete our picture. The fuel of worship is a true vision of the greatness of God; the fire that makes the fuel burn white hot is the quickening of the Holy Spirit; the furnace made alive and warm by the flame of truth is our renewed spirit; and the resulting heat of our affections is powerful worship, pushing its way out in confessions, longings, acclamations, tears, songs, shouts, bowed heads, lifted hands and obedient lives.

From Matters of Food to Matters of Faith

Now back to Samaria for a moment. The disciples had gone into town for food. Jesus had been alone with the woman by the well. When the disciples returned they offered Jesus lunch. But he did the same thing with them that he did with the woman — he jumped from matters of food to matters of faith. "I have food to eat which you do not know." Jesus had been eating the whole time they were gone. But what? "My food is to do the will of him who sent me, and to accomplish his work." And what is the work of the Father? The Father is seeking people to worship him in spirit and truth.

The whole interchange between Jesus and the Samaritan adultress is the work of God to make a genuine worshiper. Then Jesus applies the episode to the disciples — and to us! "Do you not say there are yet four months and then comes the harvest? I tell you, lift up your eyes and see how the fields are already white for harvest." He is saying, "There is a white harvest of harlots in

Samaria. I have just made one into a worshiper of God. That is why the Father sent me — so send I you. God seeks people to worship him in spirit and truth. Here comes the city of Sychar white unto harvest. If you love the glory of God make ready to reap."

Christ has set a course for us in the rest of this chapter on worship. What does it really mean to worship "in spirit and truth"? What is the response of the Spirit-quickened spirit of man? What is the relationship of truth to this experience? That's our plan: to ponder the nature of worship as an affair of the heart, and then as an affair of the mind. Then at the end we will briefly consider the external form of worship.

An Affair of the Heart

Almost everyone would agree that biblical worship involves some kind of outward act. The very word in Hebrew means to bow down. Worship is bowing, lifting hands, praying, singing, reciting, preaching, performing rites of eating, cleansing, ordaining, and so on.

But the startling fact is that all these things can be done in vain. They can be pointless and useless and empty. This is the warning of Jesus in Matthew 15:8-9 when he devastates the Pharisees with God's word from Isaiah 29:13,

> "These people honor me with their lips but their heart is far
> from me; in vain do they worship me."

First, notice that the parallel between the phrases "honor me" and "worship me" shows that worship is essentially a way of honoring God. Of course, that doesn't mean making him honorable or increasing his honor. It means recognizing it and feeling the worth of it and ascribing it to him in all the ways appropriate to his character.

> Honor and majesty are before him, strength and beauty are in
> his sanctuary. Ascribe to the LORD, O families of the peoples,
> ascribe to the LORD glory and strength! Ascribe to the LORD the
> glory due his name. (Psalm 96:6-8)

So the first thing to see in Jesus' words is that worship is a way of gladly reflecting back to God the radiance of his worth.

The reason for saying "gladly" is that even mountains and trees reflect back to God the radiance of his worth: "Praise the LORD from the earth . . . mountains and all hills, fruit trees and all cedars!" (Psalm 148:7,9). Yet this reflection of God's glory in nature is not conscious. The mountains and hills do not willingly worship. In all the earth, only humans have this unique capacity.

If we do not gladly reflect God's glory in worship, we will nevertheless reflect the glory of his justice in our own condemnation. "Surely the wrath of men shall praise thee" (Psalm 76:10). But this unwilling reflection of God's worth is *not* worship. Therefore it is necessary to define worship not simply as a way of reflecting back to God the radiance of his worth, but, more precisely, as a way of doing it *gladly.*

The word "gladly" is liable to misunderstanding because (as we will see in a moment) worship at times involves contrition and brokenness, which we do not usually associate with gladness. But I keep the word because if we say only, for example, that worship is a "willing" reflection back to God of his worth, then we are on the brink of a worse misunderstanding, namely, that worship can be willed when the heart has no real desire, or as Jesus says, when the heart is "far from God." Moreover, I think we will see that in genuine biblical contrition there is at least a seed of gladness that comes from the awakening hope that "God revives the spirit of the contrite" (Isaiah 57:15).

How to Worship God in Vain

This leads to the second thing to see in Matthew 15:8, namely, that we can "worship" God in vain. "These people honor me with their lips but their heart is far from me." An act of worship is vain and futile when it does not come from the heart. This was implied in the words of Jesus to the Samaritan adultress: "True worshipers will worship the Father in spirit and truth, for such the Father seeks to worship him" (John 4:23). Now what is this experience of the spirit? What goes on in the heart when worship is *not* in vain?

It is more than an act of mere willpower. All the outward acts of worship are performed by acts of will. But that does not make them authentic. The will can be present (for all kinds of reasons) while the heart is not truly engaged (or, as Jesus says, is "far away"). The engagement of the heart in worship is the coming alive of the feelings and emotions and affections of the heart.[1] Where feelings for God are dead, worship is dead.

The Affections That Make Worship Authentic

Now let's be specific. What are these feelings or affections that make the outward acts of worship authentic? For an answer we turn to the inspired psalms and hymns of the Old Testament. An array of different and intertwined affections may grip the heart at any time. So the extent and order of the following list is not intended to limit the possibilities of pleasure in anyone's heart.

Perhaps the first response of the heart at seeing the majestic holiness of

God is stunned silence. "Be still and know that I am God!" (Psalm 46:10). "The LORD is in his holy temple; let all the earth keep silence before him" (Habakkuk 2:20).

In the silence rises a sense of awe and reverence and wonder at the sheer magnitude of God. "Let all the earth fear the LORD, let all the inhabitants of the world stand in awe of him" (Psalm 33:8).

And because we are all sinners there is in our reverence a holy dread of God's righteous power. "The LORD of hosts, him you shall regard as holy; let him be your fear, and let him be your dread" (Isaiah 8:13). "I will worship toward thy holy temple in the fear of thee" (Psalm 5:7).

But this dread is not a paralyzing fright full of resentment against God's absolute authority. It finds release in brokenness and contrition and grief for our ungodliness. "The sacrifice acceptable to God is a broken spirit; a broken and contrite heart, O God, thou wilt not despise" (Psalm 51:17). "Thus says the high and lofty One who inhabits eternity, whose name is Holy: 'I dwell in the high and holy place, and also with him who is of a contrite and humble spirit, to revive the spirit of the humble, and to revive the heart of the contrite' " (Isaiah 57:15).

Mingled with the feeling of genuine brokenness and contrition there arises a longing for God. "As a hart longs for the flowing streams, so longs my soul for thee, O God. My soul thirsts for God, for the living God" (Psalm 42:1-2). "Whom have I in heaven but thee? And there is nothing on earth that I desire besides thee. My flesh and my heart may fail, but God is the strength of my heart and my portion forever" (Psalm 73:25-26). "O God, thou art my God, I seek thee, my soul thirsts for thee; my flesh faints for thee, as in a dry and weary land where no water is" (Psalm 63:1).

God is not unresponsive to the contrite longing of the soul. He comes and lifts the load of sin and fills our heart with gladness and gratitude. "Thou hast turned for me my mourning into dancing; thou hast loosed my sackcloth and girded me with gladness, that my soul may praise thee and not be silent. O LORD my God, I will give thanks to thee forever" (Psalm 30:11-12).

But our joy does not just rise from the backward glance in gratitude. It also rises from the forward glance in hope.

"Why are you downcast, O my soul, and why are you disquieted within me? Hope in God; for I shall again praise him, my help and my God" (Psalm 42:5). "I wait for the LORD, my soul waits, and in his word I hope" (Psalm 130:5).

In the end the heart longs not for any of God's good gifts, but for God himself. To see him and know him and be in his presence is the soul's final feast. Beyond this there is no quest. Words fail. We call it pleasure, joy, delight. But these are weak pointers to the unspeakable experience.

"One thing have I asked of the LORD, that will I seek after; that I may dwell in the house of the LORD all the days of my life, to behold the beauty of the LORD, and to inquire in his temple" (Psalm 27:4). "In thy presence there is fullness of joy, in thy right hand are pleasures for evermore" (Psalm 16:11). "Take delight in the LORD . . ." (Psalm 37:4).

These are some of the affections of the heart that keep worship from being "in vain." Worship is a way of gladly reflecting back to God the radiance of his worth. It is not a mere act of willpower by which we perform outward acts. Without the engagement of the heart, we do not really worship. The engagement of the heart in worship is the coming alive of the feelings and emotions and affections of the heart. *Where feelings for God are dead, worship is dead.*

True worship must include inward feelings that reflect the worth of God's glory. If this were not so, the word *hypocrite* would have no meaning. But there is such a thing as hypocrisy — going through outward motions (like singing, praying, giving, reciting) which signify affections of the heart that are not there. "These people honor me with their lips, but their heart is far from me."

Worship as an End in Itself

Now what does this imply about the feast of worship? Surprisingly, it implies that worship is an end in itself. We do not eat the feast of worship as a means to anything else. If what transforms outward ritual into authentic worship is the quickening of the heart's affections, then true worship cannot be performed as a means to some other experience. Feelings are not like that. Genuine feelings of the heart cannot be manufactured as stepping stones to something else.

For example: My brother-in-law called me long-distance in 1974 to tell me my mother had just been killed. I recall his breaking voice as I took the phone from my wife: "Johnny, this is Bob, good buddy. I've got bad news . . . Your mother and dad were in a serious bus accident. Your mom didn't make it, and your dad is hurt bad."

One thing is for sure. When I hear news like that, I do not sit down and say, "Now to what end shall I feel grief?" As I pull my baby son off my leg and hand him to my wife and walk to the bedroom to be alone, I do not say, "What good end can I accomplish if I cry for the next half-hour?" The feeling of grief is an end in itself, as far as my conscious motivation is concerned.

It is there spontaneously. It is not performed as a means to anything else. It is not consciously willed. It is not decided upon. It comes from deep within, from a place beneath the conscious will. It will no doubt have many byproducts — most of them good. But that is utterly beside the point as I kneel by my bed and weep. The feeling is there, bursting out of my heart. And it is an end in itself.

Grief is not the only example. If you have been floating on a raft without water for three days after a shipwreck on the ocean, and there appears a speck of land on the horizon, you do not say, "Now to what end shall I feel desire for that land? What good end should now prompt me to decide to feel hope?" Even though the longing in your heart may give you the renewed strength to get to land, you do *not* perform the act of desire and hope and longing in order to get there.

The longing erupts from deep in your heart because of the tremendous value of water (and life!) on that land. It is not planned and performed (like the purchase of a plane ticket) as a means to getting what we desire. It rises spontaneously in the heart. It is not a decision made in order to . . . anything! As a genuine feeling of the heart it is an end in itself.

Or consider fear. If you are camping in the Boundary Waters of Minnesota, and waken in the night to the sound of snorting outside, and then see in the moonlight the silhouette of a huge bear coming toward your tent, you do not say, "Now to what end shall I feel fear?" You do not calculate the good results that might come from the adrenaline that fear produces, and then decide that fear would be an appropriate and helpful emotion to have. It is just there!

When you stand at the edge of the Grand Canyon for the first time and watch the setting sun send the darkness down through the geological layers of time, you do not say, "Now to what end shall I feel awe and wonder before this beauty?"

When a little child on Christmas morning opens his first gift and finds his "most favoritest" rocket that he has wanted for months, he does not think, "Now to what end shall I feel happy and thankful?" We call a person an ingrate when words of gratitude are dutifully forced instead of coming spontaneously from the heart.

When a five-year-old enters kindergarten and starts getting picked on by some second-graders, and his big fourth-grade brother comes over and takes his side, he does not "decide" to feel confidence and love welling up in his little heart. He just does.

All genuine emotion is an end in itself. It is not consciously caused as a means to something else. This does not mean we cannot or should not seek to have certain feelings. We should and we can. We can put ourselves in situations where the feeling may more readily be kindled. We may indeed prize some of the results of these feelings as well as the feelings themselves. But in the moment of authentic emotion, the calculation vanishes. We are transported (perhaps only for seconds) above the reasoning work of the mind and we experience feeling without reference to logical or practical implications.

This is what keeps worship from being "in vain." Worship is authentic when affections for God arise in the heart as an end in themselves. In worship God is the dreaded voice on the phone. God is the island on the horizon. God is the bear and the setting sun and the "most favoritest" rocket and the mother who gave it and the big, strong fourth-grade brother.

If God's reality is displayed to us in his Word or his world, and we do not then feel in our heart any grief or longing or hope or fear or awe or joy or gratitude or confidence, then we may dutifully sing and pray and recite and gesture as much as we like, but it will not be real worship. We cannot honor God if our "heart is far from him."

Worship is a way of gladly reflecting back to God the radiance of his worth. This cannot be done by mere acts of duty. It can be done only when spontaneous affections arise in the heart.

You Must Kiss Me, but Not That Kind of Must

Consider the analogy of a wedding anniversary. Mine is on December 21. Suppose on this day I bring home a dozen long-stemmed red roses for Noël. When she meets me at the door I hold out the roses, and she says, "O Johnny, they're beautiful, thank you," and gives me a big hug. Then suppose I hold up my hand and say matter-of-factly, "Don't mention it; it's my duty."

What happens? Is not the exercise of duty a noble thing? Do not we honor those we dutifully serve? Not much. Not if there's no heart in it. Dutiful roses are a contradiction in terms. If I am not moved by a spontaneous affection for her as a person, the roses do not honor her. In fact they belittle her. They are a very thin covering for the fact that she does not have the worth or beauty in my eyes to kindle affection. All I can muster is a calculated expression of marital duty.

Here is the way Edward John Carnell puts it:

> Suppose a husband asks his wife if he must kiss her good night.
> Her answer is, "You must, but not that kind of a must." What
> she means is this: "Unless a spontaneous affection for my per-
> son motivates you, your overtures are stripped of all moral
> value."[2]

The fact is, many of us have failed to see that duty toward God can never be restricted to outward action. Yes, we must worship him. "But not that kind of must." What kind then? The kind C. S. Lewis described to Sheldon Vanauken: "It is a Christian duty, as you know, for everyone to be as happy as he can."[3]

The real duty of worship is not the outward duty to say or do the liturgy. It is the inward duty, the command — "Delight yourself in the LORD!" (Psalm 37:4). "Be glad in the LORD and rejoice!" (Psalm 32:11).

The reason this is the real duty of worship is that this honors God, while the empty performance of ritual does not. If I take my wife out for the evening on our anniversary and she asks me, "Why do you do this?" the answer that honors her most is, "Because nothing makes me happier tonight than to be with you."

"It's my duty" is a dishonor to her.

"It's my joy" is an honor.

There it is! The feast of Christian Hedonism. How shall we honor God in worship? By saying, "It's my duty"? Or by saying, "It's my joy"?

Worship is a way of reflecting back to God the radiance of his worth. Now we see that the mirror that catches the rays of his radiance and reflects them back in worship is the joyful heart. Another way of saying this is to say

The chief end of man is to glorify God
BY
enjoying him forever.

Beware of Giving to God

Now it becomes clear why it is significant that worship is an end in itself. Worship is an end in itself because it is the final end for which we were created.

It also becomes clear why it is not idolatrous and man-centered to say that our emotions are ends in themselves. It is not man-centered because the emotions of our worship are centered on *God!* We look away from ourselves to him, and only then do the manifold emotions of our heart erupt in worship.[4]

Nor is it idolatrous to say our affections in worship are ends in themselves, because our affections for God glorify God, not us. Whoever thought he was glorifying himself and not the Grand Canyon when he stood at its edge for hours in silent awe? Whoever would accuse me of glorifying myself and not my wife when I tell her, "I delight to spend this evening with you"? Who would accuse a little child of self-centeredness on Christmas morning if he runs away from his new rocket to hug his mother and say thank you because he is bursting with joyful gratitude?

Someone might object that in making the joy of worship an end in itself, we make God a means to our end rather than our being a means to his end. Thus we seem to elevate ourselves above God. But consider this question: Which glorifies God more — that is, which reflects back to God more clearly the greatness of his glory — (1) a worship experience that comes to climax with joy in the wonder of God, or (2) an experience that comes to climax in a noble attempt to free itself from rapture in order to make a contribution to the goal of God?

This is a subtle thing. We strive against God's all-sufficient glory if we think we can become a means to *his* end without making joy in him *our* end. Christian Hedonism does not put us above God when it makes the joy of worship its goal. It is precisely in confessing our frustrated, hopeless condition without him that we honor him. A patient is not greater than his doctor because he longs to be made well. A child is not greater than his father when he wants the fun of playing together with him.

On the contrary, the one who actually sets himself above God is the person who presumes to come to God to give rather than get. With a pretense of self-denial he positions himself as God's benefactor — as if the world and all it contains were not already God's (Psalm 50:12)!

No, the hedonistic approach to God in worship is the only humble approach because it is the only one that comes with empty hands. Christian Hedonism pays God the respect of acknowledging (and really feeling!) that he alone can satisfy the heart's longing to be happy. Worship is an end in itself because we glorify God *by* enjoying him forever.

Three Stages of Worship

But this is liable to be misunderstood. It might give the impression that we cannot come to God in real worship unless we are overflowing with the affections of delight and joy and hope and gratitude and wonder and awe and reverence. I do not believe this is necessarily implied in what I have said.

I see three stages of movement toward the ideal experience of worship. We may experience all three in one hour, and God is pleased with all three — if indeed they are stages on the way to full joy in him. I will mention them in reverse order.

1. There is the final stage in which we feel an unencumbered joy in the manifold perfections of God — the joy of gratitude, wonder, hope, admiration. "My soul is feasted as with marrow and fat and my mouth praises thee with joyful lips" (Psalm 63:5). In this stage we are satisfied with the excellency of God, and we overflow with the joy of his fellowship. This is the feast of Christian Hedonism.

2. In a prior stage that we often taste, we do not feel fullness, but rather longing and desire. Having tasted the feast before, we recall the goodness of the Lord — but it seems far off. We preach to our souls not to be downcast, because we are sure we shall again praise the Lord (Psalm 42:5). Yet for now our hearts are not very fervent.

Even though this falls short of the ideal of vigorous, heartfelt adoration and hope, yet it is a great honor to God. We honor the water from a mountain spring not only by the satisfied "ahhh" after drinking our fill, but also by the unquenched longing to be satisfied while still climbing to it.

In fact, these two stages are not really separable in the true saint, because all satisfaction in this life is still shot through with longing and all genuine longing has tasted the satisfying water of life. David Brainerd expressed the paradox:

> Of late God has been pleased to keep my soul hungry almost continually, so that I have been filled with a kind of pleasing pain. When I really enjoy God, I feel my desires of Him the more insatiable and my thirstings after holiness more unquenchable.[5]

3. The lowest stage of worship — where all genuine worship starts, and where it often returns for a dark season — is the barrenness of soul that scarcely feels any longing, and yet is still granted the grace of repentant sorrow for having so little love. "When my soul was embittered, when I was pricked in heart, I was stupid and ignorant, I was like a beast toward thee" (Psalm 73:22).

E. J. Carnell points toward these same stages when he says,

> Rectitude, we know, is met in one of two ways: either by a spontaneous expression of the good or by spontaneous sorrow for having failed. The one is a direct fulfillment; the other is indirect fulfillment.[6]

Worship is a way of gladly reflecting back to God the radiance of his worth. This is the ideal. For God surely is more glorified when we delight in his magnificence than when we are so unmoved by it we scarcely feel anything, and only wish we could. Yet he is also glorified by the spark of anticipated gladness that gives rise to the sorrow we feel when our hearts are lukewarm. Even in the miserable guilt we feel over our beast-like insensitivity, the glory of God shines. If God were not gloriously desirable, why would we feel sorrowful for not feasting fully on his beauty?

Yet even this sorrow, to honor God, must in one sense be an end in itself — not that it shouldn't lead on to something better, but that it must be real and spontaneous. The glory from which we fall short cannot be reflected in a calculated sorrow. As Carnell says, "Indirect fulfillment is stripped of virtue whenever it is made a goal of conscious striving. Whoever deliberately tries to be sorry will never be sorry. Sorrow cannot be induced by human effort."[7]

The Moral Enemy of Worship

I conclude from this meditation on the nature of worship that the revolt against hedonism has killed the spirit of worship in many churches and many hearts. The widespread notion that high moral acts must be free from self-interest is a great enemy of true worship. Worship is the highest moral act a human can perform; so the only basis and motivation for it that many people can conceive is the notion of morality as the disinterested performance of duty. But when worship is reduced to disinterested duty, it ceases to be worship. For worship is a feast.

Neither God nor my wife is honored when we celebrate the high days of our relationship out of a sense of duty. They are honored when I delight in them! Therefore to honor God in worship we must not seek him disinterestedly, for fear of gaining some joy in worship and so ruining the moral value of the act. But instead we must seek him hedonistically, the way a thirsty deer seeks the stream, precisely for the joy of seeing and knowing him! Worship is nothing less than obedience to the command of God, "Delight yourself in the LORD!"

Misguided virtue smothers the spirit of worship. The person who has the vague notion that it is virtue to overcome self-interest, and that it is vice to seek pleasure, will scarcely be able to worship. For worship is the most hedonistic affair of life and must not be ruined with the least thought of disinterestedness. The great hindrance to worship is not that we are a pleasure-seeking people, but that we are willing to settle for such pitiful pleasures.

The prophet Jeremiah put it like this:

> "My people have exchanged their glory for that which does not profit. Be appalled, O heavens, at this; be shocked, be utterly desolate," says the LORD; "for my people have committed two evils: they have forsaken me, the fountain of living waters, and hewed out cisterns for themselves, broken cisterns that can hold no water." (Jeremiah 2:11-13)

The heavens are appalled and shocked when people give up soon on their quest for pleasure and settle for broken cisterns.

We Are Far Too Easily Pleased

One of the most important things I ever read on my pilgrimage toward Christian Hedonism was from a sermon preached by C. S. Lewis in 1941. He said,

> If there lurks in most modern minds the notion that to desire our own good and earnestly to hope for the enjoyment of it is a bad thing, I submit that this notion has crept in from Kant and the Stoics and is no part of the Christian faith. Indeed, if we consider the unblushing promises of reward and the staggering nature of the rewards promised in the Gospels, it would seem that our Lord finds our desires, not too strong, but too weak. We are half-hearted creatures, fooling about with drink and sex and ambition when infinite joy is offered us, like an ignorant child who wants to go on making mud pies in a slum because he cannot imagine what is meant by the offer of a holiday at the sea. We are far too easily pleased.[8]

That's it! The enemy of worship is not that our desire for pleasure is too strong but too weak! We have settled for a home, a family, a few friends, a job, a television, a microwave oven, an occasional night out, a yearly vacation, and perhaps a new personal computer. We have accustomed ourselves to such meager, short-lived pleasures that our capacity for joy has shriveled. And so our worship has shriveled. Many can scarcely imagine what is meant by "a holiday at the sea" — worshiping the living God!

The Shriveling of Darwin's Soul

Through long drinking at the broken cistern of mud-pie pleasures, many have lost almost all capacity for delighting in God — not unlike what happened to Charles Darwin. Near the end of his life he wrote an autobiography for his children and expressed one regret:

> Up to the age of 30 or beyond it, poetry of many kinds . . . gave me great pleasure, and even as a schoolboy I took intense delight in Shakespeare. . . . formerly pictures gave me considerable, and music very great, delight. But now for many years I cannot endure to read a line of poetry: I have tried to read Shakespeare, and found it so intolerably dull that it nauseated

me. I have also almost lost any taste for pictures or music. . . . I retain some taste for fine scenery, but it does not cause me the exquisite delight which it formerly did. . . . My mind seems to have become a kind of machine for grinding general laws out of large collections of facts, but why this should have caused the atrophy of that part of the brain alone, on which the higher tastes depend, I cannot conceive. . . . The loss of these tastes is a loss of happiness, and may possibly be injurious to the intellect, and more probably to the moral character, by enfeebling the emotional part of our nature.[9]

Worship services across the land bear the scars of this process. For many, Christianity has become the grinding out of general doctrinal laws from collections of biblical facts. But childlike wonder and awe have died. The scenery and poetry and music of the majesty of God have dried up like a forgotten peach at the back of the refrigerator.

And the irony is that we have aided and abetted the desiccation by telling people they ought not seek their own pleasure, especially in worship.[10] We have implied in a thousand ways that the virtue of an act diminishes to the degree you enjoy doing it, and that doing something because it yields happiness is bad. The notion hangs like a gas in the Christian atmosphere.

Immanuel Kant and Hebrews 11:6 in Combat

C. S. Lewis thought Immanuel Kant (who died in 1804) was a culprit in this confusion. So did the atheist Ayn Rand. Her striking description of Kant's ethics, if not historically precise, is at least a good description of the paralyzing effects it seems to have had in the church:

> An action is moral, said Kant, only if one has no desire to perform it, but performs it out of a sense of duty and derives no benefit from it of any sort, neither material nor spiritual. A benefit destroys the moral value of an action. (Thus if one has no desire to be evil, one cannot be good; if one has, one can.)[11]

Ayn Rand equated this notion of virtue with Christianity and rejected the whole thing out of hand. But this is not Christianity! It was tragic for her and it is tragic for the church that this notion pervades the air of Christendom — the notion that the pursuit of joy is submoral, if not immoral.

Would that Ayn Rand had understood her Christian contemporary Flannery O'Connor:

I don't assume that renunciation goes with submission or even that renunciation is good in itself. Always you renounce a lesser good for a greater; the opposite is what sin is. . . . The struggle to submit . . . is not a struggle to submit but a struggle to accept and with passion. I mean, possibly, with joy. Picture me with my ground teeth stalking joy — fully armed too as it's a highly dangerous quest.[12]

Amen!

Every Sunday morning at 11 A.M., Hebrews 11:6 enters combat with Immanuel Kant. "Without faith it is impossible to please God. For whoever would draw near to God must believe that he exists and that *he is the rewarder of those who seek him.*" You cannot please God if you do not come to him for reward! Therefore, worship that pleases God is the hedonistic pursuit of God. He is our exceeding great reward! In his presence is fullness of joy and at his right hand are *pleasures* for evermore. Worship is the feast of Christian Hedonism.

An Affair of the Mind

God seeks people to worship him "in spirit and truth" (John 4:23). I have put tremendous emphasis on the "spirit" of worship in the previous section. Now I must balance the scales and reassert that true worship always combines heart and head, emotion and thought, affection and reflection, doxology and theology.

"True worshipers will worship the Father in spirit and truth." True worship does not come from people whose feelings are like air ferns with no root in the solid ground of biblical doctrine. The only affections that honor God are those rooted in the rock of biblical truth.

Else what meaning have the words of the apostle, "They have a zeal for God, but it is not according to knowledge" (Romans 10:2)? And did not the Lord pray, "Sanctify them by the truth; your word is truth" (John 17:17)? And did he not say, "You will know the truth and the truth shall make you free" (John 8:32)? Holy freedom in worship is the fruit of truth. Religious feelings that do not come from a true apprehension of God are neither holy nor truly free, no matter how intense.

The pastoral testimony of Jonathan Edwards has therefore always seemed to me inescapably biblical. He was the foremost defender of the Great Awakening in New England in the early 1740s. It had come under severe criticism because of apparent emotional excesses.

Charles Chauncy, pastor of the old First Church in Boston, opposed the revival strenuously. He pointed out all of its excesses like the "swooning away and falling to the ground . . . bitter shriekings and screamings; convulsion-like tremblings and agitations, strugglings and tumblings."[13]

Edwards did not defend the excesses, but he earnestly defended the deep and genuine engagement of the affections based on truth. He argued with these carefully chosen words:

> I should think myself in the way of my duty, to raise the affections of my hearers as high as I possibly can, provided they are affected with nothing but truth, and with affections that are not disagreeable to the nature of what they are affected with.[14]

Edwards was utterly convinced of the crucial importance of powerful affections in worship because

> The things of religion are so great, that there can be no suitableness in the exercises of our hearts, to their nature and importance, unless they be lively and powerful. In nothing is vigor in the actings of our inclinations so requisite, as in religion; and in nothing is lukewarmness so odious.[15]

Yet the only heat he valued in worship was the heat that comes with light. In 1744 he preached an ordination sermon from the text about John the Baptist, "He was a burning and shining light" (John 5:35). There must be heat in the heart and light in the mind — and no more heat than justified by the light!

> If a minister has light without heat, and entertains his [hearers] with learned discourses, without a savour of the power of godliness, or any appearance of fervency of spirit, and zeal for God and the good of souls, he may gratify itching ears, and fill the heads of his people with empty notions; but it will not be very likely to reach their souls. And if, on the other hand, he be driven on with a fierce and intemperate zeal, and vehement heat, without light, he will be likely to kindle the like unhallowed flame in his people, and to fire their corrupt passions and affections; but will make them never the better, nor lead them a step towards heaven, but drive them apace the other way.[16]

Strong affections for God, rooted in and shaped by the truth of Scripture — this is the bone and marrow of biblical worship.

Therefore Christian Hedonism is passionately opposed to all attempts to drive a wedge between deep thought and deep feeling. It rejects the common notion that profound reflection dries up fervent affection. It resists the assumption that intense emotion thrives only in the absence of coherent doctrine.

On the contrary, Christian Hedonists are persuaded with Edwards that the only affections that magnify God's value are those which come from true apprehensions of his glory. If the feast of worship is rare in the land, it is because there is a famine of the Word of God (Amos 8:11-12).

The Form of Worship

It follows that forms of worship should provide two things: channels for the mind to apprehend the truth of God's reality, and channels for the heart to respond to the beauty of that truth — that is, forms to ignite the affections with biblical truth, and forms to express the affections with biblical passion.

Of course, good forms do both. Good sermons and hymns and prayers express and inspire worship. And they do it best when they are unabashedly hedonistic and therefore God-centered.

Take preaching, for example. John Broadus was on target when he wrote a hundred years ago,

> The minister may lawfully appeal to the desire for happiness and its negative counterpart, the dread of unhappiness. Those philosophers [Kant?] who insist that we ought always to do right simply and only because it is right are not philosophers at all, for they are either grossly ignorant of human nature [and I would add: Scripture] or else indulging in mere fanciful speculations.[17]

Or take hymns! How unabashedly hedonistic they are! Hymns are the voices of the church's lovers; and lovers are the least duty-oriented and most God-besotted people in the world.

> Jesus, Thou joy of loving hearts
> Thou fount of life, Thou light of men
> From the best bliss that earth imparts
> We turn unfilled to Thee again.
> Bernard of Clairvaux

> Jesus, priceless treasure
> Source of purest pleasure,

Truest friend to me:
Long my heart hath panted,
'Til it well-nigh fainted,
Thirsting after Thee.
Thine I am,
O spotless Lamb,
I will suffer nought to hide Thee,
Ask for nought beside Thee.

Johann Franck

Jesus, I am resting, resting
In the joy of what Thou art;
I am finding out the greatness
Of Thy loving heart.
Thou hast bid me gaze upon Thee,
And Thy beauty fills my soul,
For by Thy transforming power,
Thou hast made me whole.

Jean Sophia Pigott

And for the prayers of the church what could suffice better than the inspired (hedonistic!) prayers of the psalmists!

Thou hast put more joy in my heart than they have when their grain and wine abound! (Psalm 4:7)

Let all who take refuge in thee rejoice, let them ever sing for joy; and do thou defend them, that those who love thy name may exult in thee. (Psalm 5:11)

I will be glad and exult in thee, I will sing praise to thy name, O Most High. (Psalm 9:2)

As for me, I shall behold thy face in righteousness; when I awake, I shall be satisfied with beholding thy form. (Psalm 17:15)

I delight to do thy will, O my God; thy law is within my heart. (Psalm 40:8)

Create in me a clean heart, O God, and put a new and right spirit within me. . . . Restore to me the joy of thy salvation, and uphold me with a willing spirit. (Psalm 51:10,12)

O God, thou art my God, I seek thee, my soul thirsts for thee; my flesh faints for thee, as in a dry and weary land where no water is. So I have looked upon thee in the sanctuary, beholding thy power and glory. Because thy steadfast love is better than life, my lips shall praise thee. (Psalm 63:1-3)

Whom have I in heaven but thee? And there is nothing upon earth that I desire besides thee. My flesh and my heart may fail, but God is the strength of my heart and my portion forever. (Psalm 73:25-26)

When the people of God — and especially the lead worshipers — begin to pray in this hedonistically God-centered way, then the form will both express and inspire authentic worship.

But in the end the form is not the issue. The issue is whether the excellency of Christ is seen. Worship will happen when the God who said, "Let light shine out of darkness," shines in our hearts to give us "the light of the knowledge of the glory of God in the face of Christ" (2 Corinthians 4:6).

We must see and feel the incomparable excellency of the Son of God. Incomparable because in him meet infinite glory and lowest humility, infinite majesty and transcendent meekness, deepest reverence toward God and equality with God, infinite worthiness of good and greatest patience to suffer evil, supreme dominion and exceeding obedience, divine self-sufficiency and childlike trust.[18]

The irony of our human condition is that God has put us within sight of the Himalayas of his glory in Jesus Christ, but we have chosen to pull down the shades of our chalet and show slides of Buck Hill — even in church. We are content to go on making mud pies in the slums because we cannot imagine what is meant by the offer of a holiday at the sea.

An Exhortation and an Experience

I close this chapter with an exhortation and experience. Don't let your worship decline to the performance of mere duty. Don't let the childlike awe and wonder be choked out by unbiblical views of virtue. Don't let the scenery and poetry and music of your relationship with God shrivel up and die. You have capacities for joy which you can scarcely imagine. They were made for the enjoyment of God. He can awaken them no matter how long they have lain asleep. Pray for his quickening power. Open your eyes to his glory. It is all around you. "The heavens declare the glory of God and the firmament proclaims his handiwork."

I was flying at night from Chicago to Minneapolis, almost alone on the plane. The pilot announced that there was a thunderstorm over Lake Michigan and into Wisconsin. He would skirt it to the west to avoid turbulence. As I sat there staring out into the total blackness, suddenly the whole sky was brilliant with light and a cavern of white clouds fell away four miles beneath the plane and then vanished. A second later, a mammoth white tunnel of light exploded from north to south across the horizon, and again vanished into blackness. Soon the lightning was almost constant and volcanoes of light burst up out of cloud ravines and from behind distant white mountains. I sat there shaking my head almost in unbelief. "O Lord, if these are but the sparks from the sharpening of your sword, what will be the day of your appearing!" And I remembered the word of Christ,

> As the lightning comes from the east,
> and shines as far as the west,
> so will be the coming of the Son of Man.
> (Luke 17:24)

Even now as I recollect that sight, the word *glory* is full of feeling for me. I thank God that again and again he has awakened my heart to desire him, to see him, and to sit down to the feast of Christian Hedonism and worship the King of Glory. The banquet hall is very large.

> The Spirit and the Bride say, "Come. . . . Let him who is thirsty come, let him who desires take the water of life without price." (Revelation 22:17)

In some sense the most benevolent, generous person in the world
seeks his own happiness in doing good to others, because he places
his happiness in their good. His mind is so enlarged as to take
them, as it were, into himself. Thus when they are happy, he
feels it; he partakes with them, and is happy in their happiness.
This is so far from being inconsistent with the freeness of
beneficence, that, on the contrary, free benevolence and
kindness consists in it.

JONATHAN EDWARDS

God loves a cheerful giver.

THE APOSTLE PAUL

CHAPTER 4

LOVE

The Labor of Christian Hedonism

I have argued so far that disinterested benevolence toward God is evil. If you come to God dutifully offering him the reward of your fellowship instead of thirsting after the reward of his fellowship, then you exalt yourself above God as his benefactor and belittle him as a needy beneficiary — and that is evil.

The only way to glorify the all-sufficiency of God in worship is to come to him because "in his presence is fullness of joy and at his right hand are pleasures for evermore" (Psalm 16:11). This has been the main point so far, and we could call it vertical Christian Hedonism. Between man and God, on the vertical axis of life, the pursuit of pleasure is not just tolerable; it is mandatory — "Delight yourself in the LORD!" The chief end of man is to glorify God *by* enjoying him forever.

But now what about horizontal Christian Hedonism? What about our relationships with other people? Is disinterested benevolence the ideal among men? Or is the pursuit of pleasure proper and indeed mandatory for every kind of human love which pleases God?

This chapter's answer is that the pursuit of pleasure is an essential motive for every good deed. Or, to put it another way, if you aim to abandon the pursuit of full and lasting pleasure, you cannot love people or please God.

Does Love Seek Its Own?

This will take some explaining and defending! I plead your patience and openness. I am swimming against the current of a revered river in this chapter. When I preached on this once, a philosophy professor wrote a letter to me with the following criticism:

> Is it not the contention of morality that we should do the good because it is the good? . . . We should do the good and perform virtuously, I suggest, because it is good and virtuous; that God will bless it and cause us to be happy is a consequence of it, but not the motive for doing it.

Another popular writer says,

> For the Christian, happiness is never a goal to be pursued. It is always the unexpected surprise of a life of service.

I regard these quotes as contrary to Scripture and contrary to love, and in the end (though unintentionally) dishonoring to God.

No doubt, biblical passages come to mind that seem to say exactly the opposite of what I am saying. For example, in the great "love chapter" the apostle Paul says, "Love does not seek its own" (1 Corinthians 13:5). Earlier in the same book he admonished the church, "Let no one seek his own [good] but that of the other. . . . I try to please all men in everything, not seeking my own advantage, but that of many, that they may be saved" (10:24,33). In Romans 15:1-3 he says, "We who are strong ought to bear with the failings of the weak, and not to please ourselves; let each of us please his neighbor for his good, to edify him. For Christ did not please himself."

An isolated and unreflective focus on texts like these gives the impression that the essence of Christian morality is to free ourselves of all self-interest when it comes to good deeds for other people. But there is good reason to think this impression is wrong. It does not take all of the context into account, and it certainly cannot account for many other teachings in the New Testament.

Take the context of 1 Corinthians 13, for example. Verse 5 says love seeks not its own. But is this meant so absolutely that it would be wrong to enjoy being loving? First consider the wider biblical context.

Should We Delight in Being Merciful?

According to the prophet Micah, God has commanded us not simply to be merciful but to "love mercy." "He has showed you, O man, what is good; and what does the LORD require of you but to do justice, and to love mercy, and to walk humbly with your God" (Micah 6:8). In other words, the command is not just to do acts of mercy, but to *delight* to be merciful or to *want* to be merciful. If you love being merciful, how can you keep from satisfying your own desire in doing acts of mercy? How can you keep from seeking your own joy in acts of love when your joy consists in being loving? Does obedience to the command to "love mercy" mean you must disobey the teaching of 1 Corinthians 13:5 that love should not "seek its own"?

No. The more immediate context gives several clues that the point of 1 Corinthians 13:5 is not to forbid the pursuit of the joy of loving. Jonathan Edwards gives the true sense when he says that the error 1 Corinthians 13:5 opposes is not:

the degree in which [a person] loves his own happiness, but in his placing his happiness where he ought not, and in limiting and confining his love. Some, although they love their own happiness, do not place that happiness in their own confined good, or in that good which is limited to themselves, but more in the common good — in that which is the good of others, or in the good to be enjoyed in and by others. . . . And when it is said that Charity seeketh not her own, we are to understand it of her own private good — good limited to herself.[1]

Does Paul Assume We Will Want to Gain Nothing?

One clue that this is in fact what Paul means is the way he tries to motivate genuine love in verse three. He says, "If I give away all I have, and if I deliver my body to be burned, but have not love, *I gain nothing.*" If genuine love dare not set its sights on its own gain, isn't it strange that Paul should warn us that not having love will rob us of "gain"? But this is in fact what he says: "If you don't have real love, you won't have real gain."

Someone no doubt will say that the gain is a sure result of genuine love, but if it is the motive of love, then love is not really love. In other words, it is good for God to reward acts of love, but it is not good for us to be drawn into love by the promise of reward. But if this is true, then why did Paul tell us in verse three that we would lose our reward if we were not really loving? If longing for the "gain" of loving ruins the moral value of love, it is very bad pedagogy to tell someone to be loving lest he lose his "gain."

Giving Paul the benefit of the doubt, should we not rather say there is a kind of "gain" that is wrong to be motivated by (hence "Love seeks not its own"), as well as a kind of "gain" that is right to be motivated by (hence "If I do not have love, I gain nothing")? Edwards says the proper "gain" to be motivated by is the happiness one gets in the act of love itself or in the good achieved by it.

Can Disinterested Love Rejoice in the Truth?

The second clue that Edwards is on the right track is verse six: "Love does not rejoice at wrong, but rejoices in the right [or: the truth]." Love is not a bare choice or mere act. It involves the affections. It does not just *do* the truth. Nor does it just choose the right. It rejoices in the way of truth. So Micah 6:8 was not a strained parallel at all: We must "love mercy"!

But if love rejoices in the choices it makes, it cannot be disinterested. It cannot be indifferent to its own joy! To rejoice in an act is to get joy from it. And this joy is "gain." It may be that there is much more gain than this, or that this joy is in fact the firstfruits of an indestructible and eternal joy. At this point, though, the least we can say is that Paul does not think the moral value of an act of love is ruined when we are motivated to do it by the anticipation of our own joy in it and from it. If it were, then a bad man, who hated the prospect of loving, could engage in pure love, since he would take no joy in it; while a good man, who delighted in the prospect of loving, could not love, since he would "gain" joy from it and thus ruin it.

Therefore 1 Corinthians 13:5 ("Love seeks not its own") does not stand in the way of the thesis that *the pursuit of pleasure is an essential motive for every good deed.* In fact, surprisingly, the context supports it by saying that "love *rejoices* in the truth," and by implying that one should be vigilant in love so as not to lose one's "gain" — the gain of joy that comes in being a loving person, both now and forever.

If this is Paul's intention in 1 Corinthians 13:5, the same thing can be said of 10:24 and 33. These are simply specific instances of the basic principle laid down in 13:5, "Love seeks not its own." When Paul says we should not seek our own advantage but that of our neighbors so that they may be saved, he does not mean we should not *delight* in the salvation of our neighbors.

In fact Paul said of his converts, "You are our glory and our *joy*" (1 Thessalonians 2:20). In another place he said, "My heart's *desire* and prayer to God is that they may be saved" (Romans 10:1).

This is not the voice of disinterested benevolence. The salvation of others was the joy and passion of his life! When he denied himself comforts for this he was a Christian Hedonist, not a dutiful stoic. So the point of 1 Corinthians 10:24 and 33 is that we should not count any private comfort a greater joy than the joy of seeing our labor lead to another's salvation.

This is also the point of Romans 15:1-3, where Paul says we should not please ourselves but instead should please our neighbor for his good to edify him. This too is an application of the principle of "Love seeks not its own." He does not mean we shouldn't seek the joy of edifying others, but that we should let *this* joy free us from bondage to private pleasures that make us indifferent to the good of others. Love does not seek its own *private, limited* joy, but instead seeks its own joy in the good — the salvation and edification — of others.[2]

In this way we begin to love the way God loves. He loves because he delights to love. He does not seek to hide from himself the reward of love lest his act be ruined by the anticipated joy that comes from it.

> "I am the LORD, who practice steadfast love, justice, and right-eousness in the earth; *for in these things I delight,"* says the LORD. (Jeremiah 9:24)

Love Is More than Deeds

We turn now from defense to offense. There are texts that seem to be a problem, but many others point positively to the truth of Christian Hedonism. We can take 1 Corinthians 13:3 as a starting point: "If I give away all I have, and if I deliver my body to be burned, but have not love, I gain nothing." This is a startling text. For Jesus himself said, "Greater love has no man than this, that a man lay down his life for his friends" (John 15:13). How can Paul say that laying down your life may in fact be a loveless act?

One thing is for sure: Love cannot be equated with sacrificial action! It cannot be equated with *any* action! This is a powerful antidote to the common teaching that love is not what you feel but what you do. The good in this popular teaching is the twofold intention to show (1) that mere warm feelings can never replace actual deeds of love (James 2:16; 1 John 3:18), and (2) that efforts of love must be made even in the absence of the joy that one might wish were present. But it is careless and inaccurate to support these two truths by saying that love is simply what you do and not what you feel. (See Epilogue, Reason Four, for a further discussion of how to obey when you don't feel like it.)

The very definition of love in 1 Corinthians refutes this narrow conception of love. For example, Paul says love is not *jealous* and not easily *provoked,* and that it *rejoices* in the truth and *hopes* all things (13:4-7). All these are *feelings!* If you feel certain things such as unholy jealousy and irritation, you are not loving. And if you do not feel certain things such as joy in the truth and hope, you are not loving. In other words, YES, love is more than feelings; but, NO, love is not less than feelings.

This may help account for the startling statement that it is possible to give your body to be burned and yet not have love. Evidently an act does not qualify as love unless it involves right motives. But isn't the willingness to die a sign of good motives? You would think so if the essence of love were disinterestedness. But someone might say that what ruined the self-sacrificing act of apparent love was the intention to inherit reward after death or to leave a noble memory on earth.

That may be part of the answer. But it is not complete. It does not distinguish what sort of reward after death might be appropriate to aim at in an act of love (if any!). Nor does it describe what feelings if any must accompany an outward "act" of love for it to be truly loving.

In answering these questions we need to ask another: What does love to man have to do with our love for God and his grace toward us? Could it be that the reason a person could give his body to be burned and not have love is that his act had no connection to a genuine love for God? Could it be that Paul's conception of horizontal love between people is such that it is authentic only when it is the extension of a vertical love for God? It would be strange indeed if the apostle who said "Whatever does not proceed from faith is sin" (Romans 14:23) could define genuine love without reference to God.

Love Is the Overflow of Joy in God

2 Corinthians 8:1-4, 8 shows that Paul thinks of genuine love only in relation to God.

> We want you to know, brethren, about the grace of God which has been shown in the churches of Macedonia, for in a severe test of affliction their abundance of joy and their extreme poverty have overflowed in a wealth of liberality on their part. For they gave according to their means, as I can testify, and beyond their means, of their own accord, begging us earnestly for the favor of taking part in the relief of the saints.

The reason Paul wanted the Corinthians to know about this remarkable work of grace among the Macedonians is that he hopes the same will prove true among them. He is traveling among the churches collecting funds for the poor saints in Jerusalem (Romans 15:26; 1 Corinthians 16:1-4). He writes 2 Corinthians 8 and 9 to motivate the Corinthians to be generous. The crucial thing for our purpose is to notice that in 8:8 he says this is a test of their *love:* "I say this not as a command, but to prove by the earnestness of others that your *love also* is genuine."

The clear implication of 8:8 (especially the word "also") is that the Macedonians' generosity is a model of love that the Corinthians "also" should copy. By recounting the earnest love of the Macedonians, Paul aims to stir up the Corinthians to genuine love *also.* So here we have a test case to see just what the love of 1 Corinthians 13 looks like in real life. The Macedonians have given away their possesions just as 1 Corinthians 13:3 says ("If I give away all I have"). But *here* it is real love, while *there* it was not love at all. What makes the Macedonian generosity a genuine act of love?

The nature of genuine love can be seen in four things:

First, it is a work of divine *grace.* "We want you to know, brethren, about the *grace* of God which has been shown in the churches of Macedonia" (8:1). The generosity of the Macedonians was not of human origin. Even though verse three says they gave "of their own accord," the willingness was a gift of God — a work of grace.

You can see this same combination of God's sovereign grace resulting in man's willingness in 8:16-17.

Thanks be to *God* who *puts the same earnest care for you into the heart of Titus.* For he . . . is going to you *of his own accord.*

God put it in his heart. So he goes of his *own* accord. The willingness is a gift — a work of divine grace.

Second, this experience of God's grace filled the Macedonians with joy. "In a severe test of affliction, their abundance of joy and extreme poverty have overflowed in a wealth of liberality" (8:2). Note that their joy was not owing to the fact that God had prospered them financially. He hadn't! In "extreme poverty" they had joy. Therefore the joy was a joy in God — in the experience of his grace.

Third, their joy in God's grace *overflowed* in generosity to meet the needs of others. "Their abundance of joy . . . *overflowed* in a wealth of liberality" (8:2). Therefore the liberality expressed horizontally toward men was an overflow of joy in God's grace.

Fourth, the Macedonians begged for the opportunity to sacrifice their meager possessions for the saints in Jerusalem. "They gave . . . beyond their means, of their own accord, *begging us earnestly for the favor of taking part in the relief of the saints*" (8:3-4). In other words, the way their joy in God overflowed was in the joy of giving. They *wanted* to give. It was their joy!

Now we can give a definition of love that takes God into account and also includes the feelings that should accompany the outward acts of love: *Love is the overflow of joy in God which gladly meets the needs of others.*

Paul did not set the Macedonians up as a model of love just because they sacrificed in order to meet the needs of others. What he stresses is how they *loved* doing this (remember Micah 6:8!). It was the overflow of JOY! They "begged earnestly" to give. They found their pleasure in channeling the grace of God through their poverty to the poverty in Jerusalem. It is simply astonishing!

This is why a person can give his body to be burned and not have love. Love is the overflow of joy *in God!* It is not duty for duty's sake, or right for right's sake. It is not a resolute abandoning of one's own good with a view solely to the good of the other person. It is first a deeply satisfying experience of the fullness of God's grace, and then a doubly satisfying experience of sharing that grace with another person.

When poverty-stricken Macedonians beg Paul for the privilege of giving money to other poor saints, we may assume that this is what they want to do, not just ought to do, or have to do, but really long to do. It is their joy— an extension of their joy in God. To be sure, they are "denying themselves" whatever pleasures or comforts they could have from the money they give away, but the joy of extending God's grace to others is a far better reward than anything money could buy. The Macedonians have discovered the labor of Christian Hedonism: Love! It is the overflow of joy in God which gladly meets the needs of others.

God Loves a Cheerful Giver

In 2 Corinthians 9:6-7 we get a confirmation that we are on the right track. Paul continues to motivate the Corinthians to be generous. He says,

> He who sows sparingly will also reap sparingly, and he who sows bountifully will also reap bountifully. Each one must do as he has made up his mind, not reluctantly or under compulsion, for *God loves a cheerful giver.*

I take this to mean God is not pleased when people act benevolently but don't do it gladly. When people don't find pleasure (Paul's word is "cheer"!) in their acts of service, God doesn't find pleasure in them. He loves cheerful givers, cheerful servants. What sort of cheer? Surely the safest way to answer that question is to remember what sort of cheer moved the Macedonians to be generous. It was the overflow of joy in the grace of God. Therefore, the giver God loves is the one whose joy in him overflows "cheerfully" in generosity to others.

Perhaps it is becoming clear why part of the thesis of this chapter is that if you try to abandon the pursuit of your full and lasting joy, you cannot love people or please God. If love is the overflow of joy in God which gladly meets the needs of others, then to abandon the pursuit of *this* joy is to abandon the pursuit of love! And if God is pleased by cheerful givers, then to abandon the pursuit of *this* cheerfulness sets you on a course where God takes no delight. If we are indifferent to whether we do a good deed cheerfully, we are indifferent to what pleases God. For God loves a cheerful giver.

Therefore it is essential that we be Christian Hedonists on the horizontal level in our relationships with other people and not just on the vertical axis in our relationship with God. If love is the overflow of joy in God that gladly meets the needs of other people, and if God loves such joyful givers, then this joy in giving is a Christian duty, and the effort not to pursue it is sin.

Love Rejoices in the Joy of the Beloved

Before we leave 2 Corinthians, consider one more passage that brims with implications about the nature of love. In 1:23–2:4 Paul writes about a visit he didn't make and a painful letter he had to send. He explains the inner workings of his heart in all this.

(23) But I call God to witness against me—it was to spare you that I refrained from coming to Corinth. (24) Not that we lord it over your faith; we work with you *for your joy,* for you stand firm in your faith. (2:1) For I made up my mind not to make you another painful visit. (2) For if I cause you pain, *who is there to make me glad* but the one whom I have pained? (3) And I wrote as I did, so that when I came *I might not be pained* by those who should have *made me rejoice,* for I felt sure of all of you, that *my joy would be the joy of you all.* (4) For I wrote you out of much affliction and anguish of heart and with many tears, not to cause you pain but to let you know *the abundant love that I have for you.*

Notice how Paul's pursuit of their joy and his own joy relate to love. In verse two he gives the reason he did not make another painful visit to Corinth: "For if I cause you pain, who is there to *make me glad* but the one whom I have pained?" In other words, Paul's motive here is to preserve his own joy. He says in effect: "If I destroy your joy, then my joy goes too." Why? Because their joy is precisely what gives him joy!

It is clear from 1:24 that the joy in view is the joy of faith. It is the joy of knowing and resting in God's grace — the same joy that moved the Macedonians to be generous (8:1-3). When *this* joy abounds in his converts, Paul feels great joy himself. And he unashamedly tells them that the reason he does not want to rob them of their joy is that this would rob him of *his* joy. This is the way a Christian Hedonist talks.

In verse three he tells the reason he sent them a painful letter. "I wrote as I did, so that when I came I might not be pained by those who should have made me rejoice, for I felt sure of all of you, that *my joy would be the joy of you all.*" Here his motive is the same, up to a point. He says he did not want to be pained. He wants joy, not pain. He is a Christian Hedonist! But he goes a step further here than in verse two. He says the reason he wants joy, not pain, is that he is confident his joy is also their joy: "For I felt sure of all of you, that my joy would be the joy of you all."

So verse three is the converse of verse two. In verse two the point is that *their* joy is his joy; that is, when they are glad he feels glad in their gladness. And the point of verse three is that *his* joy is their joy; that is, when he is glad they feel glad in his gladness.

Then verse four makes the connection with love explicit. He says the reason he had written them was "to let you know the abundant *love* I have for you." So what is love? Love abounds between us when your joy is mine and my joy is yours. I am not loving just because I seek your joy, but because I seek it as *mine*.

Suppose I tell one of my sons, "Be nice to your brother, help him clean up the room, try to make him happy, not miserable." What if he does help his brother clean up the room, but pouts the whole time and generally exudes unhappiness? Is there virtue in his effort? Not much. What's wrong is that his brother's happiness is not his own happiness. When he helps his brother, he does not pursue his joy in his brother's happiness. He is not acting like a Christian Hedonist. His labor is not the labor of love. It is the labor of legalism — he acts out of mere duty to escape punishment.

Love Delights to Cause and Contemplate Joy in Others

Now consider the relationship between the images of love in 2 Corinthians 8 and 2. In chapter 8, love is the overflow of joy in God which gladly meets the needs of others. It is the impulse of a fountain to overflow. It originates in the grace of God which overflows freely because it delights to fill the empty. Love shares the nature of that grace, because it too delights to overflow freely to meet the needs of others.

In chapter 2, love is what exists between people when they find their joy in each other's joy. Is this in contradiction to the love of chapter 8, where joy comes from God and overflows to others? It sounds in chapter 2 like joy is coming from the joy of other people, not from God. How do these two ways of talking about love relate to each other?

I think the answer is that love not only delights to cause joy in those who are empty (2 Corinthians 8), but also delights to contemplate joy in those who are full (2 Corinthians 2). And these two delights are not at all in contradiction. The grace of God delights to grant repentance (2 Timothy 2:25) *and* it rejoices over one sinner who repents (Luke 15:7). Therefore when our hearts are filled with joy in the grace of God, we not only want to cause the joy of others, but also to contemplate it when it exists in others.

So it is not inconsistent to say love is the overflow of joy in God that gladly meets the needs of others, *and* to say love is finding your joy in the joy of another. If love is the *labor* of Christian Hedonism which delights to beget its joy in others, then it is also the *leisure* of Christian Hedonism which delights to behold this joy begotten in others.[3]

Love Weeps

But Paul's words in 2 Corinthians 2 raise another question. In verse 4 he says he wrote "out of much affliction and anguish of heart and with many tears." Is this a heart of love? I have stressed so heavily that love is the overflow of joy that someone might think there is no place for grief or anguish in the heart of love, and no place for tears on its face. That would be very wrong.

The contentment of a Christian Hedonist is not a Buddha-like serenity, unmoved by the hurts of others. It is a profoundly dissatisfied contentment. It is constantly hungry for more of the feast of God's grace. And even the measure of contentment that God grants contains an insatiable impulse to expand itself to others (2 Corinthians 8:4; 1 John 1:4). Christian joy reveals itself as dissatisfied contentment whenever it perceives human need. It starts to expand in love to fill that need and bring about the joy of faith in the heart of the other person. But since there is often a time lapse between our perception of a person's need and our eventual rejoicing in the person's restored joy, there is a place for weeping in that interval. The weeping of compassion is the weeping of joy impeded in the extension of itself to another.

Love Keeps the Reward of Love in Mind

Another tearful experience comes when Paul uncovers his commitment to Christian Hedonism. In Acts 20 he gathers for the last time with elders of the church of Ephesus. There are many tears and much embracing as Paul finishes his farewell address (20:37). But these tears only accent the poignancy of affection the elders have for one who taught them the joy of ministry.

In verse 35 Paul says, "In all things I have shown you that by so toiling one must help the weak, *remembering* the words of the Lord Jesus, how he said, 'It is more blessed to give than to receive.'" The last thing Paul left ringing in their ears on the beach at Miletus was the ministerial charge of Christian Hedonism. "It is more blessed to give than to receive.'"

Most people do not feel the hedonistic force of these words because they do not meditate on the meaning of the word "remembering." Literally Paul says, "In all things I have shown you that, so laboring, it is necessary to help the weak and to *remember* the words of the Lord Jesus, that he himself said, 'It is more blessed to give than to receive.'"

In other words, Paul says two things are *necessary:* (1) to help the weak, and (2) to remember that Jesus said it is more blessed to give than to receive. Why are both of these things necessary? Why not just help the weak? Why must one also remember that giving brings blessing?

Most Christians today think that while it is true that giving brings blessing, it is not true that one should "remember" this. Popular Christian wisdom says that blessing will come as a *result* of giving, but that if you keep this fact before you as a motive, it will ruin the moral value of your giving and turn you into a mercenary. The word "remember" in Acts 20:35 is a great obstacle to this popular wisdom. Why would Paul tell church elders to *keep in mind* the benefits of ministry, if in fact their doing so would turn ministers into mercenaries?

Christian Hedonism's answer is that it is necessary to keep in mind the *true* rewards of ministry so we will *not* become mercenaries. C. S. Lewis sees this clearly:

> We must not be troubled by unbelievers when they say that this promise of reward makes the Christian life a mercenary affair. There are different kinds of reward. There is the reward which has no natural connection with the things you do to earn[4] it, and is quite foreign to the desires that ought to accompany those things. Money is not the natural reward of love; that is why we call a man mercenary if he marries a woman for the sake of her money. But marriage is the proper reward for a real lover, and he is not mercenary for desiring it. A general who fights well in order to get a peerage is mercenary; a general who fights for victory is not, victory being the proper reward of battle as marriage is the proper reward of love. The proper rewards are not simply tacked on to the activity for which they are given, but are the activity itself in consummation.[5]

I do not see how anyone can honor the word "remember" in Acts 20:35 and still think it is wrong to pursue the reward of joy in the ministry. On the contrary, Paul thinks it is necessary to keep the joy set firmly before us. This is the last and perhaps most important thing he has to say to the Ephesian elders before he departs. "REMEMBER! It is more blessed to give than to receive."

Love Enjoys Ministry

Nor is Paul the only apostle who counseled elders to remember and pursue the blessedness of ministry. In 1 Peter 5:1-2, Peter writes,

> I exhort the elders among you, as a fellow elder . . . tend the flock of God that is your charge, not under constraint, but willingly, not for shameful gain but eagerly.

In other words, "God loves a cheerful pastor." Notice how hedonistic these admonitions are. Peter does not admonish pastors to simply do their work, come what may. Perseverance through the hard times is good. It is essential! But it is not all that is commanded of pastors. We are commanded to enjoy our work!

Peter condemns two motives. One is "constraint." Don't do your work under constraint. This means the impulse should come gladly from within, not oppressively from without. Parental pressure, congregational expectations, fear of failure or divine censure — these are not good motives for staying in the pastoral ministry. There should be an inner willingness. We should *want* to do the ministry. It should be our joy. Joy in ministry is a duty! — a light burden and an easy yoke.

The other motive Peter condemns is the desire for money — "not for shameful gain but eagerly." If money is the motive, your joy comes not from the ministry but from the stuff you can buy with your salary. This is what Lewis calls mercenary. The "eagerness" of ministry should not come from the extrinsic reward of money, but from the intrinsic reward of seeing God's grace flow through you to others.

John gives a good example of this joy in 3 John 4: "No greater joy can I have than this, to hear that my children follow the truth." When this kind of reward creates joyful eagerness in ministry, *Christ* is honored (since he is the "truth" that our people follow) and *they* are loved (since they can receive no greater benefit than the grace to follow Christ).

So the command of the apostle Peter is to pursue joy in the ministry. It is not optional. It is not a mere unexpected result. It is a duty. To say you are indifferent to what the apostle commands you to experience is to be indifferent to the will of God. And that is sin.

Phillips Brooks, an Episcopalian pastor in Boston a hundred years ago, caught the spirit of Peter's counsel to pastors:

> I think, again, that it is essential to the preacher's success that he should thoroughly enjoy his work. I mean in the actual doing of it, and not only in its idea. No man to whom the details of his task are repulsive can do his task well constantly, however full he may be of its spirit. He may make one bold dash at it and carry it over all his disgusts, but he cannot work on at it year after year, day after day. Therefore, count it not merely a perfectly legitimate pleasure, count it an essential element of your power, if you can feel a simple delight in what you have to do as a minister, in the fervor of writing, in the glow of speaking, in standing before men and moving them, in contact with the young. The more thoroughly you enjoy it, the better you will do it all.
>
> This is all true of preaching. Its highest joy is in the great ambition that is set before it, the glorifying of the Lord and the saving

of the souls of men. No other joy on earth compares with that. The ministry that does not feel that joy is dead. But in behind that highest joy, beating in humble unison with it, as the healthy body thrills in sympathy with the deep thoughts and pure desires of the mind and soul, the best ministers have always been conscious of another pleasure which belonged to the very doing of the work itself. As we read the lives of all the most effective preachers of the past, or as we meet the men who are powerful preachers of the Word today, we feel how certainly and how deeply the very exercise of their ministry delights them.[6]

Love Is Not Easily Pleased

Can we not, then, say that the hindrance to loving other people, whether through the pastoral ministry or any other avenue of life, is the same as the hindrance to worship we discovered in chapter three? The obstacle that keeps us from obeying the first (vertical) commandment is the same obstacle that keeps us from obeying the second (horizontal) commandment. It is *not* that we are all trying to please ourselves, but that we are all far too easily pleased. We do not believe Jesus when he says there is more blessedness, more joy, more lasting pleasure in a life devoted to helping others than there is in a life devoted to our material comfort. And therefore the very longing for content-ment which ought to drive us to simplicity of life and labors of love contents itself instead with the broken cisterns of prosperity and comfort.

The message that needs to be shouted from the houses of high finance is this: Secular man, you are not nearly hedonistic enough!

> "Do not lay up for yourselves treasures on earth where moth and rust consume and where thieves break in and steal, but lay up for yourselves treasures in heaven, where neither moth nor rust consumes and where thieves do not break in and steal." (Matthew 6:19-20)

Quit being satisfied with little 5 percent yields of pleasure that get eaten up by the moths of inflation and the rust of death. Invest in the blue-chip, high-yield, divinely insured securities of heaven. A life devoted to material comforts and thrills is like throwing money down a rathole. But a life invested in the labor of love yields dividends of joy unsurpassed and unending.

> "Sell your possessions, give alms; [and *thus*] provide yourselves with purses that do not grow old, with a treasure in the heavens that does not fail." (Luke 12:33)

This message is very good news: Come to Christ in whose presence are fullness of joy and pleasures for evermore. Join us in the labor of Christian Hedonism. For the Lord has spoken: It is more blessed to love than to live in luxury!

Love Suffers for Joy

Love is costly. It always involves some kind of self-denial. It often demands suffering. But Christian Hedonism insists that the gain outweighs the pain. It affirms that there are rare and wonderful species of joy that flourish only in the rainy atmosphere of suffering. "The soul would have no rainbow if the eye had no tears."

The costly joy of love is illustrated repeatedly in Hebrews 10–12. Consider three examples.

HEBREWS 10:32-35

> But recall the former days when, after you were enlightened, you endured a hard struggle with sufferings, sometimes being publicly exposed to abuse and affliction, and sometimes being partners with those so treated. For you had compassion on the prisoners, and you *joyfully* accepted the plundering of your property, since you knew that you yourselves had a better possession and an abiding one. Therefore do not throw away your confidence, which has a great reward.

Based on my limited experience with suffering, I would have no right in myself to say such a thing is possible — to accept *joyfully* the plundering of your property. But the authority of Christian Hedonism is not in me; it is in the Bible. I have no right in myself to say, "Rejoice insofar as you share Christ's sufferings" (1 Peter 4:13). But Peter does because he and the other apostles were beaten for the gospel and "left the presence of the council, *rejoicing* that they were counted worthy to suffer dishonor for the name" (Acts 5:40-41).

And the Christians in Hebrews 10:32-35 have earned the right to teach us about costly love. The situation appears to be this: in the early days of their conversion, some of them had been imprisoned for the faith. The others were confronted with a difficult choice: Shall we go underground and stay "safe," or shall we visit our brothers and sisters in prison and risk our lives and our property? They chose the way of love and accepted the cost. "For you had compassion on the prisoners, and you joyfully accepted the plundering of your property."

But were they losers? No. They lost property and gained *joy!* They joyfully accepted the loss. In one sense they denied themselves. But in another they did not. They chose the way of joy. Evidently these Christians were motivated for prison ministry the same way the Macedonians (of 2 Corinthians 8:1-8) were motivated to relieve the poor. Their joy in God overflowed in love for others.

They looked at their own lives and said, "The steadfast love of the Lord is better than life" (Psalm 63:3). They looked at all their possessions and said, "We have a possession in heaven that is better and that lasts longer than any of this" (verse 34). Then they looked at each other and said,

> Let goods and kindred go,
> This mortal life also;
> The body they may kill;
> God's truth abideth still,
> His kingdom is forever.
>   Martin Luther

With *joy* they "renounced all they had" (Luke 14:33) and followed Christ into the prison to visit their brothers and sisters. Love is the overflow of joy in God that meets the needs of others.

HEBREWS 11:24-26

To drive the point home, the author of Hebrews gives Moses as an example of this sort of Christian Hedonism. Notice how similar the motivation is to the early Christians of chapter 10.

> By faith Moses, when he was grown up, refused to be called the son of Pharaoh's daughter, choosing rather to share ill-treatment with the people of God than to enjoy the fleeting pleasures of sin. He considered abuse suffered for the Christ greater wealth than the treasures of Egypt, for he looked to the reward.

In 10:34 the author said the desire of the Christians for a better and lasting possession overflowed in joyful love which cost them their property. Here in chapter 11, Moses is a hero for the church because his delight in the promised reward overflowed in such joy that he counted the pleasures of Egypt rubbish by comparison, and was bound forever to God's people in love.

There is nothing here about ultimate self-denial. He was given eyes to see that the pleasures of Egypt were "fleeting," not eternal. He was granted to see that suffering for the cause of the Messiah was "greater wealth than all the treasures of Egypt." As he considered these things, he was constrained to give himself to the labor of Christian Hedonism — love. And he spent the rest of his days channeling the grace of God to the people of Israel. His joy in God overflowed in a lifetime of service to a recalcitrant and needy people. He chose the way of maximum joy, not the way of "fleeting pleasures."

HEBREWS 12:1-2

We raised the question earlier whether the example of Jesus contradicts the principle of Christian Hedonism, namely, that love is the way of joy and that one should choose it for that very reason, lest one be found begrudging obedience to the Almighty, or chafing under the privilege of being a channel of grace, or belittling the promised reward. Hebrews 12:2 seems to say fairly clearly that Jesus did not contradict this principle.

> Therefore, since we are surrounded by so great a cloud of witnesses, let us also lay aside every weight, and sin which clings so closely, and let us run with perseverance the race that is set before us, looking to Jesus the pioneer and perfecter of our faith, who *for the joy that was set before him* endured the cross, despising the shame, and is seated at the right hand of the throne of God.

The greatest labor of love that ever happened was possible because Jesus pursued the greatest imaginable joy, namely, the joy of being exalted to God's right hand in the assembly of a redeemed people. "For the joy that was set before him, he endured the cross!"

Back in 1978 I was trying to explain some of these things to a college class. As usual I found some of them quite skeptical. One of the more thoughtful wrote me a letter to express his disagreement. Since this is one of the most serious objections raised against Christian Hedonism, I think it will be helpful to others if I print Ronn's letter here and my response.

> Dr. Piper:
>
> I disagree with your position that love seeks or is motivated by its own pleasure. I suggest that all of your examples are true: You have cited many cases in which personal joy is increased and *may even* be the motivation for a person to love God or another human.
>
> But you cannot establish a doctrine on the fact that some evidence supports it unless you can show that no evidence contradicts it.

Two examples of the second type:

Picture yourself in Gethsemane with Christ. He is about to perform the supreme act of love in all of history. Walking up to him,
you decide to test your position on Christian Hedonism. Should
not this supreme love bring great pleasure, abundant joy? Yet
what is this you see? Christ is sweating terribly, in anguish, cry-
ing. Joy is nowhere to be found. Christ is praying. You hear him
ask God if there is any way out. He tells God the upcoming act
will be so hard, so painful. Can't there be a fun way?

Thank God that Christ chose the hard way.

My second example is not biblical, though there are many more
of them. Are you familiar with Dorothy Day? She is a very old
woman who has devoted her life to loving others, especially the
poor, displaced, downtrodden. Her experience of loving when
there was no joy has led her to say this: "Love in action is a harsh
and dreadful thing."

I could not agree more with her than I do.

I would like to know your response to these thoughts. In truth,
I do feel this presentation is too simplistic. But it is sincere.

Ronn

I responded to Ronn the same week back in December of 1978. Since
then Dorothy Day has died, but I will leave the references as they were back
then. Incidentally, to this day I count Ronn a friend and a sharp thinker about
the Christian worldview.

Ronn,

Thanks very much for your concern to have a fully biblical
stance on this matter of Christian Hedonism — a stance which
honors all the evidence. This is my concern, too. So I must ask
whether your two examples (Christ in Gethsemane and
Dorothy Day in painful service of love) contradict or confirm
my position.

(1) Take Gethsemane first. For my thesis to stand I need to be
able to show that in spite of the horror of the cross, Jesus' decision to accept it was motivated by his conviction that this way

would bring him more joy than the way of disobedience. Hebrews 12:2 says, "For the joy that was set before him Christ endured the cross, despising the shame." In saying this, the writer means to give Jesus as another example, along with the saints of Hebrews 11, of those who are so eager for, and confident in, the joy God offers that they reject the "fleeting pleasures of sin" (11:25) and choose ill-treatment in order to be aligned with God's will. It is not unbiblical, therefore, to say that what sustained Christ in the dark hours of Gethsemane was the hope of joy beyond the cross.

This does not diminish the reality and greatness of his love for us, because the joy in which he hoped was the joy of leading many sons to glory (Hebrews 2:10). His joy is in *our* redemption which redounds to *God's* glory. To abandon the cross and thus to abandon us and the Father's will was a prospect so horrible in Christ's mind that he repulsed it and embraced death.

But my essay on "Dissatisfied Contentment" [this is what Ronn was responding to; its content has been incorporated into this chapter] suggests even more: namely, that in some profound sense there must be joy in the very act of love, if it is to be pleasing to God.

You have shown clearly that if this is true in the case of Jesus' death, there must be a radical difference between joy and "fun." But we all know that there is.

It is not fair when you shift from saying there is no "fun way" in Gethsemane, to saying "Joy is nowhere to be found." I know that at those times in my life when I have chosen to do the most costly good deeds, I have (with and under the hurts) felt a very deep joy at doing good.

I think that when Jesus rose from his final prayer in Gethsemane with the resolve to die, there flowed through his soul a glorious sense of triumph over the night's temptation. Did he not say, "My food is to do the will of him who sent me and to accomplish his work" (John 4:34)? Jesus cherished his Father's will like we cherish food. To finish his Father's work was what he fed upon; to abandon it would be to choose starvation. I think there was joy in Gethsemane as Jesus was led away — not fun, not sensual pleasure, not laughter, in fact not anything that this world can offer. *But there was a good feeling deep in Jesus' heart that his action was pleasing to his Father, and that the reward to come would outweigh all the pain.* This profoundly good feeling is the joy that enabled Jesus to do for us what he did.

(2) You say of Dorothy Day: "Her experience of loving [the poor, displaced, downtrodden] when there was no joy has led her to say this: 'Love in action is a harsh and dreadful thing.'" I will try to respond in two ways.

First, don't jump to the conclusion that there is no joy in things that are "harsh and dreadful." There are mountain climbers who have spent sleepless nights on the faces of cliffs, have lost fingers and toes in sub-zero temperatures, and have gone through horrible misery to reach a peak. They say, "It was harsh and dreadful." But if you ask them why they do it, the answer will come back in various forms: "There is an exhilaration in the soul that feels so good it is worth all the pain."

If this is how it is with mountain climbing, cannot the same be true of love? Is it not rather an indictment of our own worldliness that we are more inclined to sense exhilaration at mountain climbing than at conquering the precipices of un-love in our own lives and in society? Yes, love is often a "harsh and dreadful" thing, but I do not see how a person who cherishes what is good and admires Jesus can help but sense a joyful exhilaration when (by grace) he is able to love another person.

Now let me approach Dorothy Day's situation in another way. Let's pretend that I am one of the poor that she is trying to help at great cost to herself. I think a conversation might go like this:

Piper: Why are you doing this for me, Miss Day?

Day: Because I love you.

Piper: What do you mean, you love me? I don't have anything to offer. I'm not worth loving.

Day: Perhaps. But there are no application forms for my love. I learned that from Jesus. What I mean is, I want to *help* you because Jesus has helped me so much.

Piper: So you are trying to satisfy your "wants"?

Day: I suppose so, if you want to put it like that. One of my deepest wants is to make you a happy and purposeful person.

Piper: Does it upset you that I *am* happier and that I feel more purposeful since you've come?

Day: Heavens, no! What could make me happier?

Piper: So you really spend all those sleepless nights here for what makes you happy, don't you?

Day: If I say yes, someone might misunderstand me. They might think I don't care for *you* at all, but only for myself.

Piper: But won't you say it at least for me?

Day: Yes, I'll say it for you: I work for what brings me the greatest joy: your joy.

Piper: Thank you. Now I know that you love me.

Love's Deed and Reward Are Organically Related

One thing touched on briefly in this letter that might need a brief elaboration is the question concerning the relationship between the joy that comes in the actual deed of love and the joy that comes from the reward promised in the more distant future. The reason I think this question is important is that the motivation of receiving a future reward could turn love into a mercenary affair (as we have seen) if the hoped-for reward were not somehow organically related to the act one is doing to get the reward.

If the nature of the deed did not partake of the nature of the reward, you could do things you thought were stupid or evil to get the reward you considered wise or good. But it would be stretching the word *love* beyond biblical limits to say one is loving when he does a thing he thinks is stupid or evil. A loving act (even if very painful) must be approved by our conscience.

So to say it is right and good to be motivated by the hope of reward (as Moses and the early Christians and Jesus were, according to Hebrews 11:26 and 10:34 and 12:2) does not mean that this view to the future nullifies the need to choose acts which in their nature are organically related to the hoped-for reward.

What I mean by organically related is this: Any act of love we choose for the sake of a holy reward must compel us because we see in that act the moral traits of that promised reward. Or to put it the other way around, the only fitting reward for an act of love is the experience of divine glory whose moral dimension is what made the chosen act attractive.

The reward to which we look as Christian Hedonists for all the good we are commanded to do is distilled for us in Romans 8:29 — "Those whom he foreknew he predestined to be conformed to the image of his Son, in order that he might be the first-born among many brethren." There are two goals of our predestination mentioned here: one highlighting *our* glory and one highlighting Christ's.

The first goal of our predestination is to be like Christ. This includes new resurrection bodies of glory like his (Philippians 3:21; 1 Corinthians 15:49). But most importantly, it includes spiritual and moral qualities and capacities like Christ's (1 John 3:2-3).

The second and more ultimate goal of our predestination is "that Christ might be the first-born among many brethren." In other words, God aims to surround his Son with living images of himself so that the preeminent excellency of the original will shine the more brightly in his images. The goal of predestination is (1) our delight in becoming holy as he is holy and (2) his delight in being exalted as preeminent over all in the midst of a transformed, joyful people.

But if the reward we long for is to behold and be like the preeminent Christ, then it would be a contradiction if the actions we choose were not morally consistent with the character of Christ. If we really are being attracted by the reward of being made holy as he is holy, then we will be attracted to those acts which partake of his holiness. If we delight in the prospect of knowing Christ even as we are known, we will delight in the sorts of acts and attitudes that reflect his moral character.

So in true Christian Hedonism there is an organic relationship between the love Christ commands and the reward he promises. It is never a mercenary affair in which we do what we despise to get what we enjoy. Jesus illustrates this connection between act and reward in Luke 6:35.

> "Love your enemies, and do good, and lend, expecting nothing
> in return; *and your reward will be great* and you will be sons of
> the Most High: for he is kind to the ungrateful and the selfish."

Even though we should not care about human reward ("expecting nothing in return"), the Lord himself gives us an incentive to love by promising his reward, namely, that we will be sons of the Most High. This sonship implies likeness ("for he is kind to the ungrateful"). So the command and the reward are one piece of fabric. The command is to love. The reward is to become like one who loves.

So it is important to emphasize on the one hand that the reward a Christian Hedonist pursues is the incomparable delight of being like God and loving what he loves with an intensity approaching his own (John 17:26). And it is important to emphasize on the other hand that the acts of love which a Christian Hedonist performs are themselves therefore delightful in measure, because they have about them the aroma of this final reward. This, as we saw, was also C. S. Lewis's point when he spoke of an activity's "proper rewards" which "are the activity itself in consummation."

Love Longs for the Power of Grace

One last question belongs to this chapter. I have defined love as the overflow of joy in God that meets the needs of others. It will be practically helpful in conclusion to ask how this actually works in experience. What is the psychological process that moves from joy in God to the actual deed of love?

We start with a miracle, namely, that I, a sinner, should delight in God! Not just in his material rewards, but in him, in all his manifold excellencies! This conversion experience, as we saw, is the "creation" of a Christian Hedonist. Now how does practical love emerge from this heart of joy in God?

When the object of our delight is moral beauty, the longing to *behold* is inseparable from the longing to *be*. When the Holy Spirit awakens the heart of a person to delight in the holiness of God, an insatiable desire is born not only to *behold* that holiness but also to *be* holy as God is holy. Our joy is incomplete if we can only stand outside beholding the glory of God, but are not allowed to share it. It is one thing for a little boy to cheer in the grandstands at a football game. But his joy is complete if he can go home and get a team together and actually play the game.

We don't want to just *see* the grace of God in all its beauty, saving sinners and sanctifying saints. We want to share the power of that grace. We want to feel it saving.

We want to feel it conquer temptation in *our* lives. We want to feel it using *us* to save others. But why? Because our joy in God is insatiably greedy. The more you have, the more you want. The more you see, the more you want to see. The more you feel, the more you want to feel.

This means that the holy greed for joy in God that wants to see and feel more and more manifestations of his glory will push a person into love. My desire to feel the power of God's grace conquering the pride and selfishness in my life inclines me to behavior that demonstrates the victory of grace, namely love. Genuine love is so contrary to human nature that its presence bears witness to an extraordinary power. The Christian Hedonist pursues love because he is addicted to the experience of that power. He wants to feel more and more of the grace of God reigning in his life.

Conquering the Internal Mountain of Pride

There is an analogy here to a powerful motive that exists in unbelieving hearts as well. Virtually all people outside Christ are possessed by the desire to find happiness by overcoming some limitation in their lives and having the sensation of power. Heinrich Harrer, a member of the first team to climb the north wall of the Eiger in the Swiss Alps, confessed that his reason for attempting such a climb was to overcome a sense of insecurity. "Self-confidence," he said, "is the most valuable gift a man can possess . . . but to possess this true confidence it is necessary to have learned to know oneself at moments when one was standing at the very frontier of things. . . . On the 'Spider' in the Eiger's North Face, I experienced such borderline situations, while the avalanches were roaring down over us, endlessly."[7]

The all-important difference between the non-Christian and the Christian Hedonist in this pursuit of joy is that the Christian Hedonist has discovered that self-confidence will never satisfy the longing of his heart to overcome finitude.

He has learned that what we are really made for is not the thrill of feeling our own power increase, but the thrill of feeling God's power increase — conquering the precipices of un-love in our sinful hearts.

As I said in the letter to my friend Ronn, it is an indictment of our own worldliness that we feel more exhilaration when we conquer an external mountain of granite in our own strength than when we conquer the internal mountain of pride in God's strength. The miracle of Christian Hedonism is that overcoming obstacles to love by the grace of God has become more enticing than every form of self-confidence. The joy of experiencing the power of God's grace defeating selfishness is an insatiable addiction.

Joy Doubled in the Joy of Another

But there is another way of describing the psychological process that leads from delight in God to labors of love. When a person delights in the display of the glorious grace of God, that person will want to see as many displays of it as possible in other people. If I can be God's means of another person's miraculous conversion, I will count it all joy, because what would I rather see than another display of the beauty of God's grace in the joy of another person? My joy is doubled in his.

When the Christian Hedonist sees a person without hope or joy, that person's need becomes like a low-pressure zone approaching the high-pressure zone of joy in God's grace. In this spiritual atmosphere, a draft is created from the Christian Hedonist's high-pressure zone of joy to the low-pressure zone of need, as joy tends to expand to fill the need. That draft is called love.

Love is the overflow of joy in God that meets the needs of others. The overflow is experienced consciously as the pursuit of our joy in the joy of another. We double our delight in God as we expand it in the lives of others. If our ultimate goal were anything less than joy in God, we would be idolaters and would be no eternal help to anyone. Therefore, the pursuit of pleasure is an essential motive for every good deed. And if you aim to abandon the pursuit of full and lasting pleasure, you cannot love people or please God.

The precepts of the LORD are right,
rejoicing the heart . . .
More to be desired are they than gold,
even much fine gold;
sweeter also than honey
and drippings of the honeycomb.
Moreover by them is thy servant warned;
in keeping them there is great reward.

PSALM 19:8,10-11

I saw more clearly than ever, that the first great and primary business to
which I ought to attend every day was, to have my soul happy in the Lord.
The first thing to be concerned about was not, how much I might serve the
Lord, how I might glorify the Lord; but how I might get my soul into a
happy state, and how my inner man may be nourished. . . . I saw that the
most important thing I had to do was to give myself to the reading of the
Word of God and to meditation on it.

GEORGE MUELLER OF BRISTOL

CHAPTER 5

SCRIPTURE

Kindling for Christian Hedonism

Christian Hedonism is much aware that every day with Jesus is *not* "sweeter than the day before." Some days with Jesus our disposition is sour. Some days with Jesus we are so sad we feel our heart will break open. Some days with Jesus we are so depressed and discouraged that between the garage and the house we just want to sit down on the grass and cry.

Every day with Jesus is not sweeter than the day before. We know it from experience and we know it from Scripture. For David says in Psalm 19:7, "The law of the LORD is perfect, *reviving* the soul." If every day with Jesus were sweeter than the day before, if life were a steady ascent with no dips in our affection for God, we wouldn't need to be *re*-vived.

In another place David extolled the Lord with similar words: "He leads me beside still waters, he *restores* my soul" (Psalm 23:2-3). This means David must have had bad days.

There were days when his soul needed to be re-stored. It's the same phrase used in Psalm 19:7 — "the law of the LORD is perfect, *reviving the soul.*" Normal Christian life is a repeated process of restoration and renewal. Our joy is not static. It fluctuates with real life. It is vulnerable to Satan's attacks.

When Paul says in 2 Corinthians 1:24, "Not that we lord it over your faith, but we are *workers* with you for your joy," we should emphasize it this way: "We are workers with you for your joy." The preservation of our joy in God takes *work.* It is a fight. Our adversary the devil prowls around like a roaring lion, and he has an insatiable appetite to destroy one thing: the joy of faith. But the Holy Spirit has given us a sword called the Word of God for the defense of our joy.

Or, to change the image, when Satan huffs and puffs and tries to blow out the flame of your joy, you have an endless supply of kindling in the Word of God. Even on days when every cinder in our soul feels cold, if we crawl to the Word of God and cry out for ears to hear, the cold ashes will be lifted and the tiny spark of life will be fanned. For "the law of the LORD is perfect, *reviving the soul.*" The Bible is the kindling of Christian Hedonism.

My aim in this chapter is to help you wear the sword of the Spirit, the

Word of God, and wield it to preserve your joy in God. There are three steps we need to climb together:

First, we need to know why we accept the Bible as the reliable Word of God.

Second, we need to see the benefits and power of Scripture and how it kindles our joy.

Third, we need to hear a practical challenge to renew our daily meditation in the Word of God, and to bind that sword so closely around our waist that we are never without it.

How Trustworthy Is the Bible?

Almost everybody in the world would agree that if the one and true God has spoken, then people who ignore his Word can have no lasting happiness. But not everyone really believes the Bible is the Word of the living God. Nor should someone believe it without sufficient reasons.

Some who read this book will share my persuasion that the Bible is the Word of God. They will want to get on with the use of it. Others will be struggling with whether to give the Bible such a powerful place in their lives. They may want to hear me give a reasonable account of my persuasion. I feel deeply the duty to honor this request for the ground of my confidence in Scripture. So I have added Appendix 2, "Is the Bible a Reliable Guide to Lasting Joy?" I hope it will help some to stand confidently on the Scriptures as the very Word of God.

If our quest for lasting happiness is to succeed, we must seek it in relationship with our Creator. We can do that only by listening to his Word. This we have in the Bible. And the best news of all is that what God has said in his book is the kindling of Christian Hedonism.

THE BENEFITS AND POWER OF HOLY SCRIPTURE

In the Bible are many confirmations that its purpose is to kindle, and not kill, our joy. We find them when we set our sights on the benefits of Scripture which sustain and deepen our true happiness.

The Bible Is Your Life

Moses says in Deuteronomy 32:46-47, "Lay to heart all the words which I enjoin upon you this day, that you may command them to your children, that they may be careful to do all the words of this law. For it is no trifle for you, but *it is your life.*" The Word of God is not a trifle; it is a matter of life and death. If you treat the Scripture as a trifle, you forfeit life.

Even our physical life depends on God's Word, because by his Word we were created (Psalm 33:6; Hebrews 11:3), and "He upholds the universe by the Word of his power" (Hebrews 1:3). Our spiritual life begins by the Word of God: "By his own will he brought us forth by the Word of truth" (James 1:18). "You have been born anew . . . through the living and abiding Word of God" (1 Peter 1:23).

Not only do we *begin* to live by God's Word, but we also *go on* living by God's Word: "Man shall not live by bread alone, but by every Word that proceeds from the mouth of God" (Matthew 4:4; Deuteronomy 8:3). Our physical life is created and upheld by the Word of God, and our spiritual life is quickened and sustained by the Word of God.

How many stories could be gathered to bear witness to the life-giving power of the Word of God! Consider the story of "Little Bilney," an early English Reformer born in 1495. He studied law and was outwardly rigorous in his efforts at religion. But there was no life within. Then he happened to receive a Latin translation of Erasmus's Greek New Testament. Here is what happened:

> I chanced upon this sentence of St. Paul (O most sweet and comfortable sentence to my soul!) in 1 Timothy 1: "It is a true saying, and worthy of all men to be embraced, that Christ Jesus came into the world to save sinners; of whom I am the chief and principal." This one sentence, through God's instruction and inward working, which I did not then perceive, did so exhilarate my heart, being before wounded with the guilt of my sins, and being almost in despair, that . . . immediately I . . . felt a marvelous comfort and quietness, in so much that "my bruised bones leaped for joy." After this, the Scriptures began to be more pleasant to me than the honey or the honeycomb.[1]

Indeed, the Bible is "no trifle for you, it is your life!" The foundation of all joy is life. Nothing is more fundamental than sheer existence — our creation and our preservation. All this is owing to the Word of God's power. By that same power he has spoken in Scripture for the creation and sustenance of our spiritual life. Therefore the Bible is no trifle, it is your life — the kindling of your joy!

Faith Comes by Hearing

The Word of God begets and sustains spiritual *life* because it begets and sustains *faith*. "These things are written," John says, "that you might *believe* that Jesus is the Christ, the Son of God, and that *believing* you might have *life* in his name" (John 20:31). "Faith comes by hearing," writes the apostle Paul, "and hearing by the Word of Christ" (Romans 10:17). The faith that starts our life in Christ and by which we go on living comes from hearing the Word of God.

And there is no true joy without faith. "May the God of hope fill you with all joy and peace *in believing*" (Romans 15:13). "I know that I will remain and continue with you all for your advancement and *joy of faith*" (Philippians 1:25). How else can we sustain our joy in dark hours except by the promises of God's Word that he will work it all together for our good (Romans 8:28)?

A great testimony to the power of the Word to beget and sustain faith is found in the story of the conversion and execution of Tokichi Ichii — a man who was hanged for murder in Tokyo in 1918. He had been sent to prison more than twenty times and was known as being cruel as a tiger. On one occasion, after attacking a prison official, he was gagged and bound, and his body suspended in such a way that "my toes barely reached the ground." But he stubbornly refused to say he was sorry for what he had done.

Just before being sentenced to death, Tokichi was sent a New Testament by two Christian missionaries, Miss West and Miss McDonald. After a visit from Miss West, he began to read the story of Jesus' trial and execution. His attention was riveted by the sentence, "And Jesus said, 'Father, forgive them, for they know not what they do.' " This sentence transformed his life.

> I stopped: I was stabbed to the heart, as if by a five-inch nail. What did the verse reveal to me? Shall I call it the love of the heart of Christ? Shall I call it His compassion? I do not know what to call it. I only know that with an unspeakably grateful heart I believed.

Tokichi was sentenced to death and accepted it as "the fair, impartial judgment of God." Now the Word that brought him to faith also sustained his faith in an amazing way. Near the end, Miss West directed him to the words of 2 Corinthians 6:8-10 concerning the suffering of the righteous. The words moved him very deeply, and he wrote,

> "As sorrowing, yet always rejoicing." People will say that I must have a very sorrowful heart because I am daily awaiting the execution of the death sentence. This is not the case. I feel neither sorrow nor distress nor any pain. Locked up in a prison cell six feet by nine in size I am infinitely happier than I was in the days of my sinning when I did not know God. Day and night . . . I am talking with Jesus Christ.

"As poor, yet making many rich." This certainly does not apply to the evil life I led before I repented. But perhaps in the future, someone in the world may hear that the most desperate villain that ever lived repented of his sins and was saved by the power of Christ, and so may come to repent also. Then it may be that though I am poor myself, I shall be able to make many rich.

The Word sustained him to the end, and on the scaffold with great humility and earnestness he uttered his last words, "My soul, purified, today returns to the City of God."[2]

Faith is born and sustained by the Word of God, and out of faith grows the flower of joy.

God Supplies the Spirit through the Hearing of Faith

We are commanded to be filled with the Holy Spirit: "Do not get drunk with wine, for that is debauchery; but be filled with the Spirit" (Ephesians 5:18). How does the Spirit come? In Galatians 3:2, Paul asks, "Did you receive the Spirit by works of the law or by hearing with faith?" The answer, of course, is "hearing with faith." Hearing what? The Word of God!

The Spirit inspired the Word and therefore he goes where the Word goes. The more of God's Word you know and love, the more of God's Spirit you will experience. Instead of drinking wine we should drink the Spirit. How? By setting our minds on the things of the Spirit: "Those who live according to the Spirit set their minds on the things of the Spirit" (Romans 8:5).

What are the things of the Spirit? When Paul said in 1 Corinthians 2:14, "The natural man does not welcome the things of the Spirit," he was referring to his own Spirit-inspired teachings (2:13). Therefore, above all, the teachings of Scripture are the "things of the Spirit." We drink in the Spirit by setting our minds on the things of the Spirit, namely the Word of God. And the fruit of the Spirit is joy (Galatians 5:22).

The Scriptures Give Hope

Sometimes faith and hope are virtual synonyms in Scripture. "Faith is the assurance of things *hoped* for" (Hebrews 11:1). Without this hope for the future we get discouraged and depressed and our joy drains away. Hope is absolutely essential to Christian joy. "We rejoice in our sufferings, knowing that suffering produces . . . hope" (Romans 5:3-4; 15:13).

And how do we maintain hope? The psalmist puts it like this: "He established a testimony in Jacob and appointed a law in Israel which he commanded our fathers to teach to their children . . . so that they might set their *hope* in God" (78:5,7). In other words the "testimony" and the "law" — the Word of God — are kindling for the hope of our children.

Paul puts it so plainly: "Whatever was written in former days was written for our instruction, that by the steadfastness and by the encouragement of the Scriptures we might have *hope*" (Romans 15:4). The whole Bible has this aim and this power: to create hope in the hearts of God's people. And when hope abounds, the heart is filled with joy.

The Truth Shall Make You Free

Another essential element of joy is freedom. None of us would be happy if we were not free from what we hate and free for what we love. And where do we find true freedom? Psalm 119:45 says, "I shall walk in freedom, for I sought thy precepts." The picture is one of open spaces. The Word frees us from smallness of mind (1 Kings 4:29) and from threatening confinements (Psalm 18:19).

Jesus says, "You shall know the truth, and the truth shall make you *free*" (John 8:32). The freedom he has in mind is freedom from the slavery of sin (verse 34). Or, to put it positively, it is freedom for holiness. The promises of God's grace provide the power that makes the demands of God's holiness an experience of freedom rather than fear. "Through his precious and very great promises you escape from the corruption that is in the world . . . and become partakers of the divine nature" (2 Peter 1:4; cf. John 15:3). Freed from corruption, freed to share the likeness of God — by the precious and very great promises!

Therefore we should pray for each other the way Jesus prays for us in John 17:17 — "Sanctify them in the truth; thy Word is truth." There is no abiding joy without holiness, for the Scripture says, "Strive for the holiness without which no one will see the Lord" (Hebrews 12:14). How important then is the truth that sanctifies! How crucial is the Word that breaks the power of counterfeit pleasures! And how vigilant we should be to light our paths and load our hearts with the Word of God! "Thy Word is a lamp to my feet and a light to my path" (Psalm 119:105). "I have laid up thy Word in my heart, that I might not sin against thee" (Psalm 119:11; cf. v. 9).

The Testimony of the Lord Makes Wise the Simple

Of course, the Bible does not answer every question about life. Not every fork in the road has a biblical arrow. We have need of wisdom in ourselves to know the path of lasting joy. But that, too, is a gift of Scripture. "The testimony of the LORD is sure, making *wise* the simple. . . . The commandment of the LORD is pure, *enlightening the eyes*" (Psalm 19:7-8; 119:98). People whose minds are saturated with God's Word and submissive to his thoughts have a wisdom that in eternity will prove superior to all the secular wisdom in the world. "Happy is the man who finds wisdom, and the man who gets understanding" (Proverbs 3:13).

Written that You Might Have Assurance

Nevertheless, our perverted will and imperfect perceptions lead us time and again into foolish acts and harmful situations. The day this happens is not sweeter than the day before, and we need restoration and comfort. Where can we turn for comfort? We can follow the psalmist again: "This is my *comfort* in my affliction, that thy *promises* give me life. . . . When I think of thy *ordinances* from of old, I take comfort, O LORD" (Psalm 119:50,52).

And when our failures and our afflictions threaten our assurance of faith, where do we turn to rebuild our confidence? John invites us to turn to the Word of God: "I *write* this to you who believe in the name of the Son of God, that you may *know* that you have eternal life" (1 John 5:13). The Bible is written to give us assurance of eternal life.

The Evil One Is Overcome by the Word of God

Satan's number-one objective is to destroy our joy of faith. We have one offensive weapon: the sword of the Spirit, the Word of God (Ephesians 6:17). But what many Christians fail to realize is that we can't draw the sword from someone else's scabbard. If we don't wear it, we can't wield it. If the Word of God does not abide in us (John 15:7), we will reach for it in vain when the enemy strikes. But if we do wear it, if it lives within us, what mighty warriors we can be! "I write to you, young men, because you are strong and the Word of God abides in you, and you have overcome the evil one" (1 John 2:14).

This has been the secret of God's great spiritual warriors. They have saturated themselves with the Word of God. Hudson Taylor, founder of the China Inland Mission, sustained himself through incredible hardships by a disciplined meditation on the Bible every day. Dr. and Mrs. Howard Taylor give us a glimpse of this discipline:

> It was not easy for Mr. Taylor, in his changeful life, to make time
> for prayer and Bible study, but he knew that it was vital. Well do
> the writers remember traveling with him month after month in
> northern China, by cart and wheelbarrow with the poorest of
> inns at night. Often with only one large room for coolies and
> travelers alike, they would screen off a corner for their father

and another for themselves, with curtains of some sort; and then, after sleep at last had brought a measure of quiet, they would hear a match struck and see the flicker of candlelight which told that Mr. Taylor, however weary, was poring over the little Bible in two volumes always at hand. From two to four A.M. was the time he usually gave to prayer; the time he could be most sure of being undisturbed to wait upon God.[3]

The Sword of the Spirit is full of victory. But how few will give themselves to the deep and disciplined exercise of soul to take it up and wield it with joy and power!

An Earnest Exhortation

So the Bible is the Word of God. And the Word of God is no trifle. It is the source of life and faith and power and hope and freedom and wisdom and comfort and assurance and victory over our greatest enemy. Is it any wonder then that those who knew best said, "The precepts of the LORD are right, *rejoicing* the heart" (Psalm 19:8)? "I will *delight* in thy statutes, I will not forget thy Word" (Psalm 119:16).

"Oh, how I *love* thy law! It is my meditation all the day" (Psalm 119:97). "Thy testimonies are my heritage for ever, yea, they are the *joy* of my heart" (Psalm 119:111). "Thy words were found, and I ate them, and thy words became to me a *joy* and the *delight* of my heart; for I am called by Thy name" (Jeremiah 15:16).

But are we to pursue this joy like Christian Hedonists? Are we to throw the kindling of God's Word every day on the fire of joy? Indeed, we are! Not only every day, but day and night: "Blessed is the man who walks not in the counsel of the wicked, nor stands in the way of sinners, nor sits in the seat of scoffers; but *his delight is in the law of the LORD and on his law he meditates day and night*" (Psalm 1:1-2). This delight is the very design of our Lord in speaking to us: "These things I have *spoken* to you, *that my joy may be in you and your joy may be full*" (John 15:11). Not to pursue our joy every day in the Word of God is an abandonment of the revealed will of God. It is sin.

Oh, that we might not treat the Bible as a trifle! If we do, we oppose ourselves and despise the saints who labored and suffered for the Word of God. Think of the courage of Martin Luther standing before the secular and ecclesiastical rulers of his day, who had power to banish and even to execute him for his views of the Word of God. The Archbishop of Trier poses Luther the question one last time:

"Do you or do you not repudiate your books and the errors which they contain?"

Luther replies, "Since, then, Your Majesty and Your Lordships desire a simple reply, I will answer without horns and without teeth. Unless I am convicted by Scripture and plain reason — I do not accept the authority of popes and councils, for they have contradicted each other — my conscience is captive to the Word of God. I cannot and I will not recant anything, for to go against conscience is neither right nor safe. Here I stand, I cannot do otherwise. God help me."[4] Luther disappeared abruptly after the edict of his condemnation was released. The great artist Albrecht Dürer reflected in his diary,

> I know not whether he lives or is murdered, but in any case he has suffered for the Christian truth. If we lose this man, who has written more clearly than any other in centuries, may God grant his spirit to another. . . . O God, if Luther is dead, who will henceforth explain to us the gospel? What might he not have written for us in the next ten or twenty years?[5]

He was not dead. And he did keep writing — for another twenty-five years. And along with many other bold reformers he recovered for us the Word of God from the bondage of ecclesiastical tradition. O, that we might cherish the Word of God today the way they did! O, that we might wield it the way they did! For them it was such a mighty sword against the Enemy!

Martin Luther knew as well as any man that every day with Jesus is not sweeter than the day before. And according to his biographer, Roland Bainton, he wrote these famous lines in the year of his deepest depression:

> And though this world, with devils filled,
> Should threaten to undo us,
> We will not fear, for God has willed
> His truth to triumph through us.
> The prince of darkness grim,
> We tremble not for him —
> His rage we can endure,
> For lo! his doom is sure:
> One little word shall fell him.

To Wield It We Must Wear It

But if we intend to wield it, we must wear it. We must be like Ezra: "The good hand of God was upon him. For *Ezra had set his heart to study the law of the*

LORD, and to do it, and to teach his statutes and ordinances in Israel" (Ezra 7:9,10). And we must get a heart like the saint who wrote the great love song to the law in Psalm 119, "Oh, how I love thy law! It is my meditation all the day" (verse 97). Let us labor to memorize the Word of God — for worship and for warfare. If we do not carry it in our heads, we cannot savor it in our hearts or wield it in the Spirit. If you go out without the kindling of Christian Hedonism, the fire of Christian happiness will be quenched before mid-morning.

How George Mueller Started His Day

I close this chapter with a testimony from a great man of prayer and faith. George Mueller (1805-1898) is famous for establishing orphanages in England and for joyfully depending on God for all his needs. How did he kindle this joy and faith? In 1841 he made a life-changing discovery. The testimony of this from his autobiography has proved to be of tremendous value in my life, and I pray it will also bear fruit in yours:

> While I was staying at Nailsworth, it pleased the Lord to teach me a truth, irrespective of human instrumentality, as far as I know, the benefit of which I have not lost, though now . . . more than forty years have since passed away.
>
> The point is this: I saw more clearly than ever, that the first great and primary business to which I ought to attend every day was, to have my soul happy in the Lord. The first thing to be concerned about was not, how much I might serve the Lord, how I might glorify the Lord; but how I might get my soul into a happy state, and how my inner man might be nourished. For I might seek to set the truth before the unconverted, I might seek to benefit believers, I might seek to relieve the distressed, I might in other ways seek to behave myself as it becomes a child of God in this world; and yet, not being happy in the Lord, and not being nourished and strengthened in my inner man day by day, all this might not be attended to in a right spirit.
>
> Before this time my practice had been, at least for ten years previously, as an habitual thing, to give myself to prayer, after having dressed in the morning. Now I saw, that the most important thing I had to do was to give myself to the reading of the Word of God and to meditation on it, that thus my heart might be comforted, encouraged, warned, reproved, instructed; and that thus, whilst meditating, my heart might be brought into

experimental, communion with the Lord. I began therefore, to meditate on the New Testament, from the beginning, early in the morning.

The first thing I did, after having asked in a few words the Lord's blessing upon His precious Word, was to begin to meditate on the Word of God; searching, as it were, into every verse, to get blessing out of it; not for the sake of the public ministry of the Word; not for the sake of preaching on what I had meditated upon; but for the sake of obtaining food for my own soul. The result I have found to be almost invariably this, that after a very few minutes my soul has been led to confession, or to thanksgiving, or to intercession, or to supplication; so that though I did not, as it were, give myself to *prayer,* but to *meditation,* yet it turned almost immediately more or less into prayer.

When thus I have been for awhile making confession, or intercession, or supplication, or have given thanks, I go on to the next words or verse, turning all, as I go on, into prayer for myself or others, as the Word may lead to it; but still continually keeping before me, that food for my own soul is the object of my meditation. The result of this is, that there is always a good deal of confession, thanksgiving, supplication, or intercession mingled with my meditation, and that my inner man almost invariably is even sensibly nourished and strengthened and that by breakfast time, with rare exceptions, I am in a peaceful if not happy state of heart. Thus also the Lord is pleased to communicate unto me that which, very soon after, I have found to become food for other believers, though it was not for the sake of the public ministry of the Word that I gave myself to meditation, but for the profit of my own inner man.

The difference between my former practice and my present one is this. Formerly, when I rose, I began to pray as soon as possible, and generally spent all my time till breakfast in prayer, or almost all the time. At all events I almost invariably began with prayer. . . . But what was the result? I often spent a quarter of an hour, or half an hour, or even an hour on my knees, before being conscious to myself of having derived comfort, encouragement, humbling of soul, etc.; and often after having suffered much from wandering of mind for the first ten minutes, or a quarter of an hour, or even half an hour, I only then began *really to pray.*

I scarcely ever suffer now in this way. For my heart being nourished by the truth, being brought into experimental fellowship with God, I speak to my Father, and to my Friend (vile though I am, and unworthy of it!) about the things that He has brought before me in His precious Word.

It often now astonishes me that I did not sooner see this. In no book did I ever read about it. No public ministry ever brought the matter before me. No private intercourse with a brother stirred me up to this matter. And yet now, since God has taught me this point, it is as plain to me as anything, that the first thing the child of God has to do morning by morning is to *obtain food for his inner man.*

As the outward man is not fit for work for any length of time, except we take food, and as this is one of the first things we do in the morning, so it should be with the inner man. We should take food for that, as every one must allow. Now what is the food for the inner man: not *prayer,* but the *Word of God:* and here again not the simple reading of the Word of God, so that it only passes through our minds, just as water runs through a pipe, but considering what we read, pondering over it, and applying it to our hearts. . . .

I dwell so particularly on this point because of the immense spiritual profit and refreshment I am conscious of having derived from it myself, and I affectionately and solemnly beseech all my fellow-believers to ponder this matter. By the blessing of God I ascribe to this mode the help and strength which I have had from God to pass in peace through deeper trials in various ways than I had ever had before; and after having now above forty years tried this way, I can most fully, in the fear of God, commend it. How different when the soul is refreshed and made happy early in the morning, from what it is when, without spiritual preparation, the service, the trials and the temptations of the day come upon one![6]

"Hitherto you have asked nothing in my name;
ask, and you will receive,
that your joy may be full."

JOHN 16:24

"But when you pray, go into your room and shut the door
and pray to your Father who is in secret;
and your Father who sees in secret will reward you."

MATTHEW 6:6

O what peace we often forfeit,
O what needless pain we bear,
All because we do not carry
Everything to God in prayer!

JOSEPH SCRIVEN

CHAPTER 6

PRAYER

The Power of Christian Hedonism

O ne common objection against Christian Hedonism is that it puts the interests of man above the glory of God — that it puts my happiness above God's honor. But Christian Hedonism most emphatically does *not* do this.

To be sure, we Christian Hedonists endeavor to pursue our interest and our happiness with all our might. We endorse the resolution of the young Jonathan Edwards — "Resolved: To endeavor to obtain for myself as much happiness in the other world as I possibly can, with all the power, might, vigor, and vehemence, yea violence, I am capable of, or can bring myself to exert, in any way that can be thought of."

But we have learned from the Bible (and from Edwards!) that God's interest is to magnify the fullness of his glory by spilling over in mercy to us. Therefore the pursuit of our interest and our happiness is never *above* God's, but always *in* God's. The most precious truth in the Bible is that God's greatest interest is to glorify the wealth of his grace by making sinners happy in him — in HIM!

When we humble ourselves like little children and put on no airs of self-sufficiency, but run happily into the joy of our Father's embrace, the glory of his grace is magnified and the longing of our soul is satisfied. Our interest and his glory are one. Therefore, Christian Hedonists do not put their happiness above God's glory when they pursue their happiness *in him*.

Why the Hedonist Is on His Knees

One piece of evidence that the pursuit of *our* joy and the pursuit of *God's* glory are meant to be one and the same is the teaching of Jesus on prayer in the Gospel of John. The two key sayings are in John 14:13 and 16:24. The one shows that prayer is the pursuit of God's glory. The other shows that prayer is the pursuit of our joy.

In John 14:13 Jesus says, "Whatever you ask in my name, I will do it, *that the Father may be glorified in the Son.*" In John 16:24 he says, "Hitherto you have asked nothing in my name; ask, and you will receive, *that your joy may be full.*" The unity of these two goals — the glory of God and the joy of his children — is clearly preserved in the act of *prayer.* Therefore Christian

Hedonists will, above all, be people devoted to earnest prayer. Just as the thirsty deer buckles down to drink at the brook, so the characteristic posture of the Christian Hedonist is on his knees.

Let's look more closely at prayer as the pursuit of God's glory and the pursuit of our joy, in that order.

Prayer as the Pursuit of God's Glory

Once again, hear Jesus' words in John 14:13: "Whatever you ask in my name, I will do it, *that the Father may be glorified in the Son.*" Suppose you are totally paralyzed and can do nothing for yourself but talk. And suppose a strong and reliable friend promised to live with you and do whatever you needed done. How could you glorify your friend if a stranger came to see you? Would you glorify his generosity and strength by trying to get out of bed and carry him?

No! You would say, "Friend, please come lift me up, and would you put a pillow behind me so I can look at my guest. And would you please put my glasses on for me?" And so your visitor would learn from your requests that you are helpless and that your friend is strong and kind. You glorify your friend by needing him and asking him for help and counting on him.

In John 15:5 Jesus says, "I am the vine, you are the branches. He who abides in me and I in him, he it is that bears much fruit, for apart from me you can do nothing." So we really are paralyzed. Without Christ we are capable of no good. As Paul says in Romans 7:18, "There dwells in me, that is in my flesh, no good thing."

But according to John 15:5, God intends for us to do something good — namely, bear fruit. So as our strong and reliable friend — "I call you friends" (John 15:15) — he promises to do for us what we can't do for ourselves.

How then do we glorify him? Jesus gives the answer in John 15:7 — "If you abide in me, and my words abide in you, ask whatever you will and it shall be done for you." We *pray!* We ask God to do for us through Christ what we can't do for ourselves — bear fruit. Verse 8 gives the result: "By this is my Father glorified, that you bear much fruit." So how is God glorified by prayer? Prayer is the open admission that without Christ we can do nothing. And prayer is the turning away from ourselves to God in the confidence that he will provide the help we need. Prayer humbles us as needy, and exalts God as wealthy.

If You Knew Him You Would Ask!

In another text in John that shows how prayer glorifies God, Jesus asks a woman for a drink of water.

The Samaritan woman said to him, "How is it that you, a Jew, ask a drink of a woman of Samaria?" For Jews have no dealings with Samaritans. Jesus answered her, "If you knew the gift of God, and who it is that is saying to you, give me a drink, *you would have asked him,* and he would have given you living water!" (John 4:9-10)

If you were a sailor severely afflicted with scurvy, and a generous man came aboard ship with his pockets bulging with vitamin C and asked you for an orange slice, you might give it to him. But if you knew he was generous, and that he carried all you needed to be well, you would turn the tables and ask him for help.

Jesus says to the woman, "If you just knew the gift of God and who I am, you would ask me — you would pray to me!" There is a direct correlation between not knowing Jesus well and not asking much from him. A failure in our prayer life is generally a failure to know Jesus. "If you knew who was talking to you, you would ask me!" A prayerless Christian is like a bus driver trying alone to push his bus out of a rut because he doesn't know Clark Kent is on board. "If you knew, you would ask." A prayerless Christian is like having your room wallpapered with Sak's Fifth Avenue gift certificates but always shopping at Ragstock because you can't read. "If you knew the gift of God and who it is that speaks to you, you would ask — *you would ask!*"

And the implication is that those who do ask — Christians who spend time in prayer — do it because they see that God is a great Giver and that Christ is wise and merciful and powerful beyond measure. And therefore their prayer glorifies Christ and honors his Father. The chief end of man is to glorify God. Therefore, when we become what God created us to be we become people of prayer.

Robinson Crusoe's Text

Charles Spurgeon once preached a sermon on this very topic and called it "Robinson Crusoe's Text." He began like this:

Robinson Crusoe has been wrecked. He is left on the desert island all alone. His case is a very pitiable one. He goes to his bed, and he is smitten with fever. This fever lasts upon him long, and he has no one to wait upon him — none even to bring him a drink of cold water. He is ready to perish. He had been accustomed to sin, and had all the vices of a sailor; but his hard case brought him to think. He opens a Bible which he finds in his chest, and he lights upon this passage, "Call upon me in the day of trouble: I will deliver thee, and thou shalt glorify me." That night he prayed for the first time in his life, and ever after there was in him a hope in God, which marked the birth of the heavenly life.[1]

Robinson Crusoe's text was Psalm 50:15. It is God's way of getting glory for himself — *Pray to me! I will deliver you!* And the result will be, *you will glorify me!*

Spurgeon's explanation is penetrating:

> God and the praying man take shares. . . . First, here is your share: "Call upon me in the day of trouble." Secondly, here is God's share: "I will deliver thee." Again, you take a share — for you shall be delivered. And then again it is the Lord's turn — "Thou shalt glorify me." Here is a compact, a covenant that God enters into with you who pray to him, and whom he helps. He says, "You shall have the deliverance, but I must have the glory. . . ." Here is a delightful partnership: we obtain that which we so greatly need, and all that God getteth is the glory which is due unto his name.[2]

A delightful partnership indeed! Prayer is the very heart of Christian Hedonism. God gets the glory; we get the delight. He gets the glory precisely because he shows himself full and strong to deliver us into joy. And we attain fullness of joy precisely because he is the all-glorious source and goal of life.

Here is a great discovery. We do not glorify God by providing his needs, but by praying that he would provide ours — and trusting him to answer.

Is Prayer Self-Centered?

Someone may say that this is self-centered. But what does "self-centered" mean? If it means I passionately desire to be happy, then yes, prayer is self-centered.

But is this a bad thing, if what I cry for is that God's name be hallowed in my life? If my cry is for his reign to hold sway in my heart? If my cry is for his will to be done in my life as it is done by angels in heaven? If I crave the happiness of seeing and experiencing these things in my life, is that bad?

How is the will of God done in heaven? Sadly? Burdensomely? Begrudgingly? No! It is done gladly! If I then pray, "Thy will be done on earth as it is in heaven," how can I not be motivated by a desire to be glad? It is a contradiction to pray for the will of God to be done in my life the way it is in heaven, and then to say I am indifferent to whether I am glad or not. When the earth *rejoices* to do his will and does it perfectly, his will shall be done on earth as it is in heaven.

But surely we should not call this pursuit of happiness in prayer "self-centered." It is radically God-centered. In my craving to be happy, I acknowledge that at the center of my life there is a gaping hole of emptiness. I long to have it filled. I know that if it is filled with God, my joy will be full. "Self-centered" is not a good way to describe this passion to be happy in God.

Praying Like an Adultress

But someone will say, "Yes, but not all prayers are prayers for God's name to be hallowed, or his kingdom to come. Many prayers are for food and clothing and protection and healing. Is this sort of praying not self-centered?"

It may be. James did condemn a certain kind of prayer. He said,

> You ask and do not receive, because you ask wrongly, to spend it on your passions [literally: on your pleasures]. Adultresses! Do you not know that friendship with the world is enmity with God? Therefore, whoever wishes to be a friend of the world makes himself an enemy of God. Or do you suppose it is in vain that the Scripture says, "He yearns jealously over the spirit which he has made to dwell in us"? (James 4:3-5)

So there is a kind of praying that is wrong, because it makes a cuckold out of God. We use our Husband's generosity to hire prostitutes for private pleasures. These are startling words. James calls us "adultresses" if we pray like this.

He pictures the church as the wife of God. God has made us for himself and has given himself to us for our enjoyment. Therefore it is adultery when we try to be "friends" with the world. If we seek from the world the pleasures we should seek in God, we are unfaithful to our marriage vows. And, what's worse, when we go to our Heavenly Husband and actually pray for the resources with which to commit adultery with the world, it is a very wicked thing. It is as though we should ask our husband for money to hire male prostitutes to provide the pleasure we don't find in him!

So, yes, there is a kind of praying that is self-centered in an evil sense. Now the question becomes, What keeps all of our praying for "things" from being adulterous?

Enjoying Creation without Committing Idolatry

This is really part of a much larger question, namely, how is it possible for a creature to desire and enjoy the creation without committing idolatry (which is adultery)? This may seem like an irrelevant question to some. But for people who long to sing like the psalmists it is very relevant. They sing like this:

> Whom have I in heaven but thee?
> And there is nothing upon earth
> that I desire besides thee.
> My flesh and my heart may fail,
> but God is the strength of my heart
> and my portion for ever.
> (Psalm 73:25-26)

> One thing have I asked of the LORD
> that will I seek after;
> that I may dwell in the house of the LORD
> all the days of my life,
> to behold the beauty of the LORD,
> and to inquire in his temple.
> (Psalm 27:4)

If your heart longs to be this focused on God, then how to desire and enjoy "things" without becoming an idolater is a crucial question. How can prayer glorify God if it is a prayer for things? It seems to glorify things.

Of course, part of the answer was given in Robinson Crusoe's text, namely, that God gets glory as the all-sufficient Giver. But this is only part of the answer, because there can be a misuse of things even when we thank God as the Giver.

The rest of the answer is expressed by Thomas Traherne and Saint Augustine. Traherne said,

> You never Enjoy the World aright, till you see how a Sand Exhibiteth the Wisdom and Power of God: And Prize in every Thing the Service which they do you, by Manifesting His Glory and Goodness to your Soul, far more than the Visible Beauty on their Surface, or the Material Services, they can do your Body.[3]

And Augustine prayed the following words, which have proved immensely important in my effort to love God with *all* my heart.

> He loves Thee too little
> who loves anything together with Thee,
> which he loves not for Thy sake.[4]

In other words, if created things are seen and handled as gifts of God and as mirrors of his glory, they need not be occasions of idolatry — *if* our delight in them is always also a delight in their Maker.

C. S. Lewis put it like this in a "Letter to Malcolm":

> We can't — or I can't — hear the song of a bird simply as a sound. Its meaning or message ("That's a bird") comes with it inevitably — just as one can't see a familiar word in print as a merely visual pattern. The reading is as involuntary as the see-ing. When the wind roars I don't just hear the roar; I "hear the wind." In the same way it is possible to "read" as well as to "have" a pleasure. Or not even "as well as." The distinction ought to become, and sometimes is, impossible; to receive it and to recognize its divine source are a single experience. This heavenly fruit is instantly redolent of the orchard where it grew. This sweet air whispers of the country from whence it blows. It is a message. We know we are being touched by a finger of that right hand at which there are pleasures for evermore. There need be no question of thanks or praise as a separate event, something done afterwards. To experience the tiny theophany is itself to adore.[5]

If our experience of creation becomes an experience of the heavenly orchard, or the divine finger, then it may be worship and not idolatry. Lewis says it yet another way in his meditations on the Psalms:

> By emptying Nature of divinity — or, let us say, of divinities — you may fill her with Deity, for she is now the bearer of mes-sages. There is a sense in which Nature-worship silences her — as if a child or a savage were so impressed with the postman's uniform that he omitted to take in the letters.[6]

Therefore it may or may not be idolatry to pray for the mailman to come. If we are only enamored by the short-term worldly pleasures his uni-form gives, it is idolatry. But if we consider the uniform a gracious bonus to the real delight of the divine messages, then it is not idolatry. If we can pray for a spouse or job or physical healing or food or shelter for God's sake, then even here we are God-centered and not "self-centered." We are agreeing with the Psalmist, "There is nothing on earth I desire besides Thee!" That is, there is nothing I want more than You, and there is nothing I want that does not show me more of You.

Glorifying God by Not Serving Him, but Being Served by Him

But now back to the main train of thought. I said a moment ago that Robinson Crusoe's text opened for us a great discovery. (And just then someone objected that all this is self-centered.) The discovery was that we do not glorify God by providing his needs, but by praying that he would provide ours — and trusting him to answer. Here we are at the heart of the good news of Christian Hedonism.

God's insistence that we ask him to give us help so that he gets glory (Psalm 50:15) forces on us the startling fact that we must *beware of serving God,* and must take special care to let him serve us, lest we rob him of his glory.

This sounds very strange. Most of us think serving God is a totally positive thing; we have not considered that serving God may be an insult to him. But meditation on the meaning of prayer demands this consideration.

Acts 17:24-25 makes this plain.

"The God who made the world and everything in it, being Lord of heaven and earth, does not live in shrines made by man, nor is he served by human hands as though he needed anything, since he himself gives to all men life and breath and everything."

This is the same reasoning as in Robinson Crusoe's text on prayer:

"If I were hungry, I would not tell you; for the world and all that is in it is mine. . . . Call upon me in the day of trouble; I will deliver you, and you shall glorify me." (Psalm 50:12,15)

Evidently there is a way to serve God that would belittle him as needy of our service. "The Son of Man came not to be served" (Mark 10:45). He aims to be the servant. He aims to get the glory as Giver.

Still Servant at the Second Coming!

Even in his glory at the close of the age this is true, and not just in the days of his earthly humiliation. To me the Bible's most astonishing image of Christ's second coming is in Luke 12:35-37, which pictures the return of a master from a marriage feast.

"Let your loins be girded and your lamps burning, and be like men who are waiting for their master to come home from the marriage feast, so that they may open to him at once when he comes and knocks. Blessed are those servants whom the master finds awake when he comes; truly, I say to you, he will gird himself and have them sit at table, and he will come and serve them."

How Is God Different from All the Other Gods?

To be sure, we are called servants — and that no doubt means we are to do exactly as we are told. But the wonder of this picture is that the "master" insists on "serving" even in the age to come when he appears in all his glory "with his mighty angels in flaming fire" (2 Thessalonians 1:7). Why? Because the very heart of his glory is the fullness of grace that overflows in kindness to needy people. Therefore he aims "in the coming ages to display the immeasurable riches of his grace in kindness to us in Christ Jesus" (Ephesians 2:7).

What is the greatness of our God? What is his uniqueness in the world? Isaiah answers,

> From of old no one has heard or perceived by the ear, no eye has seen a God besides Thee, who works for those who wait for him. (Isaiah 64:4)

All the other so-called gods try to exalt themselves by making man work for them. In doing so they only show their weakness. Isaiah derides the gods who need the service of their people:

> Bel bows down, Nebo stoops, their idols are on beasts and cattle; these things you carry are loaded as burdens on weary beasts. (Isaiah 46:1)

Jeremiah joins the derision:

> "Their idols are like scarecrows in a cucumber field, and they cannot speak; they have to be carried, for they cannot walk." (Jeremiah 10:5)

God is unique. "From of old no one has heard or perceived by the ear . . ." And his uniqueness is that he aims to be the Workman for us, not vice versa. Our job is to "wait for him."

God Works for Those Who Wait for Him

To wait! That means to pause and soberly consider our own inadequacy and the Lord's all-sufficiency, and to seek counsel and help from the Lord, and to hope in him (Psalm 33:20-22; Isaiah 8:17). Israel is rebuked that "they did not wait for his counsel" (Psalm 106:13). Why? Because in not seeking and waiting for God's help, they robbed God of an occasion to glorify himself.

For example, in Isaiah 30:15, 16 the Lord says to Israel, "In returning and rest you shall be saved; in quietness and in trust shall be your strength." But Israel refused to wait for the Lord, and said, "No! We will speed upon horses."

Then in verse 18 the folly and evil of this self-initiated frenzy is revealed: "The LORD waits to be gracious to you; therefore he exalts himself to show mercy to you. For the LORD is a God of justice; blessed are all those who wait for him." The folly of not waiting for God is that we forfeit the blessing of having God work for us. The evil of not waiting for God is that we oppose God's will to exalt himself in mercy.

God aims to exalt himself by working for those who wait for him. Prayer is the essential activity of waiting for God: acknowledging our helplessness and his power, calling upon him for help, seeking his counsel. So it is evident why prayer is so often commanded by God, since his purpose in the world is to be exalted for his mercy. Prayer is the antidote for the disease of self-confidence that opposes God's goal of getting glory by working for those who wait for him.

"The eyes of the LORD run to and fro throughout the whole earth, to show his might on behalf of those whose heart is whole toward him" (2 Chronicles 16:9). God is not looking for people to work for him, so much as he is looking for people who will let him work for them. The gospel is not a Help Wanted ad. Neither is the call to Christian service. On the contrary, the gospel commands us to give up and hang out a Help Wanted sign (this is the basic meaning of prayer). Then the gospel promises that God will work for us if we do. He will not surrender the glory of being the Giver.

But is there not anything we can give him that won't belittle him to the status of beneficiary? Yes — our anxieties. It's a command: "Cast all your anxieties on him" (1 Peter 5:7). God will gladly receive anything from us that shows our dependence and his all-sufficiency.

The Difference between Uncle Sam and Jesus Christ

The difference between Uncle Sam and Jesus Christ is that Uncle Sam won't enlist you in his service unless you are healthy, and Jesus won't enlist you unless you are sick. "Those who are well have no need of a physician, but those who are sick; I came not to call the righteous, but sinners" (Mark 2:17). Christianity is fundamentally convalescence ("Pray without ceasing" = Keep buzzing the nurse). Patients do not serve their physicians. They trust them for good prescriptions. The Sermon on the Mount and the Ten Commandments are the Doctor's prescribed health regimen, not the Employer's job description.

Therefore our very lives hang on not working for God. "To one who works, his wages are not reckoned as a gift, but as his due. And to one who does not work but trusts him who justifies the ungodly, his faith is reckoned as righteousness" (Romans 4:4-5). Workmen get no gifts. They get their due. If we would have the gift of justification, we dare not work. God is the Workman in this affair. And what he gets is the trust of his client and the glory of being the benefactor of grace, not the beneficiary of service.

Nor should we think that after justification our labor for God's wages begins. "Did you receive the Spirit by works of the law, or by hearing with faith? Are you so foolish? Having begun with the Spirit, are you now ending with the flesh?" (Galatians 3:2-3). God was the Workman in our justification, and he will be the Workman in our sanctification.

Religious "flesh" always wants to work for God (rather than humbling itself to realize God must work for it in free grace). But "if you live according to the flesh you will die" (Romans 8:13). That is why our very lives hang on not working for God.

Then shall we not serve Christ? It is commanded: "Serve the Lord!" (Romans 12:11). Those who do not serve Christ are rebuked (Romans 16:18). Yes, we must serve him. But we will beware of serving in a way that implies a deficiency on his part or exalts our indispensability.

Serving God Is Always Receiving

How then shall we serve? Psalm 123:2 points the way. "Behold, as the eyes of servants look to the hand of their master, as the eyes of a maid to the hand of her mistress, so our eyes look to the LORD our God, till he have mercy upon us." The way to serve God so that he gets the glory is to look to him for mercy. Prayer prevents service from being an expression of pride.

Any servant who tries to get off the divine dole and strike up a manly partnership with his Heavenly Master is in revolt against the Creator. God does not barter. He gives the mercy of life to servants who will have it, and the wages of death to those who won't. Good service is always and fundamentally receiving mercy, not rendering assistance. So there is no good service without prayer.

How Do You Serve Money?

Matthew 6:24 gives another pointer toward good service. "No one can serve two masters; for either he will hate the one and love the other, or he will be devoted to the one and despise the other. You cannot *serve* God and mammon." How does a person serve money? He does not assist money. He does not enrich money. He is not the benefactor of money. How then do we serve money?

Money exerts a certain control over us because it seems to hold out so much promise of happiness. It whispers with great force, "Think and act so as to get into a position to enjoy my benefits." This may include stealing, borrowing, or working. Money promises happiness, and we serve it by believing the promise and walking by that faith. So we don't serve money by putting our power at its disposal for its good. We serve money by doing what is necessary so that money's power will be at our disposal for our good.

The same sort of service to God must be in view in Matthew 6:24, since Jesus puts the two side by side: "You cannot serve God and money." So if we are going to serve God and not money, then we are going to have to open our eyes to the vastly superior promise of happiness which God offers. Then God will exert a greater control over us than money does.

And so we will serve God by believing his promise of fullest joy and walking by that faith. We will not serve by trying to put our power at his disposal for his good, but by doing what is necessary so that his power will be ever at our disposal for our good. And of course, God has appointed that his power be at our disposal through prayer. "Ask and you will receive!" So we serve by the power that comes through prayer, when we serve for the glory of God.

Without doubt this sort of serving also means obedience. A patient who trusts his doctor's prescriptions obeys them. A convalescent sinner trusts the painful directions of his therapist, and follows. Only in this way do we keep ourselves in a position to benefit from what the divine Physician has to offer. In all this obedience it is we who are the beneficiaries. God is ever the Giver. For it is the Giver who gets the glory.

The Giver Gets the Glory

First Peter 4:11 states the principle so well: "Let him who serves serve in the strength which God supplies in order that in everything God may be glorified through Jesus Christ, to whom belong glory and power forever and ever. Amen." The Giver gets the glory. So all serving that honors God must be a receiving. Which means that all service must be performed by prayer.

To be sure, let us work hard; but never let us forget that it is not we, but the grace of God which is with us (1 Corinthians 15:10). Let us obey now, as always, but never forget that it is God who works in us, both to will and to do his good pleasure (Philippians 2:13). Let us spread the gospel far and wide, and spend ourselves for the sake of God's elect, but never venture to speak of anything except what Christ has wrought through us (Romans 15:18). Let us be ever praying for his power and wisdom, so that all our serving is the overflow of righteousness, joy and peace from the Holy Spirit. "For he who thus serves Christ is acceptable to God and approved by men" (Romans 14:17-18).

So the astonishing good news implied in the duty of prayer is that God will never give up the glory of being our Servant. "No eye has seen a God besides thee, who works for those who wait for him" (Isaiah 64:4).

Prayer as the Pursuit of Our Joy

Uniquely preserved in the act of prayer is the unity of two goals — the pursuit of God's glory and the pursuit of our joy. So far in this chapter we have meditated on prayer as the pursuit of God's glory, with John 14:13 as our starting point — "Whatever you ask in my name, I will do it, that the Father may be glorified in the Son." Now we turn to Jesus' words in John 16:24 — "Hitherto you have asked nothing in my name; ask, and you will receive *that your joy may be full.*"

Is this not a clear invitation to Christian Hedonism? Pursue the fullness of your joy! *Pray!*

From this sacred Word and from experience we can draw a simple rule: Among professing Christians, prayerlessness produces joylessness. Why? Why is it that a deep life of prayer leads to fullness of joy, and a shallow life of prayerlessness produces joylessness? Jesus gives at least two reasons in the context of John 16:24.

Prayer Is the Nerve Center of Fellowship with Jesus

The first reason prayer leads to joy is given in John 16:20-22. Jesus alerts the disciples that they will grieve at his death, but then rejoice again at his resurrection:

> "Truly, truly, I say to you, you will weep and lament, but the world will rejoice; you will be sorrowful, but your sorrow will be turned to joy. When a woman is in travail, she has sorrow because her hour has come; but when she is delivered of the child, she no longer remembers the anguish for joy that a child is born into the world. So you have sorrow now but I will see you again, and your hearts will rejoice."

Separation from Jesus means sadness. Restoration of fellowship means joy. Therefore we learn that no Christian can have fullness of joy without a vital fellowship with Jesus Christ. Knowledge about him will not do. Work for him will not do. We must have personal, vital fellowship with him; otherwise Christianity becomes a joyless burden.

In his first letter, John wrote, "Our fellowship is with the Father and with his Son, Jesus Christ. And we are writing this that our joy may be full" (1 John 1:3,4). Fellowship with Jesus shared with others is essential to fullness of joy.

The first reason, then, why prayer leads to fullness of joy is that prayer is the nerve center of our fellowship with Jesus. He is not here physically to see. But in prayer we speak to him just as though he were. And in the stillness of those sacred times we listen to his Word and we pour out to him our longings.

Perhaps John 15:7 is the best summary of this two-sided fellowship of prayer: "If you abide in me and my words abide in you, ask whatever you will and it shall be done for you." When the biblical words of Jesus abide in our mind, we hear the very thoughts of the living Christ, for he is the same yesterday, today, and forever. And out of that deep listening of the heart comes the language of prayer which is a sweet incense before God's throne. The life of prayer leads to fullness of joy because prayer is the nerve center of our vital fellowship with Jesus.

Jonathan Edwards gives us an account of his early years to illustrate the height and intensity to which this fellowship can rise.

> I had vehement longings of soul after God and Christ, and after more holiness, wherewith my heart seemed to be full, and ready to break. . . . I spent most of my time in thinking of divine things, year after year; often walking alone in the woods, and solitary places, for meditation, soliloquy, and prayer, and converse with God; and it was always my manner, at such times, to sing forth my contemplations. I was almost constantly in ejaculatory prayer, wherever I was. Prayer seemed to be natural to me, as the breath by which the inward burnings of my heart had vent.[7]

Prayer is God's appointed way to fullness of joy because it is the vent of the inward burnings of our heart for Christ. If we had no vent, if we could not commune with him in response to his Word, we would be miserable indeed.

Prayer Empowers for the Mission of Love

But there is a second reason prayer leads to joy's fullness: It provides the power to do what we love to do, but can't do without God's help. The text says, "Ask, and you will receive, that your joy may be full." Receive what? What would bring us fullness of joy? Not a padded and protected and comfortable life. Rich people are as miserably unhappy as poor people. What we need in answer to prayer to fill our joy is the power to love. Or as John puts it, the power to bear fruit. Prayer is the fountain of joy because it is the source of power to love.

We see this twice in John 15. First in verses 7-8:

"If you abide in me, and my words abide in you, ask whatever you will, and it shall be done for you. By this my Father is glorified, that you bear much fruit."

The connection is clear between prayer and fruit-bearing. God promises to answer prayers for people who are pursuing fruit that abounds to his glory.

Verses 16-17 point in the same direction.

"You did not choose me, but I chose you and appointed you that you should go and bear fruit and that your fruit should abide; so that whatever you ask the Father in my name, he may give it to you. This I command you, to love one another."

The logic here is crucial. Notice: Why is the Father going to give the disciples what they ask in Jesus' name? Answer: Because they have been sent to bear fruit. The reason the Father gives the disciples the gift of prayer is because Jesus has given them a mission. In fact, the grammar of John 15:16 implies that the reason Jesus gives them their mission is so that they will be able to enjoy the power of prayer. "I send you to bear fruit . . . so that whatever you ask the Father . . . he may give you."

Isn't it plain that the purpose of prayer is to accomplish a mission? A mission of love — "This I command you, to love one another." It is as though the field commander (Jesus) called in the troops, gave them a crucial mission (go and bear fruit), handed each of them a personal transmitter coded to the frequency of the general's headquarters, and said, "Comrades, the general has a mission for you. He aims to see it accomplished. And to that end he has authorized me to give each of you personal access to him through these transmitters. If you stay true to his mission and seek his victory first, he will always be as close as your transmitter, to give tactical advice and to send in air cover when you need it."

Can a Wartime Walkie-Talkie Be a Domestic Intercom?

Could it be that many of our problems with prayer and much of our weakness in prayer come from the fact that we are not all on active duty, and yet we still try to use the transmitter? We have taken a wartime walkie-talkie and tried to turn it into a civilian intercom to call the servants for another cushion in the den.

There are other examples in Scripture of the wartime significance of prayer. In Luke 21:34-36 Jesus warns his disciples that times of great distress and opposition were coming. Then he said, "But watch at all times, praying that you may have strength to escape all these things that will take place, and to stand before the Son of man."

In other words, following Jesus will inevitably lead us into severe conflict with evil. This evil will surround us and attack us and threaten to destroy our faith. So God has given us a transmitter. If we go to sleep it will do us no good, but if we are alert and call for help in the conflict, the reinforcements will come, and the general will not let his faithful soldiers be denied their crown of victory before the Son of man.

Life is war. And "we are not contending against flesh and blood, but against principalities and against the powers, and against the world rulers of this present darkness, against the spiritual hosts of wickedness in the heavenly places." Therefore Paul commands us to "take the helmet of salvation, and the sword of the Spirit, which is the word of God, *with all prayer* and supplication praying on every occasion in the Spirit, and keeping awake for this with all perseverance" (Ephesians 6:12,17-18).

So we see repeatedly in Scripture that prayer is a walkie-talkie for warfare, not a domestic intercom for increasing our conveniences. The point of prayer is empowering for mission. "Pray for me that utterance may be given me in opening my mouth boldly to proclaim the mystery of the gospel" (Ephesians 6:19). "Pray for us that God may open to us a door for the word, to declare the mystery of Christ" (Colossians 4:3). "Strive together with me in your prayers to God on my behalf . . . that my service for Jerusalem may be acceptable to the saints" (Romans 15:30-31). "Pray for us that the word of the Lord may run and be glorified" (2 Thessalonians 3:1). "Pray the Lord of the harvest to send out laborers into his harvest!" (Matthew 9:38).

The fullness of joy we seek is the joy of overflowing love to other people. No amount of *getting* can satisfy the soul until it overflows in *giving*. And no sacrifice will destroy the soul-delights of an obedient people on a mission of love from God, for which prayer is his strategic provision. So the reason we pray is "that our joy may be full."

Fellowship with Jesus is essential to joy, but there is something about it that impels us outward to share his life with others. A Christian can't be happy and stingy. "It is more blessed to give than to receive." Therefore, the second reason a life of prayer leads to fullness of joy is that it gives us the power to love. If the pump of love runs dry it is because the pipe of prayer isn't deep enough.

Love is the fruit of the Spirit (Galatians 5:22), and the Spirit is given in answer to prayer (Luke 11:13). Love is the outworking of faith (Galatians 5:6), and faith is sustained by prayer (Mark 9:24; Luke 22:32). Love is rooted in hope (Colossians 1:4-5), and hope is preserved by prayer (Ephesians 1:18). Love is guided and inspired by knowledge of the Word of God (Philippians 1:9; John 17:17), and prayer opens the eyes of the heart to the wonders of the Word (Psalm 119:18). If love is the path of fullest joy, then let us pray for the power to love "that our joy might be full!"

The Final Joy of God's People

What will be the final joy of God's people? Will it not be the day when the glory of the Lord fills the earth as the waters cover the sea? Will it not be the day when our mission is completed and the children of God are gathered in from every people and tongue and tribe and nation (John 11:52; Revelation 5:9; 7:9) — when all causes of sin and all evildoers are taken out of Christ's kingdom and the righteous will shine like the sun in the kingdom of their Father (Matthew 13:42-43)?

And is not Frontier Missions a road to that ultimate joy? And is not Frontier Missions quickened and carried by a movement of prayer? This was the conviction of the early church (Acts 1:14; 4:23-31; 6:4; 10:9; 12:5; 13:3; 14:23 and so on) and of the seventeenth-century Puritans,[8] and of the eighteenth-century European Moravians[9] and American Evangelicals,[10] and of the nineteenth-century student and laymen's movements.[11] It is also the deepening conviction of many mission leaders today.[12]

How a Great Awakening Came

Rightly so. For history testifies to the power of prayer as the prelude to spiritual awakening and missions advance. One example from New York City history: Approaching the middle of the nineteenth century, the glow of earlier religious awakenings had faded. The city, like most of America, was prosperous and felt little need to call on God. Then came the late 1850s:

Secular and religious conditions combined to bring about a crash. The third great panic in American history swept away the giddy structure of speculative wealth. Thousands of merchants were forced to the wall as banks failed, and railroads went into bankruptcy. Factories were shut down and vast numbers thrown out of employment, New York City alone having 30,000 idle men. In October 1857, the hearts of the people were thoroughly weaned from speculation and uncertain gain, while hunger and despair stared them in the face.

On 1st July, 1857, a quiet and zealous businessman named Jeremiah Lanphier took up an appointment as a City Missionary in downtown New York. Lanphier was appointed by the North Church of the Dutch Reformed denomination. This church was suffering from depletion of membership due to the removal of the population from the downtown to the better residential quarters, and the new City Missionary was engaged to make diligent visitation in the immediate neighborhood with a view to enlisting church attendance among the floating population of the lower city. The Dutch Consistory felt that it had appointed an ideal layman for the task in hand, and so it was.

Burdened so by the need, Jeremiah Lanphier decided to invite others to join him in a noonday prayer meeting, to be held on Wednesdays once a week. He therefore distributed a handbill:

HOW OFTEN SHALL WE PRAY?

As often as the language of prayer is in my heart; as often as I see my need of help; as often as I feel the power of temptation; as often as I am made sensible of any spiritual declension or feel the aggression of a worldly spirit.

In prayer we leave the business of time for that of eternity, and intercourse with men for intercourse with God.

A day Prayer Meeting is held every Wednesday, from 12 to 1 o'clock, in the Consistory building in the rear of the North Dutch Church, corner of Fulton and William Streets (entrance from Fulton and Ann Streets).

This meeting is intended to give merchants, mechanics, clerks, strangers, and businessmen generally an opportunity to stop and call

*upon God amid the perplexities incident to their respective avoca-
tions. It will continue for one hour; but it is also designed for those
who may find it inconvenient to remain more than five or ten minutes, as well as for those who can spare the whole hour.*

Accordingly, at twelve noon, 23rd September, 1857 the door
opened and the faithful Lanphier took his seat to await the
response to his invitation. . . . Five minutes went by. No one
appeared. The missionary paced the room in a conflict of fear
and faith. Ten minutes elapsed. Still no one came. Fifteen minutes passed.

Lanphier was yet alone. Twenty minutes; twenty-five; thirty;
and then at 12:30 a step was heard on the stairs, and the first
person appeared, then another, and another and another, until
six people were present and the prayer meeting began. On the
following Wednesday . . . there were forty intercessors.

Thus in the first week of October 1857, it was decided to hold
a meeting daily instead of weekly . . .

Within six months, ten thousand businessmen were gathering
daily for prayer in New York, and within two years, a million
converts were added to the American churches. . . .

Undoubtedly the greatest revival in New York's colorful history
was sweeping the city, and it was of such an order to make the
whole nation curious. There was no fanaticism, no hysteria,
simply an incredible movement of the people to pray.[13]

And the joy of Jeremiah Lanphier was very great. "Ask and you will
receive, that your joy may be full."

Summary and Exhortation

The Bible plainly teaches that the goal of all we do should be to glorify God.
But it also teaches that in all we do we should pursue the fullness of our joy.
Some theologians have tried to force these two pursuits apart. But the Bible
does not force us to choose between God's glory and our joy. In fact, it forbids
us to choose. And what we have seen in this chapter is that prayer, perhaps
more clearly than anything else, preserves the unity of these two pursuits.

Prayer pursues joy in fellowship with Jesus and in the power to share
his life with others. And prayer pursues God's glory by treating him as the

inexhaustible reservoir of hope and help. In prayer we admit our poverty and God's prosperity, our bankruptcy and his bounty, our misery and his mercy. Therefore, prayer highly exalts and glorifies God precisely by pursuing everything we long for in him and not in ourselves. "Ask and you will receive . . . that the Father may be glorified in the Son and . . . that your joy may be full."

I close this chapter with an earnest exhortation. Unless I'm badly mistaken, one of the main reasons so many of God's children don't have a significant life of prayer is not so much that we don't want to, but that we don't plan to. If you want to take a four-week vacation, you don't just get up one summer morning and say, "Hey, let's go today!" You won't have anything ready. You won't know where to go. Nothing has been planned.

But that is how many of us treat prayer. We get up day after day and realize that significant times of prayer should be a part of our life, but nothing's ever ready. We don't know where to go. Nothing has been planned. No time. No place. No procedure. And we all know that the opposite of planning is not a wonderful flow of deep, spontaneous experiences in prayer. The opposite of planning is the rut. If you don't plan a vacation you will probably stay home and watch TV. The natural, unplanned flow of spiritual life sinks to the lowest ebb of vitality. There is a race to be run and a fight to be fought. If you want renewal in your life of prayer you must *plan* to see it.

Therefore, my simple exhortation is this: Let us take time this very day to rethink our priorities and how prayer fits in. Make some new resolve. Try some new venture with God. Set a time. Set a place. Choose a portion of Scripture to guide you. Don't be tyrannized by the press of busy days. We all need mid-course corrections. Make this a day of turning to prayer — for the glory of God and for the fullness of your joy.

"Provide yourselves with purses
that do not grow old."

LUKE 12:33

"Make friends for yourselves
by means of unrighteous mammon,
so that when it fails
they may receive you into the eternal habitations."

LUKE 16:9

CHAPTER 7

MONEY

The Currency of Christian Hedonism

M oney is the currency of Christian Hedonism. What you do with it — or desire to do with it — can make or break your happiness forever. The Bible makes clear that what you feel about money can destroy you:

> Those who desire to be rich fall into temptation, into a snare, into many senseless and hurtful desires that plunge men into ruin and destruction. (1 Timothy 6:9)

Or what you do with your money can secure the foundation of eternal life:

> They are to be liberal and generous, thus laying up for themselves a good foundation for the future, so that they may take hold of the life which is life indeed. (1 Timothy 6:18,19)

These verses teach us to use our money in a way that will bring us the greatest and longest gain. That is, they advocate Christian Hedonism. They confirm that it is not only permitted but commanded by God that we flee from destruction and pursue our full and lasting pleasure. They imply that all the evils in the world come not because our desires for happiness are too strong, but because they are so weak that we settle for fleeting pleasures that do not satisfy our deepest souls, but in the end destroy them. The root of all evil is that we are the kind of people who settle for the love of money instead of the love of God (1 Timothy 6:10).

Beware the Desire to Be Rich

This text in 1 Timothy 6 is so crucial that we should meditate on it in more detail. Paul is warning Timothy against

> (5) . . . men who are depraved in mind and bereft of the truth, imagining that godliness is a means of gain. (6) There is great gain in godliness with contentment; (7) for we brought nothing into the world, and we cannot take anything out of the world; (8) but if we have food and clothing, with these we shall be

content. (9) But those who desire to be rich fall into temptation, into a snare, into many senseless and hurtful desires that plunge men into ruin and destruction. (10) For the love of money is the root of all evils; it is through this craving that some have wandered away from the faith and pierced their hearts with many pangs.

Paul writes to Timothy a word of warning about slick deceivers who discovered they could cash in on the upsurge of godliness in Ephesus. According to verse five, these puffed-up controversialists treat godliness as a means of gain. They are so addicted to the love of money that truth occupies a very subordinate place in their affections. They don't "rejoice in the truth." They rejoice in tax evasion. They are willing to use any new, popular interest to make a few bucks.

Nothing is sacred. If the bottom line is big and black, the advertising strategies are a matter of indifference. If godliness is in, then sell godliness.

This text is very timely. Ours are good days for profits in godliness. The godliness market is hot for booksellers and music makers and dispensers of silver crosses and fish buckles and olivewood letter-openers and bumper stickers and lucky-water crosses with Jesus on the front and miracle water inside guaranteed to make you win at Bingo or your money back in ninety days. These are good days for gain in godliness!

He Didn't Say, "Don't Live for Gain."

In his day or in ours, Paul could have responded to this effort to turn godliness into gain by saying, "Christians don't live for gain. Christians do what's right for its own sake. Christians aren't motivated by profit." But that's *not* what Paul said. He said (in verse 6), "There is great gain in godliness with contentment."

Instead of saying Christians don't live for gain, he says Christians ought to live for greater gain than the slick money lovers do. Godliness is the way to get this great gain, but only if we are content with simplicity rather than greedy for riches. "Godliness *with contentment* is great gain."

If your godliness has freed you from the desire to be rich and has helped you be content with what you have, then your godliness is tremendously profitable. "For while physical training is a little profitable, godliness is profitable for all things, as it holds promise for the present life and also for the life to come" (1 Timothy 4:8). Godliness that overcomes the craving for material wealth produces great spiritual wealth. The point of verse 6 is that it is very profitable not to pursue wealth.

What follows in verses 7-10 are three reasons why we should not pursue riches.

Getting Raises Is Not the Same as Getting Rich

But first let me insert a clarification. We live in a society in which many legitimate businesses depend on large concentrations of capital. You can't build a new manufacturing plant without millions of dollars in equity. Therefore, financial officers in big businesses often have the responsibility to build reserves, for example, by selling shares to the community. When the Bible condemns the desire to get rich, it is not necessarily condemning a business which aims to expand and therefore seeks larger capital reserves. The officers of the business may be greedy for more personal wealth, or they may have larger, nobler motives of how their expanded productivity will benefit people.

Even when a competent person in business is offered a raise or a higher paying job and accepts it, that is not enough to condemn him for the desire to be rich. He may have accepted the job because he craves the power and status and luxuries the money could bring. Or, content with what he has, he may intend to use the extra money for founding an adoption agency or giving a scholarship or sending a missionary or funding an inner-city ministry.

Working to earn money for the cause of Christ is not the same as desiring to be rich. What Paul is warning against is not the desire to earn money to meet our needs and the needs of others; he is warning against the desire to *have* more and more money and the ego boost and material luxuries it can provide.

There Are No U-Hauls behind Hearses

Let's look at the three reasons Paul gives in verses 7-10 for why we should not aspire to be rich.

(1) In verse seven he says, "For we brought nothing into the world and we cannot take anything out of the world." There are no U-Hauls behind hearses.

Suppose someone passes empty-handed through the turnstiles at a big city art museum and begins to take the pictures off the wall and carry them importantly under his arm. You come up to him and say, "What are you doing?"

He answers, "I'm becoming an art collector."

"But they're not really yours," you say, "and besides, they won't let you take any of those out of here. You'll have to go out just like you came in."

But he answers again, "Sure, they're mine. I've got them under my arm. People in the halls look at me as an important dealer. And I don't bother myself with thoughts about leaving. Don't be a kill-joy."

We would call this man a fool! He is out of touch with reality. So is the person who spends himself to get rich in this life. We will go out just the way we came in.

Or picture 269 people entering eternity in a plane crash in the Sea of Japan. Before the crash there is a noted politician, a millionaire corporate executive, a playboy and his playmate, a missionary kid on the way back from visiting grandparents.

After the crash they stand before God utterly stripped of Mastercards, checkbooks, credit lines, image clothes, how-to-succeed books, and Hilton reservations. Here are the politician, the executive, the playboy, and the missionary kid, all on level ground with nothing, absolutely nothing in their hands, possessing only what they brought in their hearts. How absurd and tragic the lover of money will seem on that day — like a man who spends his whole life collecting train tickets and in the end is so weighed down by the collection he misses the last train. Don't spend your precious life trying to get rich, Paul says, "for we brought nothing into the world and we can take nothing out of the world."

Simplicity Is Possible and Good

(2) Then in verse eight Paul adds the second reason not to pursue wealth: "If we have food and clothing, with these we shall be content." Christians can be and ought to be content with the simple necessities of life.

I'll mention three reasons why such simplicity is possible and good.

First, when you have God near you and for you, you don't need extra money or extra things to give you peace and security.

> Keep your life free from the love of money. Be content with what you have. For he has said, "I will never fail you nor forsake you." Hence we can confidently say, "The Lord is my helper, I will not be afraid; what can man do to me?" (Hebrews 13:5-6)

No matter which way the market is moving, God is always better than gold. Therefore, by God's help we can be and we should be content with the simple necessities of life.

Second, we can be content with simplicity because the deepest, most satisfying delights God gives us through creation are free gifts from nature and from loving relationships with people. After your basic needs are met, accumulated money begins to diminish your capacity for these pleasures rather than increase them. Buying things contributes absolutely nothing to the heart's capacity for joy.

There is a deep difference between the temporary thrill of a new toy and a homecoming hug from a devoted friend. Who do you think has the deepest, most satisfying joy in life, the man who pays $140 for a fortieth-floor suite downtown and spends his evening in the half-lit, smoke-filled lounge impressing strange women with ten-dollar cocktails, or the man who chooses the Motel 6 by a vacant lot of sunflowers and spends his evening watching the sunset and writing a love letter to his wife?

Third, we should be content with the simple necessities of life because we could invest the extra we make for what really counts. Three billion people today are outside Jesus Christ. Two-thirds of them have no viable Christian witness in their culture. If they are to hear — and Christ commands that they hear — then cross-cultural missionaries will have to be sent and paid for. All the wealth needed to send this new army of good news ambassadors is already in the church.

If we, like Paul, are content with the simple necessities of life, hundreds of millions of dollars in the church would be released to take the gospel to the frontiers. The revolution of joy and freedom it would cause at home would be the best local witness imaginable. The biblical call is that you can and ought to be content with life's simple necessities.

How to Pierce the Heart with Many Pangs

(3) The third reason not to pursue wealth is that the pursuit will end in the destruction of your life. This is the point of verses nine and ten:

> Those who desire to be rich fall into temptation, into a snare, into many senseless and hurtful desires that plunge men into ruin and destruction. For the love of money is the root of all evils. It is through this craving that some have wandered away from the faith and pierced their hearts with many pangs.

No Christian Hedonist wants to plunge into ruin and destruction and be pierced with many pangs. Therefore, no Christian Hedonist desires to be rich.

Test yourself. Have you learned your attitude toward money from the Bible, or have you absorbed it from contemporary American merchandising? When you ride an airplane and read the airline magazine, almost every page teaches and pushes a view of wealth exactly opposite from the view in 1 Timothy 6:9 that those desiring to be rich will fall into ruin and destruction. Paul makes vivid the peril of the same desire which the airline magazines exploit and promote.

The Images of Wealth

I recall a full-page ad for a popular office chair which showed a man in a plush office. The ad's headline read, "His suits are custom tailored. His watch is solid gold. His office chair is _____." Below the man's picture was this quote:

> I've worked hard and had my share of luck: my business is a success. I wanted my office to reflect this and I think it does. For my chair I chose a _____. It fits the image I wanted. . . . If you can't say this about your office chair, isn't it about time you sat in a _____? After all, haven't you been without one long enough?

The philosophy of wealth in those lines goes like this: If you've earned them, you would be foolish to deny yourself the images of wealth. If 1 Timothy 6:9 is true, and the desire to be rich brings us into Satan's trap and the destruction of hell, then this advertisement, which exploits and promotes that desire, is just as destructive as anything you might read in the sex ads of a big city daily.

Are you awake and free from the false messages of American merchandising? Or has the omnipresent economic lie deceived you so that the only sin you can imagine in relation to money is stealing? I believe in free speech and free enterprise because I have no faith whatsoever in the moral capacity of sinful civil government to improve upon the institutions created by sinful individuals. But for God's sake let us use our freedom as Christians to say *no* to the desire for riches and *yes* to the truth: There is great gain in godliness when we are content with the simple necessities of life.

What Should the Rich Do?

So far we have been pondering the words addressed in 1 Timothy 6:6-10 to people who are not rich but who may be tempted to want to be rich. In 1 Timothy 6:17-19 Paul addresses a group in the church who are already rich. What should a rich person do with his money if he becomes a Christian? And what should a Christian do if God prospers his business so that great wealth is at his disposal? Paul answers like this:

> (17) As for the rich in this world, charge them not to be haughty, nor to set their hopes on uncertain riches but on God who richly furnishes us with everything to enjoy. (18) They are to do good, to be rich in good deeds, liberal and generous, (19) thus

laying up for themselves a good foundation for the future, so that they may take hold of the life which is life indeed.

The words of verse 19 simply paraphrase Jesus' teaching. Jesus said

Do not lay up for yourselves treasures on earth, where moth and rust consume and where thieves break in and steal, but lay up for yourselves treasures in heaven, where neither moth nor rust consumes and where thieves do not break in and steal. For where your treasure is there will your heart be also. (Matthew 6:19-21)

Jesus is not against investment. He is against bad investment — namely, setting your heart on the comforts and securities that money can afford in this world. Money is to be invested for eternal yields in heaven — "Lay up for yourselves treasures in heaven!" How?
Luke 12:32-34 gives one answer:

"Fear not, little flock, for it is your Father's good pleasure to give you the kingdom. Sell your possessions, and give alms; provide yourselves with purses that do not grow old, with a treasure in the heavens that does not fail, where no thief approaches and no moth destroys. For where your treasure is, there will your heart be also."

So the answer to how to lay up treasures in heaven is to spend your earthly treasures for merciful purposes in Christ's name here on earth. Give alms — that is, provide yourself with purses in heaven. Notice carefully that Jesus does not merely say that treasure in heaven will be the unexpected result of generosity on earth. No, he says we should pursue treasure in heaven. Lay it up! Provide yourselves with unfailing purses and treasures! This is pure Christian Hedonism.

You Will Be Repaid at the Resurrection of the Just

Another instance of it in the teaching of Jesus is Luke 14:13-14, where he is more specific about how to use our resources to lay up treasures in heaven.

"Whenever you give a feast, invite the poor, the crippled, the lame and the blind, and you will be blessed, because they cannot pay you back, for it will be paid back to you in the resurrection of the just."

This is virtually the same as saying, "Give alms; provide yourselves purses in heaven." Don't seek the reward of an earthly tit for tat. Be generous. Don't pad your life with luxuries and comforts. Look to the resurrection and the great reward in God "whose presence is fullness of joy and at whose right hand are pleasures for evermore" (Psalm 16:11).

Beware of Being Wiser than the Bible

Beware of commentators who divert attention from the plain meaning of these texts. What would you think, for example, of the following typical comment on Luke 14:13-14: "The promise of reward for this kind of life is there as a fact. You do not live this way for the sake of reward. If you do you are not living in this way but in the old selfish way."[1]

Is this true — that we are selfish and not loving if we are motivated by the promised reward? If so, why did Jesus entice us by mentioning the reward, even giving it as the basis ("for") of our action? And what would this commentator say concerning Luke 12:33, where we are not told that reward will result from our giving alms, but we are told to actively seek to get the reward — "Provide yourselves with purses!"?

And what would he say concerning the parable of the unrighteous steward (Luke 16:1-13), where Jesus concludes, "Make friends for yourselves by means of unrighteous mammon, so that when it fails they may receive you into the eternal habitations" (16:9)? The aim of this parable is to instruct the disciples in the right and loving use of worldly possessions. Jesus does not say the result of such use is to receive eternal habitations. He says, Make it your aim to secure an eternal habitation by the use of your possessions.

So it is simply wrong to say that Jesus does not want us to pursue the reward he promises. He commands that we pursue it (Luke 12:33; 16:9). More than forty times in the Gospel of Luke there are promises of reward and threats of punishment connected with the commands of Jesus.[2]

Of course, we must not seek the reward of earthly praise or material gain. This is clear not only from Luke 14:14, but also from Luke 6:35, "Love your enemies, and do good, expecting nothing in return; and *your reward will be great, and you will be sons of the Most High.*" In other words, don't care about earthly reward; look to the heavenly reward, namely, the infinite joys of being a son of God!

Or, as Jesus put it in Matthew 6:3-4, don't care about human praise for your merciful acts. If that is your goal, that's all you will get, and that will be a pitiful reward compared to the reward of God. "When you give alms, do not let your left hand know what your right hand is doing, so that your alms may be in secret; and *your Father who sees in secret will reward you.*"

Luring Others to the Reward by Loving It Ourselves

The reason our generosity toward others is not a sham-love when we are motivated by the longing for God's promise is that we are aiming to take those others with us into that reward. We know our joy in heaven will be greater if the people we treat with mercy are won over to the surpassing worth of Christ, and join us in praising him.

But how will we ever point them to Christ's infinite worth if we are not driven, in all we do, by the longing to have more of him? It would only be unloving if we pursued our joy at the expense of others. But if our very pursuit includes the pursuit of their joy, how is that selfish? How am I the less loving if my longing for God moves me to give away my earthly possessions so that my joy in him can be forever doubled in your partnership of praise?

Laying Up for Yourself a Good Foundation

Paul's teaching to the rich in 1 Timothy 6:19 continues and applies these teachings of Jesus from the Gospels. He says rich people should use their money in a way that "lays up for themselves a good foundation for the future and takes hold on life which is life indeed." In other words, there is a way to use your money that forfeits eternal life.[3]

We know Paul has eternal life in view because seven verses earlier he uses the same kind of expression in reference to eternal life: "Fight the good fight of faith; take hold of the eternal life to which you were called when you made the good confession in the presence of many witnesses" (1 Timothy 6:12).

The reason the use of your money provides a good foundation for eternal life is not that generosity earns eternal life, but that it shows where your heart is. Generosity confirms that our hope is in God and not in ourselves or our money. We don't earn eternal life. It is a gift of grace (2 Timothy 1:9). We receive it by resting in God's promise. Then how we use our money confirms or denies the reality of that rest.

Pride of Possessions

Paul gives three directions to the rich about how to use their money to confirm their eternal future.

First, don't let your money produce pride. "As for the rich in this world, charge them not to be haughty" (1 Timothy 6:17). How deceptive our hearts are when it comes to money! Every one of us has felt the smug sense of superiority that creeps in after a clever investment or new purchase or a big deposit. Money's chief attractions are the power it gives and the pride it feeds. Paul says, don't let this happen.

Why It Is Hard for the Rich to Inherit Life

Second, he adds in verse 17, "Don't set your hope on uncertain riches, but on God who richly furnishes you all things to enjoy." This is not easy for the rich to do. That's why Jesus said it is hard for a rich man to enter the kingdom of God (Mark 10:23). It is hard to look at all the earthly hope that riches offer and then turn away from that to God, and rest all your hope on him. It is hard not to love the gift instead of the Giver. But this is the only hope for the rich. If they can't do it, they are lost.

They must remember the warning Moses gave the people of Israel as they entered the promised land:

> Beware lest you say in your heart, "My power and the might of my hand have gotten me this wealth." You shall remember the LORD your God, for it is he who gives you power to get wealth; that he may confirm his covenant which he swore to your fathers, as at this day. (Deuteronomy 8:17-18)

The great danger of riches is that our affections will be carried away from God to his gifts.

Is This a Health-Wealth-and-Prosperity Teaching?

Before moving on to Paul's third exhortation for the rich, we must consider a common abuse of verse 17. The verse says that "God richly furnishes us with everything to enjoy." This means, first, that God is usually generous in the provision he makes to meet our needs. He furnishes things "richly." Second, it means we need not feel guilty for enjoying the things he gives us. They are given "for enjoyment." Fasting, celibacy, and other forms of self-denial are right and good in the service of God, but they must not be elevated as the spiritual norm. The provisions of nature are given for our good and, by our Godward joy, can become occasions of thanksgiving and worship (1 Timothy 4:2-5).

But a wealth-and-prosperity doctrine is afoot today, shaped by the half-truth that says, "We glorify God with our money by enjoying thankfully all the things he enables us to buy. Why should a son of the King live like a pauper?" And so on. The true half of this is that we should give thanks for every good thing God enables us to have. That does glorify him. The false half is the subtle implication that God can be glorified in this way by all kinds of luxurious purchases.

If this were true, Jesus would not have said, "Sell your possessions and give alms" (Luke 12:33). He would not have said, "Do not seek what you are to eat and what you are to drink" (Luke 12:29). John the Baptist would not have said, "He who has two coats, let him share with who has none" (Luke 3:11). The Son of Man would not have walked around with no place to lay his head (Luke 9:58). And Zacchaeus would not have given half his goods to the poor (Luke 19:8).

God is not glorified when we keep for ourselves (no matter how thankfully) what we ought to be using to alleviate the misery of unevangelized, uneducated, unmedicated, and unfed millions. The evidence that many professing Christians have been deceived by this doctrine is how little they give and how much they own. God *has* prospered them. And by an almost irresistible law of consumer culture (baptized by a doctrine of health, wealth, and prosperity) they have bought bigger (and more) houses, newer (and more) cars, fancier (and more) clothes, better (and more) meat, and all manner of trinkets and gadgets and containers and devices and equipment to make life more fun.

Why God Prospers Many Saints

They will object: does not the Old Testament promise that God will prosper his people? Indeed! God increases our yield so that by giving we can prove our yield is not our god. God does not prosper a man's business so he can move from a Ford to a Cadillac. God prospers a business so that thousands of unreached peoples can be reached with the gospel. He prospers a business so that twelve percent of the world's population can move a step back from the precipice of starvation.

I am a pastor, not an economist. Therefore I see my role today the way James Stewart saw it in Scotland thirty years ago.

> It is the function of economists, not the pulpit, to work out plans of reconstruction. But it is emphatically the function of the pulpit to stab men broad awake to the terrible pity of Jesus, to expose their hearts to the constraint of that divine compassion which halos the oppressed and the suffering, and flames in judgment against every social wrong. . . . There is no room for a preaching devoid of ethical directness and social passion, in a day when heaven's trumpets sound and the Son of God goes forth to war.[4]

Our Calling: A Wartime Lifestyle

The mention of "war" is not merely rhetorical. What is specifically called for today is a "wartime lifestyle." I have used the phrase "simple necessities of life" earlier in this chapter because Paul said in 1 Timothy 6:8, "If we have food and clothing, with these we shall be content." But this idea of simplicity can be very misleading. I mean it to refer to a style of life that is unencumbered with nonessentials — and the criterion for "essential" should not be primitive "simplicity," but wartime effectiveness.

Ralph Winter illustrates this idea of a wartime lifestyle:

> The Queen Mary, lying in repose in the harbor at Long Beach, California, is a fascinating museum of the past. Used both as a luxury liner in peacetime and a troop transport during the Second World War, its present status as a museum the length of three football fields affords a stunning contrast between the lifestyles appropriate in peace and war. On one side of a partition you see the dining room reconstructed to depict the peacetime table setting that was appropriate to the wealthy patrons of high culture for whom a dazzling array of knives and forks and spoons held no mysteries. On the other side of the partition the evidences of wartime austerities are in sharp contrast. One metal tray with indentations replaces fifteen plates and saucers. Bunks, not just double but eight tiers high, explain why the peacetime complement of 3000 gave way to 15,000 people on board in wartime. How repugnant to the peacetime masters this transformation must have been! To do it took a national emergency, of course. The survival of a nation depended upon it. The essence of the Great Commission today is that the survival of many millions of people depends on its fulfillment.[5]

There is a war going on. All talk of a Christian's right to live luxuriantly "as a child of the King" in this atmosphere sounds hollow — especially since the King himself is stripped for battle. It is more helpful to think of a "wartime" lifestyle than a merely "simple" lifestyle. Simplicity can be very inward directed, and may benefit no one else. A wartime lifestyle implies that there is a great and worthy cause for which to spend and be spent (2 Corinthians 12:15).

Winter continues:

> America today is a save-yourself society if there ever was one. But does it really work? The underdeveloped societies suffer from one set of diseases: tuberculosis, malnutrition, pneumonia, parasites, typhoid, cholera, typhus, etc. Affluent America has

virtually invented a whole new set of diseases: obesity, arteriosclerosis, heart disease, stroke, lung cancer, venereal disease, cirrhosis of the liver, drug addiction, alcoholism, divorce, battered children, suicide, murder. Take your choice. Laborsaving machines have turned out to be body-killing devices. Our affluence has allowed both mobility and isolation of the nuclear family, and as a result our divorce courts, our prisons and our mental institutions are flooded. In saving ourselves we have nearly lost ourselves.

How hard have we tried to save others? Consider the fact that the U.S. evangelical slogan, "Pray, give, or go" allows people merely to pray, if that is their choice! By contrast the Friends Missionary Prayer Band of South India numbers 8000 people in their prayer bands and supports 80 full-time missionaries in North India. If my denomination (with its unbelievably greater wealth per person) were to do that well, we would not be sending 500 missionaries, but 26,000. In spite of their true poverty, those poor people in South India are sending 50 times as many cross-cultural missionaries as we are.[6]

The point here is to show that those who encourage Christians to pursue a luxuriant peacetime lifestyle are missing the point of all Jesus taught about money. He called us to lose our lives in order that we might gain them again (and the context is indeed money — "What does it profit a man, to gain the whole world and forfeit his life?" — Mark 8:36). And the way he means for us to lose our lives is in fulfilling the mission of love he gave us.

Be Rich in Good Deeds

Which leads us to the final admonition Paul makes to the rich: "They are to do good, to be rich in good deeds, liberal and generous" (1 Timothy 6:18). Once they are liberated from the magnet of pride and once their hope is set on God, not money, only one thing can happen: their money will flow freely to multiply the manifold ministries of Christ.

What about the Lake Home?

So what does a pastor say to his people concerning the purchase and ownership of two homes in a world where 2,000 people starve to death every day and mission agencies cannot penetrate more unreached peoples for lack of funds? First, he may quote Amos 3:15 — "I will smite the winter house and the summer house; and the houses of ivory shall perish; and the great houses shall come to an end." Then he may read Luke 3:11, "He who has two coats, let him share with him who has none."

Then he might tell about the family in St. Petersburg, Florida, who caught a vision for the housing needs of the poor. They sold their second home in Ohio and used the funds to build houses for several families in Immokalee, Florida.

Then he will ask, Is it wrong to own a second home that sits empty part of the year? And he will answer, Maybe and maybe not. He will not make it easy by creating a law. Laws can be obeyed under constraint with no change of heart; prophets want new hearts for God, not just new real estate arrangements. He will empathize with their uncertainty and share his own struggle to discover the way of love. He will not presume to have a simple answer to every lifestyle question.

But he will help them decide. He will say, "Does your house signify or encourage a level of luxury enjoyed in heedless unconcern of the needs of others? Or is it a simple, oft-used retreat for needed rest and prayer and meditation that sends people back to the city with a passion to deny themselves for the evangelization of the unreached and the pursuit of justice?"

He will leave the arrow lodged in their conscience and challenge them to seek a lifestyle in sync with the teaching and life of the Lord Jesus.

Why Has God Given Us So Much?

In Ephesians 4:28, Paul says, "Let the thief no longer steal, but rather let him labor, doing honest work with his hands, so that he may be able to give to those in need." In other words, there are three levels of how to live with things: (1) you can steal to get; (2) or you can work to get; (3) or you can work to get in order to give.

Too many professing Christians live on level two. Almost all the forces of our culture urge them to live on level two. But the Bible pushes us relentlessly to level three. "God is able to provide you with every blessing in abundance, so that you may always have enough of everything and may provide in abundance for every good work" (2 Corinthians 9:8). Why does God bless us with abundance? So we can have enough to live on and then use the rest for all manner of good works that alleviate spiritual and physical misery. Enough for us; abundance for others.

The issue is not how much a person makes. Big industry and big salaries are a fact of our times, and they are not necessarily evil. The evil is in being deceived into thinking a $100,000 salary must be accompanied by a $100,000 lifestyle. God has made us to be conduits of his grace. The danger is in thinking the conduit should be lined with gold. It shouldn't. Copper will do.

Living on the Brink of Eternity

Our final summary emphasis should be this: In 1 Timothy 6, Paul's purpose is to help us lay hold on eternal life and not lose it. Paul never dabbles in unessentials. He lives on the brink of eternity. That's why he sees things so clearly. He stands there like God's gatekeeper and treats us like reasonable Christian Hedonists: you want life which is life indeed, don't you (verse 19)? You don't want ruin, destruction and pangs of heart, do you (verses 9-10)? You do want all the gain that godliness can bring, don't you (verse 6)? Then use the currency of Christian Hedonism wisely: do not desire to be rich, be content with the wartime necessities of life, set your hope fully on God, guard yourself from pride and let your joy in God overflow in a wealth of liberality to a lost and needy world.

He who loves his wife loves himself.

EPHESIANS 5:28

A good wife who can find?
She is far more precious than jewels.

PROVERBS 31:10

CHAPTER 8

MARRIAGE

A Matrix for Christian Hedonism

The reason there is so much misery in marriage is not that husbands and wives seek their own pleasure, but that they do not seek it in the pleasure of their spouses. The biblical mandate to husbands and wives is to seek your own joy in the joy of your spouse. Make marriage a matrix for Christian Hedonism.

To Make a Wife of Splendor

There is scarcely a more hedonistic passage in the Bible than the one on marriage in Ephesians 5:25-30.

> (25) Husbands, love your wives, as Christ loved the church and gave himself up for her, (26) that he might sanctify her, having cleansed her by the washing of water with the word, (27) that he might present the church to himself in splendor, without spot or wrinkle or any such thing, but that she might be holy and without blemish. (28) Even so husbands should love their wives as their own bodies. He who loves his wife loves himself. (29) For no man ever hates his own flesh, but nourishes and cherishes it, as Christ does the church, (30) because we are members of his body.

Husbands are told to love their wives the way Christ loved the church. How did he love the church? "He gave himself up for her." But why? "That he might sanctify and cleanse her." But why did he want to do that? "That he might present the church to himself in splendor!"

Ah! There it is! "For the joy that was set before him, he endured the cross" (Hebrews 12:2). What joy? The joy of marriage to his bride the church. Jesus does not want a dirty and unholy wife. Therefore he was willing to die to "sanctify and cleanse" his betrothed so he could present to himself a wife "in splendor."

Pursuing Joy in the Joy of the Beloved

And what is the church's ultimate joy? Is it not to be cleansed and sanctified and then presented as a bride to the sovereign, all-glorious Christ? So Christ sought his own joy, yes — but he sought it in the joy of the church! That is what love is: the pursuit of our own joy in the joy of the beloved.

In Ephesians 5:29-30, Paul pushes the hedonism of Christ even further: "No man ever hates his own flesh, but nourishes and cherishes it, as Christ does the church, because we are members of his body." Why does Christ nourish and cherish the church? Because we are members of his own body, and no man ever hates his own body. In other words, the union between Christ and his bride is so close ("one flesh") that any good done to her is a good done to himself. The blatant assertion of this text is that this fact motivates the Lord to nourish, cherish, sanctify, and cleanse his bride.

By some definitions this cannot be love. Love, they say, must be free of self-interest — especially Christ-like love, especially Calvary love. I have never seen such a view of love made to square with this passage of Scripture. Yet what Christ does for his bride, this text plainly calls love. "Husbands love your wives as Christ loved the church. . . ." Why not let the text define love for us, instead of bringing our definition from ethics or philosophy?

According to this text, love is the pursuit of our joy in the holy joy of the beloved. There is no way to exclude self-interest from love, for self-interest is not the same as selfishness. Selfishness seeks its own private happiness at the expense of others. Love seeks its happiness in the happiness of the beloved. It will even suffer and die for the beloved in order that its joy might be full in the life and purity of the beloved.

But Did Not Jesus Say, "Hate Your Life"?

When Paul says, "No man ever hates his own flesh but nourishes and cherishes it," and then uses Christ himself as an example, is he contradicting John 12:25 where Jesus said, "He who loves his life loses it, and he who hates his life in this world will keep it for eternal life"? No! There is no contradiction. On the contrary, the agreement is remarkable.

The key phrase is "in this world": he who hates his life in this world will keep it for eternal life. This is not an ultimate hating, because by doing it you keep your life forever. So there is a kind of hating of life that is good and necessary, and this is not what Paul denies when he says no one hates his life. This kind of hating is a means to saving, and is therefore a kind of love. That's why Jesus has to limit the hating he commends with the words "in this world." If you take the future world into view, it can't be called hating anymore. Hating life in this world is what Jesus did when he "gave himself for the church." But he did it for the joy set before him. He did it that he might present his bride to himself in splendor. Hating his own life was the deepest love for his own life — and for the church!

Nor is Paul's word here a contradiction of Revelation 12:11: "And they have conquered him by the blood of the Lamb and by the word of their testimony, for *they loved not their lives even unto death.*" They were willing to be killed for Jesus, but by hating their lives in this way they "conquered" Satan and gained the glory of heaven: "Be faithful unto death and I will give you the crown of life" (Revelation 2:10). This "not loving life unto death" was indeed a loving of life beyond death.

Everyone Seeks Happiness

No man in this world ever hates his own flesh in the ultimate sense of choosing what he is sure will produce the greater misery. This has been the conclusion of many great knowers of the human heart. Blaise Pascal put it like this,

> All men seek happiness. This is without exception. Whatever different means they employ, they all tend to this end. The cause of some going to war, and of others avoiding it, is the same desire in both, attended with different views. The will never takes the least step but to this object. This is the motive of every action of every man, even of those who hang themselves.[1]

Jonathan Edwards tied it to the Word of Christ:

> Jesus knew that all mankind were in the pursuit of happiness. He has directed them in the true way to it, and He tells them what they must become in order to be blessed and happy.[2]

Edward Carnell generalizes the point,

> The Christian ethic, let us remember, is premised on the self's love for the self. Nothing motivates us unless it appeals to our interests.[3]

Karl Barth, in his typically effusive manner, writes for pages on this truth. Here is an excerpt:

> The will for life is the will for joy, delight, happiness. . . . In every real man the will for life is also the will for joy. In everything he wills, he wills and intends also that this, too, exist for him in some form. He strives for different things with the spoken or unspoken, but very definite, if unconscious, intention of securing for himself this joy. . . . It is hypocrisy to hide this from oneself. And the

hypocrisy would be at the expense of the ethical truth that he should will to enjoy himself, just as he should will to eat, drink, sleep, be healthy, work, stand for what is right and live in fellowship with God and his neighbor. A person who tries to debar himself from this joy is certainly not an obedient person.[4]

For a husband to be an obedient person he must love his wife the way Christ loved the church. That is, he must pursue his own joy in the holy joy of his wife.

> Even so husbands should love their wives as their own bodies.
> He who loves his wife loves himself. (Ephesians 5:28)

This is clearly Paul's paraphrase of Jesus' command which he took from Leviticus 19:18, "Love your neighbor as yourself" (Matthew 22:39). The popular misconception is that this command teaches us to learn to esteem ourselves so we can love others. This is not what the command means. (See Appendix 3.) Jesus does not command us to love ourselves. He assumes that we do. That is, he assumes, as Edwards said, that we all pursue our own happiness, then he makes the measure of our innate self-love the measure of our duty to love others. "As you love yourself, so love others."

Paul now applies this to marriage. He sees it illustrated in Christ's relationship to the church. And he sees it illustrated in the fact that husbands and wives become "one flesh" (verse 31). "Husbands should love their wives as their own bodies. He who loves his wife loves himself." In other words, husbands should devote the same energy and time and creativity to making their wives happy that they devote naturally to making themselves happy. The result will be that in doing this they will make themselves happy. For he who loves his wife loves himself. Since the wife is one flesh with her husband, the same applies to her love for him.

Paul does not build a dam against the river of hedonism; he builds a channel for it. He says, "Husbands and wives, recognize that in marriage you have become one flesh. If you live for your private pleasure at the expense of your spouse, you are living against yourself and destroying your joy. But if you devote yourself with all your heart to the holy joy of your spouse, you will also be living for your joy and making a marriage after the image of Christ and his church."

The Pattern for Christian Hedonism in Marriage

Now what does this love between husband and wife look like? Does Paul teach a pattern for married love in this text?

Ephesians 5:31 is a quotation of Genesis 2:24 — "For this reason a man shall leave his father and mother and be joined to his wife, and the two shall become one flesh." Paul adds in verse 32, "This is a great mystery, and I am speaking with reference to Christ and the church." Why does he call Genesis 2:24 a great "mystery"?

Before we answer, let's go back to the Old Testament context and see more clearly what Genesis 2:24 meant.

The Old Testament Context

According to Genesis 2, God created Adam first and put him in the garden alone. Then the Lord said, "It is not good that the man should be alone; I will make a helper fit for him" (2:18). This is not necessarily an indictment of Adam's fellowship with God, nor proof that care for the garden was too hard for one person. Rather, the point is that God made man to be a sharer. God created us not to be cul-de-sacs of his bounty, but conduits. No man is complete unless he is conducting grace (like electricity) between God and another person. (No single person should conclude that this can happen only in marriage!)

It must be another person, not an animal. So in Genesis 2:19-20 God paraded the animals before Adam to show him that animals would never do as a "helper fit for him." Animals help plenty, but only a person can be a fellow-heir of the grace of life (1 Peter 3:7). Only a person can receive and appreciate and enjoy grace. What a man needs is another person with whom he can share the love of God. Animals will not do! There is an infinite difference between sharing the northern lights with your beloved and sharing them with your dog.

Therefore, according to verse 21, "The LORD God caused a deep sleep to fall upon the man, and while he slept took one of his ribs and closed up its place with flesh; and the rib which the LORD God had taken from the man, he made into a woman and brought her to the man." Having shown the man that no animal would do for his helper, God made another human from man's own flesh and bone to be like him — and yet very unlike him. He did not create another male. He created a female. And Adam recognized in her the perfect counterpart to himself — utterly different from the animals: "This at last is bone of my bones and flesh of my flesh; she shall be called Woman, because she was taken out of Man" (Genesis 2:23).

By creating a person *like* Adam yet very *unlike* Adam, God provided the possibility of a profound unity that otherwise would have been impossible. There is a different kind of unity enjoyed by the joining of diverse counterparts than is enjoyed by joining two things just alike. When we all sing the same melody line it is called unison, which means "one sound." But when we unite diverse lines of soprano and alto and tenor and bass, we call it harmony; and everyone who has an ear to hear knows that something deeper in us is touched by great harmony than by mere unison. So God made a woman and not another man. He created heterosexuality, not homosexuality.

Notice the connection between verses 23 and 24, signaled by the word "therefore" in verse 24:

> (23) Then the man said, "This at last is bone of my bones and flesh of my flesh; she shall be called Woman, because she was taken out of Man." (24) Therefore a man leaves his father and his mother and cleaves to his wife and they become one flesh.

In verse 23 the focus is on two things: objectively, the fact that woman is part of man's flesh and bone; and subjectively, the joy Adam has in being presented with the woman. "*At last,* this is bone of my bones and flesh of my flesh!" From these two things the writer draws an inference about marriage in verse 24: "Therefore a man leaves his father and his mother and cleaves to his wife and they become one flesh."

In other words, in the beginning God took woman out of man as bone of his bone and flesh of his flesh, and then God presented her back to the man to discover in living fellowship what it means to be one flesh. Verse 24 draws out the lesson that marriage is just that: a man leaving father and mother, because God has given him another; a man cleaving to this woman alone and no other; and a man discovering the experience of being one flesh with this woman.

The Great Mystery of Marriage

Paul looks at this and calls it a "great mystery." Why?

He had learned from Jesus that the church is Christ's body (Ephesians 1:23). By faith a person is joined to Jesus Christ. Thus a person becomes one with all other believers, so that we "are all one in Christ Jesus" (Galatians 3:28). Believers in Christ are the body of Christ. We are the organism through which he manifests his life and in which his Spirit dwells.

Knowing this about the relationship between Christ and the church, Paul sees a parallel with marriage. He sees that husband and wife become one flesh and that Christ and the church become one body. So in 2 Corinthians 11:2, for example, he says to the church, "I feel a divine jealousy for you, for I betrothed you to Christ to present you as a pure bride to her one husband." He pictures Christ as the husband, the church as the bride, and conversion as an act of betrothal which Paul had helped bring about. The bride's presentation to her husband probably will happen at the Lord's second coming, referred to in Ephesians 5:27 ("that he might present the church to himself in splendor").

It looks as though Paul uses the relationship of human marriage, learned from Genesis 2, to describe and explain the relationship between Christ and the church. But if that were the case, *marriage* would not be a mystery, as Paul calls it in Ephesians 5:32; it would be the clear and obvious thing that explains the mystery of Christ and the church. So there is more to marriage than meets the eye. What is it?

The mystery is this: God did not create the union of Christ and the church after the pattern of human marriage; just the reverse! He created human marriage on the pattern of Christ's relation to the church.

The mystery of Genesis 2:24 is that the marriage it describes is a parable or symbol of Christ's relation to his people. There was more going on in the creation of woman than meets the eye. God doesn't do things willy-nilly. Everything has purpose and meaning. When God engaged to create man and woman and to ordain the union of marriage, he didn't roll dice or draw straws or flip a coin as to how they might be related to each other. He patterned marriage very purposefully after the relationship between his Son and the church, which he had planned from all eternity.[5]

Therefore marriage is a mystery — it contains and conceals a meaning far greater than what we see on the outside. God created man male and female, and ordained marriage so that the eternal covenant relationship between Christ and his church would be imaged forth in the marriage union. As Geoffrey Bromiley has written, "As God made man in his own image, so he made marriage in the image of his own eternal marriage with his people."[6]

The inference Paul draws from this mystery is that the roles of husband and wife in marriage are not arbitrarily assigned, but are rooted in the distinctive roles of Christ and his church. Those of us who are married need to ponder again and again how mysterious and wonderful it is that God grants us in marriage the privilege to image forth stupendous divine realities, infinitely bigger and greater than ourselves.

This is the foundation of the pattern of love that Paul describes for marriage. It is not enough to say each spouse should pursue his or her own joy in the joy of the other. It is also important to say husbands and wives should consciously copy the relationship God intended for Christ and the church.

The Wife Takes Her Special Cues from the Church

Accordingly, wives are to take their cues from the purpose of the church in its relation to Christ: "Wives, be subject to your husbands, as to the Lord. For the husband is the head of the wife as Christ is the head of the church, his body, and is himself its Savior. As the church is subject to Christ, so let wives also be subject in everything to their husbands" (Ephesians 5:22-24).

To understand the wife's submission we need to understand the husband's "headship," because her submission is based on his headship. ("Wives be subject . . . for the husband is the head.") What is the meaning of "head" in Ephesians 5:23?

The Greek word for "head" (*kephalē*) is used in the Old Testament sometimes to refer to a chief or leader (Judges 10:18; 11:8-9; 2 Samuel 22:44; Psalm 18:43; Isaiah 7:8). But it is not at first obvious why "head" should be used to refer to a leader. Perhaps its position at the top of the body gave the head its associations with high rank and power.

For some ancients the leading faculty of thought was in the heart, not the head, though according to Charles Singer in the *Oxford Classical Dictionary*, Aristotle's opinion that intelligence is in the heart "was contrary to the views of some of his medical contemporaries, contrary to the popular view, and contrary to the doctrine of [Plato's] Timaeus."[7] The most pertinent Greek witness for the meaning of "head" in Paul's time would be his contemporary, Philo, who said,

> Just as nature conferred the sovereignty of the body on the head when she granted it also possession of the citadel as the most suitable for its kingly rank, conducted it thither to take command and established it on high with the whole framework from neck to foot set below it, like the pedestal under the statue, so too she has given the lordship of the senses to the eyes.[8]

This was the popular view in Paul's day, according to Heinrich Schlier, as is evident from Stoic sources besides Philo.[9] Therefore, contemporary critics are wrong when they claim that "for Greek speaking people in New Testament times, who had little opportunity to read the Greek translation of the Old Testament, there were many possible meanings for 'head' but 'supreme over' or 'being responsible to' were not among them."[10]

"Supremacy" is precisely the quality given to the head by Philo and others. But most important is that Paul's own use of the word "head" in Ephesians 1:22 "unquestionably carries with it the idea of authority."[11]

In Ephesians 1:20-22, Paul says that God raised Christ:

> from the dead and made him sit at his right hand in the heavenly places, far above all rule and authority and power and dominion and above every name that is named . . . and he has

put all things under his feet and has made him the head over all things for the church.

Even if the word "head" could mean "source" as some claim,[12] this would be a foreign idea here where Christ is installed as supreme over all authorities. Nor is it at all likely that this idea was in Paul's mind in Ephesians 5:23 where the wife's "subordination" suggests most naturally that her husband is "head" in the sense of leader or authority.

But, let's just suppose that "source" were the sense of "head" in this passage. What would that mean in this context? The husband is pictured as the head of his wife as Christ is pictured as the head of the church, *his body* (Ephesians 5:29-30). You cannot say that "head" is the head of a river or something like that. Paul is very specific what kind of "head" he has in mind. It is the head connected to a neck on top of a "body."

Now if the head means "source," what is the husband the source of? What does the body get from the head? It gets *nourishment* (that's mentioned in verse 29, "No one ever hates his own flesh but *nourishes* it, just as Christ does the church"). And we can understand this, because the *mouth* is in the head, and nourishment comes through the mouth to the body. But that's not all the body gets from the head. It gets *guidance* because the eyes are in the head. And it gets *alertness* and *protection* because the ears are in the head.

In other words, if the husband as head is one flesh with his wife, his body, and if he is therefore her source of guidance and food and alertness, then the natural conclusion is that the head, the husband, has a primary responsibility for leadership and provision and protection.

So even if you give "head" the meaning "source," the most natural interpretation of these verses is that husbands are called by God to take primary responsibility for Christlike, servant leadership and protection and provision in the home. And wives are called to honor and affirm the husband's leadership and help carry it through according to her gifts.

Therefore when Paul says, "Wives, be subject to your husbands . . . for the husband is the head of the wife," he means a wife should recognize and honor her husband's greater responsibility to lead the home. She should be disposed to yield to her husband's authority and should be inclined to follow his leadership.

The reason I say a *disposition* to yield and an *inclination* to follow is that no submission of one human being to another is absolute. The husband does not replace Christ as the woman's supreme authority. She must never follow her husband's leadership into sin. But even where a Christian wife may have to stand with Christ against the sinful will of her husband, she can still have a spirit of submission. She can show by her attitude and behavior that she does not like resisting his will and that she longs for him to forsake sin and lead in righteousness so that her disposition to honor him as head can again produce harmony.

Another reason for stressing the disposition and inclination of submission, rather than any particular acts, is that the specific behaviors growing out of this spirit of submission are so varied from marriage to marriage. They can even appear contradictory from culture to culture.

The Husband Takes His Special Cues from Christ

So in this mysterious parable of marriage, the wife is to take her special cue from God's purpose to the church in its relation to Christ. And to the husbands Paul says, Take your special cue from Christ — "Husbands, love your wives, as Christ loved the church and gave himself up for her" (verse 25). If the husband is the head of the wife as verse 23 says, let it be very plain to all husbands that this means primarily leading out in the kind of love that is willing to die to give her life.

As Jesus says in Luke 22:26, "Let the leader become as one who serves." The husband who plops himself down in front of the TV and orders his wife around like a slave has abandoned the way of Christ. Jesus bound himself with a towel and washed the apostles' feet. Woe to the husband who thinks his maleness requires of him a domineering, demanding attitude toward his wife. If you want to be a Christian husband, you become a servant, not a boss.

It is true that verse 21 puts this whole section under the sign of mutual submission. "Be subject to one another out of reverence for Christ." But it is utterly unwarranted to infer from this verse that the *way* Christ submits himself to the church and the way the church submits herself to Christ are the same. The church submits to Christ by a disposition to follow his leadership. Christ submits to the church by a disposition to exercise his leadership in humble service to the church. (See pp. 144-149.)

When Christ said, "Let the leader become as one who serves," he did not mean, let the leader cease to be leader. Even while he was on his knees washing their feet, no one doubted who the leader was. Nor should any Christian husband shirk his responsibility under God to provide moral vision and spiritual leadership as the humble servant of his wife and family.

I address the men directly for a moment: do not let the rhetoric of unbiblical feminism cow you into thinking that Christlike leadership from husbands is bad. It is what our homes need more than anything. For all your meekness and all your servanthood and all your submission to your wife's deep desires and needs, you are still the head, the leader.

What I mean is this: You should feel the greater responsibility to take the lead in the things of the Spirit; you should lead the family in a life of prayer, in the study of God's Word, and in worship; you should lead out in giving the family a vision of its meaning and mission; you should take the lead in shaping the moral fabric of the home and in governing its happy peace. I have never met a woman who chafes under such Christlike leadership. But I know of too many wives who are unhappy because their husbands have abdicated their God-ordained leadership and have no moral vision, no spiritual conception of what a family is for, and therefore no desire to lead anyone anywhere.

A famous cigarette billboard pictures a curly-headed, bronze-faced, muscular macho with a cigarette hanging out the side of his mouth. The sign says, "Where a man belongs." That is a lie. Where a man belongs is at the bedside of his children, leading in devotion and prayer. Where a man belongs is leading his family to the house of God. Where a man belongs is up early and alone with God seeking vision and direction for the family.

Forms of Submission

To the wife it should be said that the form your submission takes will vary according to the quality of your husband's leadership. If the husband is a godly man who has a biblical vision for the family and leads out in the things of the Spirit, a godly woman will rejoice in this leadership and support him in it. You will no more be squelched by this leadership than the disciples were squelched by the leadership of Jesus.

If you think your husband's vision is distorted or his direction is unbiblical, you will not sit in dumb silence, but query him in a spirit of meekness and may often save his foot from stumbling. The husband's headship does not mean infallibility or hostility to correction. Nor does a wife's involvement in shaping the direction of the family involve insubordination.

There is no necessary correlation between leadership and intelligence or between submission and the lack of intelligence. A wife will always be superior in some things and a husband in others. But it is a mistake to ignore the God-ordained pattern of husband leadership on the grounds that the woman is a more competent leader. Any man with zeal to obey the Word of God can be a leader, no matter how many superior competencies his wife has.

A small example: suppose the husband has a hard time reading. When he tries to read the Bible aloud it gets all twisted and he pronounces the words wrong. His wife, meanwhile, is a gifted reader. Leadership does not require that he do all the reading during family devotions. Leadership may consist in this one announcement: "Hey, kids, come on into the living room. It's time for devotions. Let's pick up where we left off last time. Mama will read it for us." Dad may even be an invalid and still be recognized as the leader. It has to do with the spirit of initiative and responsibility, and with the wife's open support for this spirit.

But what if a Christian woman is married to a man who provides no vision and gives no moral direction, takes no lead in the things of the Lord? First Peter 3:1 makes plain that submission is still the will of God. ("Wives, be submissive to your husbands, so that some, though they do not obey the word, may be won without a word by the behavior of their wives.") Yet the form of submission in this case will be different.

Under the Lordship of Christ she will not join her husband in sin even if he wants her to, since she is called to submit to Christ who forbids sinning (Ephesians 5:22). But she will go as far as her conscience allows in supporting her husband and doing with him what he likes to do.

Where she can she will give a spiritual vision and moral direction to her children, without communicating a cocky spirit of insubordination to her unbelieving husband. Even when, for Christ's sake, she must do what her husband disapproves, she can try to explain in a tranquil and gentle spirit that it is not because she wants to go against him, but because she is bound to Christ. Yet it will do no good to preach at him. At the root of his being there is guilt that he is not assuming the moral leadership of his house. She must give him room and win him in quietness by her powerful and sacrificial love (1 Peter 3:1-6).

Redeeming Fallen Headship and Fallen Submission

I have argued that there is a pattern of love in marriage ordained by God. The roles of husband and wife are not the same. The husband is to take his special cues from Christ as the head of the church. The wife is to take her special cues from the church as submissive to Christ. In doing this the sinful and damaging results of the Fall begin to be reversed. The Fall twisted man's loving headship into hostile domination in some men and lazy indifference in others. The Fall twisted woman's intelligent, willing submission into manipulative obsequiousness in some women and brazen insubordination in others.

The redemption we anticipate with the coming of Christ is not the dismantling of the created order of loving headship and willing submission,[13] but a *recovery* of it. This is precisely what we find in Ephesians 5:21-33. Wives, redeem your fallen submission by modeling it after God's intention for the church! Husbands, redeem your fallen headship by modeling it after God's intention for Christ!

The point of all of this has been to give direction to those who are persuaded that married love is the pursuit of our own joy in the holy joy of our spouses. I find in Ephesians 5:21-33 these two things: (1) the display of Christian Hedonism in marriage, and (2) the direction its impulses should take. Wives, seek your joy in the joy of your husband by affirming and honoring his God-ordained role as leader in your relationship. Husbands, seek your joy in the joy of your wife by accepting the responsibility to lead as Christ led the church and gave himself for her.

Not that my personal testimony could add anything to the weight of the Word of God, yet I would like to bear witness to God's goodness in my life. I discovered Christian Hedonism the same year I got married, in 1968. Since then Noël and I, in obedience to Jesus Christ, have pursued as passionately as we could the deepest, most lasting joys possible. All too imperfectly, all too half-heartedly at times, we have stalked our own joy in the joy of each other. And we can testify together: for those who marry, this is the path to the heart's desire. For us, marriage has been a matrix for Christian Hedonism. As each pursues joy in the joy of the other and fulfills a God-ordained role, the mystery of marriage as a parable of Christ and the church becomes manifest for his great glory and for our great joy.[14]

Most men are not satisfied with the permanent output of their lives. Nothing can wholly satisfy the life of Christ within his followers except the adoption of Christ's purpose toward the world he came to redeem. Fame, pleasure and riches are but husks and ashes in contrast with the boundless and abiding joy of working with God for the fulfillment of his eternal plans. The men who are putting everything into Christ's undertaking are getting out of life its sweetest and most priceless rewards.

J. CAMPBELL WHITE (1909)
SECRETARY OF THE LAYMEN'S MISSIONARY MOVEMENT

Surely there can be no greater joy
than that of saving souls.

LOTTIE MOON (1887)
"PATRON SAINT OF BAPTIST MISSIONS"

CHAPTER 9

MISSIONS

The Battle Cry of Christian Hedonism

What Is Frontier Missions?

> Most men don't die of old age, they die of retirement. I read somewhere that half of the men retiring in the state of New York die within two years. Save your life and you'll lose it. Just like other drugs, other psychological addictions, retirement is a virulent disease, not a blessing.[1]

These are the words of Ralph Winter, founder of the United States Center for World Mission. His life and strategy have been a constant summons to young and old that the only way to find life is to give it away. He is one of my heroes. He says so many things that Christian Hedonists ought to say (although he wishes I would not use the word "hedonist")!

Not only does he call retired Christians to quit throwing their lives away on the golf course when they could be giving themselves to the global cause of Christ, but he also calls students to go hard after the fullest and deepest joy of life. In his little pamphlet, "Say Yes to Missions," he says, "Jesus, for the joy that was set before him, endured the cross, despising the shame. . . . To follow him is your choice. You're warned! But don't forget the joy."

In fact, in all my reading outside the Bible over the past fifteen years, the greatest source of affirmation for my emerging Christian Hedonism has been from missionary literature, especially biographies. And those who have suffered most seem to state the truth most unashamedly. I will tell you some of my findings in this chapter.

But first, back to the issue of retirement. Winter asks, "Where in the Bible do they see that? Did Moses retire? Did Paul retire? Peter? John? Do military officers retire in the middle of a war?"[2] Good questions. If we try to answer them in the case of the apostle Paul, we bump right into a definition of "missions" which is what we need here at the beginning of this chapter.

As Paul writes his letter to the Romans, he has been a missionary for about twenty years. He was between twenty and forty years old (that's the range implied in the Greek word for "young man" in Acts 7:58) when he was converted. We may guess, then, that he was perhaps around fifty as he writes this great letter.

That may sound young to us. But remember two things: In those days, life expectancy was less, and Paul had led an incredibly stressful life — five times whipped with thirty-nine lashes, three times beaten with rods, once stoned, three times shipwrecked, constantly on the move and constantly in danger (2 Corinthians 11:24-29).

By our contemporary standards he should perhaps be "letting up" and planning for retirement. But in Romans 15 he says he is planning to go to Spain! In fact, the reason for writing to the Romans was largely to enlist their support for this great new frontier mission. Paul is not about to retire. Vast areas of the empire are unreached, not to mention the regions beyond! So he says,

> Now, since I no longer have any room for work in these regions, and since I have longed for many years to come to you, I hope to see you in passing as I go to Spain, and to be sped on my journey there by you, once I have enjoyed your company for a little. (Romans 15:23-24)

Paul was probably killed in Rome before he could ever fulfill his dream of preaching in Spain. But one thing is certain: He was cut down in combat, not in retirement. He was moving on to the frontier instead of settling down to bask in his amazing accomplishments. Right here we learn the meaning of missions.

How could Paul possibly say in Romans 15:23, "I no longer have any room for work in these regions"? There were thousands of unbelievers left to be converted in Judea and Samaria and Syria and Asia and Macedonia and Achaia. That is obvious from Paul's instructions to the churches on how to relate to unbelievers. But Paul has no room for work!

The explanation is given in verses 19-21,

> From Jerusalem and as far round as Illyricum I have fully preached the gospel of Christ, thus making it my ambition to preach the gospel, not where Christ has already been named, lest I build on another man's foundation, but as it is written,

> "They shall see who have never been told of him, and they shall understand who have never heard of him."

Paul's missionary strategy is to preach where nobody has preached before. This is what we mean by Frontier Missions. Paul had a passion to go where there were no established churches — that meant Spain.

What is amazing in these verses is that Paul can say he has *fully preached* (literally: "fulfilled") the gospel from Jerusalem in southern Palestine to Illyricum northwest of Greece! To understand this is to understand the meaning of Frontier Missions. Frontier Missions is very different from domestic evangelism. There were thousands of people yet to be converted from Jerusalem to Illyricum. But the task of Frontier Missions was finished. Paul's job of "planting" was done and would now be followed by someone else's "watering" (1 Corinthians 3:6).

So when I speak of missions in this chapter, I generally refer to the Christian church's ongoing effort to carry on Paul's strategy: preaching the gospel of Jesus Christ and planting his church among groups of people who have not yet been reached.

The Need for Frontier Missions

My assumption is that people without the gospel are without hope, because only the gospel can free them from their sin. Therefore missions is utterly essential in the life of a loving church, though not all Christians believe this.

Walbert Buhlmann, a Catholic missions secretary in Rome, spoke for many mainline denominational leaders when he said,

> In the past we had the so-called motive of saving souls. We were convinced that if not baptized, people in the masses would go to hell. Now, thanks be to God, we believe that all people and all religions are already living in the grace and love of God and will be saved by God's mercy.[3]

Sister Emmanuelle of Cairo, Egypt, said, "Today we don't talk about conversion any more. We talk about being friends. My job is to prove that God is love and to bring courage to these people."[4]

It is natural to want to believe in a God who saves all men no matter what they believe or do. But it is not biblical.[5] Essential teachings of Scripture must be rejected to believe in such a God. Listen to the words of the Son of God when he called the apostle Paul into missionary service:

> "I have appeared to you for this purpose, to appoint you to serve and bear witness to the things in which you have seen me and

to those in which I will appear to you, delivering you from the people and from the Gentiles — to whom I send you to open their eyes, that they may turn from darkness to light and from the power of Satan to God, that they may receive forgiveness of sins and a place among those who are sanctified by faith in me." (Acts 26:16-18)

This is an empty commission if in fact the eyes of the nations don't need to be opened, and they don't need to turn from darkness to light, and don't need to escape the power of Satan to come to God, and don't need the forgiveness of sins that comes only by faith in Christ who is preached by the Lord's ambassadors. Paul did not give his life as a missionary to Asia and Macedonia and Greece and Rome and Spain to inform people they were already saved. He gave himself that "by any means [he] might save some" (1 Corinthians 9:22).

So when Paul's message about Christ was rejected (for example, at Antioch by the Jews), he said, "Since you thrust the word of God from you and judge yourselves unworthy of eternal life, behold, we turn to the Gentiles" (Acts 13:46). At stake in missionary outreach to unreached peoples is *eternal life*! Conversion to Christ from any and every other allegiance is precisely the aim. "For there is salvation in no one else, for there is no other name under heaven given among men by which we must be saved" (Acts 4:12).

The Justice of God in Judgment and Salvation

God is not unjust. No one will be condemned for not believing a message they have never heard. Those who have never heard the gospel will be judged by their failure to own up to the light of God's grace and power in nature and in their own conscience. This is the point of Romans 1:20-21.

> Ever since the creation of the world his invisible nature, namely his eternal power and deity, have been clearly perceived in the things that have been made. So they are without excuse: for although they knew God they did not glorify him as God or give thanks to him.

Apart from the special, saving grace of God, people are dead in sin, darkened in their understanding, alienated from the life of God and hardened in heart (Ephesians 2:1; 4:18). And the means God has ordained to administer that special saving grace is the preaching of the gospel of Jesus Christ.

I am a debtor both to the Greeks and to the barbarians, both to
the wise and to the foolish; so I am eager to preach the gospel
to you also who are in Rome. For I am not ashamed of the
gospel: It is the power of God for salvation to everyone who
believes. (Romans 1:14-16)

The Effects of Universalism on Missions

The notion that people are saved without hearing the gospel has wreaked
havoc in the missions effort of denominations and churches that minimize the
biblical teaching of human lostness without Christ. Between 1953 and 1980,
the overseas missionary force of mainline Protestant churches of North America decreased from 9,844 to 2,813, while the missionary force of evangelical
Protestants, who take this biblical teaching more seriously, increased by more
than 200 percent. The Christian and Missionary Alliance, for example, with
its 200,000 members, supports forty percent more missionaries than the
United Methodist Church with its 9.5 million members. There is amazing
missionary power in taking seriously all the Word of God.[6]

Many Christians thought the end of the colonial era after the Second
World War was also the end of foreign missions. The gospel had more or less
penetrated every country in the world. But what we have become keenly
aware of in the last generation is that the command of Jesus to make disciples
of "every nation" does not refer to political nations as we know them today.
Nor does it mean every individual, as though the great commission could not
be completed until every individual were made a disciple.

What Are People Groups?

We are increasingly aware that the intention of God is for every "people
group" to be evangelized — that a thriving church be planted in every group.
No one can exactly define what a people group is. But we get a rough idea
from passages like Revelation 7:9.

After this I looked, and behold, a great multitude which no man
could number from every nation, from all tribes and peoples
and tongues, standing before the throne and before the
Lamb . . .

It is almost impossible to draw precise distinctions between "nations,"
"tribes," "peoples," and "tongues." But what is clear is that God's redemptive
purpose is not complete just because there are disciples of Jesus in all

twentieth-century "nations," i.e., political states. Within those countries are thousands of tribes and castes and subcultures and languages.

So the remaining task of Frontier Missions no longer is conceived mainly in geographic terms. The question now is, "Where are the unreached people groups?"[7]

Since the first edition of *Desiring God* appeared in 1986 there has been tremendous progress in the cooperation of mission agencies, denominations and churches in the tasks of researching and evangelizing the unreached peoples of the world. There is now basic agreement that "of the 12,000 known ethno-linguistic peoples in the world, 10,000 already have a church-planting movement in their midst. . . . [At the end of 1994, of the 2,000 groups remaining] only 1,000 have virtually no penetration. . . . Today we have a target list of least-evangelized peoples that is being revised each year to reflect greater accuracy. The 100 largest of these peoples . . . represent almost two billion people."[8] They are found mainly in the Muslim, Hindu, Buddhist and Animist peoples of the so-called 10/40 Window.[9] It seems to me that Rick Wood is not overstating things when he says, "Never before in Christian history has there been such a large movement with so many sincere believers, churches denominations and agencies working together toward the common goal of a church for every people. This level of global cooperation is unprecedented."[10]

Missions Is Finishable, but Not Evangelism

To keep us sober in our estimates of the remaining task of reaching the unreached people groups of the world, Ralph Winter reminds us of two facts.

First, evangelism can never be finished, but missions can be finished. The reason is this: missions has the unique task of crossing language and culture barriers to penetrate a people group and establish a church movement; but evangelism is the ongoing task of sharing the gospel among people within the same culture. This fact allows us to talk realistically about "closure" — the completion of the missionary task, even if there may be millions of people yet to be won to Christ in all the people groups of the world where the church has been planted.

The second fact Winter reminds us of is that there are probably more people groups than the ones listed among the 12,000 ethno-linguistic groups mentioned above. He illustrates by pointing out that tribal divisions along the lines of mutually unintelligible dialects may vary depending on whether the dialect is spoken or written. So, for example, Wycliffe Bible Translators may detect that a translation of the Bible is readable in a dialect covering a wide area, while Gospel Recordings may determine that seven or more different audio recordings are needed because of the audible distinctions in the larger dialect.

Thus Winter asks, which level of people group did Jesus have in mind when he said, "This gospel of the kingdom will be preached in the whole world as a testimony to all the peoples, and then the end will come" (Matthew 24:14)? His answer: "We'll find out . . . the closer we get to the situation. In the meantime we need to live with guesses. . . . We can only learn more as we go! And at this hour greater human resources are looming into view than have ever been available to the unfinished task!"[11]

The point of these observations is that the job of Frontier Missions is not complete. In fact the vast majority of missionaries are working on "fields" where the church has been planted for decades. The need for frontier missionaries is great. The Lord's command to disciple the remaining unreached groups is still in force. And my burden in this chapter is to kindle a desire in your heart to be part of the last chapter of the greatest story in the world.

Dramatic Growth

There are historical as well as theological reasons for hope that the task of world missions is finishable. The following chart is truly amazing. It shows that the number of unreached peoples is decreasing dramatically in proportion to the number of evangelical congregations available to evangelize them.

The Proportion of Unreached Peoples
to Congregations of Christians[12]

Year A.D.	Non-Christians per believer[13]	Unreached People Groups[14]	Congregations per Unreached People Group[15]
100	360 to 1	60,000	1 to 12
1000	220 to 1	50,000	1 to 5
1500	69 to 1	44,000	1 to 1
1900	27 to 1	40,000	10 to 1
1950	21 to 1	24,000	33 to 1
1980	11 to 1	17,000	162 to 1
1989	7 to 1	12,000	416 to 1
2000	?	0?	?

Ralph Winter has observed that the drop from 11 to 7 (62 percent) between 1980 and 1989 (in the second column) is equivalent to the drop from

360 to 220 (62 percent) in the first nine hundred years of church history! The two measurements in the second and fourth columns, and the trends that they reveal, are two of the most hopeful insights in the study of church growth. Even though there is an ongoing and urgent need for more frontier missionaries to penetrate the final unreached peoples with the gospel, it seems that the momentum of closure is accelerating. In addition to the ironclad promise of Jesus in Matthew 24:14, that the gospel will penetrate all the peoples, there is the empirical evidence that this is in fact happening, and at an increasing rate. It is "A Finishable Task"!

Becoming World Christians

I would like to believe that many of you who read this chapter are on the brink of setting a new course of commitment to missions: some a new commitment to go to a frontier people, others a new path of education, others a new use of your vocation in a culture less saturated by the church, others a new lifestyle and a new pattern of giving and praying and reading. I want to push you over the brink. I would like to make the cause of missions so attractive that you will no longer be able to resist its magnetism.

Not that I believe everyone will become a missionary, or even should become one. But I pray that every reader of this book might become what David Bryant calls a *World Christian* — that you would reorder your life around God's global cause. In his inspiring book *In the Gap*, Bryant defines World Christians as that group of Christians who say,

> We want to accept personal responsibility for reaching some of earth's unreached, especially from among the billions at the widest end of the Gap who can only be reached through major new efforts by God's people. Among every people-group where there is no vital, evangelizing Christian community there should be one, there must be one, there shall be one. Together we want to help make this happen.[16]

The Rich Young Ruler

The biblical basis for the missions commitment of a Christian Hedonist is found in the story of the rich young ruler (Mark 10:17-31).

> As [Jesus] was setting out on his journey, a man ran up and knelt before him, and asked him, "Good Teacher, what must I do to inherit eternal life?" And Jesus said to him, "Why do you call me good? No one is good but God alone. You know the

commandments: 'Do not kill, Do not commit adultery, Do not steal, Do not bear false witness, Do not defraud, Honor your father and mother.' "

And he said to him, "Teacher, all these I have observed from my youth." And Jesus looking upon him loved him, and said to him, "You lack one thing; go, sell what you have, and give to the poor, and you will have treasure in heaven; and come, follow me." At that saying his countenance fell, and he went away sorrowful; for he had great possessions.

And Jesus looked around and said to his disciples, "How hard it will be for those who have riches to enter the kingdom of God!" And the disciples were amazed at his words. But Jesus said to them again, "Children, how hard it is to enter the kingdom of God! It is easier for a camel to go through the eye of a needle than for a rich man to enter the kingdom of God."

And they were exceedingly astonished, and said to him, "Then who can be saved?" Jesus looked at them and said, "With men it is impossible, but not with God; for all things are possible with God." Peter began to say to him, "Look, we have left everything and followed you." Jesus said, "Truly, I say to you, there is no one who has left house or brothers or sisters or mother or father or children or lands, for my sake and for the gospel, who will not receive a hundredfold now in this time, houses and brothers and sisters and mothers and children and lands, with persecutions, and in the age to come eternal life. But many that are first will be last, and the last first."

This story contains at least two great incentives for being totally dedicated to the cause of Frontier Missions.

With Men It Is Impossible, but Not with God

First, in Mark 10:25-27 Jesus said to his disciples, "It is easier for a camel to go through the eye of a needle than for a rich man to enter the kingdom of God."

And they were astonished and said to him, "Then who can be saved?" Jesus looked at them and said, "With men it is impossible, but not with God; for all things are possible with God."

This is one of the most encouraging missionary conversations in the Bible. What missionary has not looked on his work and said, "It's impossible!"? To which Jesus agrees, "Yes, with men it is impossible." No mere human being can liberate another human being from the enslaving power of the love of money. The rich young ruler went away sorrowful because the bondage to things cannot be broken by man. With man it is impossible! And therefore missionary work, which is simply liberating the human heart from bondage to allegiances other than Christ, is impossible — with men!

If God were not in charge in this affair, doing the humanly impossible, the missionary task would be hopeless. Who but God can raise the spiritually dead and give them an ear for the gospel? "Even when we were dead through our trespasses, God made us alive together with Christ" (Ephesians 2:5). The great missionary hope is that when the gospel is preached in the power of the Holy Spirit, God himself does what man cannot do — he creates the faith which saves.

The call of God does what the call of man can't. It raises the dead. It creates spiritual life. It is like the call of Jesus to Lazarus in the tomb, "Come forth!" (John 11:43). We can waken someone from sleep with our call, but God's call can summon into being things that are not (Romans 4:17).

God's call is irresistible in the sense that it can overcome all resistance. It is infallibly effective according to God's purpose — so much so that Paul can say, "Those whom God called he also justified." In other words, God's call is so effectual that it infallibly creates the faith through which a person is justified. All the called are justified. But none is justified without faith (Romans 5:1). So the call of God cannot fail in its intended effect. It irresistibly secures the faith that justifies.

This is what man cannot do. It is impossible. Only God can take out the heart of stone (Ezekiel 36:26). Only God can draw people to the Son (John 6:44,65). Only God can open the heart so that it gives heed to the gospel (Acts 16:14). Only the Good Shepherd knows his sheep by name. He calls them and they follow (John 10:3-4, 14). The sovereign grace of God, doing the humanly impossible, is the great missionary hope.

What Christian Hedonists Love Best

It is also the spring of life for the Christian Hedonist. For what the Christian Hedonist loves best is the experience of the sovereign grace of God filling him and overflowing for the good of others. Christian Hedonist missionaries love the experience of "not I, but the grace of Christ which is with me" (1 Corinthians 15:10). They bask in the truth that the fruit of their missionary labor is entirely of God (1 Corinthians 3:7; Romans 11:36). They feel only gladness when the Master says, "Without me you can do nothing" (John 15:5). They leap like lambs over the truth that God has taken the impossible weight of new creation off their shoulders and put it on his own.

Without begrudging, they say, "Not that we are sufficient of ourselves to claim anything as coming from us; our sufficiency is from God!" (2 Corinthians 3:5). When they come home on furlough, nothing gives them more joy than to say to the churches, "I will not venture to speak of anything except what *Christ* has wrought through me to win obedience from the Gentiles" (Romans 15:18). "All things are possible with God!" — in front the words give hope, and behind they give humility. They are the antidote to despair and pride — the perfect missionary medicine.

Missionary Incentives of Sovereign Grace

This great confidence of the missionary enterprise is given again by Jesus in John 10:16 with different words:

> "I have other sheep that are not of this fold; I must bring them
> also, and they will heed my voice. So there shall be one flock,
> one shepherd."

Notice three powerful encouragements in this text for frontier missionaries:

1. *Christ does indeed have other sheep outside the present fold!* They have been "ransomed from every tribe and tongue and people and nation" (Revelation 5:9). The children of God are "scattered abroad" (John 11:52). No missionary will ever reach a hidden group and be able to say God has no people there.

This is precisely how the Lord encouraged Paul when he was downcast in Corinth and confronted by the "impossibility" of planting a church in that rocky soil.

> And the Lord said to Paul one night in a vision, "Do not be
> afraid, but speak and do not be silent; for I am with you, and
> no man shall attack you to harm you; *for I have many people in
> this city*." (Acts 18:9-10)

In other words, take heart! It may look impossible, but God has a chosen people (the "other sheep" of John 10:16), and the Good Shepherd knows his own and will call them by name when you faithfully preach the gospel.

Jesus Must Bring His Other Sheep

2. This leads to the second encouragement for missions in John 10:16, namely the words, "I must bring them also." *Christ is under a divine necessity to gather his own sheep. He* must do it. He *must* do it. But of course this does not lead to the hyper-Calvinistic[17] notion that he will do it without using us as means. William Carey, "father of modern missions," did a great service to the cause of Frontier Missions when he published in 1792 his little book entitled, *An Enquiry into the Obligation of Christians to Use Means for the Conversion of the Heathens.*

God will always use means. Jesus makes this plain when he says, "I do not pray for these only, but also for those who believe in me *through their word*" (John 17:20). Nevertheless, Carey believed, as the Lord taught, that he was helpless and that it is really Christ who calls and saves and works in us what is pleasing in his sight (Hebrews 13:21). After forty years of spectacular accomplishment (for example, he translated the entire Bible into Bengali, Oriya, Marathi, Hindi, Assamese, and Sanskrit, and parts of it into twenty-nine other languages), William Carey died; yet the simple tablet on his grave reads, at his own request,

WILLIAM CAREY
Born August 17th, 1761
Died June, 1834
A wretched, poor and helpless worm,
On Thy kind arms I fall.

The great encouragement from John 10:16 is that the Lord himself will do what is impossible for "poor helpless worms" like us. "I have other sheep that are not of this fold; I must bring them also."

They Will Hear His Voice

3. The third encouragement from this verse is that the sheep he calls will surely come. "I must bring them also, and *they will heed my voice*." What is impossible with men is possible with God! When Paul was finished preaching in the city of Antioch, Luke describes the result like this: "As many as were ordained to eternal life believed" (Acts 13:48). God has a people in every people group. He will call them with Creator power. And they *will* believe!

What a power is in these words for overcoming discouragement in the hard places of the frontiers! The story of Peter Cameron Scott is a good illustration of the power of John 10:16.

He was born in Glasgow in 1867 and became the founder of the Africa

Inland Mission. But his beginnings in Africa were anything but auspicious. His first trip to Africa ended in a severe attack of malaria that sent him home. He resolved to return after recuperation.

This return was especially gratifying to Scott, because this time his brother John joined him. But before long John was struck down by fever. All alone, Peter buried his brother, and in the agony of those days recommitted himself to preach the gospel in Africa. Yet again his health gave way and he had to return to England.

How would he ever pull out of the desolation and depression of those days? He had pledged himself to God. But where could he find the strength to go back again to Africa? With man it was impossible!

He found the strength in Westminster Abbey. David Livingstone's tomb is there. Scott entered quietly, found the tomb, and knelt in front of it to pray. The inscription reads,

> OTHER SHEEP I HAVE
> WHICH ARE NOT OF THIS FOLD;
> THEM ALSO I MUST BRING.

He rose from his knees with a new hope. He returned to Africa. And the mission he founded is a vibrant, growing force for the gospel today in Africa.

If your greatest joy is to experience the infilling grace of God overflowing from you for the good of others, then the best news in all the world is that God will do the impossible through you for the salvation of the hidden peoples. "With men it is impossible, but not with God; for all things are possible with God."

You Will Receive Back a Hundredfold

The second great incentive in Mark 10:17-31 for being dedicated to the cause of Frontier Missions is found in verses 28-30.

> Peter began to say to [Jesus], "Look, we have left everything and followed you." Jesus said, "Truly, I say to you, there is no one who has left house or brothers or sisters or mother or father or children or lands, for my sake and for the gospel, who will not receive a hundredfold now in this time, house and brothers and sisters and mothers and children and lands, with persecutions, and in the age to come eternal life.

This text does not mean you get materially rich by becoming a missionary — at least not in the sense that your own private possessions increase.

If you volunteer for mission service with such a notion, the Lord will confront you with these words: "Foxes have holes, and birds of the air have nests; but the Son of Man has nowhere to lay his head" (Luke 9:58).

Instead, the point seems to be that if you are deprived of your earthly family in the service of Christ, it will be made up a hundredfold in your spiritual family, the church. But even this may be too limiting. What about the lonely missionaries who labor for years without being surrounded by hundreds of sisters and brothers and mothers and children in the faith? Is the promise not true for them?

He Makes Up for Every Sacrifice

Surely it is. Surely what Christ means is that he himself makes up for every sacrifice. If you give up a mother's nearby affection and concern, you get back one hundred times the affection and concern from the ever-present Christ. If you give up the warm comradeship of a brother, you get back one hundred times the warmth and comradeship of Christ. If you give up the sense of at-homeness you had in your house, you get back one hundred times the comfort and security of knowing that your Lord owns every house and land and stream and tree on earth. To prospective missionaries Jesus says, I promise to *work* for and *be* for you so much that you will not be able to speak of having sacrificed anything.

What was Jesus' attitude to Peter's "sacrificial" spirit? Peter said, "We have left everything and followed you." Is this spirit of "self-denial" commended by Jesus? No, it is rebuked. Jesus says, "No one ever sacrifices anything for me which I do not pay back a hundredfold — yes, in one sense even in this life, not to mention eternal life in the age to come." Why does Jesus rebuke Peter for thinking in terms of sacrifice? Jesus himself had demanded "self-denial" (Mark 8:34). The reason seems to be that Peter did not yet think about sacrifice the way a Christian Hedonist is supposed to.

How is that?

The response of Jesus indicates that the way to think about self-denial is to deny yourself only a lesser good for a greater good. You deny yourself one mother in order to get one hundred mothers. In other words, Jesus wants us to think about sacrifice in a way that rules out all self-pity. This is, in fact, just what the texts on self-denial teach.

> "If any man would come after me, let him deny himself and take
> up his cross and follow me. For whoever would save his life will
> lose it; and whoever loses his life for my sake and the gospel's
> will save it." (Mark 8:34-35)[18]

The argument is inescapably hedonistic. Saint Augustine captured the paradox in these words:

> If you love your soul, there is danger of its being destroyed. Therefore you may not love it, since you do not want it to be destroyed. But in not wanting it to be destroyed you love it.[19]

Jesus knew this. It was the basis of his argument. He does not ask us to be indifferent to whether we are destroyed. On the contrary, he assumes that the very longing for true life (1 Peter 3:10) will move us to deny ourselves all the lesser pleasures and comforts of life. If we were indifferent to the value of God's gift of life, we would dishonor it. The measure of your longing for life is the amount of comfort you are willing to give up to get it. The gift of eternal life in God's presence is glorified if we are willing to "hate our lives in this world" in order to get it (John 12:25). Therein lies the God-centered value of self-denial.

Two Kinds of Self-Love

When Peter blurted out that he had sacrificed everything, he had not thought as deeply as David Brainerd and David Livingstone. As a young missionary to the Indians of New England, Brainerd wrestled with the issue of self-love and self-denial. On January 24, 1744, he wrote in his diary,

> In the evening, I was unexpectedly visited by a considerable number of people, with whom I was enabled to converse profitably of divine things. Took pains to describe the difference between a regular and irregular self love; the one consisting with a supreme love to God, but the other not; the former uniting God's glory and the soul's happiness that they become one common interest, but the latter disjoining and separating God's glory and man's happiness, seeking the larger with a neglect of the former. Illustrated this by that genuine love that is founded between the sexes, which is diverse from that which is wrought up towards a person only by rational argument, or hope of self-interest.[20]

Brainerd knew in his soul that in seeking to live for the glory of God, he was loving himself! He knew there was no ultimate sacrifice going on, though he was dying of tuberculosis. Yet he knew that Jesus condemned some form of self-love and commended some form of self-denial. So he endorsed a distinction between a self-love that separates our pursuit of happiness from our pursuit of God's glory, and a self-love that combines these pursuits into "one common interest." In other words, he did not make Peter's mistake of thinking his suffering for Christ was ultimately sacrificial. With everything he gave up there came new experiences of the glory of God. A hundredfold!

"I Never Made a Sacrifice"

On December 4, 1857, David Livingstone, the great pioneer missionary to Africa, made a stirring appeal to the students of Cambridge University, showing that he had learned through years of experience what Jesus was trying to teach Peter:

> For my own part, I have never ceased to rejoice that God has appointed me to such an office. People talk of the sacrifice I have made in spending so much of my life in Africa. Can that be called a sacrifice which is simply paid back as a small part of a great debt owing to our God, which we can never repay? Is that a sacrifice which brings its own blest reward in healthful activity, the consciousness of doing good, peace of mind, and a bright hope of a glorious destiny hereafter? Away with the word in such a view, and with such a thought! It is emphatically no sacrifice. Say rather it is a privilege. Anxiety, sickness, suffering, or danger, now and then, with a foregoing of the common conveniences and charities of this life, may make us pause, and cause the spirit to waver, and the soul to sink; but let this only be for a moment. All these are nothing when compared with the glory which shall be revealed in and for us. I never made a sacrifice.[21]

One sentence of this quote is, I think, unhelpful and inconsistent: "Can that be called a sacrifice which is simply paid back as a small part of a great debt owing to our God, which we can never repay?" I don't think it is helpful to describe our obedience as an attempt (albeit impossible) to pay God back for his grace. It is a contradiction of free grace to think of it that way. Not only is it unhelpful, it is inconsistent with the rest of what Livingstone says. He says his obedience is in fact more receiving — healthful, peaceful, hopeful. It would honor God's grace and value more if we dropped the notion of paying him back at all. We are not involved in a trade or purchase. We have received a gift. But this reservation aside, the last line is magnificent: "I never made a sacrifice."

This is what Jesus' rebuke to Peter's sacrificial (self-pitying?) spirit was supposed to teach. Our great incentive for throwing our lives into the cause of Frontier Missions is the 10,000 percent return on the investment. Missionaries have borne witness to this from the beginning — since the apostle Paul.

Paul was bold to say that everything was garbage compared to knowing and suffering with Jesus:

> But whatever gain I had, I counted as loss for the sake of Christ. Indeed I count everything as loss because of the surpassing worth of knowing Christ Jesus my Lord. For his sake I have suffered the loss of all things, and count them as refuse, in order that I may gain Christ . . . that I may know him and the power of his resurrection, and may share his sufferings. (Philippians 3:7-10)

> This slight momentary affliction is preparing for us an eternal weight of glory beyond all comparison. (2 Corinthians 4:17)

> I consider that the sufferings of this present time are not worth comparing with the glory that is to be revealed to us. (Romans 8:18)

> I do it all for the sake of the gospel, that I may share in its blessings. (1 Corinthians 9:23)[22]

Holy Missionaries Are Most Hedonistic

It is simply amazing how consistent are the testimonies of missionaries who have suffered for the gospel. Virtually all of them bear witness of the abundant joy and overriding compensations (a hundredfold!).

Colin Grant describes how the Moravian Brethren were sending missionaries out from the mountains of Saxony in central Europe sixty years before William Carey set out for India. With utter abandon they reached the West Indies, Surinam, North America, Greenland, South Africa, China and Persia between 1732 and 1742 — "a record without parallel in the post-New Testament era of world evangelization." In recounting the main characteristics of this movement, Grant puts "glad obedience" at the top of the list. "In the first place, the missionary obedience of the Moravian Brethren was essentially glad and spontaneous, 'the response of a healthy organism to the law of its life.' "[23]

Andrew Murray refers to this "law of life" in his missionary classic *Key to the Missionary Problem*. Nature teaches us that every believer should be a soul-winner: "It is an essential part of the new nature. We see it in every child who loves to tell of his happiness and to bring others to share his joys."[24]

Missions is the automatic outflow and overflow of love for Christ. We delight to enlarge our joy in him by extending it to others. As Lottie Moon said, "Surely there can be no greater joy than that of saving souls."[25]

What Lottie Moon did in promoting the cause of foreign missions among Southern Baptist women in the United States, Amy Carmichael did among the Christian women of all denominations in the United Kingdom. She wrote thirty-five books detailing her fifty-five years in India. Sherwood Eddy, a missionary statesman and author who knew her well, said, "Amy Wilson Carmichael was the most Christlike character I ever met, and . . . her life was the most fragrant, the most joyfully sacrificial, that I ever knew."[26] "Joyfully sacrificial!" That is what Jesus was after when he rebuked Peter's sacrificial spirit in Mark 10:29-30.

John Hyde, better known as "Praying Hyde," led a life of incredibly intense prayer as a missionary to India at the turn of the century. Some thought him morose. But a story about him reveals the true spirit behind his life of sacrificial prayer.

A worldly lady once thought she would have a little fun at Mr. Hyde's expense. So she asked, "Don't you think, Mr. Hyde, that a lady who dances can go to heaven?" He looked at her with a smile, said quietly, "I do not see how a lady can go to heaven *unless* she dances." Then he dwelt on the joy of sin forgiven.[27]

Samuel Zwemer, famous for his missionary work among the Muslims, gives a stirring witness to the joy of sacrifice. In 1897 he and his wife and two daughters sailed to the Persian Gulf to work among the Muslims of Bahrein. Their evangelism was largely fruitless. The temperatures soared regularly to 107 "in the coolest part of the verandah." In July 1904 both the daughters, ages four and seven, died within eight days of each other. Nevertheless, fifty years later Zwemer looked back on this period and wrote, "The sheer joy of it all comes back. Gladly would I do it all over again."[28]

In the end, the reason Jesus rebukes us for a self-pitying spirit of sacrifice is that he aims to be glorified in the great missionary enterprise. And the way he aims to be glorified is by keeping himself in the role of benefactor and keeping us in the role of beneficiaries. He never intends for the patient and the physician to reverse roles. Even if we are called to be missionaries, we remain invalids in Christ's sanatorium. We are still in need of a good physician. We are still dependent on him to do the humanly impossible in us and through us. We may sacrifice other things to enter Christ's hospital, but we are there for our spiritual health, not to pay back a debt to the doctor!

Invalids Make the Best Missionaries

Daniel Fuller uses this picture of patient and doctor to show how the effective missionary avoids the presumption of assisting God:

> An analogy for understanding how to live the Christian life without being a legalist is to think of ourselves as being sick and needing a doctor's help in order to get well. Men begin life with a disposition so inclined to evil that Jesus called them "children of hell" (Matthew 23:15). . . . In Mark 2:17 and elsewhere Jesus likened Himself to a doctor with the task of healing man's sins; He received the name "Jesus" because it was His mission to "save His people from their sins" (Matthew 1:21). The moment we turn from loving things in this world to bank our hope on God and His promises summed up in Jesus Christ, Jesus takes us, as it were, into His clinic to heal us of our hellish dispositions. . . . True faith means not only being confident that one's sins are forgiven but also means believing God's promises that we will have a happy future through eternity. Or, to revert to the metaphor of medicine and the clinic, we must entrust our sick selves to Christ as the Great Physician, with confidence that He will work until our hellishness is transformed into godliness.
>
> [One] implication to be drawn from the doctor analogy is that while he will prescribe certain general instructions for all his patients to follow, he will also make up individual health regimens for the particular needs of each patient. For example, he may direct some to leave their homeland to go to proclaim the Gospel in a foreign land. There is great temptation in such circumstances for people to revert to the legalism of thinking that they are being heroes for God because they are leaving their homeland to endure the rigors of living in a foreign land [this was Peter's problem]. Those who are directed to do hard jobs for God must remind themselves that these rigors are simply for their health. As these difficulties help them become more like Christ, they will sing a song of praise unto God, and as a result "many will see it and fear and put their trust in the LORD" (Psalm 40:3). People who regard themselves as invalids rather than heroes will make excellent missionaries.[29]

For the Increase of Our Most Holy Faith

As strange as this may sound to self-reliant, self-esteeming secular people, it is in fact the way many missionaries have conceived of their labor. Francis Xavier (1506-1552), who founded the Jesuit missionary movement and served in India and Japan, was always in pursuit of a deeper life with God. He died at forty-six awaiting passage to the great forbidden China. Keep in mind the doctor-patient analogy as you read one of his last letters concerning his desire to enter China. We need not minimize the serious theological problems with sixteenth century Roman Catholic teaching in order to see the truth expressed about missionary motivation in this quotation.

> The danger of all dangers would be to lose trust and confidence in the mercy of God for whose love and service we came to manifest the law of Jesus Christ, His Son, our Redeemer and Lord, as He well knows. . . . To distrust Him would be a far more terrible thing than any physical evil which all the enemies of God put together could inflict on us, for without God's permission neither the devils nor their human ministers could hinder us in the slightest degree. . . . We are therefore determined to make our way into China at all costs, and *I hope in God that the upshot of our journey will be the increase of our holy faith*, however much the devil and his ministers may persecute us. If God is for us who can overthrow us?[30]

Expecting First, Then Attempting

William Carey, at first glance, may appear to be an exception to the idea that missionaries should see their ministry as God's treatment for their spiritual disease of sin. On Wednesday, May 31, 1792, he preached his famous sermon from Isaiah 54:2-3 ("Enlarge the place of thy tent . . . ") in which his most famous dictum was pronounced: "Expect great things from God; attempt great things for God." Is this the way an invalid talks about his relationship with his physician-therapist?

Yes! Emphatically, yes! If a therapist says to a partially paralyzed invalid, "Hold on to me and stand up out of your chair," the invalid must first trust the therapist and "expect great help." Mary Drewery's interpretation of Carey's motto surely accords with his intention:

> Once he was convinced of his missionary call, Carey put his complete faith in God to guide him and to supply all his needs. "Expect great things from God" had been the first part of his

command at the Association Meeting in Nottingham in 1792. Though the expectations were not always met in the form or at the time Carey anticipated, nonetheless, he would claim that the help did always come and to an ever-increasing extent. Thus he was able to "achieve great things for God." The blessings were not a reward for work done; they were a prerequisite for carrying out the work.[31]

Confirmation of this interpretation from Carey himself is found in the words he requested on his tombstone, as we have seen: "A wretched, poor and helpless worm, On Thy kind arms I fall." This is a perfect description of an invalid and his kind and loving physician-therapist. It was true in life ("Expect great things from God"), and it was true in death ("On Thy kind arms I fall").

The Powerful Resting of Hudson Taylor

The same was true of Hudson Taylor, founder of the China Inland Mission. His son compiled a short work in 1932 called *Hudson Taylor's Spiritual Secret*. The secret is simply that Hudson Taylor learned to be a happy patient in the Savior's clinic of life.

> Frequently those who were wakeful in the little house at Chinkiang might hear, at two or three in the morning, the soft refrain of Mr. Taylor's favorite hymn ["Jesus, I am resting, resting in the joy of what Thou art . . . "]. He had learned that for him, only one life was possible — just that blessed life of resting and rejoicing in the Lord under all circumstances, while He dealt with the difficulties, inward and outward, great and small.[32]

It almost goes without saying that every therapy is painful. "Through many tribulations we must enter the kingdom of God" (Acts 14:22). This is what Jesus meant when he said our hundredfold benefit in mission therapy would be "with persecutions" (Mark 10:30). No naiveté here. For some the therapy includes even death, for the clinic bridges heaven and earth: "They will lay their hands on you and persecute you . . . and some of you they will put to death. . . . But not a hair of your head will perish. By your endurance you will gain your lives" (Luke 21:12,16,18-19).

Calling Death Sweet Names

This is why martyr missionaries have often called death sweet names. "Though we have but a hard breakfast, yet we shall have a good dinner, we shall very soon be in heaven."[33] The faithful missionary invalid is promised a hundredfold improvement in this life, with persecutions, and in the age to come eternal life.

Missionaries are not heroes who can boast in great sacrifice for God. They are the true Christian Hedonists. They know the battle cry of Christian Hedonism is missions. They have discovered a hundred times more joy and satisfaction in a life devoted to Christ and the gospel than in a life devoted to frivolous comforts and pleasures and worldly advancements. And they have taken to heart the rebuke of Jesus: Beware of a self-pitying spirit of sacrifice! Missions is gain! Hundredfold gain!

Summary and Exhortation

These, then, are two great incentives from Jesus to become a World Christian and to dedicate yourself to the cause of Frontier Missions as the twentieth century comes to a close.

(1) Every impossibility with men is possible with God (Mark 10:27). The conversion of hardened sinners will be the work of God and will accord with his sovereign plan. We need not fear or fret over our weakness. The battle is the Lord's and he will give the victory.

(2) Christ promises to work for us and to be for us so much that when our missionary life is over, we will not be able to say we've sacrificed anything (Mark 10:29-30). When we follow his missionary prescription, we discover that even the painful side effects work to improve our condition. Our spiritual health, our joy, improves a hundredfold. And when we die, we do not die. We gain eternal life.

I do not appeal to you to screw up your courage and sacrifice for Christ. I appeal to you to renounce all you have to obtain life that satisfies your deepest longings. I appeal to you to count all things as rubbish for the surpassing value of standing in the service of the King of kings. I appeal to you to take off your store-bought rags and put on the garments of God's ambassadors. I promise you persecutions and privations, but "remember the joy!" "Blessed are those who are persecuted for righteousness' sake, for theirs is the kingdom of heaven" (Matthew 5:10).

On January 8, 1956, five Auca Indians of Ecuador killed Jim Elliot and his four missionary companions as they were trying to bring the gospel to the Auca tribe of sixty people. Four young wives lost husbands and nine children lost their fathers. Elisabeth Elliot wrote that the world called it a nightmare of tragedy. Then she added, "The world did not recognize the truth of the second clause in Jim Elliot's credo:

He is no fool who gives what he cannot keep
to gain what he cannot lose.[34]

If only for this life we have hope in Christ,
we are to be pitied more than all men.

1 CORINTHIANS 15:19

The noble army of the martyrs praise thee

TE DEUM

I rejoice in my sufferings for you
and I complete in my flesh
what is lacking in the afflictions of Christ
on behalf of his body,
which is the church.

COLOSSIANS 1:24

CHAPTER 10

SUFFERING

The Sacrifice of Christian Hedonism

Sitting at the Feet of a Suffering Saint

I have never been the same since sitting at the feet of Richard Wurmbrand. It was literally at his feet. He took off his shoes and sat in a chair on the slightly raised platform at Grace Baptist Church in south Minneapolis. (I learned later it had to do with damage to his feet during the torture that he had received in a Romanian prison.) Before him — and below him — sat about a dozen pastors. He spoke of suffering. Again and again he said that Jesus "chose" suffering. He "chose" it. It did not merely happen to him. He "chose" it. "No one takes my life from me. I lay it down of my own will" (John 10:18). He asked us if we would choose suffering for the sake of Christ.

Wurmbrand's devotional book, *Reaching toward the Heights*, introduces him like this: Richard Wurmbrand is an evangelical Lutheran pastor of Jewish origin who was born in 1909 in Romania. When the Communists seized his native land in 1945, he became a leader in the underground church. In 1948 he and his wife, Sabina, were arrested, and he served fourteen years in Red Prisons, including three years in solitary confinement in a subterranean cell, never seeing the sun, the stars, or flowers. He saw no one except his guards and torturers. Christian friends in Norway purchased his freedom for $10,000 in 1964.[1]

How Beautiful Is Sacrifice?

One of the stories he tells is about a Cistercian abbot who was interviewed on Italian television. The interviewer was especially interested in the Cistercian tradition of living in silence and solitude. So he asked the abbot, "And what if you were to realize at the end of your life that atheism is true, that there is no God? Tell me, what if it were true?"

The Abbot replied, "Holiness, silence, and sacrifice are beautiful in themselves, even without promise of reward. I still will have used my life well."

Few glimpses into the meaning of life have had a greater impact on my contemplations about suffering. The first impact of the abbot's response was a superficial, romantic surge of glory. But then something stuck. It did not sit well. Something was wrong. At first I could not figure it out. Then I turned to the great Christian sufferer, the apostle Paul, and was stunned by the gulf between him and the abbot.

Paul's answer to the interviewer's question was utterly contrary to the abbot's answer. The interviewer had asked, "What if your way of life turns out to be based on a falsehood, and there is no God?" The abbot's answer in essence was, "It was a good and noble life anyway." Paul gave his answer in 1 Corinthians 15:19, "If for this life only we have hoped in Christ, we are of all men most to be pitied." This is the exact opposite of the abbot's answer.

Why did Paul not agree with the monk? Why didn't Paul say, "Even if Christ is not raised from the dead, and even if there is no God, a life of love and labor and sacrifice and suffering is a good life"? Why didn't he say that "even without the reward of resurrection, we are not to be pitied"? Why did he say instead, "If our hope in Christ proves false in the end, we are to be pitied more than anyone"?

Does Life Go Better with Christ?

This is an utterly crucial question for the Christian Church, especially in prosperous, comfortable lands like America and Western Europe. How many times do we hear Christian testimonies to the effect that becoming a Christian has made life easier? I recently heard the quarterback of a professional football team say that after he prayed to receive Christ, he felt good about the game again and was proud of their 8 and 8 record because he was able to go out every Sunday and give it his best.

It seems that most Christians in the prosperous West describe the benefits of Christianity in terms that would make it a good life, even if there were no God and no resurrection. Think of all the psychological benefits and relational benefits. And of course these are true and biblical: the fruit of the Holy Spirit is love, joy, and peace. So if we get love, joy, and peace from believing these things, then is it not a good life to live, even if it turns out to be based on a falsehood? Why should we be pitied?

What's wrong with Paul, then? Was he not living the abundant life? Why would he say that, if there is no resurrection, we are of all men most to be pitied? It does not seem to be pitiable to live your three score and ten in a joyful and satisfying delusion, if that delusion makes no difference whatever for the future. If delusion can turn emptiness and meaninglessness into happiness, then why not be deluded?

The answer seems to be that the Christian life for Paul was not the so-called good life of prosperity and ease. Instead it was a life of freely chosen suffering beyond anything we ordinarily experience. Paul's belief in God, and his confidence in resurrection, and his hope in eternal fellowship with Christ, did not produce a life of comfort and ease that would have been satisfying even without resurrection. No, what his hope produced was a life of chosen suffering. Yes, he knew joy unspeakable. But it was a "rejoicing in hope" (Romans 12:12). And that hope freed him to embrace sufferings that he never would have chosen apart from the hope of his own resurrection and the resurrection of those for whom he suffered. If there is no resurrection, Paul's sacrificial choices, by his own testimony, were pitiable.

Yes, there was joy and a sense of great significance in his suffering. But the joy was there only because of the joyful hope beyond suffering. This is the point of Romans 5:3-4. "We exult in our afflictions, knowing that affliction produces endurance, and endurance produces proven genuineness, and genuineness produces *hope*." So there *is* joy in affliction. But the joy comes because of the hope that affliction itself is helping to secure and increase. So if there is no hope, Paul is a fool to embrace this affliction, and even more foolish to rejoice in it. But there is hope. And so Paul chooses a way of life that would be foolish and pitiable without the hope of joy beyond the grave. He answers Richard Wurmbrand's question, Yes. He chooses suffering.

Is There a Difference between Conflict and Cancer?

Let's take a brief detour for a moment. Someone may ask at this point, "What about suffering I do not choose? Like cancer. Or the death of my child in a car accident? Or a severe depression? Is this chapter about any of that?" My answer is that most of this chapter is about the suffering Christians accept as part of a choice to be openly Christian in risky situations. And all situations are risky, one way or the other.

The most significant difference between sickness and persecution is that persecution is an intentional hostility from someone because we are known to be Christians, but sickness is not. Therefore, in some situations, to choose to be public Christians is to choose a way of life that accepts suffering, if God wills (1 Peter 4:19). But suffering may result from living as a Christian even when there is no intentional hostility from unbelievers. For example, a Christian may go to a disease-ridden village to minister, and contract the disease. This is suffering as a Christian, but it is not "persecution." It is a choice to suffer, if God wills, but not from the hostility of others.

But then, when you stop to think about it, all of life, if it is lived earnestly by faith in the pursuit of God's glory and the salvation of others, is like the Christian who goes to the disease-ridden village. The suffering that comes is part of the price of living where you are in obedience to the call of

God. In choosing to follow Christ in the way he directs, we choose all that this path includes under his sovereign providence. Thus all suffering that comes in the path of obedience is suffering with Christ and for Christ — whether it is cancer or conflict. And it is "chosen" — that is, we willingly take the path of obedience where the suffering befalls us, and we do not murmur against God. We may pray — as Paul did — that the suffering be removed (2 Corinthians 12:8); but if God wills, we embrace it in the end, as part of the cost of discipleship in the path of obedience on the way to heaven.

All Suffering in a Christian Calling Is with Christ and for Christ

All experiences of suffering in the path of Christian obedience, whether from persecution or sickness or accident, have this in common: they all threaten our faith in the goodness of God and tempt us to leave the path of obedience. Therefore, every triumph of faith and all perseverance in obedience are testimonies to the goodness of God and the preciousness of Christ — whether the enemy is sickness, Satan, sin, or sabotage.

Therefore all suffering, of every kind, that we endure in the path of our Christian calling is a suffering "with Christ" and "for Christ." *With* him in the sense that the suffering comes to us as we are walking with him by faith, and in the sense that it is endured in the strength that he supplies through his sympathizing high-priestly ministry (Hebrews 4:15). *For* him in the sense that the suffering tests and proves our allegiance to his goodness and power, and in the sense that it reveals his worth as an all-sufficient compensation and prize.

Satan's and God's Design in the Same Suffering

Not only that, the suffering of sickness and the suffering of persecution have this in common: they are both intended by Satan for the destruction of our faith, and governed by God for the purifying of our faith.

Take first the case of persecution. In 1 Thessalonians 3:4-5 Paul describes his concern for the faith of the Thessalonians in the face of persecution:

> When we were with you, we told you in advance that we were going to suffer affliction; and so it happened, as you know. On account of this, when I could endure it no longer, I also sent to find out about your faith, lest somehow the tempter might have tempted you, and our labor should be in vain.

What is plain here is that the design of the "tempter" in this affliction is to destroy faith.

But Satan is not the only designer in this affair. God rules over Satan and gives him no more leash than can accomplish his ultimate purposes. Those purposes are the opposite of Satan's, even in the very same experience of suffering. For example, the writer of Hebrews 12 shows his readers how not to lose heart in persecution, because of God's loving purposes in it.

> Consider [Christ] who has endured such hostility by sinners against himself, so that you may not grow weary and lose heart. You have not yet resisted to the point of shedding blood in your striving against sin; and you have forgotten the exhortation which is addressed to you as sons, "My son, do not regard lightly the discipline of the Lord, nor faint when you are reproved by him; for those whom the Lord loves he disciplines, and he scourges every son whom he receives" [Proverbs 3:11-12]. It is for discipline that you endure. . . . All discipline for the moment seems not to be joyful, but sorrowful; yet to those who have been trained by it, afterwards it yields the peaceful fruit of righteousness.

Here is suffering that is coming from "hostility by sinners." This means that Satan has a hand in it, just as he did in the suffering of Jesus (Luke 22:3). Nevertheless, this very suffering is described as governed by God in such a way that it has the loving and fatherly design of purifying discipline. So Satan has one design for our suffering in persecution and God has a different design for that very same experience.

But persecution is not unique in this. The same is true of sickness. Both the design of Satan and the design of God are evident in 2 Corinthians 12:7-10.

> There was given me a thorn in the flesh, a messenger of Satan to buffet me — to keep me from exalting myself! Concerning this I entreated the Lord three times that it might depart from me. And He has said to me, "My grace is sufficient for you, for power is perfected in weakness." Most gladly, therefore, I will rather boast about my weaknesses, that the power of Christ may dwell in me. Therefore I am well content with weaknesses, with insults, with distresses, with persecutions, with difficulties, for Christ's sake; for when I am weak, then I am strong.

Here Paul's physical suffering — the thorn in the flesh — is called "a messenger of Satan." But the design of this suffering is "to keep [Paul] from exalting [himself]," which never would have been Satan's design. So the point is that Christ sovereignly accomplishes his loving, purifying purpose, by overruling Satan's destructive attempts. Satan is always aiming to destroy our faith; but Christ magnifies his power in weakness.

Are Suffering from Persecution and Sickness Distinguishable?

Another reason for not distinguishing sharply between persecution and sickness is that the pain from persecution and the pain from sickness are not always distinguishable. Decades after his torture for Christ in a Romanian prison, Richard Wurmbrand still suffered from the physical effects. Was he being "persecuted" as he endured the pain in his feet thirty years later? Or consider the apostle Paul. Among the sufferings that he listed as a "servant of Christ" was the fact that he was shipwrecked three times and spent a night and a day in the water. He also says his sufferings for Christ included "labor and hardship, through many sleepless nights, in hunger and thirst, often without food, in cold and exposure" (2 Corinthians 11:25,27).

Suppose that he got pneumonia from all this work and exposure. Would that pneumonia have been "persecution"? Paul did not make a distinction between being beaten by rods, or having a boating accident, or being cold while traveling between towns. For him any suffering that befell him while serving Christ was part of the "cost" of discipleship. When a missionary's child gets diarrhea, we think of this as part of the price of faithfulness. But if any parent is walking in the path of obedience to God's calling, it is the same price. What turns sufferings into sufferings "with" and "for" Christ is not how intentional our enemies are, but how faithful we are. If we are Christ's, then what befalls us is for his glory and for our good whether it is caused by enzymes or by enemies.

Is Gluttony the Alternative to Resurrection?

Now we turn from our brief detour to Paul's amazing statement in 1 Corinthians 15:19 that the life he has chosen is pitiable if there is no resurrection. In other words Christianity, as Paul understands it, is not the best way to maximize pleasure, if this life is all that there is. Paul tells us the best way to maximize our pleasures in this life. "If the dead are not raised, let us eat and drink, for tomorrow we die" (1 Corinthians 15:32). He does not mean something so naive as sheer epicureanism and debauchery. That is not the best way to maximize your pleasures, as anyone one knows who has followed the path of alcoholism and gluttony. Drunks and gluttons are to be pitied just like Christians, if there is no resurrection.

But what he does mean by the phrase, "Let us eat and drink," is that, without the hope of resurrection, one should pursue ordinary pleasures and avoid extraordinary suffering. This is the life Paul has rejected as a Christian.

Thus, if the dead are not raised, and if there is no God and no heaven, he would not have pummeled his body the way he did. He would not have turned down wages for his tentmaking the way he did. He would not have walked into five whippings of thirty-nine lashes. He would not have endured three beatings with rods. He would not have risked his life from robbers and deserts and rivers and cities and seas and angry mobs. He would not have accepted sleepless nights and cold and exposure. He would not have endured so long with backsliding and hypocritical Christians (2 Corinthians 11:23-29). Instead he would have simply lived the good life of comfort and ease as a respectable Jew with the prerogatives of Roman citizenship.

When Paul says, "If the dead are not raised, let us eat and drink," he does not mean, "Let's all become lechers." He means, there is a normal, simple, comfortable, ordinary life of human delights that we may enjoy with no troubling thoughts of heaven or hell or sin or holiness or God — if there is no resurrection from the dead. And what stunned me about this train of thought is that many professing Christians seem to aim at just this, and call it Christianity.

Paul did not see his relation to Christ as the key to maximizing his physical comforts and pleasures in this life. No, Paul's relation to Christ was a call to choose suffering — a suffering that was beyond what would make atheism "meaningful" or "beautiful" or "heroic." It was a suffering that would have been utterly foolish and pitiable to choose if there is no resurrection into the joyful presence of Christ.

An Almost Unbelievable Indictment of Western Christianity

This was the astonishing thing I finally saw in pondering Wurmbrand's story about the Cistercian abbot. In Paul's radically different viewpoint I saw an almost unbelievable indictment of Western Christianity. Am I overstating this? Judge for yourself. How many Christians do you know who could say, "The lifestyle I have chosen as a Christian would be utterly foolish and pitiable if there is no resurrection"? How many Christians are there who could say, "The suffering I have freely chosen to embrace for the cause of Christ would be a pitiable life if there is no resurrection"? As I see it, these are shocking questions.

Christianity: A Life of Chosen Suffering

"If we have hoped in Christ in this life only, we are of all men most to be pitied" (1 Corinthians 15:19). The Christian life for Paul was a life of chosen sacrifice on earth, that we might gain the joy of fellowship with Christ in the age to come. Here is how he put it:

219

> Whatever things were gain to me, these things I have counted
> as loss for the sake of Christ. More than that, I count all things
> to be loss on account of the surpassing value of knowing Christ
> Jesus my Lord, for whom I have suffered the loss of all things,
> and count them but rubbish in order that I may gain Christ. . . .
> I share his sufferings . . . that if possible I may attain the resur-
> rection from the dead. (Philippians 3:7-11)

I say it again: the call of Christ is a call to live a life of sacrifice and loss and suffering that would be foolish to live, if there were no resurrection from the dead. This is a conscious choice for Paul. Listen to his protest: "If the dead are not raised . . . why am I in peril every hour? I protest, brothers, by my exultation in you which I have in Christ Jesus our Lord, I die every day!" (1 Corinthians 15:29-31). This is what Paul has chosen. He "protests" because he does not *have* to live this way. He chooses it: "In peril every hour!" "Dying every day!" This is why he says he should be pitied if there is no resurrection from the dead. He chooses a path that leads to trouble and pain virtually every day of his life. "I die every day."

Why? Why Does He Do It?

This is not normal. Human beings flee suffering. We move to safer neighborhoods. We choose milder climates. We buy air conditioners. We take aspirin. We come in out of the rain. We avoid dark streets. We purify our water. We do not normally choose a way of life that would put us in "peril every hour." Paul's life is out of sync with ordinary human choices. Virtually no advertising slogans lure us into daily dying.

So what is driving the apostle Paul to "share abundantly in Christ's sufferings" (2 Corinthians 1:5) and to be a "fool for Christ's sake" (1 Corinthians 4:10)? Why would he make choices that expose him to being "hungry and thirsty . . . poorly clothed . . . roughly treated . . . homeless . . . reviled . . . persecuted . . . slandered . . . as the scum of the world, the dregs of all things" (1 Corinthians 4:11-13)?

"I Will Show Him How Much He Must Suffer."

Perhaps it was simple obedience to Christ's commission expressed in Acts 9:15-16. When Jesus sent Ananias to open Paul's eyes after he was blinded on the road to Damascus, he said, "Go, for [Paul] is a chosen instrument of mine, to bear my name before the Gentiles and kings and the sons of Israel; for *I will show him how much he must suffer for my name's sake.*" In other words, suffering was simply part of Paul's apostolic calling. To be faithful to his calling, he had to embrace what Christ gave him, much suffering.

"Gave" is the right word. Because when writing to the Philippians, Paul, incredibly, calls suffering a gift, just like faith is a *gift*. "To you it has been *granted* (*echaristhē* = freely given) for Christ's sake, not only to believe in Him, but also to *suffer* for His sake" (Philippians 1:29). But this would mean that the "gift" given to him as part of his apostleship is not viewed by Paul as limited to apostles. It is "granted" to the Philippian believers, the whole church.

Others have made the same strange discovery, that suffering is a gift to be embraced. Alexander Solzhenitsyn spoke of his time in prison, with all its pain, as a gift. "It was only when I lay there on rotting prison straw that I sensed within myself the first stirrings of good. Gradually, it was disclosed to me that the line separating good and evil passes, not through states, nor between classes, nor between political parties either, but right through every human heart — and through all human hearts. . . . Bless you, prison, for having been in my life."[2] Solzhenitsyn agrees with the apostle Paul that suffering is — or can be — a gift not just for apostles, but for every Christian.

To Show He Was Simply a Christian

Which raises the question: did Paul, then, embrace his suffering because it would confirm that he was simply a faithful disciple of Jesus? Jesus had said, "If anyone wishes to come after me, let him deny himself, and take up his cross daily, and follow me. For whoever wishes to save his life shall lose it, but whoever loses his life for my sake, he will save it" (Luke 9:23-24). So there is no true Christianity without cross-bearing and a *daily* dying — which sounds very much like Paul's "I die daily" (1 Corinthians 15:31). Moreover, Jesus had told his disciples, "A slave is not greater than his master. If they persecuted me, they will also persecute you" (John 15:20). So something would be amiss if Paul did not share in the sufferings of Jesus. Jesus gave his disciples an ominous image of their ministry: "Behold, I send you out as lambs in the midst of wolves" (Luke 10:3). And so he promised them, "You will be delivered up even by parents and brothers and relatives and friends, and they will put some of you to death . . . you will be hated by all nations on account of my name" (Luke 21:16; Matthew 24:9).

Evidently Paul did not consider these promises of suffering as limited to the original twelve apostles, because he passed them on to his churches. For example, he strengthened all his converts by telling them, "Through many tribulations we must enter the kingdom of God" (Acts 14:22). And he encouraged the suffering Thessalonian believers by exhorting them not to be "disturbed by these afflictions; for you yourselves know that we have been destined for this" (1 Thessalonians 3:3). And when he wrote to Timothy he made it a general principle: "Indeed, all who desire to live godly in Christ Jesus will be persecuted" (2 Timothy 3:12). When he spoke of his sufferings he did not treat them as unique, but said to the churches, "Be imitators of me" (1 Corinthians 4:16). So it would be understandable if Paul embraced a life of suffering because it would simply confirm that he was a Christian. "If they persecuted me, they will also persecute you."

Weaning Christians off the Breast of Self-Reliance

Since he believed that suffering was part of faithful Christian living, he probed into why this might be so. His own experience of suffering drove him deep into the ways of God's love with his children. For example, he learned that God uses our suffering to wean us from self-reliance and cast us on himself alone. After suffering in Asia he says, "We do not want you to be unaware, brethren, of our affliction which came to us in Asia, that we were burdened excessively, beyond our strength, so that we despaired even of life; indeed, we had the sentence of death within ourselves *in order that we should not trust in ourselves, but in God* who raises the dead" (2 Corinthians 1:8-9). This is God's universal purpose for all Christian suffering: more contentment in God and less satisfaction in self and the world.

I have never heard anyone say, "The really deep lessons of life have come through times of ease and comfort." But I have heard strong saints say, "Every significant advance I have ever made in grasping the depths of God's love and growing deep with him, has come through suffering." Samuel Rutherford said that when he was cast into the cellars of affliction, he remembered that the great King always kept his wine there. Charles Spurgeon said that those who dive in the sea of affliction bring up rare pearls.

To Magnify Christ As a Superior Satisfaction

The pearl of greatest price is the glory of Christ. Thus Paul stresses that in our sufferings the glory of Christ's all-sufficient grace is magnified. If we rely on him in our calamity, and he sustains our "rejoicing in hope," then he is shown to be the all-satisfying God of grace and strength that he is. If we hold fast to him "when all around our soul gives way," then we show that he is more to be desired than all we have lost. Christ said to the suffering apostle, "My grace is sufficient for you, for *[my] power is perfected in weakness*." Paul responded to this: "Gladly, then, I will boast about my weaknesses, *that the power of Christ may dwell in me.* Therefore I am content with weaknesses, with insults, with distresses, with persecutions, with difficulties, for Christ's sake; for when I am weak, then I am strong" (2 Corinthians 12:9-10). So suffering clearly is designed by God not only as a way to wean Christians off of self and onto grace, but also as a way to spotlight that grace and make it shine. That is precisely what faith does; it magnifies Christ's future grace.

The deep things of life in God are discovered in suffering. So it was with Jesus himself. "Although he was a Son, Jesus learned obedience through what he suffered" (Hebrews 5:8). The same book where we read this also tells us Jesus never sinned (Hebrews 4:15). So "learning obedience" does not mean switching from disobedience to obedience. It means growing deeper and deeper with God in the experience of obedience. It means experiencing depths of yieldedness to God that would not have been otherwise demanded.

The Unspeakable Words of Christian Suffering

As Paul contemplated the path of his Master, he was moved to follow. But just at this point I have been astonished again by Paul's words. When he describes the relationship between Christ's sufferings and his own, he speaks what seems unspeakable. He says to the Colossian church: "Now I rejoice in my sufferings for you and I complete in my flesh what is lacking in the afflictions of Christ on behalf of his body, which is the church" (Colossians 1:24). This may be the most powerful motive for Paul's choosing a life of suffering. These words have filled me with longing for the Church of Jesus Christ. O that we would embrace the necessary suffering appointed for the advancement of Christ's kingdom in the world!

How Can We Complete the Sufferings of Christ?

What does Paul mean that he "completes what is lacking in the afflictions of Christ"? Is this an unspeakable belittling of the all-sufficient, atoning worth of the death of Jesus? Did not Jesus himself say as he died, "It is finished" (John 19:30)? Is it not true that "by one offering [Christ] *has perfected for all time* those who are sanctified" (Hebrews 10:14)? And that "through his own blood, he entered the holy place *once for all*, having obtained *eternal* redemption" (Hebrews 9:12)? Paul knew and taught that the afflictions of Christ were a complete and sufficient ground for our justification. We are "justified by his blood" (Romans 5:9). Paul taught that Christ chose suffering and was "obedient unto death" (Philippians 2:8). That obedience of suffering was the all-sufficient ground of our righteousness before God. "As through [Adam's] disobedience the many were made sinners, even so through the obedience of [Christ] the many will be made righteous" (Romans 5:19). So Paul does not mean that his sufferings complete the atoning worth of Jesus' afflictions.

There is a better interpretation. Paul's sufferings complete Christ's afflictions *not* by adding anything to their worth, but by extending them to the people they were meant to save. What is lacking in the afflictions of Christ is not that they are deficient in worth, as though they could not sufficiently cover the sins of all who believe. What is lacking is that the infinite value of Christ's afflictions is not known and trusted in the world. These afflictions and what they mean are still hidden to most peoples. And God's intention is that the mystery be revealed to all the nations. So the afflictions of Christ are "lacking" in the sense that they are not seen and known and loved among the nations. They must be carried by ministers of the word. And those ministers of the word "complete" what is lacking in the afflictions of Christ by extending them to others.

Epaphroditus Is the Key

There is a strong confirmation of this interpretation in the use of similar words in Philippians 2:30. There was a man named Epaphroditus in the church at Philippi. When the church there gathered support for Paul (perhaps money or supplies or books), they decided to send them to Paul in Rome by the hand of Epaphroditus. In his travels with this supply, Epaphroditus almost lost his life. He was sick to the point of death, but God spared him (Philippians 2:27).

So Paul tells the church in Philippi to honor Epaphroditus when he comes back (v. 29), and he explains his reason with words very similar to Colossians 1:24. He says, "He came close to death for the work of Christ, risking his life to *complete* (similar word to the one in Colossians 1:24) *what was lacking* (same word as in Colossians 1:24) in your service to me." In the Greek original the phrase *"complete what was lacking* in your service to me" is almost identical with *"complete what is lacking* in Christ's afflictions."

In what sense, then, was the service of the Philippians to Paul "lacking" and in what sense did Epaphroditus "complete" what was lacking in their service? A hundred years ago a commentator Marvin Vincent explained it like this:

> The gift to Paul was a gift of the church as a body. It was a sacrificial offering of love. What was lacking, and what would have been grateful to Paul and to the church alike, was the church's presentation of this offering in person. This was impossible, and Paul represents Epaphroditus as supplying this lack by his affectionate and zealous ministry.[3]

I think that is exactly what the same words mean in Colossians 1:24. Christ has prepared a love offering for the world by suffering and dying for sinners. It is full and lacking in nothing — except one thing, a personal presentation by Christ himself to the nations of the world. God's answer to this lack is to call the people of Christ (people like Paul) to make a personal presentation of the afflictions of Christ to the world.

In doing this we "complete what is lacking in the afflictions of Christ." We finish what they were designed for, namely, a personal presentation to the people who do not know about their infinite worth.

Filling Afflictions with Afflictions

But the most amazing thing about Colossians 1:24 is *how* Paul completes what is lacking in Christ's afflictions. He says that it is *his own sufferings* that complete Christ's afflictions. "I rejoice in *my sufferings* for you and I complete *in my flesh* what is lacking in the afflictions of Christ." This means, then, that Paul exhibits the sufferings of Christ by suffering *himself* for those he is trying to win. In *his* sufferings they see Christ's sufferings. Here is the astounding upshot: *God intends for the afflictions of Christ to be presented to the world through the afflictions of his people.* God really means for the body of Christ, the church, to experience some of the suffering he experienced so that when we proclaim the cross as the way to life, people will see the marks of the cross in us and feel the love of the cross from us. Our calling is to make the afflictions of Christ real for people by the afflictions we experience in bringing them the message of salvation.

Since Christ is no longer on the earth, he wants his body, the church, to reveal *his* suffering in *its* suffering. Since we are his body, our sufferings are his sufferings. Romanian pastor Joseph Tson put it like this: "I am an extension of Jesus Christ. When I was beaten in Romania, He suffered in my body. It is not my suffering: I only had the honor to share His sufferings."[4] Therefore our sufferings testify to the kind of love Christ has for the world.

"I Bear on My Body the Marks of Jesus"

This is why Paul spoke of his scars as the "marks of Jesus." In his wounds people could see Christ's wounds. "I bear on my body the marks of Jesus" (Galatians 6:17). The point of bearing the marks of Jesus is that Jesus might be seen and his love might work powerfully in those who see. "[We always] carry in our body the death of Jesus, so that the life of Jesus may also be manifested in our bodies. For while we live we are always being given up to death for Jesus' sake, so that the life of Jesus may be manifested in our mortal flesh. So death is at work in us, but life in you" (2 Corinthians 4:10-12).

"The Blood of the Martyrs Is Seed"

The history of the expansion of Christianity has proved that "the blood of the martyrs is seed" — the seed of new life in Christ spreading through the world. For almost three hundred years Christianity grew in soil that was wet with the blood of the martyrs. In his *History of Christian Missions,* Stephen Neil mentions the sufferings of the early Christians as one of the six main reasons the church grew so rapidly.

> Because of their dangerous situation vis-á-vis the law, Christians were almost bound to meet in secret. . . . Every Christian knew that sooner or later he might have to testify to his faith at the cost of his life. . . . When persecution did break out, martyrdom could be attended by the utmost possible publicity. The Roman public was hard and cruel, but it was not altogether without compassion; and there is no doubt that the attitude of the martyrs, and particularly of the young women who suffered along with the men, made a deep impression. . . . In the earlier records what we find is calm, dignified, decorous behaviour; cool courage in the face of torment, courtesy towards enemies, and a joyful acceptance of suffering as the way appointed by the Lord to lead to his heavenly kingdom. There are a number of well-authenticated cases of conversion of pagans in the very moment of witnessing the condemnation and death of Christians; there must have been far more who received impressions that in the course of time would be turned into a living faith.[5]

"How Can I Blaspheme My King Who Saved Me?"

One example of such a powerful witness through suffering was the martyrdom of Polycarp, the Bishop of Smyrna who died in A.D. 155. His student Irenaeus said that Polycarp had been the student of the apostle John. We know he was very old when he died because, when the Proconsul commanded him to recant and curse Christ, he said, "Eighty and six years have I served him and he hath done me no wrong; how then can I blaspheme my king who saved me?"[6]

During one season of persecution a frenzied crowd in Smyrna cried out for a search to be made for Polycarp. He had moved to a town just outside the city, and three days before his death he had a dream from which he concluded, "I must needs be burned alive." So when the search was finally made, instead of fleeing he said, "The will of God be done." The ancient account of the martyrdom gives the following record:

So, hearing of their arrival, he came down and talked with them, while all that were present marveled at his age and constancy, and that there was so much ado about the arrest of such an old man. Then he ordered that something should be served for them to eat and drink, at that late hour, as much as they wanted. And he besought them that they should grant him an hour that he might pray freely. They gave him leave, and he stood and prayed, being so filled with the grace of God that for two hours he could not hold his peace, while they that heard were amazed, and the men repented that they had come after so venerable an old man.[7]

When he was finally taken away and condemned to burning, they tried to nail his hands to the stake, but he pled against it and said, "Let me be as I am. He that granted me to endure the fire will grant me also to remain at the pyre unmoved without being secured with nails."[8] When his body seemed not to be consumed by the fire, an executioner drove a dagger into his body. The ancient account concludes, "All the multitude marveled at the great difference between the unbelievers and the elect."[9] In large measure this is what explains the triumph of Christianity in the early centuries. They triumphed by their suffering. It did not just accompany their witness, it was the capstone of their witness. "They overcame [Satan] because of the blood of the Lamb and because of the word of their testimony, and *they did not love their life even to death*" (Revelation 12:11).

Not Till the Number of the Martyrs Is Complete

It is not a fluke of history that the church expands and is strengthened by suffering and martyrdom. This is the way God means it to be. One of the most powerful evidences that God intends to complete his saving purposes in the world by means of suffering is found in the book of Revelation. The setting is a vision of heaven where the souls of the martyrs cry out, "How long O Lord?" In other words, when will history be complete and your purposes of salvation and judgment be accomplished? The answer is ominous for all of us who want to be a part of the completion of the Great Commission. "They were told to rest a little longer, until the number of their fellow servants and their brothers should be complete, who were to be killed as they themselves had been" (Revelation 6:11).

What this means is that God has planned to complete his purposes by appointing a certain number of martyrs. When that number is complete, then the end will come. George Otis shocked many at the second Lausanne

Congress on World Evangelization in Manila in 1989 when he asked, "Is our failure to thrive in Muslim countries owing to the absence of martyrs? Can a covert church grow in strength? Does a young church need martyr models?" Fittingly he concludes his book, *The Last of the Giants*, with a chapter titled "Risky Safety."

> Should the Church in politically or socially trying circumstances remain covert to avoid potential eradication by forces hostile to Christianity? Or would more open confrontation with prevailing spiritual ignorance and deprivation — even if it produced Christian martyrs — be more likely to lead to evangelistic breakthroughs? Islamic fundamentalists claim that their spiritual revolution is fueled by the blood of martyrs. Is it conceivable that Christianity's failure to thrive in the Muslim world is due to the notable absence of Christian martyrs? And can the Muslim community take seriously the claims of a Church in hiding? . . . The question is not whether it is wise at times to keep worship and witness discreet, but rather how long this may continue before we are guilty of "hiding our light under a bushel. . . . The record shows that from Jerusalem and Damascus to Ephesus and Rome, the apostles were beaten, stoned, conspired against and imprisoned for their witness. Invitations were rare, and never the basis for their missions."[10]

Otis would no doubt agree with Gregory the Great (pope from 590 to 604), when he said, "The death of the martyrs blossoms in the lives of the faithful."[11]

The Blood Flowed from Our Wounds like a Fountain

There are countless examples in our own day of *choosing* to suffer for the purpose of Colossians 1:24 — to complete what is lacking in Christ's afflictions by presenting them to others through suffering.[12] As I was writing this chapter in late 1995, a missionary letter describing such suffering came to my attention. I quickly E-mailed the missionary in Africa to confirm the facts. He spoke personally with Dansa, the man in question, and got his permission for me to quote this story in Dansa's words from the letter.

> Around 1980 there was a time of severe persecution from the local officials of the communist government in my area of Wolayta. At the time, I was working in a government office, but

I was also serving as the leader of the Christian youth association for all the churches in my area. The communist officials repeatedly came to me to ask for my help in teaching the doctrines of the revolution among the youth. Many other Christians were giving in because the pressure was very great, but I could only say no.

At first, their approach was positive: they offered me promotions and pay increases. But then the imprisonments began. The first two were fairly short. The third time lasted an entire year. During this time communist cadres would regularly come to brainwash the nine of us believers (six men and three women — one of whom would later become my wife) who were being held together. But when one of the cadres converted to Christ, we were beaten and forced to haul water from long distances and carry heavy stones to clear farm land.

The worst time came during a two-week period in which the prison official would wake us early while it was still dark when no one could see and force us to walk on our bare knees over a distance of up to 1 1/2 kilometers on the gravel road of the town. It would take us about three hours. After the first day, the blood flowed from our wounds like a fountain, but we felt nothing.

On another occasion one particularly brutal prison official forced us to lie on our backs under the blazing sun for six straight hours. I don't know why I said it, but when we finished I told him, "You caused the sun's rays to strike us, but God will strike you." A short time later, the official contracted severe diabetes and died.

When the communist government fell several years later, the head official invited us back to preach in the jail. At that time, twelve prisoners being held for murder received Christ. We have continued to minister in the prison, and there are now 170 believers. Most of the prison officials have also believed.

Only God can sort out all the influences that led to this remarkable time of harvest among the prison inmates and officials. But surely it would be naive to think that the suffering of Dansa was not part of the compelling presentation of the reality of Christ in the lives of those who believed.

Demoted for Christ and for Salvation

Joseph Tson has thought deeply about the issue of suffering for Christ as a way to show Christ to the world. He was the pastor of the Second Baptist Church of Oradea, Romania, until 1981 when he was exiled by the government. I have heard him interpret Colossians 1:24 by saying that Christ's suffering is for *propitiation,* our suffering is for *propagation.* He points out that not only Colossians 1:24, but also 2 Timothy 2:10 makes suffering the means of evangelism: "I endure all things of the sake of the elect, so that they may obtain the salvation which is in Jesus Christ." According to Joseph Tson, Paul is saying,

> If I had remained a pastor in Antioch, in that affluent and peaceful city, in that wonderful church with so many prophets and such great blessings, nobody in Asia Minor or Europe would have been saved. In order for them to be saved, I have had to accept being beaten with rods, scourged, stoned, treated as the scum of the earth, becoming a walking death. But when I walk like this, wounded and bleeding, people see the love of God, people hear the message of the cross, and they are saved. If we stay in the safety of our affluent churches and we do not accept the cross, others may not be saved. How many are not saved because we don't accept the cross?[13]

He illustrates how the very suffering of Christians itself is what often provides the means of fruitful evangelism.

> I had a man in an important position whom I baptized come to me and ask, "Now what shall I do? They will convene three or four thousand people to expose me and mock me. They will give me five minutes to defend myself. How should I do it?"
>
> "Brother," I told him, "defending yourself is the only thing you shouldn't do. This is your unique chance to tell them who you were before, and what Jesus made of you; who Jesus is, and what he is for you now."
>
> His face shone and he said, "Brother Joseph, I know what I am going to do." And he did it well — so well that afterwards he was severely demoted. He lost almost half of his salary. But he kept coming to me after that saying, "Brother Joseph, you know I cannot walk in that factory now without someone coming up

to me. Wherever I go, somebody pulls me in a corner, looks around to see that nobody sees him talking to me, and then whispers, 'Give me the address of your church,' or 'Tell me more about Jesus,' or 'Do you have a Bible for me?' "

Every kind of suffering can become a ministry for other people's salvation.[14]

Choosing to Suffer for the Sake of the Nations

I conclude, then, that when Paul said, "If for this life only we have hoped in Christ, we are of all men most to be pitied," he meant that Christianity means choosing and embracing a life of suffering for Christ that would be pitiable if Christ proved false. Christianity is not a life that one would embrace as abundant and satisfying without the hope of fellowship with Christ in the resurrection. And what we have seen is that this embracing of suffering is not just an accompaniment of our witness to Christ, it is the visible expression of it. Our sufferings make Christ's sufferings known, so that people can see the kind of love Christ offers. We complete Christ's afflictions by providing what they do not have, namely, a personal, vivid presentation to those who did not see Christ suffer in person.

The startling implication of this is that the saving purposes of Christ among the nations and in our neighborhoods will not be accomplished unless Christians choose to suffer. At the extreme end of this suffering, the number of martyrs is not yet complete (Revelation 6:11). Without them, the final frontiers of world evangelization will not be crossed. Less extreme is the simple costliness in time and convenience and money and effort to replace excessive and addictive leisure with acts of servant love: "Let your light so shine that men may see your good deeds and give glory to your Father in heaven" (Matthew 5:16).

But Is This Christian Hedonism?

I have titled this chapter "Suffering: the Sacrifice of Christian Hedonism" even though on page 204 I quoted David Livingstone as saying that the sufferings of his missionary service were not a "sacrifice." This is not a contradiction or a disagreement with Livingstone. Words are like that. Context is almost everything. When he says suffering is not a sacrifice, he means the blessings outweigh the losses. When I say that suffering is a sacrifice, I mean that there are losses — great losses. When you realize that I agree with Livingstone, it simply implies that I see the blessings as massive.

But I am going to retain the use of the word sacrifice. The pain is too great, the losses too real to pretend that we can only talk in terms of no-sacrifice. We must simply keep our definitions clear.

My answer is, Yes, this is Christian Hedonism. The entire New Testament treats suffering in a Christian Hedonist context.

Was Paul pursuing deep and lasting joy when he chose suffering — so much suffering that his life would have been utterly foolish and pitiable if there were no resurrection from the dead? The question virtually answers itself. If it is the resurrection alone that makes Paul's painful life-choices *not* pitiable but praiseworthy (and possible!), then it is precisely his hope and quest for that resurrection that sustains and empowers his suffering. This is, in fact, exactly what he says: he counts all ordinary human privileges as loss "that I may know [Christ] and the power of his resurrection and the fellowship of his sufferings, being conformed to his death; *in order that I may attain to the resurrection from the dead*" (Philippians 3:10-11). His aim is to so live — and suffer — that he is assured of resurrection from the dead.

Giving All to Gain Christ

Why? Because resurrection meant full, bodily, eternal fellowship with Christ. That was the center of Paul's hope: "I count [all things] but rubbish in order that I may gain Christ" (Philippians 3:8). Gaining Christ was Paul's great passion and goal in all he did. "To live is Christ and to die is gain" (Philippians 1:21). Gain! Gain! This is the goal of his life and suffering. Paul "desired to depart and be with Christ, for that is *very much better.*" (Philippians 1:23). "Very much better" is not an altruistic motive. It is a Christian Hedonist motive. Paul wanted what would bring the deepest and most lasting satisfaction to his life, namely, being with Christ in glory.

But not alone with Christ in glory!

No one who knows and loves Christ can be content to come to him alone. The apex of his glory is this: "You were slain, and purchased for God, with your blood, persons from every tribe and tongue and people and nation" (Revelation 5:9). If this is the summit of Christ's glorious mercy, then those who count it their infinite gain, cannot live for private pleasures. The pleasures at Christ's right hand are public pleasures, shared pleasures, communal pleasures. When Paul said that he counted everything as loss in order to gain Christ, his losses were all for the sake of bringing others with him to Christ. "If I am to be poured upon the sacrifice and service of *your faith,* I rejoice, indeed I rejoice with you all" (Philippians 2:17). The pouring out of his life in sufferings was, to be sure, "that he might gain Christ," but it was also that he might gain *the faith* of the nations that magnifies the mercy of Christ.

My Joy, My Crown of Exultation!

This is why Paul called the people he had won to faith *his joy.* "My loved brothers, my desired ones, *my joy* and crown, so stand firm in the Lord, my loved ones" (Philippians 4:1). "Who is our hope or *joy* or crown of exultation? Is it not even you, in the presence of our Lord Jesus at His coming? For you are our glory and *joy*" (1 Thessalonians 2:19-20). The church was his joy because in their joy in Christ his joy in Christ was greater. More of Christ's mercy was magnified in multiplied converts of the cross. So when Paul chose suffering in the cause of world evangelization and said that his aim was to "gain Christ," he meant that his own personal enjoyment of fellowship with Christ would be eternally greater because of the great assembly of the redeemed enjoying Christ with him.

Even though I am not as far along as Paul was in his passionate love for the church, I thank God that there have been key points in my life where God has rescued me from the pit of cynicism. I recall the days as I was finishing college and starting seminary. The mood in the late sixties was inhospitable to the local church. I can remember walking the streets of Pasadena on Sunday mornings in the fall of 1968, wondering if there was any future for the church — like a fish doubting the worth of water, or a bird wondering about the reason for wind and air. It was a precious work of grace that God rescued me from that folly and gave me a home with the people of God at Lake Avenue Church for three years, and let me see in the heart of Ray Ortlund, my pastor, a man who exuded the spirit of Paul when he looked out on his flock and said, "My joy, my crown of exultation."

Ten years later there was another moment of crisis as I stood at my table late at night in October of 1979 writing in my journal. The issue was, would I remain as a professor at Bethel College teaching Biblical Studies, or would I resign and look for a pastorate? One of the things God was doing in those days was giving me a deeper love for the church — the gathered, growing, ministering body of people that meet week in and week out and move into the likeness of Christ. Teaching had its joys. It is a great calling. But that night another passion triumphed, and God led me, over the next months, to Bethlehem Baptist Church. As I write these words, it has been over fifteen years. If I allow myself, the tears come fairly easily when I think about what these people mean to me. They know, I hope, that my great passion is to "gain Christ." And unless I am mistaken, they also know that I live for "the advancement and joy of their faith" (Philippians 1:25). It is the aim of my writing and preaching to show that these two aims are one. I gain more of Christ in one converted sinner and growing saint than in a hundred ordinary chores. To say that Christ is my joy and Bethlehem is my joy is not double talk.

If Joy in Suffering Is Admirable, Pursue It

It should not surprise us, even though it is utterly unnatural, that Paul should say in Colossians 1:24, "I *rejoice* in my sufferings for you and I complete in my flesh what is lacking in the afflictions of Christ." In other words, when I complete Christ's afflictions by making a personal presentation of them to you in my own afflictions and pain, I rejoice. I rejoice.

Christian Hedonism simply says this is a good and admirable thing that Paul is doing, and we should go and do likewise. To treat this magnificent spiritual event of joy in suffering as something small or incidental or not-to-be-pursued is close to blasphemy. I say this carefully. When the Holy Spirit himself does such a great thing, and thus magnifies the all-sufficiency of Christ in suffering, it is close to blasphemy to say, "It is permissible to experience suffering for others, but not to pursue the joy." The Christ-exalting miracle is not just the suffering, but the joy in suffering. And we are meant to pursue it. In 1 Thessalonians 1:6-7 Paul says, "You . . . received the word in much tribulation with the *joy of the Holy Spirit,* so that you *became an example* to all the believers in Macedonia and in Achaia." Notice two crucial things: First, joy in tribulation is the work of the Holy Spirit; second, it is an example for others to follow. Beware of those who belittle the miracles of the Spirit of God by saying they are good gifts but not good goals.

Rejoice in Persecution, Your Reward Is Great!

Christian Hedonism says that there are different ways to rejoice in suffering as a Christian. All of them are to be pursued as an expression of the all-sufficient, all-satisfying grace of God. One way is expressed by Jesus in Matthew 5:11-12. "Blessed are you when men cast insults at you, and persecute you, and say all kinds of evil against you falsely, on account of me. *Rejoice, and be glad,* for *your reward in heaven is great*" (cf. Luke 6:22-23). One way of rejoicing in suffering comes from fixing our minds firmly on the greatness of the reward that will come to us in the resurrection. The effect of this kind of focus is to make our present pain seem small by comparison to what is coming. "I consider that the sufferings of this present time are not worthy to be compared with the glory that is to be revealed to us" (Romans 8:18; cf. 2 Corinthians 4:16-18). In making the suffering tolerable, rejoicing over our reward will also make love possible, as we saw in chapter four. "Love your enemies and do good, expecting nothing in return; and *your reward will be great*" (Luke 6:35). Be generous with the poor "and you will be blessed, since they do not have the means to repay you; for *you will be repaid at the resurrection of the just"* (Luke 14:14).

Rejoice in Affliction, It Deepens Assurance!

Another way of rejoicing in suffering comes from the effects of suffering on our assurance of hope. Joy in affliction is rooted in the hope of resurrection, but our experience of suffering also deepens the root of that hope. For example, Paul says, "We exult in our afflictions, knowing that affliction produces endurance, and endurance produces proven genuineness, and genuineness produces hope" (Romans 5:3-4). Here Paul's joy is not merely rooted in his great reward, but in the effect of suffering to solidify his hope in that reward. Afflictions produce endurance and endurance produces a sense that our faith is real and genuine, and that strengthens our hope that we will indeed gain Christ.

Richard Wurmbrand describes how one may survive the moments of excruciating pain of torture for Christ.

> You have been so much tortured, nothing counts any more. If nothing counts any more, my survival doesn't count either. If nothing counts any more, the fact that I should not have pain also does not count. Draw this last conclusion at the stage at which you have arrived and you will see that you will overcome this moment of crisis. If you have overcome this one moment of crisis, it gives you an intense inner joy. You feel that Christ has been with you in that decisive moment.[15]

The "intense joy" comes from the sense that you endured with the help of Christ. You have been proven in the fire and you have come through as genuine. You did not recant. Christ is real in your life. He is for you the all-satisfying God that he claims to be. This is what the apostles seemed to experience according to Acts 5:41 when, after being beaten, "they went on their way from the presence of the Council, *rejoicing that they had been considered worthy to suffer shame for his name."* The joy came from the thought that their faith was regarded by God as real and ready to be proved in the fire of affliction.

Rejoice in Suffering with Christ, It Leads to Glory!

Another way of rejoicing in suffering is kindled by the truth that our joy itself is a proven pathway to glory. Joy in suffering comes not only 1) from focusing on our reward, and 2) from the solidifying effect of suffering on our sense of genuineness, but also 3) from the promise that joy in suffering will secure eternal joy in the future. The apostle Peter expresses it like this: "To the degree that you share the sufferings of Christ, keep on rejoicing; *so that* also at the revelation of his glory, you may rejoice with exultation" (1 Peter 4:13). Joy now in suffering is the appointed pathway to the final rejoicing at the revelation of Christ. Peter is calling us to pursue joy now in suffering (he commands it!) so that we will be found among those who rejoice exceedingly at the coming of Christ.

Rejoice in Suffering for Others, They See Christ!

The fourth way of rejoicing in suffering we have seen already. It comes from realizing that through our suffering others are seeing the worth of Christ and standing firm because of our faith in the fire. Paul says to the Thessalonians, "Now we really live, if you stand firm in the Lord. For what thanks can we render to God for you in return for *all the joy with which we rejoice because of you before our God*" (1 Thessalonians 3:8-9). This is the joy of Colossians 1:24, "I rejoice in my sufferings for you." When we suffer to show others the love of Christ and the worth of Christ, it is because every new convert that stands firm in faith is a new, unique prism for refracting the all-satisfying glory of Christ. The joy we feel in them is not a different joy than we feel in Christ. The glory of Christ is our "great gain." For this we will suffer the loss of anything and everything. And everyone who sees in our suffering the superior worth of Christ, and believes, is another image and evidence of that great worth — and therefore another reason to rejoice.

The Happiest People in the World

The Calvary road with Jesus is not a joyless road. It is a painful one, but it is a profoundly happy one. When we choose the fleeting pleasures of comfort and security over the sacrifices and sufferings of missions and evangelism and ministry and love, we choose against joy. We reject the spring whose waters never fail (Isaiah 58:11). The happiest people in the world are the people who experience the mystery of "Christ in them, the hope of glory" (Colossians 1:27), satisfying their deep longings and freeing them to extend the afflictions of Christ through their own sufferings to the world.

God is calling us to live for the sake of Christ and to do that through suffering. Christ chose suffering; it didn't just happen to him. He chose it as the way to create and perfect the church. Now he calls us to choose suffering. That is, he calls us to take up our cross and follow him on the Calvary road and deny ourselves and make sacrifices for the sake of ministering to the church and presenting his sufferings to the world.

Brother Andrew, who heads a ministry called Open Doors and who is most famous for his 1967 book, *God's Smuggler*, describes Christ's call in the mid 1990s like this:

> There's not one door in the world closed where you want to witness for Jesus. . . . Show me a closed door and I will tell you how you can get in. I won't however, promise you a way to get out. . . .
>
> Jesus didn't say, "Go if the doors are open," because they weren't. He didn't say, "Go if you have an invitation or a red carpet treatment." He said, "Go," because people needed his Word. . . .
>
> We need a new approach to missions — an aggressive, experimental, evangelical, no-holds-barred approach . . . a pioneering spirit. . . .
>
> I'm afraid we'll have to go through a deep valley of need and threatening situations, blood baths; but we'll get there.
>
> God will take away what hinders us if we mean business. If we say, "Lord, at any cost . . ." — and people should never pray that unless they truly want God to take them at their word — he will answer. Which is scary. But we have to go through the process. This is how it has worked in the Bible for the last two thousand years.
>
> So we face potentially hard times, and we have to go through that. . . . We play church and we play Christianity. And we aren't even aware we are lukewarm. . . . We should have to pay a price for our faith. Read 2 Timothy 3:12: "Indeed, all who want to live a godly life in Christ Jesus will be persecuted." The church has been much purified in countries where there was a lot of pressure. . . . All I can say is to be ready.[16]

Not to Prove Our Power, but His Preciousness

The answer to this call is a radical step of Christian Hedonism. We do not choose suffering simply because we are told to, but because the one who tells us to describes it as the path to everlasting joy. He beckons us into the obedience of suffering not to demonstrate the strength of our devotion to duty, nor to reveal the vigor of our moral resolve, nor to prove the heights of our tolerance for pain; but rather to manifest, in childlike faith, the infinite preciousness of his all-satisfying promises. Moses *"chose* to share ill-treatment with the people of God rather than enjoy the fleeting pleasures of sin . . . because he looked to the reward" (Hebrews 11:25-26). Therefore his obedience glorified the God of grace, not the resolve to suffer.

The Essence of Christian Hedonism

This is the essence of Christian Hedonism. In the pursuit of joy through suffering, we magnify the all-satisfying worth of the Source of our joy. God himself shines as the brightness at the end of our tunnel of pain. If we do not communicate that he is the goal and the ground of our joy in suffering, then the very meaning of our suffering will be lost. The meaning is this: God is gain. God is gain. God is gain.

The chief end of man is to glorify God. And it is more true in suffering than anywhere else that *God is most glorified in us when we are most satisfied in him.* My prayer, therefore, is that the Holy Spirit would pour out on his people around the world a passion for the supremacy of God in all things. And I pray that he would make it plain that the pursuit of joy in God, whatever the pain, is a powerful testimony to God's supreme and all-satisfying worth. And so may it come to pass, as we "complete what is lacking in Christ's afflictions," that all the peoples of the world will see the love of Christ and magnify his grace in the gladness of faith.

WHY I HAVE WRITTEN THIS BOOK

Seven Reasons

Reason One: It's My Pleasure!

> I wrote as I did so that when I came I might not be pained by those who should have made me rejoice, for I felt sure of you, that my joy would be the joy of you all. (2 Corinthians 2:3)

> We are writing this that our joy may be complete. (1 John 1:4)

When you are a starving man among starving people, and you discover a banquet in the wilderness, you become a debtor to all. And the payment of that debt is delightful in proportion to the magnificence of the banquet.

I have felt like the lepers of Samaria. The Syrians surrounded the capital of Israel. Inside the besieged city the fourth part of a kab of dove's dung sold for five shekels, and women boiled their children for food. But outside the city, unknown to the people within, the Lord had sent the Syrians fleeing. And there in the wilderness was laid a banquet of salvation.

The lepers realized they had nothing to lose. So they ventured into the enemy camp, and found the enemy gone but all their provisions left behind. At first they began to hoard the treasures for themselves. But then the first rays of Christian Hedonism began to dawn on them:

> They said to one another, "We are not doing right. This day is a day of good news; if we are silent and wait until the morning light, punishment will overtake us; now therefore come, let us go and tell the king's household." (2 Kings 7:9)

This was the text from which Daniel Fuller preached at my ordination service in 1975. It was prophetic. For I have been a leper stumbling again and again onto the banquet of God in the wilderness of this world. And I have discovered that the banquet tastes far sweeter when I eat it with the widows of Samaria than when I hoard it in the desert.

I am radically committed to the pursuit of full and lasting joy. And so my ear has not been deaf to the wisdom of words like these from Karl Barth:

> It must be said that we can have joy, and therefore will it, only as we give it to others . . . . There may be cases where a man can be really merry in isolation. But these are exceptional and dangerous . . . . It certainly gives us ground to suspect the nature of his joy as real joy if he does not desire — "Rejoice with me" — that at least one or some or many others, as representatives of the rest, should share this joy . . . . We may succeed in willing joy exclusively for ourselves, but we have to realize that in this case, unless a miracle happens (and miracles are difficult to imagine for such a purpose), this joy will not be true, radiant and sincere.[1]

The motive for writing this book is the desire to double my joy in God's banquet of grace by sharing it with as many as I can. I write this to you that my joy might be full.

Reason Two: God Is Breathtaking!

> One thing have I asked of the Lord,
> that will I seek after;
> that I may dwell in the house of the Lord
> all the days of my life,
> to behold the beauty of the Lord,
> and to inquire in his temple.
> (Psalm 27:4)

I saw the Lord sitting upon a throne, high and lifted up; and his train filled the temple. Above him stood the seraphim; each had six wings: With two he covered his face, and with two he covered his feet, and with two he flew. And one called to another and said:

> "Holy, holy, holy is the Lord of hosts;
> the whole earth is full of his glory."
> (Isaiah 6:1-3)

If you are a guide on a sightseeing trip, and you know the people are longing to enjoy beauty, and you come upon some breathtaking ravine, then you should show it to them and urge them to enjoy it. Well, the human race does in fact crave the experience of awe and wonder. And there is no reality more breathtaking than God.

The Preacher said,

> God has made everything beautiful in its time; also he has put eternity into man's mind, yet so that he cannot find out what God has done from the beginning to the end. (Ecclesiastes 3:11)

Eternity is in the heart of man filling him with longing. But we know not what we long for until we see the breathtaking God. This is the cause of universal restlessness.

> Thou madest us for Thyself,
> and our heart is restless,
> until it rest in Thee.
> Saint Augustine

> When God at first made man,
> Having a glass of blessings standing by —
> Let us (said He) pour on him all we can;
> Let the world's riches which dispersed lie,
> Contract into a span.
> So strength first made a way;
> Then beauty flow'd, then wisdom, honour, pleasure:
> When almost all was out, God made a stay,
> Perceiving that, alone, of all His treasure,
> Rest in the bottom lay.
> For if I should (said He)
> Bestow this jewel also on My creature,
> He would adore My gifts instead of Me,
> And rest in nature, not the God of Nature:
> So both should losers be.
> Yet let him keep the rest,
> But keep them with repining restlessness;
> Let him be rich and weary, that at least,
> If goodness lead him not, yet weariness
> May toss him to My breast.
> George Herbert, "The Pulley"

The world has an inconsolable longing. It tries to satisfy the longing with scenic vacations, accomplishments of creativity, stunning cinematic productions, sexual exploits, sports extravaganzas, hallucinogenic drugs, ascetic rigors, managerial excellence, et cetera. But the longing remains. What does this mean?

> If I find in myself a desire which no experience in this world can satisfy, the most probable explanation is that I was made for another world.[2]

> It was when I was happiest that I longed most. . . . The sweetest thing in all my life has been the longing . . . to find the place where all the beauty came from.[3]

The tragedy of the world is that the echo is mistaken for the Original Shout. When our back is to the breathtaking beauty of God, we cast a shadow on the earth and fall in love with it. But it does not satisfy.

> The books or the music in which we thought the beauty was located will betray us if we trust to them; it was not in them, it only came through them, and what came through them was longing. These things — the beauty, the memory of our own past — are good images of what we really desire; but if they are mistaken for the thing itself they turn into dumb idols, breaking the hearts of their worshipers. For they are not the thing itself; they are only the scent of a flower we have not found, the echo of a tune we have not heard, news from a country we have never yet visited.[4]

I have written this book because the breathtaking Beauty has visited us. "The Word became flesh and dwelt among us, full of grace and truth; we have beheld his glory (his beauty!), glory as of the only Son from the Father" (John 1:14). How can we not cry, Look!

Reason Three: The Word of God Commands Us to Pursue Our Joy

> Delight yourself in the LORD!
> (Psalm 37:4)

> Rejoice in the Lord always;
> and again I will say, Rejoice.
> (Philippians 4:4)

And the Word of God threatens terrible things if we will not be happy:

> Because you did not serve the LORD your God with joyfulness and gladness of heart, by reason of the abundance of all things,

therefore you shall serve your enemies whom the LORD your
God will send against you. (Deuteronomy 28:47-48)

But there are numerous objections to Christian Hedonism at this point.

Objection One

Someone may object, No, you should not pursue your joy. You should pursue God. This is a helpful objection. It forces us to make several needed clarifications.

The objector is absolutely right that if we focus our attention on our own subjective experience of joy, we will most certainly be frustrated and God will not be honored. When you go to an art museum, you had better attend to the paintings and not your pulse. Otherwise there will be no delight in the beauty of the art.

But beware of jumping to the conclusion that we should no longer say, "Come and take delight in these paintings." Do not jump to the conclusion that the command to pursue joy is misleading while the command to look at the paintings is not.

What would you say is wrong with the person who comes to the art museum looking for a particular painting because he knows he can make a big profit if he buys and resells it? He goes from room to room, looking carefully at each painting. He is not the least preoccupied with his subjective, aesthetic experience. What is wrong here?

He is mercenary. His reason for looking is not the reason the painting was created. You see, it is not enough to say our pursuit should simply be the paintings. For there are ways to pursue the paintings that are bad.

One common way of guarding against this mercenary spirit is to say we should pursue art for art's sake. But what does this mean? It means, I think, pursuing art in a way that honors art and not money. But how do you honor art? I would answer: you honor art mainly by experiencing an appropriate emotion when you look at it.

We know we will miss this emotion if we are self-conscious while beholding the painting. We also know we will miss it if we are money-conscious or fame-conscious or power-conscious when we look at the painting. It seems to me therefore that a helpful way to admonish visitors to the art museum is to say, "Delight yourself in the paintings!"

The word "delight" guards them from thinking they should pursue money or fame or power with the paintings. And the phrase "in the paintings" guards them from thinking the emotion which honors the paintings could be experienced any other way than by focusing on the paintings themselves.

So it is with God. We are commanded by the Word of God, "Delight yourself in the LORD." This means: Pursue joy in God. The word "joy" or "delight" protects us from a mercenary pursuit of God. And the phrase "in God" protects us from thinking joy somehow stands alone as an experience separate from our experience of God himself.

Objection Two

The most common objection against the command to pursue joy is that Jesus commanded just the opposite when he called for our self-denial: "Whoever would save his life will lose it, and whoever loses his life for my sake and the gospel's will save it" (Mark 8:35). We have dealt with this already (p.202), but it may be helpful to draw in one other text to illustrate that *biblical self-denial* means "Deny yourselves lesser joys so you don't lose the big ones." Which is the same as saying: *Really* pursue joy! Don't settle for anything less than full and lasting joy.

Consider Hebrews 12:15-17 as an example of how one person failed to practice self-denial, to his own destruction.

> See to it that no one fail to obtain the grace of God; that no root of bitterness spring up and cause trouble, and by it the many become defiled; that no one be immoral or irreligious like Esau, who sold his birthright for a single meal. For you know that afterward, when he desired to inherit the blessing, he was rejected, for he found no chance to repent, though he sought it with tears.

Esau lost his life because he preferred the pleasure of a single meal above the blessings of his birthright in the chosen family. This is a picture of all people who refuse to deny themselves the "fleeting pleasures of sin" (Hebrews 11:25). But note well! The main evil is not in choosing a meal, but in despising his birthright. Self-denial is never a virtue in itself. It has value precisely in proportion to the superiority of the reality embraced above the one denied. Self-denial that is not based on a desire for some superior goal will become the ground of boasting.

Objection Three

The third objection to the command to seek our joy can be stated like this:

> You have argued that the pursuit of pleasure is a necessary part of all worship and virtue. You said that if we try to abandon this

pursuit we cannot honor God or love people. But can you make this square with Romans 9:3 and Exodus 32:32? It seems that Paul and Moses do indeed abandon the pursuit of their own pleasure when they express a willingness to be damned for the salvation of Israel.

These are startling verses!

In Romans 9:3, Paul expresses his heartache over the cursed condition of most of his Jewish kinsmen. He says, "I could wish that I myself were accursed and cut off from Christ for the sake of my brethren, my kinsmen by race."

In Exodus 32 the people of Israel have committed idolatry. The wrath of God burns against them. Moses takes the place of a mediator to protect the people. He prays, "Alas, these people have sinned a great sin; they have made for themselves gods of gold. But now, if thou wilt forgive their sin — and if not, blot me, I pray thee, out of thy book which thou hast written" (Exodus 32:31-32).

First, we must realize that these two instances do not present us with the same problem. Moses' prayer does not necessarily include a reference to eternal damnation like Paul's does. We must not assume that the "book" he refers to here carries the same eternal significance that the "book of life" does, say, in Philippians 4:3 and Revelation 13:8;17:8; 20:15; and 21:27.

George Bush argues that being blotted out of the book in Exodus 32:32

is tantamount to being taken out of life while others survive. There is no intimation in these words of any secret book of the divine decrees, or of anything involving the question of Moses' final salvation or perdition. He simply expressed the wish rather to die than to witness the destruction of his people. The phraseology is an allusion, probably, to the custom of having the names of a community enrolled in a register, and whenever one died, of erasing his name from the number.[5]

A person's willingness to die is not necessarily at odds with Christian Hedonism. Hebrews 11:26 says that "Moses considered abuse suffered for the Christ greater wealth than the treasures of Egypt, for he looked to the reward." There is no reason to think Moses stopped looking to the all-compensating reward when he struggled with the sin of Israel.

But this, of course, does not remove the main problem, which is Romans 9:3. Paul had written, "I could wish that I myself were accursed and cut off from Christ for the sake of my brethren." This appears to be a willingness to abandon the pursuit of happiness. Did Paul then cease to be a Christian Hedonist in expressing this kind of love for the lost?

Notice that he says, "I *could wish* that I myself were accursed." The reason for translating the verb as "I could wish . . ." is that the Greek imperfect tense is used to soften the expression and show that it cannot be carried through. Henry Alford says, "The sense of the imperfect in such expressions is the proper and strict one . . . : the act is unfinished, an obstacle intervening."[6]

The obstacle is the immediately preceding promise of Romans 8:38-39, "For I am sure that neither death nor life, nor angels, nor principalities, nor things present, nor things to come, nor powers, nor height, nor depth, nor anything else in all creation, will be able to separate us from the love of God in Christ Jesus." Paul knows it is impossible to take the place of his kinsmen in hell.

But he says he is willing to! This is the problem for Christian Hedonism. We simply must take this seriously. Paul ponders the hypothetical possibility of a world in which such a thing might be possible. Suppose there were a world in which an unconverted sinner and a man of faith could stand before the bar of God to receive judgment. And suppose that if the saint is willing, God would reverse their roles. If the saint is willing, God would withdraw his saving grace from the saint so he becomes fit for hell in unbelief and rebellion, and he would give converting grace to the unbeliever so that he trusts Christ and becomes fit for heaven.

In such a world, what would love require? It would require total self-sacrifice. And the principle of Christian Hedonism would cease to apply. But mark well! This hypothetical world does not exist! God did not create a world in which a person could be eternally damned for an act of love.

In the real world God made, we are never asked to make such a choice: Are you willing to become damnable for the salvation of others? Instead, we are constantly told that doing good to others will bring us great reward, *and* that we should pursue that reward.

Paradoxically, Paul's willingness to reach for a hypothetical case of ultimate sacrifice is a deep and dramatic way of saying with as much force as he knows how, "This, even this, is how much I delight in the prospect of Israel's salvation!" But immediately we see the impossibility of carrying through the wish: If their salvation were such a great delight to him, would hell really be hell? Could we really speak of hell as the place where Paul achieved his deepest and noblest desire of love? This is the sort of incongruity you run into in hypothetical worlds that do not exist.

Happiness would be impossible in any case in such a world. For if God gave a saint the option of becoming damnable to save another, such a saint could never live with himself if he said no. And he would suffer forever in hell if he said yes. He loses both ways.

But Christian Hedonism is not a philosophy for hypothetical worlds. It is based on the real world God has established and regulated in Holy Scripture. In this real world we are never urged or required to become evil that good may abound. We are always required to become good. This means becoming the kind of people who delight in the good, not just doing it dutifully. The Word of God commands us to pursue our joy.

Reason Four: Affections Are Essential to the Christian Life, Not Optional

It is astonishing to me that so many people try to define true Christianity in terms of decisions and not affections. Not that decisions are unessential. The problem is that they require so little transformation to achieve. They are evidence of no true work of grace in the heart. People can make "decisions" about the truth of God while their hearts are far from him.

We have moved far away from the Christianity of Jonathan Edwards. Edwards pointed to 1 Peter 1:8 and argued that "true religion, in great part, consists in the affections."

> Whom having not seen, you love; in whom, though now you
> see him not, yet believing, you rejoice with joy unspeakable,
> and full of glory. (1 Peter 1:8)

He points out that "true religion" has two kinds of operation in the souls of the saints, according to this text: love to Christ ("whom having not seen, you love"), and joy in Christ ("in whom . . . you rejoice with joy unspeakable and full of glory"). Both of these operations in the soul are affections, not merely decisions. Edward's conception of true Christianity was that the new birth really brought into being a new nature which had new affections.[7]

I find this supported throughout Scripture. We are commanded to feel, not just to think or decide. We are commanded to experience dozens of emotions, not just to perform acts of will power.

For example, we are commanded not to covet (Exodus 20:17), and it is obvious that every commandment not to have a certain feeling is also a commandment to feel a certain way. The opposite of covetousness is contentment with what we have, and this is exactly what we are commanded to experience in Hebrews 13:5 ("Be content with what you have").

We are commanded to bear no grudge but to forgive "from the heart" (Leviticus 19:17-18). Note: The law does not say, Make a mere decision to drop the matter. Rather it says, Experience an event in the heart (Matthew 18:35). Similarly, the intensity of the heart is commanded in 1 Peter 1:22 ("Love one another *earnestly* from the heart") and Romans 12:10 ("Love one another with brotherly *affection*").

Among other examples of emotions that the Scriptures command are these:

joy	(Psalm 100:2; Philippians 4:4; 1 Thessalonians 5:16; Romans 12:8,12,15)
hope	(Psalm 42:5; 1 Peter 1:13)
fear	(Luke 12:5; Romans 11:20; 1 Peter 1:17)
peace	(Romans 5:1; Colossians 3:15)
zeal	(Romans 12:11)
grief	(Romans 12:15; James 4:9)
desire	(1 Peter 2:2)
tenderheartedness	(Ephesians 4:32)
brokenness and contrition	(Psalm 51:17)
gratitude	(Ephesians 5:20; Colossians 3:17)
lowliness	(Philippians 2:3)

I do not believe it is possible to say scriptures like these all refer to optional icing on the cake of decision. They are commanded by the Lord who said, "Why do you call me Lord, Lord, and do not do what I tell you?" (Luke 6:46).

It is true our hearts are often sluggish. We do not feel the depth or intensity of affections appropriate for God or his cause. It is true that at those times we must, inasmuch as it lies within us, exert our wills and make decisions that we hope will rekindle our joy. Though joyless love is not our aim ("God loves a cheerful giver!"), nevertheless it is better to do a joyless duty than not to do it, provided there is a spirit of repentance for the deadness of our hearts.

I am often asked what a Christian should do if the cheerfulness of obedience is not there. It is a good question. My answer is not to simply get on with your duty because feelings are irrelevant! My answer has three steps. First, confess the sin of joylessness. Acknowledge the culpable coldness of your heart. Don't say it doesn't matter how you feel. Second, pray earnestly that God would restore the joy of obedience. Third, go ahead and do the outward dimension of your duty in the hope that the doing will rekindle the delight.

This is very different from saying: do your duty because feelings don't count. These steps are predicated on the assumption that there is such a thing as hypocrisy. They are based on the belief that our goal is the reunion of pleasure and duty, and that a justification of their separation is a justification of sin. John Murray puts it like this:

> There is no conflict between gratification of desire and the enhancement of man's pleasure, on the one hand, and fulfillment of God's command on the other. . . . The tension that often exists within us between a sense of duty and wholehearted spontaneity is a tension that arises from sin and a disobedient will. No such tension would have invaded the heart of unfallen man. And the operations of saving grace are directed to the end of removing the tension so that there may be, as there was with man at the beginning, the perfect complementation of duty and pleasure, of commandment and love.[8]

This is the goal of saving grace, and the goal of this book.

Reason Five: Christian Hedonism Combats Pride and Self-Pity
God does everything he does to exalt his mercy and abase man's pride.

> . . . that in the coming ages he might show the immeasurable riches of his grace . . . lest any man should boast. (Ephesians 2:7,9)

> He destined us in love to be his sons through Jesus Christ . . . to the praise of the glory of his grace. (Ephesians 1:5-6)

> God chose what is low and despised in the world . . . so that no human being might boast in the presence of God. (1 Corinthians 1:28-29)

Christian Hedonism combats pride because it puts man in the category of an empty vessel beneath the fountain of God. It guards us from the presumption of trying to be God's benefactors. Philanthropists can boast. Welfare recipients can't. The primary experience of the Christian Hedonist is *need*. When a little, helpless child is being swept off his feet by the undercurrent on the beach, and his father catches him just in time, the child does not boast; he hugs.

The nature and depth of human pride are illuminated by comparing boasting to self-pity. Both are manifestations of pride. Boasting is the response of pride to success. Self-pity is the response of pride to suffering. Boasting says, "I deserve admiration because I have achieved so much." Self-pity says, "I deserve admiration because I have sacrificed so much." Boasting is the voice of pride in the heart of the strong. Self-pity is the voice of pride in the heart of the weak. Boasting sounds self-sufficient. Self-pity sounds self-sacrificing.

The reason self-pity does not look like pride is that it appears to be needy. But the need arises from a wounded ego, and the desire of the self-pitying is not really for others to see them as helpless, but as heroes. The need self-pity feels does not come from a sense of unworthiness, but from a sense of unrecognized worthiness. It is the response of unapplauded pride.

Christian Hedonism severs the root of self-pity. People don't feel self-pity when suffering is accepted for the sake of joy.

> "Blessed are you when men revile you and persecute you and utter all kinds of evil against you falsely on my account. *Rejoice and be glad, for your reward is great in heaven,* for so men persecuted the prophets who were before you." (Matthew 5:11-12)

This is the ax laid to the root of self-pity. When we have to suffer on account of Christ, we do not summon up our own resources like heroes. Rather, we become like little children who trust the strength of their father and who want the joy of his reward. As we saw in the last chapter, the greatest sufferers for Christ have always deflected praise and pity by testifying to their Christian Hedonism.

> "I never made a sacrifice," said Hudson Taylor in later years, looking back over a life in which that element was certainly not lacking. But what he said was true, for the compensations were so real and lasting that he came to see that giving up is inevitably receiving, when one is dealing heart to heart with God. . . . The sacrifice was great, but the reward far greater.

> "Unspeakable joy [he tells us] all day long and every day, was my happy experience. God, even my God, was a living bright reality, and all I had to do was joyful service."[9]

"Giving up is inevitably receiving." This is the motto of Christian Hedonism and the demise of self-pity. You can see the principle at work among the godly again and again. For example, I knew a seminary professor who also served as an usher in the balcony of a big church. Once when he was to have part in a service, the pastor extolled him for his willingness to serve in this unglamorous role even though he had a doctorate in theology. The professor humbly deflected the praise by quoting Psalm 84:10:

> For a day in Thy courts is better than a thousand elsewhere. I would rather be a doorkeeper in the house of my God than dwell in the tents of wickedness.

In other words, don't think I am heroically overcoming great obstacles of disinclination to keep the doors of the sanctuary. The Word of God says it will bring great blessing!

Most people can recognize that doing something for the joy of it is a humbling experience. When a man takes friends out for dinner and picks up the check, his friends may begin to say how good it was of him to pay for them. But he simply lifts his hand in a gesture that says, Stop. And he says, "It's my pleasure." In other words, if I do a good deed for the joy of it, the impulse of pride is broken.

The breaking of that impulse is the will of God, and one of the reasons I have written this book.

Reason Six: Christian Hedonism Promotes Genuine Love for People

No one has ever felt unloved because he was told the attainment of his joy would make another person happy. I have never been accused of selfishness when justifying a kindness on the basis that it delights me. On the contrary, loving acts are genuine to the degree that they are not done begrudgingly. And the good alternative to begrudgingly is not neutrally or dutifully, but gladly. The authentic heart of love "loves mercy" (Micah 6:8); it doesn't just do mercy. Christian Hedonism forces this truth into consideration.

> (2) By this we know that we love the children of God, when we love God and obey his commandments. (3) For this is the love of God, that we keep his commandments. And his commandments are not burdensome. (4) For whatever is born of God overcomes the world. (1 John 5:2-4)

Read these sentences in reverse order and notice the logic. First, being born of God gives a power that conquers the world. This is given as the ground or basis ("For") for the statement that the commandments of God are not burdensome. So being born of God gives a power that conquers our worldly aversion to the will of God. Now his commandments are not "burdensome," but are the desire and delight of our heart. This is the love of God:

not just that we do his commandments, but also that they are not burdensome.

Then in verse 2 the evidence of the genuineness of our love for the children of God is said to be the love of God. What does this teach us about our love for the children of God? Since love for God is doing his will gladly rather than with a sense of burden, and since love for God is the measure of the genuineness of our love for the children of God, therefore our love for the children of God must also be done gladly rather than begrudgingly. Christian Hedonism stands squarely in the service of love, for it presses us on to glad obedience.

Jesus was big on giving alms. How did he motivate almsgiving? He said, "Sell your possessions, and give alms; provide yourselves with purses that do not grow old, with a treasure in the heavens that does not fail" (Luke 12:33). In other words, stop craving two-bit possessions on earth when you can have endless treasures in heaven by giving alms! (Remember Hudson Taylor: "Giving up is inevitably receiving.")

Or, a bit differently, but basically the same, he said, "When you give alms, do not let your left hand know what you right hand is doing, so that your alms may be in secret; and your Father who sees in secret will reward you" (Matthew 6:3-4). In other words, stop being motivated by the praises of men, and let the thought of God's reward move you to love.

Yes, it is real love when our alms are motivated by the heavenly treasure. It is not exploitation, because the loving almsgiver aims for his alms to rescue the beggar for that same reward. A Christian Hedonist is always aware that his own enjoyment of the Father's reward will be even greater when shared with the ones he has drawn into the heavenly fellowship.

My point is this: If Jesus thought it wise to motivate acts of love with promises of reward (Matthew 6:4) and treasures in heaven (Luke 12:33), it accords with his teaching to say Christian Hedonism promotes genuine love for people.

Consider another illustration. Hebrews 13:17 gives the following counsel to every local church.

> Obey your leaders and submit to them; for they are keeping
> watch over your souls, as men who will have to give account;
> that they might do this with joy and not with groaning, for that
> would not be profitable to you.

Now, if it is not profitable for pastors to do their oversight sadly instead of joyfully, then a pastor who does not seek to do his work with joy does not care for his flock. Not to pursue our joy in ministry is not to pursue the profit of our people.

This is why Paul admonished those who do acts of mercy to do them "with cheerfulness" (Romans 12:8), and why God loves a "cheerful giver" (2 Corinthians 9:7). Begrudging service does not qualify as love. The pursuit of joy through mercy is what makes love real. And that is one of the reasons I have written this book.

Reason Seven: Christian Hedonism Glorifies God

We have come back to where we began. And this is as it should be. "For from him and through him and to him are all things" (Romans 11:36).

Does Christian Hedonism put man's pleasure above God's glory? No. It puts man's pleasure *in* God's glory. Our quest is not merely joy. It is joy *in* God. And there is no way for a creature to consciously manifest the infinite worth and beauty of God without delighting in him. It is better to say that we pursue our joy *in* God than to simply say that we pursue God. For one can pursue God in ways that do not honor him.

> "What to me is the multitude of your sacrifices?" says the LORD;
> "I have had enough of burnt offerings of rams and the fat of fed
> beasts." (Isaiah 1:11)

Our solemn assemblies may be a stench in God's nose (cf. Amos 5:21-24). It is possible to pursue God without glorifying God. If we want our quest to honor God, we must pursue him for the joy in fellowship with him.

Consider the sabbath as an illustration of this. The Lord rebukes his people for seeking "their own" pleasure on his holy day. But what does he mean? He means they are delighting in their business and not in the beauty of their God. He does not rebuke their hedonism. He rebukes the weakness of it. They have settled for secular interests, and thus honor them above the Lord.

> If you turn back your foot from the sabbath,
> from doing your pleasure on my day,
> and *call the sabbath a delight*
> *and the holy day of the LORD honorable;*
> if you honor it, not going your own ways,
> or seeking your own pleasure, or talking idly;
> then you shall *take delight in the LORD,*
> and I will make you ride upon the heights of the earth;
> I will feed you with the heritage of Jacob your father,
> for the mouth of the LORD has spoken.
> (Isaiah 58:13-14)

Notice that calling the sabbath a *delight* is parallel to calling the holy day of the Lord *honorable*. This simply means you honor what you delight in. Or you glorify what you enjoy.

The enjoyment of God and the glorification of God are one. His eternal purpose and our eternal pleasure unite. To magnify his name and multiply your joy is the reason I have written this book, for

The chief end of man is to glorify God
BY
enjoying him forever.

APPENDIX 1

The Goal of God in Redemptive History

In chapter one I said God's ultimate goal in all that he does is to preserve and display his glory. I inferred from this that he is uppermost in his own affections. He prizes and delights in his own glory above all things. This appendix presents the biblical evidence for this statement. It is a brief survey of the high points of redemptive history with a view to why God does what he does.

First, a comment about terminology.

The term "glory of God" in the Bible generally refers to the visible splendor or moral beauty of God's manifold perfections. It is an attempt to put into words what cannot be contained in words — what God is like in his unveiled magnificence and excellence.

Another term which can signify much the same thing is "the name of God." When Scripture speaks of doing something "for God's name's sake" it means virtually the same as doing it "for his glory." The "name" of God is not merely his label, but a reference to his character. The term "glory" simply makes more explicit that the character of God is indeed magnificent and excellent. This is implicit in the term "name" when it refers to God.

What follows is an overview of some of the high points of redemptive history where Scripture makes clear the purpose of God. The aim is to discover the unifying goal of God in all that he does.

OLD TESTAMENT

Creation

> Then God said, "Let us make man in our image, after our likeness; and let them have dominion over the fish of the sea, and over the birds of the air, and over the cattle, and over all the earth, and over every creeping thing that creeps upon the earth." So God created man in his own image, in the image of God he created him; male and female he created them. (Genesis 1:26-27)

The biblical story of creation reaches its climax with the creation of man (male and female) in God's image. Four things should be noted about this climactic act. (1) Man is created as the last of all God's works and thus is the highest creature. (2) Only man is said to be in the image of God. (3) Only now that man is on the scene in the image of God does the writer describe the work of creation as being *very good* (1:31). (4) Man is given dominion and commanded to subdue and fill the earth (1:28).

What is man's purpose here? According to the text, creation exists for man. But since God made man like himself, man's dominion over the world and his filling the world is a display — an imaging forth — of God. God's aim, therefore, was that man would so act that he mirror forth God, who has ultimate dominion. Man is given the exalted status of image-bearer not so he would become arrogant and autonomous (as he tried to do in the Fall), but so he would reflect the glory of his Maker whose image he bears. God's purpose in creation, therefore, was to fill the earth with his own glory. This is made clear, for example, in Numbers 14:21, where the Lord says, "All the earth shall be full of the glory of the LORD," and in Isaiah 43:7, where the Lord refers to his people as those "whom I created *for my glory*."

The Tower of Babel

> Now the whole earth had one language and few words, and as men migrated from the east, they found a plain in the land of Shinar and settled there. And they said to one another, "Come, let us make bricks, and burn them thoroughly." And they had brick for stone, and bitumen for mortar. Then they said, "Come, let us build ourselves a city, and a tower with its top in the heavens, and let us make a name for ourselves, lest we be scattered abroad upon the face of the whole earth." (Genesis 11:1-4)

The point of this story is to show how fallen man thought, and still thinks. By contrast it also shows God's purpose for man. The key phrase is, "Let us make a name for ourselves, lest we be scattered" (11:4). The instinct of self-preservation in fallen man seeks fulfillment not by trusting God, and thereby exalting *his* name, but by employing his own human genius, thereby making a name *for himself*.

This was contrary to God's purpose for man and so God frustrated the effort — and has been frustrating it more or less ever since. God's purpose was that he be given credit for man's greatness and that man depend on *him*. This will be even more evident when we look at what God did next in redemptive history.

The Call of Abram

> Now the LORD said to Abram, "Go from your country and your kindred and your father's house to the land that I will show you. And I will make of you a great nation, and I will bless you, and make your name great, so that you will be a blessing." (Genesis 12:1-2)

At this major turning point in God's dealings with mankind, he calls Abram and begins his dealings with the people of Israel. There is a clear contrast between what God says here and what happened at the tower of Babel. God says that *he* will make Abram's name great, in explicit contrast to Genesis 11:4 where man wanted to make his own name great.

The key difference is this: When man undertakes to make his own name great, he takes credit for his own accomplishments and does not give glory to God. But when God undertakes to make a person great, the only proper response is trust and gratitude on the part of man, which gives all glory back to God, where it belongs. Abram proved himself to be very different from the builders of the Tower of Babel, because (as we see in Genesis 15:6) Abram trusted God.

In Romans 4:20-21, the apostle Paul shows us the link between Abram's faith and God's glory: "No distrust made him waver concerning the promise of God, *but he grew strong in his faith, giving glory to God,* fully convinced that God was able to do what he had promised." So, in contrast to the builders of the Tower of Babel, the children of Abram were chosen by God to be a people who trust him and thus give him glory. This is what God says in Isaiah 49:3, "You are my servant Israel, *in whom I will be glorified.*"

The Exodus

After the period of the patriarchs (Abraham, Isaac, and Jacob), which is recorded in the rest of the book of Genesis, the people of Israel spent several hundred years expanding in the land of Egypt, and then became slaves there. They cry to God for mercy. In response God undertakes to deliver them through the hand of Moses, and then bring them through the wilderness to the promised land of Canaan. God's purpose in this deliverance from Egypt is recorded several places besides in Exodus — for example, in Ezekiel and the Psalms:

> Thus says the LORD God: "On the day when I chose Israel, I swore to the seed of the house of Jacob, making myself known to them in the land of Egypt, I swore to them, saying, I am the

LORD your God. On that day I swore to them that I would bring them out of the land of Egypt into a land that I had searched out for them, a land flowing with milk and honey, the most glorious of all lands. And I said to them, Cast away the detestable things your eyes feast on, every one of you, and do not defile yourselves with the idols of Egypt; I am the LORD your God. But they rebelled against me and would not listen to me; they did not every man cast away the detestable things their eyes feasted on, nor did they forsake the idols of Egypt.

"Then I thought I would pour out my wrath upon them and spend my anger against them in the midst of the land of Egypt. But *I acted for the sake of my name,* that it should not be profaned in the sight of the nations among whom they dwelt, in whose sight I made myself known to them in bringing them out of the land of Egypt." (Ezekiel 20:5-9)

Both we and our fathers have sinned; we have committed iniquity, we have done wickedly. Our fathers, when they were in Egypt, did not consider thy wondrous works; they did not remember the abundance of thy steadfast love, but rebelled against the Most High at the Red Sea. Yet he saved them *for his name's sake, that he might make known his mighty power.* (Psalm 106:6-8)

It is clear that the deliverance from Egypt is not due to the worth of the Israelites, but to the worth of God's name. He acted "for the sake of his name." This is also made clear in the story of the Exodus itself in Exodus 14.

"And I will harden Pharaoh's heart, and he will pursue them and *I will get glory over Pharaoh* and all his host; and the Egyptians *shall know that I am the LORD.* . . . And the Egyptians shall know that I am the Lord, *when I have gotten glory over Pharaoh,* his chariots, and his horsemen." (14:4,18)

God's purpose is to act in a way that causes people to own up to his glory and confess that he is the only Lord of the universe. Therefore, the great event of the Exodus, which was a paradigm for all God's saving acts, should have made clear to all generations that God's purpose with Israel was to glorify himself and create a people who trust him and delight in his glory.

The Giving of the Law

When Israel reached Mount Sinai, God called Moses onto the mountain and gave him the Ten Commandments and other regulations for the new social community. At the head of this law is Exodus 20:3-5.

> "You shall have no other gods before me. You shall not make for yourself a graven image, or any likeness of anything that is in heaven above, or that is in the water under the earth; you shall not bow down to them or serve them; for I the LORD your God am a jealous God, visiting the iniquity of the fathers upon the children to the third and the fourth generation of those who hate me."

When God says we may have no other gods before him and that he is a jealous God, he means his first aim in giving the law is that we accord him the honor he alone is due. He had just shown himself gloriously gracious and powerful in the Exodus; now he simply demands in the law an appropriate response from his people — that we should love him and keep his commandments.

To love God does not mean to meet his needs, but rather to delight in him and to be captivated by his glorious power and grace, and to value him above all other things on earth. All the rest of the commandments are the kinds of things that we will do from our hearts, if our hearts are truly delighted with and resting in the glory of God's grace.

The Wilderness Wandering

God had good reason to destroy his people in the wilderness because of their repeated grumbling and unbelief and idolatry. But again the Lord stays his hand and treats them graciously for his own name's sake.

> "But the children rebelled against me; they did not walk in my statutes, and were not careful to observe my ordinances, by whose observance man shall live; they profaned my sabbaths. Then I thought I would pour out my wrath upon them and spend my anger against them in the wilderness. But I withheld my hand, and *acted for the sake of my name,* that it should not be profaned in the sight of the nations, in whose sight I had brought them out." (Ezekiel 20:21-22; cf. vv. 13-14)

This motive of God in preserving his people in the wilderness is the same one that emerges in Moses' prayer for the people in Deuteronomy 9:27-29 when God was about to destroy the people:

> "Remember thy servants, Abraham, Isaac, and Jacob; do not regard the stubbornness of this people, or their wickedness, or their sin, lest the land from which thou didst bring them say, 'Because the LORD was not able to bring them into the land which he promised them, and because he hated them, he has brought them out to slay them in the wilderness.' For they are thy people and thy heritage, whom thou didst bring out by thy great power and by thy outstretched arm." (See also Numbers 14:13-16; Exodus 32:11-14.)

Moses appeals to God's promise to the patriarchs and argues with God that *surely he does not want scorn to come upon his name,* which would certainly happen if Israel perished in the wilderness. The Egyptians would say God was not able to bring them to Canaan! In allowing Moses to pray in this way, God makes plain that his decision to relent from his wrath against Israel is for *his own name's sake.*

The Conquest of Canaan

The Book of Joshua records how God gave the people of Israel victory over the nations in the land of Canaan. At the end of the book we find a clue to why God did this for his people.

> "And I sent the hornet before you, which drove them out before you, the two kings of the Amorites; it was not by your sword or by your bow. I gave you a land on which you had not labored, and cities which you had not built, and you dwell therein; you eat the fruit of vineyards and oliveyards which you did not plant.
>
> "Now *therefore* fear the LORD, and serve him in sincerity and in faithfulness; put away the gods which your fathers served beyond the River, and in Egypt, and serve the LORD." (Joshua 24:12-14)

The words, "Now *therefore* fear the LORD" are an inference from God's grace in giving Israel the land. The logic shows that God's purpose in giving them the land of Canaan was that they might fear and honor him alone. In other words, in giving Israel the land of Canaan, God aimed to create a people who would recognize his glory and delight in it above all things. This purpose is confirmed in David's prayer recorded in 2 Samuel 7:23.

> "What other nation on earth is like thy people Israel, whom God went to redeem to be his people, *making himself a name,* and doing for them great and terrible things, by driving out before his people a nation and its gods?"

The Beginnings of Monarchy

After a period of judges (recorded in the book by that name) Israel asked for a king. Even though the motive for asking for a king was evil (Israel wanted to be like other nations), nevertheless God did not destroy his people. His motive in this gracious act of mercy is given in 1 Samuel 12:19-23.

> And all the people said to Samuel, "Pray for your servants to the LORD your God, that we may not die; for we have added to all our sins this evil, to ask for ourselves a king." And Samuel said to the people, "Fear not; you have done all this evil, yet do not turn aside from following the LORD, but serve the LORD with all your heart; and do not turn aside after vain things which cannot profit or save, for they are vain. For the LORD will not cast away his people, *for his great name's sake,* because it has pleased the LORD to make you a people for himself. Moreover as for me, far be it from me that I should sin against the LORD by ceasing to pray for you; and I will instruct you in the good and right way."

Here the preservation of the people, despite their sin at the beginning of the monarchy, is due to God's purpose to preserve and display the honor of his name. This goal is supreme.

Another way God showed mercy during the monarchy was to bring to the kingship a man after his own heart, a king whose goal was the same as God's. We can see this in how David prayed. In Psalm 25:11 he says, *"For Thy name's sake,* O LORD, pardon my guilt, for it is great." And in the most famous psalm of all, David says God's motive in leading his people is the glory of his name: "He leads me in paths of righteousness *for his name's sake"* (Psalm 23:3).

The Temple of God

The books of 1 and 2 Kings tell the story of Israel's history from David's son Solomon, who built God's temple, down to the Babylonian captivity. This was a period of about four hundred years ending in 587 B.C. In 1 Kings 8 we read

Solomon's dedicatory prayer after the building of the temple, including these words:

> "Likewise when a foreigner, who is not of thy people Israel, comes from a far country *for thy name's sake* (for they shall hear of thy great name, and thy mighty hand, and of thy outstretched arm), when he comes and prays toward this house, hear thou in heaven thy dwelling place, and do according to all for which the foreigner calls to thee; in order *that all the peoples of the earth may know thy name and fear thee,* as do thy people Israel, and that they may know that this house which I have built is *called by thy name.*
>
> "If thy people go out to battle against their enemy, by whatever way thou shalt send them, and they pray to the LORD toward the city which thou hast chosen and the house which *I have built for thy name,* then hear thou in heaven their prayer and their supplication, and maintain their cause." (1 Kings 8:41-45)

This prayer shows that Solomon's purpose for building the temple — in accord with God's own purpose: "My name shall be there!" (verse 29) — was that God's name should be exalted and all the nations should know and fear God.

Deliverance in the Time of the Kings

After the death of Solomon, the Kingdom of Israel was divided into the Northern and the Southern Kingdoms. One example of God's continued grace during this time and his continued purpose to be glorified and maintain the honor of his name is evident in the way he intervened when Hezekiah was king of Judah in the late 700s B.C.

The Assyrians, led by Sennacherib, were coming against the people of Judah. So Hezekiah prayed to the Lord for deliverance. Isaiah the prophet brought God's answer, stated in 2 Kings 19:34, "For I will defend this city to save it, *for my own sake* and for the sake of my servant David." He says the same thing again in 2 Kings 20:6, "I will deliver you and this city out of the hand of the king of Assyria, and I will defend this city *for my own sake* and for my servant David's sake."

Exile and Promised Restoration

Finally, in about 587 B.C., Jerusalem fell to the invading Babylonians (the Northern Kingdom had gone into exile with the Assyrians in 722 B.C.). The people of Judah are deported to Babylon. It looks like God may be through with his people Israel. But if so, what about his holy name, for which he has been so jealous over the centuries? We soon discover God is not finished with his people, but will again be merciful. And again, as Isaiah makes clear, God's purposes are the same as always:

> "For my name's sake I defer my anger, for the sake of my praise I restrain it for you, that I may not cut you off. Behold, I have refined you, but not like silver; I have tried you in the furnace of affliction. For my own sake, for my own sake, I do it, for how should my name be profaned? My glory I will not give to another." (Isaiah 48:9-11)

Similarly, Ezekiel, who prophesied during the Babylonian exile, tells of God's merciful restoration and why he will perform it.

> "Therefore say to the house of Israel, 'Thus says the LORD God: "It is not for your sake, O house of Israel, that I am about to act, but for the sake of my holy name, which you have profaned among the nations to which you came. And I will vindicate the holiness of my great name, which has been profaned among the nations, and which you have profaned among them; and the nations will know that I am the LORD," says the LORD God, "when through you I vindicate my holiness before their eyes. . . . It is not for your sake that I will act," says the LORD God; "let that be known to you. Be ashamed and confounded for your sins, O house of Israel." ' " (Ezekiel 36:22-23,32)

Salvation is not a ground for boasting of our worth to God. It is an occasion for self-abasement and joy in the glorious grace of God on our behalf — a grace which never depends on our distinctives but flows from God's overwhelming concern to magnify his own glory on behalf of his people.

Post-Exilic Prophets

Zechariah, Haggai, and Malachi prophesied after Israel's return from exile, representing the latest writings in the Old Testament period. Each reflects a conviction that God's goal after the exile is still his own glory.

Zechariah prophesied concerning the rebuilding of Jerusalem: "I will be the glory within her" (Zechariah 2:5).

Haggai made the same point: "Build the house that I may appear in my glory" (Haggai 1:8).

Malachi criticized the wicked priests in the new temple: They "do not lay it to heart to give glory to my name" (Malachi 2:2).

NEW TESTAMENT

Moving from the Old Testament to the New Testament, we move from an age of promise to an age of fulfillment. The hoped-for Messiah had come, Jesus Christ. But God's supreme goal did not change, only some of the circumstances in how he is achieving it.

Jesus' Life and Ministry

Two texts from the Gospel of John show that Jesus' life and ministry were devoted to glorifying his Father in heaven. In John 17:4, Jesus prayed at the end of his life, "*I glorified thee* on earth, having accomplished the work which thou gavest me to do." And in John 7:18, referring to his own ministry, Jesus said, "He who speaks on his own authority seeks his own glory; but he who *seeks the glory of him who sent him* is true, and in him there is no falsehood." Therefore, we can say with certainty that Jesus' all-consuming desire and deepest purpose on earth was to glorify his Father in heaven by doing his Father's will (John 4:34).

Jesus' Death

In John 12:27-28 Jesus weighed whether to escape the hour of his death; but he rejected that alternative knowing that precisely through dying he would finish his mission of glorifying the Father.

> "Now is my soul troubled. And what shall I say? 'Father, save me from this hour'? No, for this purpose I have come to this hour. '*Father, glorify thy name.*' " Then a voice came from heaven, "I have glorified it and *I will glorify it again.*"

The purpose of Jesus' death was to glorify the Father. To be willing as the Son of God to suffer the loss of so much glory himself in order to repair the injury done to God's glory by our sin showed how infinitely valuable the glory of God is. To be sure, the death of Christ also shows God's love for us. But we are not at the center.

God put forward his Son on the cross "*to show God's righteousness, because in his divine forbearance he had passed over former sins*" (Romans 3:25). In other words, by forgiving sin in the Old Testament and by tolerating many sinners, God had given the impression that his honor and glory were not of infinite worth. Now to vindicate the honor of his name and the worth of his glory, he required the death of his own Son. Thus Christ suffered and died for the glory of his Father. This demonstrates the righteousness of God, because God's righteousness is his unswerving allegiance to uphold the value of his glory.[1]

The Christian Life

The work of Christ for the glory of God leads inevitably to the conclusion that God's purpose for his new redeemed people, the church, is that our life goal should be to glorify God. Paul makes this explicit in 1 Corinthians 10:31 where he says, "So whether you eat or drink, or whatever you do, *do all to the glory of God.*"

Peter shows that all of our service as Christians has as its goal that God would be glorified as the One who enables all good things: "Whoever renders service [let him do it] as one who renders it by the strength which God supplies; in order that in everything God may be glorified through Jesus Christ. To him belong glory and dominion forever and ever. Amen" (1 Peter 4:11).

And when Jesus was instructing his own disciples what their goal should be in their daily living, he said in Matthew 5:16, "Let your light so shine before men, that they may see your good works and *give glory to your Father who is in heaven.*"

The Second Coming and Consummation

In 2 Thessalonians 1:9-10 the second coming of Christ is described as hope and terror. Paul says of those who do not believe the gospel,

> They shall suffer the punishment of eternal destruction and exclusion from the presence of the Lord and from the glory of his might, when he comes on that day *to be glorified in his saints, and to be marveled at in all who have believed,* because our testimony to you was believed.

Jesus Christ is coming back not only to effect the final salvation of his people, but through this salvation "to be glorified in his saints and to be marveled at in all who have believed."

A final comment concerns history's climax in the book of Revelation: John pictures the new Jerusalem, the glorified church, in 21:23 — "And the city has no need of sun or moon to shine upon it, for the glory of God is its light, and its lamp is the lamb." God the Father and God the Son are the light in which Christians will live their eternity. This is the consummation of God's goal in all of history — to display his glory for all to see and praise. The prayer of the Son confirms the final purpose of the Father: "Father, I desire that they also, whom thou hast given me, may be with me where I am, *to behold my glory,* which thou hast given me in thy love for me before the foundation of the world" (John 17:24).

Conclusion

What may we conclude from this survey of redemptive history? We may conclude that the chief end of *God* is to glorify God and enjoy himself forever. He stands supreme at the center of his own affections. For that very reason he is a self-sufficient and inexhaustible fountain of grace.

APPENDIX 2

Is the Bible a Reliable Guide to Lasting Joy?

Does God Exist?

Whole books have been written on why the Bible is trustworthy.[1] But for the sake of our own sense of integrity, we ought to review in a brief space why we bank our hope on the message of this book. I hope I can steer a course in this appendix between unsupported dogmatism on the one hand and apologetic overkill on the other.

Let's start at the most basic level of religious faith. I believe in God. There may be social and family reasons for how I got to be this way, just as there are social and family reasons for why you are the way you are. But when I try to be reasonable and test my inherited belief in God, I cannot escape his reality.

Suppose I try to go back a million billion trillion years to imagine the nature of original reality. What was it like? What I see is the stunning fact that there is a fifty-fifty possibility that original reality was a Person rather than a gas. Just think of it. Since whatever originally was has always existed, there are absolutely no causes which could have disposed that original reality to be a gas rather than a person. Every reasonable person must admit that it is a toss-up. Maybe some undefined stuff existed from eternity — or maybe it was a Person!

Admitting the reasonable possibility that ultimate reality could be personal has a way of freeing you to consider subsequent evidence more openly. My own inescapable inference from the order of the universe and the existence of human personhood and the universal sense of conscience (moral self-judgment) and the universal judicial sentiment (judgment of others who dishonor us) — my own inference from all this is that Ultimate Reality is not impersonal, but is indeed a Person. I simply find it impossible to believe that the human drama of the centuries, with its quest for meaning and beauty and truth, has no deeper root than molecular mutations.

Many Religions, Many Gods

So when I consider where enduring happiness is to be found, I am driven to search for it in relation to God — the personal Creator of all things. Nothing seems more reasonable to me than that lasting happiness will never be found by a person who ignores or opposes his Creator. I am constantly astonished at people who say they believe in God but live as though happiness were to be found by giving him 2 percent of their attention. Surely the end of the ages will reveal this to be absurd.

But once we begin to seek our happiness in relation to God, we are confronted with many different claims and religions. Why should we bank our hope on the claim that the Christian Bible is a true revelation of God? My basic answer is that Jesus Christ — the center and sum of the Bible — has won my confidence by his authenticity and love and power. I see his authenticity and love in the record of his words and deeds, and I see his power especially in his resurrection from the dead.

Listening to the Witnesses to Christ

You need not believe the Bible is infallible to discover that it presents a historical Person of incomparable qualities. On the contrary, the reasonable way to approach the Bible for the first time is to listen openly and honestly to its various witnesses to Christ, to see if these witnesses and this person authenticate themselves. If they do, the things they and Christ say about the Bible itself will take on new authority, and you may well end up accepting the whole Bible (as I do!) as God's inspired, infallible Word. But you don't need to start there.

The Incomparable Christ

Let me try to illustrate what I mean by the self-authenticating message of Christ and his witnesses. The biblical accounts present Jesus as a man of incomparable love for God and man. He became angry when God was dishonored by irreligion (Mark 11:15-17) and when man was destroyed by religion (Mark 3:4-5). He taught us to be poor in spirit, meek, hungry for righteousness, pure in heart, merciful, and peaceable (Matthew 5:3-9). He urged us to honor God from the heart (Matthew 15:8) and to put away all hypocrisy (Luke 12:1). And he practiced what he preached. His life was summed up as "doing good and healing" (Acts 10:38).

He took time for little children and blessed them (Mark 10:13-16). He crossed social barriers to help women (John 4), foreigners (Mark 7:24-30), lepers (Luke 17:11-19), harlots (Luke 7:36-50), tax collectors (Matthew 9:9-13), and beggars (Mark 10:46-52). He washed his disciples' feet like a slave and taught them to serve rather than be served (John 13:1-17). Even when he was exhausted his heart went out in compassion to the pressing crowds (Mark 6:31-34). Even when his own disciples were fickle and ready to deny him and forsake him, he wanted to be with them (Luke 22:15) and he prayed for them (Luke 22:32). He said his life was a ransom for many (Mark 10:45), and as he was being executed at age thirty-three, he prayed for the forgiveness of his murderers (Luke 23:34).

Not only is Jesus portrayed as full of love for God and man, he is also presented as utterly truthful and authentic. He did not act on his own authority to gain worldly praise. He directed men to his Father in heaven. "He who speaks on his own authority seeks his own glory; but he who seeks the glory of him who sent him is true and in him there is no falsehood" (John 7:18). He does not have the spirit of an egomaniac or a charlatan. He seems utterly at peace with himself and God. He is authentic.

This is evident in the way he saw through people's sham (Matthew 22:18). He was so pure and so perceptive that he could not be tripped up or cornered in debate (Matthew 22:15-22). He was amazingly unsentimental in his demands, even toward those for whom he had a special affection (Mark 10:21). He never softened the message of righteousness to increase his following or curry favor. Even his opponents were stunned by his indifference to human praise: "Teacher, we know that you are true, and care for no man; for you do not regard the position of men, but truly teach the way of God" (Mark 12:14). He never had to back down from a claim, and could be convicted of no wrong (John 8:46). He was meek and lowly in heart (Matthew 11:29).

But what made all this so amazing was the unobtrusive yet unmistakable *authority* that rang through all he did and said. The officers of the Pharisees speak for all of us when they say, "No man ever spoke like this man" (John 7:46). There was something unmistakably different about him: "He taught them as one who had authority, and not as their scribes" (Matthew 7:29).

His claims were not the open declaration of worldly power that the Jews expected from the Messiah. But they were unmistakable nonetheless. Though no one understood it at the time, there was no doubt that he had said, "Destroy this temple and in three days I will build it up again" (John 2:19, Matthew 26:61). They thought it was an absurd claim that he would singlehandedly rebuild an edifice that had been forty-six years in the making. But he was claiming in his typically veiled way that he would rise from the dead — and by his own power.

In his last debate with the Pharisees (Matthew 22:41-45), Jesus silenced them with this question: "What do you think of the Messiah? Whose son is he?" They answer, "David's son." In response, Jesus quoted David from Psalm 110:1 — "The LORD said to my Lord, Sit at my right hand, till I put thine enemies under thy feet." Then, with only slightly veiled authority, Jesus asked, "If David thus calls him Lord, how is he his son?" In other words, for those who have eyes to see, the son of David and far more than the son is here.

"The men of Nineveh will arise at the judgment with this generation and condemn it; for they repented at the preaching of Jonah, and behold, *something greater than Jonah is here.* The queen of the South will arise at the judgment with this generation and condemn it; for she came from the ends of the earth to hear the wisdom of Solomon, and behold, *something greater than Solomon is here*" (Matthew 12:41-42). This kind of veiled claim runs through all Jesus said and did.

Besides that, he commanded evil spirits and they obeyed him (Mark 1:27). He issued forgiveness for sins (Mark 2:5). He summoned people to leave all and follow him to have eternal life and treasure in heaven (Mark 10:17-22; Luke 14:26-33). And he made the astonishing claim that "every-one who acknowledges me before men, I also will acknowledge before my Father who is in heaven; but whoever denies me before men, I also will deny before my Father who is in heaven" (Matthew 10:32-33).

Am I Arguing in a Circle?

Perhaps someone will say I am arguing in a circle. Am I not assuming the reliability of the biblical portrait of Jesus, even as I argue for it? Not exactly. The portrait I have sketched is not isolated to one writer, nor (as critical scholars would say) to any particular layer of the tradition. No matter how far back you go through a critical study of the Gospels, you never find a Jesus of history substantially different than the one described here. In other words, you don't have to *assume* the accounts are reliable. You can assume they are not if you wish. But the more rigorously you analyze them with a fair historical procedure, the more you realize there is no point between the Jesus of history and the Jesus of the Gospels where this unequaled man was created by human artifice.

In other words, I am not starting with the assumption that the Gospels are inspired or infallible. I am trying to show that a certain portrait of Jesus is common to all the witnesses, and goes back as far as historical criticism can go.

How Do You Account for Jesus?

How is this concert and this antiquity to be explained? Did some unknown creative genius take an ordinary man, Jesus, and invent his deeds of power and his words of love and authority and authenticity, then present this invented Jesus to a church with such deceptive power that many people were willing from the outset to die for this fictional Christ? Further, must we believe that all the Gospel writers swallowed the invention — and in the space of several decades while many who knew the real Jesus were still living? Is that a more reasonable or well-founded guess than the plain assertion that a real man, Jesus Christ, did in fact say and do the sorts of things the biblical witnesses said he did?

You must decide for yourself. To my mind, an unknown inventor of this Jesus is more incredible than the possibility of Jesus' reality. So for me the question becomes, How do we account for a man who leaves a legacy like this?

I cannot morally reckon him among the poor deluded souls who suffer from pathological illusions of grandeur. Nor can I reckon him among the great con men of history, a deceiver who planned and orchestrated a worldwide movement of mission on the basis of a hoax. Instead I am constrained to acknowledge his truth. Both my mind and my heart find themselves drawn to yield allegiance to this man. He has won my confidence.

The Evidence for Jesus' Resurrection from the Dead

Alongside this line of evidence we should put the evidence for Jesus' resurrection from the dead. If he did not rise but followed the way of all flesh, the extraordinary implications of his Word and life come to nothing. But if he overcame death, his claims and his character are vindicated. And his teaching concerning the Bible becomes our standard. Without going into detail, I will mention six things that undergird my confidence in the resurrection of Jesus.

1. Jesus bore witness to his own coming resurrection.

Two separate witnesses testify in two very different ways to Jesus' statement during his lifetime that if his enemies destroyed the temple, he would build it again in three days (John 2:19; Mark 14:58; cf. Matthew 26:61). Jesus also spoke illusively of the "sign of Jonah" — three days in the heart of the earth (Matthew 12:39-40; 16:4). Therefore, the credibility of Jesus points to the reality of the resurrection to come. And he hinted at it again in Matthew 21:42 — "The very stone which the builders rejected has become the head of the corner."

2. The tomb was empty on Easter. There are four possible ways to account for this.

His foes stole the body. If they did (and they never claimed to have done so), they surely would have produced the body to stop the successful spread of the Christian faith in the very city where the crucifixion occurred. But they could not produce it.

His friends stole it. This was an early rumor (Matthew 28:11-15). Is it probable? Could they have overcome the guards at the tomb? More important, would they have begun to preach with such authority that Jesus was raised, knowing he was not? Would they have risked their lives and accepted beatings for something they knew was a fraud?

Jesus was not dead, but only unconscious when they laid him in the tomb. He awoke, removed the stone, overcame the soldiers, and vanished from history after a few meetings with his disciples in which he convinced them he was risen from the dead. Even the foes of Jesus did not try this line. He was obviously dead. The stone could not be moved by one man from within who had just spent six hours nailed to a cross and been stabbed in the side by a spear.

God raised Jesus from the dead. This is what he said would happen. It is what the disciples said did happen.

But as long as there is a remote possibility of explaining the resurrection naturalistically, modern people say we should not jump to a supernatural explanation. Is this reasonable? I don't think so. Of course, we don't want to be gullible. But neither do we want to reject the truth just because it's strange. We need to be aware that our commitments at this point are much affected by our preferences — either for the state of affairs that would arise from the truth of the resurrection, or for the state of affairs that would arise from the falsehood of the resurrection. If the message of Jesus has opened you to the reality of God and the need of forgiveness, for example, then anti-supernatural dogma might lose its power over your mind. Could it be that this openness is not prejudice for the resurrection, but freedom from prejudice against it?

3. The disciples were almost immediately transformed from men who were hopeless and fearful after the crucifixion (Luke 24:21; John 20:19) into men who were confident and bold witnesses of the resurrection (Acts 2:24; 3:15; 4:2). Their explanation was that they had seen the risen Christ and had been authorized to be his witnesses (Acts 2:32). The most popular competing explanation is that their confidence was owing to hallucinations. There are numerous problems with such a notion:

For one, hallucinations are generally private things, but Paul writes in 1 Corinthians 15:6 that Jesus "appeared to more than five hundred brethren at one time, most of whom are still alive." They were available to query.

Furthermore, the disciples were not gullible, but level-headed skeptics both before and after the resurrection (Mark 9:32; Luke 24:11; John 20:8-9,25).

Moreover, is the deep and noble teaching of those who witnessed the risen Christ the stuff of which hallucinations are made? What about Paul's great letter to the Romans?

4. The sheer existence of a thriving, empire-conquering early Christian church supports the truth of the resurrection claim. The church spread on the

power of the testimony that Jesus was raised from the dead and that God had thus made him both Lord and Christ (Acts 2:36). The Lordship of Christ over all nations is based on his victory over death. This is the message that spread all over the world. Its power to cross cultures and create one new people of God was strong testimony of its truth.

5. The apostle Paul's conversion supports the truth of the resurrection. He argues to a partially unsympathetic audience in Galatians 1:11-17 that his gospel comes from the living Jesus Christ. His argument is that before his Damascus road experience, he was utterly opposed to the Christian faith. But now, to everyone's astonishment, he is risking his life for the gospel. His explanation: The risen Jesus appeared to him and authorized him to spearhead the Gentile mission (Acts 26:15-18). Can we credit such a testimony?

This leads to my last argument for the resurrection.

6. The New Testament witnesses do not bear the stamp of dupes or deceivers. How do you credit a witness? How do you decide whether to believe a person's testimony? The decision to give credence to a person's testimony is not the same as completing a mathematical equation. The certainty is of a different kind, yet can be just as firm (I trust my wife's testimony that she is faithful).

When a witness is dead, we can base our judgment of him only on the content of his writings and the testimonies of others about him. How do Peter and John and Matthew and Paul stack up?

In my judgment (and at this point we can live authentically only by our own judgment — Luke 12:57), these men's writings do not read like the works of gullible, easily deceived or deceiving men. Their insights into human nature are profound. Their personal commitment is sober and carefully stated. Their teachings are coherent and do not look like the invention of unstable men. The moral and spiritual standard is high. And the life of these men, as it comes through their writings, is totally devoted to the truth and to the honor of God.

Jesus Is the True Revelation of God

These, then, are some (not all!) of the evidences that undergird my confidence in Jesus as the true revelation of God. Before I try to explain how this leads me to credit the whole Bible as God's Word, let me give a personal admonition.

Whenever a Christian converses with a non-Christian about the truth of the faith, every request of the non-Christian for the proof of Christianity should be met with an equally serious request for proof for the non-Christian's philosophy of life. Otherwise we get the false impression that the Christian worldview is tentative and uncertain, while the more secular worldviews are secure and sure, standing above the need to give a philosophical and historical accounting of themselves. But that is not the case.

Many people who demand that Christians produce proof of our claims do not make the same demand upon themselves. Secular skepticism is assumed to be reasonable because it is widespread, not because it is well argued. We should simply insist that the controversy be conducted with fairness. If the Christian must produce proof, so must others.

Now, if Jesus has won our confidence by his authentic love and his power over death, then his view of things will be our standard. What was his view of the Old Testament?

What Was Jesus' View of the Old Testament?

First of all, was the Old Testament he prized made up of the same books as the Old Testament that Protestants prize today? Or did it include others (like the Old Testament Apocrypha[2])? In other words, was Jesus' Bible the Hebrew Old Testament, limited to the thirty-nine books of the Protestant Old Testament, or was his Bible more like the Greek Old Testament (Septuagint) which includes an extra fifteen books? Norman Anderson, in his inspiring book, *God's Word for God's World,* states my answer and the support for it so well that I would like simply to quote him:

> So we must now consider the reciprocal witness that Jesus bore to the Bible — primarily, of course, to the Old Testament, as the only part of the Scriptures which was then in existence. That the books He had in mind spanned the whole "Hebrew Bible" is, I think, clear from two New Testament references: first, from His allusion, in Luke 24:44, to "the Law of Moses, the Prophets and the Psalms," since this was tantamount to referring to the three-fold structure of the Jewish Scriptures as the "Law," the "Prophets" and the "Writings" (in which the Psalms held pride of place); and, secondly, from His allusion to "all the righteous blood that has been shed on earth, from the blood of righteous Abel to the blood of Zechariah son of Berachiah," since the blood of Abel is mentioned early in Genesis (4:8), the first book in the Hebrew Bible, and that of Zechariah towards the end of 2 Chronicles (24:21), the last book in the Jewish Scriptures.[3]

If, then, Jesus' Bible was the same Old Testament we Protestants use today, the question now becomes, How did he regard it?

1. In quoting Psalm 110:1, he said that David spoke by the Holy Spirit: "David himself, inspired by the Holy Spirit, declared . . . " (Mark 12:36).

2. In his controversy with the Pharisees concerning their interpretation of the Old Testament, he contrasted the tradition of the elders and the commandment of God found in Scripture. "You have a fine way of rejecting the commandment of God, in order to keep your tradition!" (Mark 7:9).

3. When he answered the Pharisees concerning the problem of divorce, he referred to Genesis 2:24 as something "said" by God, though these are words of the biblical narrator and not a direct quote of God: "He who made them from the beginning made them male and female, and said, 'For this reason a man shall leave his father and mother' " (Matthew 19:4-5).

4. He makes an explicit statement concerning infallibility in John 10:35 — "The Scriptures cannot be broken."

5. An implicit claim for the inerrancy of the Old Testament is made in Matthew 22:29. "Jesus answered them, 'You err, not knowing either the Scriptures or the power of God.' " Knowing the Scriptures keeps one from erring.

6. Repeatedly Jesus treats the Old Testament as an authority that must be fulfilled. "Think not that I have come to abolish the law and the prophets; I have come not to abolish them, but to fulfill them. For truly, I say to you, till heaven and earth pass away, not an iota, not a dot, will pass from the law until all is accomplished" (Matthew 5:17-18; see Matthew 26:54,56; Luke 16:17).

7. Jesus rebuked the two disciples on the Emmaus road for being "foolish men, and slow of heart to believe all that the prophets have spoken" (Luke 24:25).

8. Jesus himself used the Old Testament as an authoritative weapon against the temptations of Satan: "But he answered, 'It is written . . . ' " (Matthew 4:4,7,10).

The diversity of this witness and its spread over all the Gospel material show that the Lord Jesus regarded the Old Testament as a trustworthy, authoritative, unerring guide in our quest for enduring happiness. Therefore we who submit to the authority of Christ will also want to submit to the authority of the book he esteemed so highly.

The Authority of the New Testament

Now what about the New Testament? It would be possible to develop a long historical argument for the inspiration and infallibility of books of the New Testament, but that would expand this appendix beyond appropriate bounds.[4] So I will give pointers that can undergird our confidence in the New Testament as being equally authoritative and reliable as the Old.

My confidence in the New Testament as God's Word rests on a group of observations.

1. Jesus chose twelve apostles to be his authoritative representatives in founding the church. At the end of his life he promised them, "The Holy Spirit . . . will teach you all things and bring to your remembrance all that I have said" (John 14:26; 16:13).

2. The apostle Paul, whose stunning conversion from a life of murdering Christians to making Christians, demands special explanation. He says he (and the other apostles) were commissioned by the risen Christ to preach "in words not taught by human wisdom but taught by the Spirit" (1 Corinthians 2:13). In other words, Christ's prediction in John 14:26 was being fulfilled through this inspiration.

3. Peter confirms this in 2 Peter 3:16, putting Paul's writings in the same category with the inspired Old Testament writings (2 Peter 1:21).

4. All the New Testament writings come from those earliest days of promised special revelation and were written by the apostles and their close associates.

5. The message of these books has the "ring of truth."[5] It makes sense out of so much reality. The message on the one hand of God's holiness and our guilt, and on the other hand of Christ's death and resurrection as our only hope—this message fits the reality we see and the hope we long for and don't see.

6. Finally, as the Catechism says, "The Bible evidences itself to be God's Word by the heavenliness of its doctrine, the unity of its parts and its power to convert sinners and edify saints."[6]

APPENDIX 3

What Does It Mean to Love Your Neighbor As You Love Yourself?[1]

For Such a Worm As I

In chapter eight I said Jesus' command (Luke 10:27) to love our neighbor as we love ourselves is widely misinterpreted today in terms of self-esteem. This appendix is the support for my statement, and presentation of a different interpretation.

According to the spirit of this age, the ultimate sin is no longer the failure to honor and thank God but the failure to esteem oneself. Self-abasement, not God-abasement, is the evil. And the cry of deliverance is not "O wretched man that I am, who will deliver me?" but "O worthy man that I am, would that I could only see it better!"

Today the first and greatest commandment is, "Thou shalt love thyself." The explanation for almost every interpersonal problem is thought to lie in someone's low self-esteem. Sermons, articles, and books have pushed this idea deep into the Christian mind. It is a rare congregation, for example, that does not stumble over the "vermicular theology" of Isaac Watts's great hymn "Alas! And Did My Savior Bleed." Hymnbooks even rewrite the line, "Would he devote that sacred head for such a *worm* as I?" We are too noble to be called worms, they say.

For many years the cult of self has been expanding phenomenally, and its professional members take every chance to put a mirror before us and to tell us to like what we see.

What distresses me in all this is not only what I regard as an unbiblical shift of focus from God to man as the goal of redemption (see Ezekiel 36:22-32), but also the paucity of opposition to it. I am eager to prevent this book from being construed as just another voice in the chorus of those who pursue self-esteem as the remedy for all our diseases. This is a book about God-esteem and grace-esteem, not self-esteem. It is a book about the pursuit of joy, not self.

A Most Misused Text

Perhaps the biblical text most commonly used in spreading the message of self-esteem is, "You shall love your neighbor as yourself" (Leviticus 19:18; Luke 10:27; Romans 13:9; Galatians 5:14; James 2:8). But this use almost always involves misinterpretation.

Even in Jesus' day this command was being misunderstood. Might there be a connection between the old misunderstanding and the new one? The ancient error hinged on the term "neighbor" and was exposed by Jesus in the Parable of the Good Samaritan (Luke 10:29-37). The modern error hinges on the term "as yourself."

In Luke 10:25, a lawyer has just asked Jesus what he must do to inherit eternal life. According to Luke, the question is not sincere. The lawyer is not seeking eternal life; he is trying to test Jesus. Under the guise of a personal question he gives Jesus an academic quiz, hoping to entangle him in some heretical contradiction of the Old Testament.

> And behold, a lawyer stood up to put him to the test, saying,
> "Teacher, what shall I do to inherit eternal life?"

With a view to exposing the man's duplicity, Jesus turns the question back: "What is written in the Law? What do you read?"

The man answers, "You shall love the Lord your God with all your heart, and with all your soul, and with all your strength, and with all your mind; and your neighbor as yourself."

Jesus simply agrees: "You have answered right; do this, and you will live."

Enslaved to Saving Face

Now the lawyer is in trouble. It is evident to everybody that he already knew the answer to his question. His motive for asking it was not a sincere desire for information, but a desire to trap Jesus in his words. The lawyer's duplicity was exposed. Everyone can see now that he was insincere, hypocritical, guilty of the injustice of deceit. What will he do? Run away shamed like the apostle Peter and weep bitterly over his sin? Or will he, with ten million other human beings before and after him, seek to save face?

> But he, desiring to justify himself, said to Jesus, [then comes the ancient error hinging on the term "neighbor"] "And who is my neighbor?"

At that threat to his reputation and self-regard, the sin of self-justification sprang up. The lawyer was deceived into thinking the problem was not his own proud unwillingness to repent and obey, but the ambiguity of the word "neighbor." The question, "Who is my neighbor?" was simply a face-saving device.

Behind the lawyer's question is such a serious misunderstanding of God's demand that Jesus will not answer it.

Often our misunderstanding of God's Word is due not to innocent intellectual slips or lack of information, but rather to a deep refusal to submit to God's demands. A person who intends to manage his own affairs, maintain his pride, and secure esteem and glory from his fellow human beings will twist the words of Jesus to support his own self-esteem. The evil of the human heart precedes and gives rise to many of our apparently intellectual misunderstandings of Scripture.

Another way of asking the lawyer's question would be, "Teacher, whom do I not have to love? Which groups in our society are exceptions to this commandment? Surely the Romans, oppressors of God's chosen people; and their despicable lackeys, the tax collectors; and those half-breed Samaritans — surely all these are not included in the term 'neighbor.' Tell me just who my neighbor is, Teacher, that as I examine various candidates for my love, I will be sure to choose him alone."

The Exposing Parable

Jesus will have nothing to do with answering outright — which was really impossible — that kind of question. Instead he tells a parable.

A man, probably a Jew, was traveling from Jerusalem to Jericho when he was attacked by robbers. They stripped and beat him, and left him half dead on the side of the road. Along came a priest, then a Levite. When they saw the man they went by on the other side. Then came a Samaritan, and when he saw the wounded man, he felt compassion for him. He went to him and treated his wounds, using his own oil and wine. Then he set him on his own beast, brought him to an inn, and took care of him till the next day. He gave the innkeeper his own money to take care of the man and said he would stop by on his way back to make up the difference if it wasn't enough.

After telling the parable, Jesus puts a question back to the lawyer: "Which of these three does it seem to you became a neighbor to the one who fell among thieves?" The lawyer answers, "The one who showed mercy on him." Jesus responds, "Go and do likewise."

The point of Jesus' parable was to show that the lawyer's request for a definition of "neighbor" was simply a skirting of the real issue: the kind of person he himself was. The lawyer's problem was not to define the word "neighbor"; his problem and the problem of every human being was becoming the kind of person who, because of compassion, cannot pass by on the other side. No truly compassionate or merciful heart can stand idly by while the mind examines a suffering candidate to see if he fits the definition of neighbor.

If the lawyer had been submissive to the intention of God's command, he would have seen how irrelevant his question about his neighbor was. God's intention is to call into being a loving, compassionate, merciful person whose heart summons him irresistibly into action when there is suffering within his reach, a person who will interrupt his schedule, risk embarrassment, use up his oil and wine, and part with his money for the sake of a suffering stranger. Become that person, Jesus says, and you will inherit eternal life: Blessed are the merciful, for they shall obtain mercy.

This, then, is the way the command, "Love your neighbor as yourself," was misunderstood in Jesus' day and how Jesus responded to it.

The Modern Error

While the old error hinged on the word "neighbor," the modern one hinges on two assumptions about "as yourself." First, the words are assumed to be a command rather than a statement. That is, it is assumed that Jesus is calling people to love themselves so they can love others as they love themselves. Second, this self-love Jesus supposedly demands is assumed to be equivalent to self-esteem, self-acceptance, a positive self-image, or the like. The proponents of this interpretation put the two assumptions together like this: A person's first task in obedience to Jesus is to develop a high self-esteem so he can fulfill the second half of the command, to love others as he now loves himself.

Is this what Jesus meant? I think not. These two assumptions depend on each other, so let us look at them together to see if the text bears them out.

Grammatically it is impossible to construe the words "as yourself" as a command. When you supply the verb, the commandment reads simply, "You shall love your neighbor as you, in fact, already love yourself." Jesus is not calling for self-love; he assumes it already exists. As far as we know, Jesus never entertained the thought that there could be someone who didn't love himself. To use Paul's words in Ephesians 5:29, "No man ever hates his own flesh but nourishes and cherishes it."

If this is so, the self-love Jesus talks about is quite different from the self-esteem so often assumed to be his meaning. To show what Jesus means by self-love we can pose the following question: Is it not reasonable to assume that the two uses of "love" in the command "Love your neighbor as you love yourself" will have the same meaning? Jesus makes it plain what he means by the verb "love" in the first half. It means to interrupt your schedule and use up your oil, wine, and money to achieve what you think best for your neighbor. It means to have a heart disposed to seek another person's good.

Giving the word "love" the same meaning in the second part of the command, we get this: "You shall seek the good of your neighbor, just as you naturally seek your own good. Nourish and cherish your needy neighbor, just as you by nature nourish and cherish yourself."

Another way in which Jesus said essentially the same thing was, "Whatever you wish that men would do to you, do so to them." "Do so to them" corresponds to "Love your neighbor." "Whatever you wish that men would do to you" corresponds to "as you love yourself." Self-love is thus defined in the Golden Rule by our desire for others to do us good.

Self-love Not Commanded but Assumed

In sum, then, "Love your neighbor as yourself" does not command, but rather presupposes, self-love. All human beings love themselves. Furthermore, the self-love Jesus speaks of has nothing to do with the common notion of self-esteem. It does not mean having a good self-image or feeling especially happy with oneself. It means simply desiring and seeking one's own good.

And we should note that Jesus' point is not affected by the fact that most people have a distorted notion of what is good for them. A man may attempt to find his good in a bottle of brandy or in illicit sex or in a fast motorcycle. Nevertheless, all human beings desire and seek what they *think*, at least in the moment of choosing, will make them happiest.

A Very Radical Command

Only when one sees "self-love" in this light will the tremendous force of the command "Love your neighbor as yourself" be apparent. This is a very radical command. What I mean by "radical" is this: it exposes the root of our sinfulness and, by God's grace, severs it. The root of our sinfulness is the desire for our own happiness apart from God and apart from the happiness of others in God. All sin comes from a desire to be happy cut off from the glory of God and cut off from the good of others.

Another name for this root of sinfulness is pride. Pride is the presumption that we can be happy without depending on God as the source of our happiness and without caring if others find their happiness in God. Pride is the passion to be happy contaminated and corrupted by two things: 1) the unwillingness to see God as the only fountain of true and lasting joy, and 2) the unwillingness to see other people as designed by God to receive our joy in him. If you take the desire to be happy and strip away from it God as the fountain of your happiness, and people as the recipients of your happiness, what you have left is pride. Pride is the pursuit of happiness anywhere but in the glory of God and the good of other people.

Now Jesus says, "Love your neighbor as yourself." And with that commandment he cuts to the root of our sinfulness. How so?

The Longing to Diminish Pain and Increase Pleasure

Jesus says in effect: I start with your inborn, deep, defining human trait — your love for yourself. This is a given. I don't command it; I assume it. All of you have a powerful instinct of self-preservation and self-fulfillment. You all want to be happy. You all want to live and to live with satisfaction. You want food for yourself. You want clothes for yourself. You want a place to live for yourself. You want protection from violence against yourself. You want meaningful or pleasant activity to fill your days. You want some friends to like you and spend some time with you. You want your life to count in some way. All this is self-love. Self-love is the deep longing to diminish pain and to increase pleasure.

Everyone, without exception, has this human trait. This is what moves us to do this or that. Even suicide is pursued out of this principle of self-love. In the midst of a feeling of utter meaninglessness and hopelessness and numbness of depression, the soul says: "It can't get any worse than this. So even if I don't know what I will gain through death, I do know what I will escape." And so suicide is an attempt to escape the intolerable. It is an act of self-love.

Now Jesus says, I start with this self-love. This is what I know about you. This is common to all people. You don't have to learn it. It comes with your humanity. My Father created it. In and of itself it is good. To hunger for food is not evil. To want to be warm in the winter is not evil. To want to be safe in a crisis is not evil. To want to be healthy during a plague is not evil. To want to be liked by others is not evil. To want your life to count in some significant way is not evil. This was a defining human trait before the fall of man into sin, and it is not evil in itself.

Make the Measure of Your Self-Seeking the Measure of Your Self-Giving

Whether it has become evil in your life will now be exposed as you hear and respond to Jesus' commandment. He commands, "As you love yourself, so love your neighbor." Which means: As you long for food when you are hungry, so long to feed your neighbor when he is hungry. As you long for nice clothes for yourself, so long for nice clothes for your neighbor. As you desire to have a comfortable place to live, so desire a comfortable place to live for your neighbor. As you seek to be safe and secure from calamity and violence, so seek comfort and security for your neighbor. As you seek friends for yourself, so be a friend to your neighbor. As you want your life to count and be significant, so desire that same significance for your neighbor. As you work to make good grades yourself, so work to help your neighbor make good grades. As you like to be welcomed into strange company, so welcome your neighbor into strange company. As you would that men would do to you, do so to them.

In other words, make the measure of your self-seeking the measure of your self-giving. The word "as" is very radical: "Love your neighbor as yourself." "As!" It means: If you are energetic in pursuing your own happiness, be energetic in pursuing the happiness of your neighbor. If you are creative in pursuing your own happiness, be creative in pursuing the happiness of your neighbor. If you are persevering in pursuing your own happiness, be persevering in pursuing the happiness of your neighbor. In other words, Jesus is not just saying: seek for your neighbor the same things you seek for yourself, but seek them in the same way — the same zeal and energy and creativity and perseverance. Make the measure of your self-seeking the measure of your self-giving. Measure your pursuit of the happiness of others by the pursuit of your own. How do you pursue your own well-being? Pursue your neighbor's well-being that way, too.

Loving Others Instead of Ourselves?

Now this is very threatening. Because we feel immediately that if we take Jesus seriously, we will not just have to love others "as we love ourselves," but we will have to love them "instead of loving ourselves." I fear that if I follow Jesus in this, and really devote myself to pursuing the happiness of others, then my own desire for happiness will always be preempted. The neighbor's claim on my time and energy and creativity will take over any time and energy and creativity I have for pursuing my own happiness. So the command to love my neighbor as I love myself really feels like a threat to my self-love. How is this even possible? If there is born in us a natural desire for our own happiness, and if this is not in itself evil, but good, how can we give it up and begin only to seek the happiness of others at the expense of our own?

The First Commandment Saves the Second

I think that is exactly the threat that Jesus wants us to feel, until we realize that this — exactly this — is why the first commandment is the first commandment. It's the first commandment that makes the second commandment doable and takes away the threat that the second commandment is really suicide to our own happiness. The first commandment is, "Love the Lord your God with all your heart and with all your soul and with all your strength and with all your mind" (Luke 10:27). The first commandment is the basis of the second commandment. The second commandment is a visible expression of the first commandment. Which means this: Before you make your self-seeking the measure of your self-giving, make God the focus of your self-seeking. This is the point of the first commandment.

"Love God with all your heart" means: find in God a satisfaction so full that it fills up all your heart. "Love God with all your soul" means: find in God a meaning so rich and so deep that it fills up all the aching corners of your soul. "Love God with all your strength" means: spare no strain or exertion to put yourself in a position to see the all-satisfying grace of God poured out on you and through you. "Love God with all your mind" means: find in God the riches of knowledge and insight and wisdom that guide and satisfy all that the human mind was meant for.

In other words, take all your self-love — all your longing for joy and hope and love and security and fulfillment and significance — take all that, and focus it on God, until he satisfies your heart and soul and mind. This is not a canceling out of self-love. This is a fulfillment of self-love. Self-love is the desire for life and satisfaction rather than frustration and death. God says, Come to me, and I will give you fullness of joy (Psalm 16:11). I will satisfy your heart and soul and strength and mind with my glory. This is the first and great commandment.

Love for God Becomes the Form of Our Love for Others

And with that great discovery — that God is the never-ending fountain of our joy — the way we love others is forever changed. Now when Jesus says, "Love your neighbor as yourself," we don't respond by saying, "Oh, this is threatening. This means my love for myself is made impossible by all the claims of my neighbor. I could never do this." Instead we say, "Oh, yes, I love myself. I have longings for joy and satisfaction and fulfillment and significance and security. But God has called me — indeed he has commanded me — to come to him first for all these things. He commands that my love for him be the form of my love for me. That all my longings for me I find in him. That is what my self-love is now. It is my love for God. They have become one. My quest for happiness is now nothing other than a quest for God. And he has been found."

What then is Jesus commanding in the second commandment — that we love our neighbor as ourselves? He is commanding that our self-love, which has now discovered its fulfillment in God-love, be the measure and the content of our neighbor-love. Or, to put it another way, he is commanding that our inborn self-seeking, which has now been transposed into God-seeking, overflow and extend itself to our neighbor. So, for example:

If you are longing to see more of God's bounty and liberality through the supply of food and rent and clothing, then seek to show others the greatness of this divine bounty by the generosity you have found in him. Let the fulfillment of your own self-love in God-love overflow into neighbor-love. Or better: seek that God, who is the fulfillment of your self-love, overflow through you and become the fulfillment of your neighbor's self-love.

If you want to enjoy more of God's compassion through the consolations he gives you in sorrow, then seek to show others more of God's compassion through the consolations you extend to them in sorrow.

If you long to savor more of God's wisdom though the counsel he gives in stressful relationships, then seek to extend more of God's wisdom to others in their stressful relationships.

If you delight in seeing God's goodness in relaxed times of leisure, then extend that goodness to others by helping them have leisure.

If you want to see more of God's saving grace powerfully manifested in your life, then stretch out that grace into the lives of others who need that saving grace.

If you enjoy the riches of God's personal friendship through thick and thin, then extend that friendship to the lonely through thick and thin.

Perplexities Will Always Remain

I don't mean that this answers all our questions about love, or that it takes away every kind of threat in loving our neighbor. There are many perplexities in the life of love. There are competing claims on our limited time. There are hard choices about what to give up and what to keep. There are different interpretations of what is good for another person. I don't mean here that all of that becomes simple.

What I do mean is this: loving God sustains us through all the joy and pain and perplexity and uncertainty of what loving our neighbor should be. When the sacrifice is great, we remember that his grace is sufficient. When the fork in the road is unmarked, we remember that his grace is sufficient. When we are distracted by the world and our hearts give way temporarily to selfishness, we remember that God alone can satisfy, and we repent and love his grace the more.

A World of Expanding Joy in God

It is a very radical command. It cuts to the root of sin, called pride. Remember, this root of pride that gives rise to all other sins, the passion to be happy, is contaminated and corrupted by two things: 1) the unwillingness to see God as the only fountain of true and lasting joy, and 2) the unwillingness to see other people as designed by God to receive our joy in him. But that is exactly the contamination and corruption that Jesus counteracts in these two commandments.

In the first commandment he focuses the passion to be happy firmly on God and God alone. In the second commandment he opens a whole world of expanding joy in God and says: people, human beings, everywhere you find them, are designed to receive your joy in God. Love them the way you love yourself. Show them, give them — through every practical means available — what you have found for yourself in God.

To sum up, the ancient misunderstanding of the command, "Love your neighbor as yourself" was the lawyer's attempt to restrict the meaning of "neighbor" to a certain group and thus to raise a question he hoped would conceal the real problem — his failure to be the person the commandment was calling him to be, one whose compassionate heart would never allow him to pass by on the other side of the road.

The modern misunderstanding of the command, most prevalent within the cult of the self, is the remarkably common notion that Jesus is not presupposing, but commanding self-love, and that self-love is equivalent to self-esteem, positive self-regard, and the like. But Jesus stated it as a fact that people love themselves. And the meaning of this self-love, (as is seen from the context, the Golden Rule, and Ephesians 5:28-29) is that all people desire and seek what they think will make them happy. This universal human trait becomes the rule to which all loving self-sacrifice must measure up.

It seems to me there is but a hair's difference between the self-justification that gave rise to the lawyer's error and the craving for self-esteem that nourishes the more modern error. Just how intimately the two errors are related I will leave for you to ponder.

APPENDIX 4

Why Call It Christian Hedonism?

I am aware that calling this philosophy of life "Christian Hedonism" runs the risk of ignoring Bishop Ryle's counsel against "the use of uncouth and new-fangled terms and phrases in teaching sanctification."[1] Nevertheless I stand by the term for at least six reasons:

1. My old *Webster's Collegiate Dictionary* of 1961, which has been within arm's reach since I was in the tenth grade, defines "hedonism" as "a living for pleasure." That is precisely what I mean by it. If the chief end of man is to enjoy God forever, human life *should* be a "living for pleasure."

2. The article on "hedonism" in *The Encyclopedia of Philosophy* shows that the term does not refer to a single precise philosophy. It is a general term to cover a wide variety of teachings which have elevated pleasure very highly. My use of the term falls inside the tolerance of this general usage.

I would be happy with the following definition as a starting point for my own usage of the word: *Hedonism* is "a theory according to which a person is motivated to produce one state of affairs in preference to another if and only if he thinks it will be more pleasant, or less unpleasant for himself."[2] I would only want to add: "forever." For there are deeds God calls us to do which in the short run are painful.

3. Other people, smarter and older than I am, have felt themselves similarly driven to use the term "hedonism" in reference to the Christian way of life.

For example, C. S. Lewis counsels his friend "Malcolm" to beware of committing idolatry in his enjoyment of nature. To be sure, he must enjoy the "sunlight in a wood." But these spontaneous pleasures are "patches of God-light" and one must let one's mind "run back up the sunbeam to the sun." Then Lewis comments,

> You notice that I am drawing no distinction between sensuous and aesthetic pleasures. But why should I? The line is almost impossible to draw and what use would it be if one succeeded in drawing it? If this is *Hedonism*, it is also a somewhat arduous discipline.[3]

We will find that it is indeed an arduous discipline!

In *The Simple Life,* Vernard Eller delights himself in some of the great parables of Søren Kierkegaard. One of his favorites is the parable of the lighted carriage and the starlit night. We could also call it the crisis of Christian Hedonism. It goes like this:

> When the prosperous man on a dark but starlit night drives comfortably in his carriage and has the lanterns lighted, aye, then he is safe, he fears no difficulty, he carries his light with him, and it is not dark close around him. But precisely because he has the lanterns lighted, and has a strong light close to him, precisely for this reason, he cannot see the stars. For his lights obscure the stars, which the poor peasant, driving without lights, can see gloriously in the dark but starry night. So those deceived ones live in the temporal existence: either, occupied with the necessities of life, they are too busy to avail themselves of the view, or in their prosperity and good days they have, as it were, lanterns lighted, and close about them everything is so satisfactory, so pleasant, so comfortable — but the view is lacking, the prospect, the view of the stars.[4]

Eller comments, "Clearly, 'the view of the stars' here intends one's awareness and enjoyment of God."[5] The rich and busy who surround themselves with the carriage lights of temporal comfort, or the busy who cover themselves with troublesome care, cut themselves off from what Kierkegaard calls "the absolute joy":

> What indescribable joy! — joy over God the Almighty. . . . For this is the absolute joy, to adore the almighty power with which God the Almighty bears all thy care and sorrow as easily as nothing.[6]

Eller applies all this to the so-called "simple life" and says,

> The motive of Christian simplicity is not the enjoyment of simplicity itself; that and any other earthly benefit that comes along are part of the 'all the rest' [Matthew 6:33]. But the sole motive of Christian simplicity is the enjoyment of God himself (and if that be *hedonism,* let's make the most of it!) — it is 'the view of the stars.'[7]

This is indeed hedonism! And I have done my best to make the most of it in this book.

Perhaps one other example will suffice. Clark Pinnock wrote a solid, popular defense of the Christian faith entitled *Reason Enough*. His second chapter is called "The Experiential Basis of Faith." It ends with a section under the heading, "Christian Hedonism?" He recounts his argument:

> I have seen the gospel as making us happy and fulfilling our needs, as giving us pleasure and satisfaction. But is this right?. . . Yes I think it is. . . . The Christian way is not hedonism in the ordinary sense, of course. It does not make a god out of sensual pleasure. But it does involve enjoying God and His gifts, pleasure deeper than all others.[8]

Precisely! Christian Hedonism does not make a god out of pleasure. It says you have already made a god out of whatever you take most pleasure in.

4. The fourth reason I use the term Christian Hedonism is that it has an arresting and jolting effect. My heart has been arrested and my life has been deeply jolted by the teaching of Christian Hedonism. It is not an easy or comfortable philosophy. It is extremely threatening to nominal Christians.

It is based on the devastating truth of Christ when he said, "Because you are lukewarm, and neither cold nor hot, I will spew you out of my mouth" (Revelation 3:16). This is utterly shocking. Should we not then find words to shock ourselves into realizing that eternity is at stake when we disobey the commandment, "Delight yourself in the LORD" (Psalm 37:4)?

Most of us are virtually impervious to the radical implications of familiar language. What language shall we borrow to awaken joyless believers to the words of Deuteronomy 28:47-48?

> Because you did not serve the LORD your God *with joyfulness and gladness of heart* . . . therefore you shall serve your enemies whom the LORD will send against you. . . and he will put a yoke of iron upon your neck, until he has destroyed you.

How shall we open their ears to the shout of Jeremy Taylor: "God threatens terrible things, if we will not be happy!"?[9]

I have found over the years that there is a correlation between people's willingness to get over the offensiveness of the term Christian Hedonism and their willingness to yield to the offensive biblical truth behind it. The chief effect of the term is not that it creates a stumbling block to the truth, but that it wakens people to the fact that the truth itself is a stumbling block — and often a very different one than they expected.

5. To the objection that the term *hedonism* carries connotations too worldly to be redeemed, I answer with the precedent of Scripture. If Jesus can describe his coming as the coming of a "thief" (Matthew 24:43-44); if he can extol a "dishonest steward" as a model of shrewdness (Luke 16:8); and if the inspired psalmist can say that the Lord awoke from sleep "like a strong man shouting because of wine" (Psalm 78:65), then it is a small thing for me to say the passion to glorify God by enjoying him forever is indeed Christian Hedonism.

6. Finally, by attaching the adjective "Christian" to the word "hedonism," I signal loud and clear that this is no ordinary hedonism. For me the word Christian carries this implication: Every claim to truth that flies under the banner of Christian Hedonism must be solidly rooted in the Christian Scriptures, the Bible. And the Bible teaches that man's chief end is to glorify God BY enjoying him forever.

A NOTE ON RESOURCES
DESIRING GOD MINISTRIES

If you would like to ponder further the vision of God and life presented in this book, we at Desiring God Ministries (DGM) would love to help you. DGM is a resource ministry of Bethlehem Baptist Church in Minneapolis, Minnesota. Our desire is to fan the flame of your passion for God and help you spread that passion to others. We have hundreds of resources available for this purpose. Most of our inventory consists of books and audiotapes by John Piper. In addition, we also produce God-centered children's curricula, host conferences, and coordinate John Piper's conference speaking schedule.

Since money is not our treasure, we try to keep our prices as low as possible. And since we don't want money to be a hindrance to the gospel, if our prices are more than you can pay at this time, our *whatever-you-can-afford* policy applies to almost all of our resources—even if you can't afford to pay anything! This policy is intended for individuals and we request that folks limit these orders to 3–4 items at a time. We also accept VISA, MasterCard, and Discover credit cards for convenience and speed, but we would rather give you resources than have you go into debt.

DGM exists to help you make God your treasure—because God is most glorified in you when you are most satisfied in him.

For more information or to request a free resource catalog, call us or visit our Web site.

1-888-346-4700 toll free in the USA
(612) 373-0651 international calls
(612) 338-4372 fax
www.desiringGOD.org
mail@desiringGOD.org

DESIRING GOD MINISTRIES
720 Thirteenth Avenue South
Minneapolis, Minnesota 55415-1793

(612) 338-7653 Bethlehem Baptist Church

NOTES

Notes, Preface (pages 9-12)

1. Richard Baxter, *The Saints' Everlasting Rest* (Grand Rapids: Baker Book House, 1978), p. 17 (emphasis added).
2. J. I. Packer, "Richard Baxter on Heaven, Hope and Holiness," in *Alive to God: Studies in Spirituality*, eds. J. I. Packer and Loren Wilkinson (Downers Grove: InterVarsity Press, 1992), p. 165.
3. Matthew Henry, *Commentary on the Whole Bible*, vol. 2 (Old Tappan, NJ: Fleming H. Revel, n.d., orig. 1708), p. 1096.

Notes, Introduction (pages 15-23)

1. Blaise Pascal, *Pascal's Pensées*, trans. by W. F. Trotter (New York: E. P. Dutton, 1958), p. 113 (thought #425).
2. C. S. Lewis, *The Weight of Glory and Other Addresses* (Grand Rapids: Eerdmans, 1965), pp. 1-2.
3. *Pascal's Pensées*, p. 113.
4. C. S. Lewis, *Reflections on the Psalms* (New York: Harcourt, Brace and World, 1958), pp. 94-95.
5. One of the most extended and serious critiques of Christian Hedonism to appear since *Desiring God* was first published is in Richard Mouw, *The God Who Commands* (Notre Dame, IN: Notre Dame Press, 1990). The quotation is taken from p. 33 (emphasis added).
6. Additional texts revealing the God-given duty of joy in God include Deuteronomy 28:47; 1 Chronicles 16:31,33; Nehemiah 8:10; Psalm 32:11; 33:1; 35:9; 40:8,16; 42:1-2; 63:1,11; 64:10; 95:1; 97:1,12; 98:4; 104:34; 105:3; Isaiah 41:16; Joel 2:23; Zechariah 2:10; 10:7; Philippians 3:1; 4:4. Additional texts mentioning the divine command of joy in loving others include 2 Corinthians 9:7; cf. Acts 20:35; Hebrews 10:34; 13:17; 1 Peter 5:2.
7. Richard Mouw, *The God Who Commands*, p. 36.

Notes, Chapter 1 (pages 33-50)

1. For a much fuller defense of God's sovereignty in all that he does, see John Piper, *The Pleasures of God: Meditations on God's Delight in Being God* (Sisters, OR: Multnomah Books, 1991), pp. 47-78, 123-160; and *The Justification of God: An Exegetical and Theological Study of Romans 9:1-23* (Grand Rapids: Baker Book House, 1993).
2. Proverbs 16:33.
3. "Personal Narrative," *Jonathan Edwards: Representative Selections*, eds. C. H. Faust, T. H. Johnson (New York: Hill and Wang, 1962), pp. 58-59.
4. Edwards treats this problem by distinguishing two kinds of willing in God (which is implied in what I have said). God's "will of command" (or revealed will) is what he commands in Scripture (Thou shalt not kill, etc.). His "will of decree" (or secret will, or sovereign will) is what he infallibly brings to pass in the world. Edwards's words are complex, but they are worth the effort if you love the deep things of God:

When a distinction is made between God's revealed will and his secret will, or his will of command and decree, "will" is certainly in that distinction taken in two senses. His will of decree, is not his will in the same sense as his will of command is. Therefore, it is no difficulty at all to suppose, that the one may be otherwise than the other: his will in both senses is his inclination. But when we say he wills virtue, or loves virtue, or the happiness of his creature; thereby is intended, that virtue, or the creature's happiness, absolutely and simply considered, is agreeable to the inclination of his nature.

His will of decree is his inclination to a thing, not as to that thing absolutely and simply, but with respect to the universality of things, that have been, are, or shall be. So God, though he hates a thing as it is simply, may incline to it with reference to the universality of things. Though he hates sin in itself, yet he may will to permit it, for the greater promotion of holiness in this universality, including all things, and at all times. So, though he has no inclination to a creature's misery, considered absolutely, yet he may will it, for the greater promotion of happiness in this universality.

"Concerning the Divine Decrees," *The Works of Jonathan Edwards*, vol. 2 (Edinburgh: Banner of Truth Trust, 1974), pp. 527-28.

5. The term "redemptive history" simply refers to the history of God's acts recorded in the Bible. It is called redemptive history not because it isn't real history, but because it is history viewed from the perspective of God's redeeming purpose.

6. Quoted from *The Four Loves*, in *A Mind Awake: An Anthology of C. S. Lewis*, ed. Clyde Kilby (New York: Harcourt, Brace and World, 1968), p. 202.

7. Hebrews 1:3.

8. Psalm 19:1.

9. If one should ask what place the Holy Spirit has in this understanding of the Trinity, I would direct attention to two works of Jonathan Edwards: "Treatise on Grace" and "An Essay on the Trinity." He sums up his understanding of the Trinity in these words:

And this I suppose to be that blessed Trinity that we read of in the Holy Scriptures. The Father is the deity subsisting in the prime, unoriginated and most absolute manner, or the deity in its direct existence. The Son is the deity generated by God's understanding, or having an idea of Himself and subsisting in that idea. The Holy Ghost is the deity subsisting in act, or the divine essence flowing out and breathed forth in God's infinite love to and delight in Himself. And I believe the whole Divine essence does truly and distinctly subsist both in the Divine idea and Divine love, and that each of them are properly distinct persons.

"An Essay on the Trinity," *Treatise on Grace and Other Posthumously Published Writings*, ed. Paul Helm (Cambridge: James Clarke and Co., 1971), p. 118.

In other words, the Holy Spirit is the delight that the Father and the Son have in each other.

So the Holy Spirit does in some ineffable and inconceivable manner proceed, and is breathed forth both from the Father and the Son, by the Divine essence being wholly poured and flowing out in that infinitely intense, holy, and pure love and delight that continually and unchangeably breathes forth from the Father and the Son, primarily towards each other, and secondarily towards the creature, and so flowing forth in a different subsistence or person in a manner to us utterly inexplicable and inconceivable, and that this is that person that is poured forth into the hearts of angels and saints.

"Treatise on Grace," *Treatise on Grace and Other Posthumously Published Writings*, p. 63.

10. I borrow this phrase from Daniel Fuller's book, *The Unity of the Bible: Unfolding God's Plan for Humanity* (Grand Rapids: Zondervan Publishing House, 1992). See especially chapters 8 and 9.

11. "Dissertation Concerning the End for Which God Created the World," *The Works of Jonathan Edwards*, vol. 1, p. 102. This "Dissertation" is of immense value in handling the whole question of God's goal in history.

12. Isaiah 48:11.

13. C. S. Lewis, *Reflections on the Psalms* (New York: Harcourt, Brace and World, 1958), pp. 93-95.

Notes, Chapter 2 (pages 53-70)

1. Romans 8:28.

2. If this summary of the gospel would be helpful in your own relationships with others, we have printed it in an attractive tract format entitled "Quest for Joy" available from Desiring God Ministries, 720 13th Avenue South, Minneapolis, MN 55415; phone: 612-338-7653; fax: 612-338-7656; E-mail: dgministry@aol. com.

3. For the biblical support against annihilationism and in support of hell as eternal conscious torment, see John Piper, *Let the Nations Be Glad: The Supremacy of God in Missions* (Grand Rapids: Baker Book House, 1993), chapter four.

4. Among evangelicals the reputation of George MacDonald's works has promoted this notion of hell as remedial and not eternal. For example, MacDonald's sermon called "Justice" in *Creation in Christ* (ed. Rolland Hein [Wheaton: Harold Shaw Publishers, 1976], pp. 63-81) argues vehemently against the orthodox view of hell:

> Mind I am not saying it is not right to punish [wicked people]; I am saying that justice is not, never can be, satisfied by suffering — nay, cannot have any satisfaction in or from suffering. . . . Such justice as Dante's keeps wickedness alive in its most terrible forms. The life of God goes forth to inform, or at least give a home to, victorious evil. Is He not defeated every time that one of these lost souls defies Him? God is triumphantly defeated, I say, throughout the hell of his vengeance. Although against evil, it is but the vain and wasted cruelty of a tyrant. . . . Punishment is for the sake of amendment and atonement. God is bound by His love to punish sin in order to deliver His creature: He is bound by his justice to destroy sin in His creation. (pp. 71-72)

> J. I. Packer discusses the contemporary forms of this view in "Good Pagans and God's Kingdom," *Christianity Today*, January 17, 1986, pp. 22-25.

5. "The Justice of God in the Damnation of Sinners," *The Works of Jonathan Edwards*, vol. 1 (Edinburgh: Banner of Truth Trust, 1974), p. 669.

6. I want to express gratitude and deep admiration for Edward John Carnell's penetrating analysis of "the judicial sentiment" and its relation to the existence of God. The judicial sentiment is the moral faculty that is duly offended when we are mistreated. Here is a taste of his words from the profound and beautiful book *Christian Commitment* (New York: Macmillan, 1957):

> Whereas conscience accuses the self the judicial sentiment accuses others. The direction of accusation is the important thing. Conscience monitors one's own moral conduct, while the judicial sentiment monitors the moral conduct of others.

> Furthermore, conscience is subject to social and cultural conditioning, whereas the judicial sentiment is not. All normal men, past, present, and future, experience an aroused judicial sentiment whenever they are personally mistreated. (p. 110)

An aroused judicial sentiment is merely heaven's warning that the image of God is being outraged. Cultural conditioning may alter the direction of the judicial sentiment, but it does not alter the faculty itself. (p. 112)

The voice of the judicial sentiment is the voice of God. (p. 136)

7. *Propitiation* is a rare word today. It has been replaced in many translations with more common words (expiation, atoning sacrifice). I keep it, in order to stress the original meaning, namely, that what Christ did by dying on the cross for sinners was to appease the wrath of God against sinners. By requiring of his Son such humiliation and suffering for the sake of God's glory, he openly demonstrated that he does not sweep sin under the rug. All contempt for his glory is duly punished, either on the cross, where the wrath of God is propitiated for those who believe, or in hell, where the wrath of God is poured out on those who don't.

8. The verb form of "conversion" (convert) is used in the Authorized Version of the New Testament in Matthew 13:15 (= Mark 4:12 = John 12:40 = Acts 28:27), Matthew 18:3, Acts 3:19, Luke 22:32, and James 5:19-20.

9. *Regeneration* is a big word for the new birth. It occurs in Greek (*palingenēsia*) only once in the New Testament (Titus 3:5) in reference to the new birth of person (also once in reference to the rebirth of the creation in the age to come, Matthew 19:28).

10. "In conversion man is active, and it wholly consists in his act; but in regeneration the Spirit of God is the only active cause." Samuel Hopkins, "Regeneration and Conversion," in *Introduction to Puritan Theology,* Edward Hindson, ed. (Grand Rapids: Baker Book House, 1976), p. 180. I recommend this entire essay as an excellent statement on the relationship between regeneration (new birth) and conversion (repentance and faith).

11. This is a great stumbling block for many people — to assert that we are responsible to do what we are morally unable to do. The primary reason for asserting it is not that it springs obviously from our normal use of reason, but that the Bible so plainly teaches it. It may help, however, to consider that the inability we speak of is not owing to a physical handicap, but to moral corruption. Our inability to believe is not the result of a physically damaged brain but of a morally perverted will. Physical inability would remove accountability. Moral inability does not. We cannot come to the light because our corrupt and arrogant nature hates the light. So when someone does come to the light "it is clearly seen that his deeds have been *wrought by God*" (John 3:21). The best treatment of this difficult subject I know of is Jonathan Edwards's *Freedom of the Will* (New Haven: Yale University Press, 1957, original 1754, also contained in *The Works of Jonathan Edwards,* vol. 1).

12. The Bible requires that we speak of God's "call" in at least two distinct senses. One call is the general or external call that goes out in the preaching of the gospel. Everyone who hears a gospel message or reads the Bible is called in this sense. But God calls in another sense to some who hear the gospel. This is God's internal or effectual call. It changes a person's heart so that faith is secured. It is like the call, "Let there be light!" or, "Lazarus, come forth!" It creates what it demands. The key passage that demands this distinction is 1 Corinthians 1:23-24, "We preach Christ crucified [general call], a stumbling block to Jews and folly to Gentiles, but to those who are called [effectual call] both Jews and Greeks, the power of God and the wisdom of God." Among the generally called there is a group who are "called" in such a way that they are enabled to esteem the gospel as wisdom and power. The change caused by the effectual call is none other than the change of regeneration.

13. The words for "grace" and "faith" are feminine in the original Greek. The word for "this" is neuter. Some have used this lack of agreement to say that the gift here is not faith. But this ignores the implication of verse 5: "*Even when you were dead!*" Grace is grace because it saved us even when we were dead. But it saves "through faith." How does it save the dead through faith? By awakening the dead into the life of faith. That is why faith is a gift in Ephesians 2:5-8. "This" refers to the whole event of salvation by grace through faith, and

therefore does include faith as a gift. (Cf. Acts 18:27, "When he arrived he greatly helped those who *through grace* had *believed*.")

14. Some have tried to argue that Romans 9 has nothing to do with individuals and their eternal destiny. But I have tried in turn to show that this is precisely what Paul has in mind because the problem he is wrestling with in this chapter is how individual Jews within God's chosen people Israel can be accursed and God's Word still stand. See Romans 9:3-6. I wrote a whole book to demonstrate this interpretation: *The Justification of God: An Exegetical and Theological Study of Romans 9:1-23*, 2nd edition (Grand Rapids: Baker Book House, 1993).

15. For a more extended treatment of the conditions of salvation and how they all resolve into faith and love, see John Piper, *The Purifying Power of Living by Faith in Future Grace*, (Sisters OR: Multnomah Books, 1995), chapters nineteen and twenty, especially pp. 255-259.

16. There is an interpretation that construes the treasure to be Israel, the field to be the world, and the man who sells all he has to buy the field to be Christ. The argument goes like this:

(a) The field is the world because the field in the parable of the weeds is the world (Matthew 13:38);

(b) the treasure is Israel because in Exodus 19:5 Israel is called God's peculiar treasure;

(c) Christ is never for sale, nor can salvation be bought.

I would construe the parable in the traditional way: The point is that the kingdom is more valuable than anything we could possibly own, and that we should be willing to joyfully give up everything to attain it. My argument goes like this:

(a) The kingdom is only *like* a man who sells all to buy a field with a treasure in it. Parables should not be pressed so hard that every word in them corresponds precisely to some particular part of reality. Pressing the details of parables opens the way for fanciful allegorizing with no control over what we make the details mean.

So the purchase of the field need not imply that salvation or Christ or the kingdom is purchased by us. It need only imply that the treasure of the kingdom is more valuable than all we have and that we should be willing to give up everything to have the kingdom.

(b) Just because the word "field" means "world" in Jesus' interpretation of the parable of the weeds (Matthew 13:38) does not mean that it must mean "world" here in Matthew 13:44. The word "field" does not mean world, for example, in the parable of the great banquet in Luke 14:18.

(c) Why should we go all the way back to Exodus 19:5 in order to determine what Jesus means by "treasure"? Isn't his ordinary use of the term a better indication of what he has in mind — especially if it occurs in contexts similar to this one?

The closest parallel to this text is Mark 10:21, where Jesus says to the rich young man, "Go and sell whatever you have and give to the poor, and you will have treasure in heaven, and come follow me." When the man turned away, Jesus said that it is indeed hard for a rich man to get into the kingdom of heaven. In other words, the kingdom is the real treasure that the man could have had if he had been willing to sell all his possessions and follow Jesus. The similarity between the wording of these two texts is so striking that I can't escape the implication that Jesus is really teaching the same thing in both places:

Matthew 13:44 — "he goes and sells all that he has"

Mark 10:21 — "Go sell whatever you have"

In both cases the reward of going and selling is the "treasure." In Mark it is explicitly called the kingdom. It would be very unlikely, then, if the treasure in Matthew 13:44 is not the kingdom.

Therefore, I conclude — (1) from Jesus' ordinary use of the word "treasure," (2) from the close similarity in wording between Mark 10:21 and Matthew 13:44, and (3) from the speculative nature of the opposite arguments — that the traditional interpretation is correct. As John Calvin said in the sixteenth century,

The straightforward meaning of the words is that the Gospel is not given its rightful honor unless we put it before all the riches, delights, honors and comforts of the world; and indeed that we should be so content with the spiritual blessings which it promises, that we neglect everything that would draw us from it. For those who aspire after heaven must be freed from all hindrances.

A Harmony of the Gospels Matthew, Mark and Luke, vol. 2, trans. by T. H. L. Parker (Grand Rapids: Eerdmans, 1975), p. 83.

17. Recalling our discussion of the Trinity in chapter one (note 5), it is worth musing over the implications that the Holy Spirit is the divine Workman who gives us a new heart of faith, and is himself the personification of the joy that the Father and the Son have in each other. We might say the change that must occur in the human heart to make saving faith possible is permeation by the Holy Spirit, which is nothing less than a permeation by the very joy that God the Father and God the Son have in each other's beauty. In other words, the taste for God that begets saving faith is God's very taste for himself, imparted to us in measure by the Holy Spirit.

Notes, Chapter 3 (pages 73-95)

1. As I use them in this book the words *feeling* and *emotion* and *affection* do not generally carry different meanings. If something distinct is intended in any given case, I will give some indication in the context. In general I use them synonymously and intend by them what Jonathan Edwards did in his great *Treatise Concerning the Religious Affections* (in *The Works of Jonathan Edwards,* vol. 1 [Edinburgh: Banner of Truth Trust, 1974], p. 237).

   Edwards defined the affections as "the more vigorous and sensible exercises of the inclination and will of the soul." To understand this we need to sum up briefly his view of the human soul or mind.

   > God has endued the soul with two principal faculties: The one, that by which it is capable of *perception* and speculation, or by which it discerns and judges of things; which is called the *understanding.* The other, that by which the soul is some way inclined with respect to the things it views or considers: or it is the faculty by which the soul beholds things — not as an indifferent unaffected spectator, but — either liking or disliking, pleased or displeased, approving or rejecting. This faculty is called by various names; it is sometimes called the *inclination;* and, as it respects the actions determined and governed by it, the *will;* and the *mind,* with regard to the exercises of this faculty, is often called the *heart . . .*

   > The will, and the affections of the soul, are not two faculties: the affections are not essentially distinct from the will, nor do they differ from the mere actings of the will and inclination, but only in the liveliness and sensibility of exercise . . .

   As examples of the affections, Edwards mentions (among others) love, hatred, desire, joy, delight, grief, sorrow, fear and hope. These are the "the more vigorous and sensible [i. e. sensed or felt] exercises of the will." Edwards is aware that there is a profound and complex relationship between the body and the mind at this point.

   > Such seems to be our nature, and such the laws of the union of soul and body, that there never is in any case whatsoever, any lively and vigorous exercise of the inclination, without some effect upon the body. . . . But yet, it is not the body, but the mind only, that is the proper seat of the affections. The body of man is no more capable of being really the subject of love or hatred, joy or sorrow, fear or hope, than the body of a tree, or than the same body of man is capable of thinking and understanding. As it is the soul only that has ideas, so it is the soul only that is pleased or displeased with

its ideas. As it is the soul only that thinks, so it is the soul only that loves or hates, rejoices or is grieved at, what it thinks of.

The biblical evidence for this is the fact that God, who has no body, nevertheless has many affections. Also Philippians 1: 23 and 2 Corinthians 5:8 teach that after a Christian's death, and before the resurrection of the body, the Christian will be with the Lord and capable of joys "far better" than what we have known here.

2. E. J. Carnell, *Christian Commitment* (New York: Macmillan, 1967), pp. 160-61. Carnell's whole book resounds with this emphasis (pp. 162, 176, 196, 206, 213, 222, 289, 301). Consider this insightful section from page 222.

> The more we make rectitude a calculated object of striving, the further we recede from moral fulfillment; for moral fulfillment is spontaneous, affectionate fulfillment. Love carries its own sense of compulsion. It is borne on the wings of the law of the spirit of life. When we must be motivated by either rational or legal necessity, love gives way to forecast, interest, and calculation. Suppose a mother rushes to help her terrified child. She acts out of spontaneous love. She would be offended by even the suggestion that she must help her child from a legal sense of duty. . . .

> Moral striving is paradoxical because we shall never love God unless we make a conscious effort; and yet because we must strive for legal righteousness, we prove that we shall never be righteous. If our affections were a fruit of the moral and spiritual environment, we should fulfill the law with the same unconscious necessity with which we breathe.

> The paradox can perhaps be illustrated by a painter who deliberately tries to become great. Unless he strives, he will never be an artist at all, let alone a great artist. But since he makes genius a deliberate goal of striving, he proves that he is not, and never will be, a genius. A master artist is great without trying to be great. His abilities unfold like the petals of a rose before the sun. Genius is a gift of God. It is a fruit, not a work.

> So is worship!

3. From a letter to Vanauken in Vanauken's book *A Severe Mercy* (New York: Harper and Row, 1977), p. 189.
4. Christian Hedonism is aware that self-consciousness kills joy and therefore kills worship. As soon as you turn your eyes in on yourself and become conscious of experiencing joy, it's gone. The Christian Hedonist knows that the secret of joy is self-forgetfulness. Yes, we go to the art museum for the *joy* of seeing the paintings. But the counsel of Christian Hedonism is: Set your whole attention on the paintings and not on your emotions, or you will ruin the whole experience. Therefore in worship there must be a radical orientation on God, not ourselves.
5. Quoted in E. M. Bounds, *The Weapon of Prayer* (Grand Rapids: Baker Book House, 1975), p. 136.
6. *Christian Commitment,* p. 213.
7. *Christian Commitment,* pp. 213-14.
8. C. S. Lewis, "The Weight of Glory" in *The Weight of Glory and other Essays* (Grand Rapids: Eerdmans, 1965), pp. 1-2.
9. Cited in Virginia Stem Owens, "Seeing Christianity in Red and Green as Well as Black and White," *Christianity Today,* September 2, 1983 (vol. 27, no. 13), p. 38.
10. For example, Carl Zylstra wrote (in "Just Dial the Lord," *The Reformed Journal* [October, 1984], p. 6): "The question is whether worship really is supposed to be a time for self-fulfillment and enjoyment or whether it should be, first of all, a time of service and honor to God, a sacrifice of praise." When the question is put like this, it cannot be answered

truthfully. It is very misleading. Of course worship is a time to honor God. But we kill that possibility by warning people not to pursue their own enjoyment. We should be telling them again and again to pursue their own enjoyment *in God!*

11. *For the Intellectual* (New York: Signet, 1961), p. 32.
12. *The Habit of Being,* ed. by Sally Fitzgerald (New York: Farrar, Straus, Giroux, 1979), p. 126.
13. Cited in C. H. Faust and T. H. Johnson, eds., *Jonathan Edwards: Selections* (New York: Hill and Wang, 1962), p. xviii.
14. Jonathan Edwards, *Some Thoughts Concerning the Revival* in *The Great Awakening,* ed. C. C. Goen (New Haven: Yale University Press, 1972), p. 387.
15. *Treatise Concerning the Religious Affections,* p. 238.
16. "The True Excellency of a Gospel Minister," *The Works of Jonathan Edwards,* vol. 2, p. 958.
17. John Broadus, *On the Preparation and Delivery of Sermons,* 4th ed., revised by Vernon Stanfield (New York: Harper and Row, 1979), p. 117.
18. These pairs are from a sermon by Jonathan Edwards entitled "The Excellency of Christ." In it Edwards meditates on the image of Christ in Revelation 5:5-6 as both the Lion of the tribe of Judah and the Lamb that was slain. The sermon is in *The Works of Jonathan Edwards,* vol. 1, pp. 680ff.

Notes, Chapter 4 (pages 97-121)

1. Jonathan Edwards, *Charity and Its Fruits* (Edinburgh: Banner of Truth Trust, 1969, original 1852), p. 164.
2. This passage in Romans includes the sentence "For even Christ did not please himself but, as it is written, 'The insults of those who insult you have fallen on me' " (15:3). Concerning this, see the discussion of Hebrews 12:1-2 under the heading "Love Suffers for Joy" later in this chapter.
3. Historically ethicists have tended to distinguish these two forms of love as *agape* and *eros,* or benevolence and complacency. But I think that both resolve into one kind of love at the root.

   God's agape does not "transcend" his eros, but expresses it. God's redeeming, sacrificial love for his sinful people is described by Hosea in the most erotic terms: "How can I give you up, O Ephraim! How can I hand you over, O Israel! . . . My heart recoils within me, my compassion grows warm and tender. I will not execute my fierce anger . . . for I am God and not man" (11:8-9). Concerning his exiled people who had sinned so grievously, God says later through Jeremiah, "I will *rejoice over them to do good to them* and I will truly plant them in this land *with all my heart and with all my soul"* (32:41).

   The divine motive of self-satisfying joy is seen also in Jesus' own ministry. When he was called to give an account of why he lowered himself to eat with tax collectors and sinners, his answer was "There will be *more joy in heaven* over one sinner who repents than over ninety-nine righteous persons who need no repentance" (Luke 15:1, 2, 7). Finally, we are told in Hebrews 12:2 by what power Jesus endured suffering: "*For the joy that was set before him* he endured the cross, despising the shame, and is seated at the right hand of the throne of God." Should we not infer that in the painful work of redeeming love, God is *very* interested in the satisfaction that comes from his efforts, and that he *does* demand the pleasure of a great return on his sacrifice?

   While there is a sense in which God has no need for creation at all (Acts 17:25) and that he is profoundly fulfilled and happy in the eternal fellowship of the Trinity, yet there is in joy an urge to increase, by expanding itself to others who, if necessary, must first be created and redeemed. This divine urge is God's desire for the compounded joy that comes from having others share the very joy he has in himself.

   It becomes evident, therefore, that one should not ask, Does God seek his own happiness as a means to the happiness of his people, or does he seek their happiness as a means to his own? For there is no either-or. They are one. This is what distinguishes a holy, divine *eros* from a fallen, human one: God's *eros* longs for and delights in the eternal and holy joy of his people.

4. I would never use the word *earn* for the way Christians come to enjoy the rewards of love. *Earn* implies the exchange of value from one to another that obligates the other to pay because of the value he has received. But in truth, everything Christians "give" to God is simply a rebound of God's gift to them. All our service is done "in the strength which he supplies" (1 Peter 4:11), so that it is in fact God who "earns" the reward for us and through us. But this does not diminish the helpfulness of Lewis's comment on the nature of rewards.

5. C. S. Lewis, *The Weight of Glory and Other Addresses* (Grand Rapids: Eerdmans, 1965), p. 2.

6. Phillips Brooks, *Lectures on Preaching* (Grand Rapids: Baker Book House, 1969, original 1907), pp. 53-54, 82-83.

7. Quoted in Daniel P. Fuller, *Hermeneutics* (Pasadena: Fuller Theological Seminary, 1969), pp. VII-4, 5.

Notes, Chapter 5 (pages 123-134)

1. From a letter cited in Norman Anderson, *God's Word for God's World* (London: Hodder and Stoughton, 1981), p. 25.

2. The story is recounted in *God's Word for God's World,* pp. 38-41.

3. *Hudson Taylor's Spiritual Secret* (Chicago: Moody Press, n.d., original 1932), p. 235.

4. Quoted in Roland Bainton, *Here I Stand* (New York: Mentor, 1950), p. 144.

5. *Here I Stand,* p. 149.

6. *Autobiography of George Mueller,* compiled by Fred Bergen, (London: J. Nisbet Co., 1906), pp. 152-54.

Notes. Chapter 6 (pages 137-156)

1. *Twelve Sermons on Prayer* (Grand Rapids: Baker Book House, 1971), p. 105.

2. *Twelve Sermons on Prayer,* p. 115.

3. Thomas Traherne, *Centuries, Poems, and Thanksgivings* (London: Oxford University Press, 1958), p. 14.

4. Augustine, quoted from the *Confessions* in *Documents of the Christian Church,* Henry Bettenson, ed., (London: Oxford University Press, 1967), p. 54.

5. Quoted from *Letters to Malcolm* in *A Mind Awake: An Anthology of C. S Lewis,* ed. Clyde Kilby (New York: Harcourt, Brace and World, 1968), p. 204.

6. C. S. Lewis, *Reflections on the Psalms* (New York: Harcourt, Brace and World, 1958), pp. 82-83.

7. "Personal Narrative" in C. H. Faust, T. H. Johnson, eds., *Jonathan Edwards* (New York: Hill and Wang, 1962), p. 61.

8. Iain H. Murray, *The Puritan Hope* (Edinburgh: Banner of Truth, 1971), pp. 99-103.

9. Colin Grant, "Europe's Moravians: A Pioneer Missionary Church" in *Perspectives on the World Christian Movement,* Ralph Winter and Steven Hawthorne eds., (Pasadena: William Carey Library, 1981), pp. 206-9.

10. Jonathan Edwards, *An Humble Attempt to Promote Explicit Agreement and Visible Union of God's People in Extraordinary Prayer for the Revival of Religion and the Advancement of Christ's Kingdom on Earth . . . in Apocalyptic Writings,* Stephen Stein ed., (New Haven: Yale University Press, 1977), pp. 309-436.

11. Winter and Hawthorne, *Perspectives on the World Christian Movement,* pp. 210-26.

12. See especially David Bryant, *Concerts of Prayer* (Ventura: Regal Books, 1984) and Dick

Eastman, *The Hour that Changes the World* (Grand Rapids: Baker Book House, 1978).

13. J. Edwin Orr, *The Light of the Nations* (Grand Rapids: Eerdmans, 1965), pp. 103-5.

Notes, Chapter 7 (pages 159-173)

1. T. W. Manson, *The Sayings of Jesus* (London: SCM Press, 1949), p. 280.

2. John Piper, *Love Your Enemies* (Cambridge: Cambridge University Press, 1979). On pages 163-65 I list and discuss these instances.

3. This does not contradict the biblical doctrine of the eternal security of God's chosen people who are truly born again, a doctrine firmly established by Romans 8:30. But it does imply there is a change of heart if we have been born of God; and this includes evidences in the way we use our money. Jesus warned repeatedly of the false confidence that bears no fruit and will forfeit life in the end (Matthew 7:15-27; 13:47-50; 22:11-14).

4. James Stewart, *Heralds of God* (Grand Rapids: Baker Book House, 1972), p. 97.

5. Ralph Winter, "Reconsecration to a Wartime, not a Peacetime, Lifestyle," in *Perspectives on the World Christian Movement,* Ralph Winter, and Steven Hawthorne, eds. (Pasadena: William Carey Library, 1981), p. 814.

6. Winter, "Reconsecration," p. 815.

Notes, Chapter 8 (pages 175-187)

1. Blaise Pascal, *Pascal's Pensées,* trans. by W. F. Trotter (New York: E. P. Dutton and Co., 1958), p. 113 (thought #425).

2. Jonathan Edwards, *The Works of Jonathan Edwards,* vol. 2 (Edinburgh: Banner of Truth, 1974), p. 905. The quote is found in a sermon on Matthew 5:8 entitled, "Blessed Are the Pure in Heart."

3. E. J. Carnell, *Christian Commitment* (New York: Macmillan, 1957), p. 96.

4. Karl Barth, *The Doctrine of Creation, Church Dogmatics,* vol. III, 4, trans. by A. T. Makay, et. al. (Edinburgh: T. and T. Clark, 1961), p. 375.

5. The covenant that binds Christ to the church is called in Hebrews 13:20 an "eternal covenant." "May the God of peace who brought again from the dead our Lord Jesus, the great shepherd of the sheep, by the blood of the eternal covenant . . ." Therefore the relationship between Christ and the church has eternally been in God's mind, and in the order of his thought it precedes and governs the creation of marriage.

6. Geoffrey Bromiley, *God and Marriage* (Grand Rapids: Eerdmans, 1980), p. 43.

7. N. G. L. Hammond and H. H. Scullard, eds., *The Oxford Classical Dictionary* (Oxtord: The Clarendon Press, 1970), p. 59.

8. *The Special Laws,* III, 184, quoted from Loeb Classical Library, vol. 8, p. 591.

9. *Theological Dictionary of the New Testament,* Gerhard Kittle, ed., vol. 3 (Grand Rapids: Eerdmans, 1965), p. 674.

10. Alvera and Berkeley Mickelsen, "Does Male Dominance Tarnish Our Translations?" *Christianity Today,* October 5, 1979, p. 25.

11. Stephen Bedale, "The Meaning of *Kephalē* in the Pauline Epistles," *Journal of Theological Studies* 5 (October, 1954), p. 215.

12. See Gilbert Bilezekian, *Beyond Sex Roles* (Grand Rapids: Baker Book House, 1985), pp. 157-162. But Wayne Grudem has shown that this is an extremely unlikely meaning for the singular use of "head" in Paul's day. See his appendix in *Recovering Biblical Manhood and Womanhood* (Wheaton, IL: Crossway Books, 1991), pp. 425-468.

13. Headship and submission did not originate with the Fall, as so many people claim, but in their pure form were part of God's intention from the beginning of creation before the Fall. See Raymond C. Ortlund Jr., "Male-Female Equality and Male Headship, Genesis 1-3," in *Recovering Biblical Manhood and Womanhood,* pp. 95-112.

14. I have tried elsewhere, with others, to give explanation and justification for the vision of manhood and womanhood in this chapter. See *Recovering Biblical Manhood and Womanhood,* John Piper and Wayne Grudem, eds.

Notes, Chapter 9 (pages 189-211)

1. Ralph Winter, "The Retirement Booby Trap," *Mission Frontiers* 7 (July 1985), p. 25.
2. "The Retirement Booby Trap," p. 25.
3. *Time* (December 27, 1982), p. 52.
4. *Time* (December 27, 1982), p. 56.
5. For the detailed support of this claim see chapter four, "The Supremacy of Christ as the Conscious Focus of All Saving Faith," in John Piper's *Let the Nations Be Glad: The Supremacy of God in Missions,* (Grand Rapids: Baker Book House, 1993), pp. 115-166.
6. In 1980 *The Division of Overseas Ministries of the National Council of Churches* had a membership of thirty-two missions representing just under 5,000 missionaries. Income approaches $200 million annually. The *Interdenominational Foreign Mission Association* represented ninety interdenominational mission boards with roughly 10,700 missionaries and an income of $150 million. The *Evangelical Foreign Missions Association* had a membership of eighty-two mission agencies representing more than 10,000 missionaries and an income of $350 million.

   > During the decade of the seventies, the DOM (the more liberal group) lost 3,462 missionaries, while the IFMA and EFMA (the more evangelical groups) gained 3,785. Incomewise, the DOM increased by $28 million or 24 percent while the IFMA/EFMA increased by $285 million or 293 percent.

   > Peter Wagner, *On the Crest of the Wave* (Ventura: Regal Books, 1983), pp. 77-78

7. For a detailed exploration of the biblical support for thinking of the Great Commission in terms of reaching people groups see Chapter Five, "The Supremacy of Christ as the Conscious Focus of All Saving Faith," in John Piper's *Let the Nations Be Glad: The Supremacy of God in Missions* (Grand Rapids: Baker Book House, 1993), pp. 167-223. An excellent discussion of the definition of "unreached peoples" and the problem of counting and locating them is given by Ralph Winter in "Unreached Peoples: The Development of the Concept," *International Journal of Frontier Missions 1* (1984), pp. 129-161.
8. Luis Bush, "What Is the Joshua Project 2000?" in *Mission Frontiers*, Vol. 17, No. 11-12, November-December, 1995, p. 9.
9. The 10/40 Window refers to the rectangular area on a global map measured horizontally from West Africa to East Asia and vertically from the 10th to the 40th latitude north of the equator.
10. Rick Wood, "MF Behind the Scenes," in *Mission Frontiers*, vol. 17, No. 11-12, November-December, 1995, p. 5.
11. "When Jesus Said . . .," *Missions Frontiers*, vol. 17, No. 11-12, November-December, 1995, p. 56.
12. These figures are taken from an article by Ralph Winter, "The Momentum Is Building in Global Missions: Basic Concepts in Frontier Missiology," *Mission Frontiers, 1990 Special Edition*, pp. 17-26. Winter said the numbers are provided by David Barrett and the Statistics Task Force of the Lausanne Committee for World Evangelization.
13. "Non-Christian" here means people who do not identify themselves as Christian. "Believer" refers to estimates of true believers among the vast multitude of people that consider themselves Christians. Another way of describing this group is "Great Commission Christians" — a term suggested by David Barrett — those who take the task of world evangelization fairly seriously.

14. These numbers are high because a narrower definition of "people group" is being used than the "ethno-linguistic" definition referred to earlier. See note 8.

15. Congregations are assumed to be an average of 100 people of the "Great Commission Christians" referred to on page 194.

16. David Bryant, *In the Gap* (Madison: InterVarsity Press, 1981), p. 62.

17. Iain Murray writes in *The Forgotten Spurgeon* (Edinburgh: Banner of Truth, 1973), p. 47:

> Hyper-Calvinism in its attempt to square all truth with God's purpose to save the elect, denies that there is a universal command to repent and believe, and asserts that we have only warrant to invite to Christ those who are *conscious* of a sense of sin and need. In other words, it is those who have been spiritually quickened to seek a Saviour and not those who are in the death of unbelief and indifference, to whom the exhortations of the Gospel must be addressed. In this way a scheme was devised for restricting the Gospel to those who there is reason to suppose are elect. This is an excellent book to show how Charles Spurgeon, the Baptist pastor in London in the latter half of the nineteenth century, held together strong (Calvinistic) views of the sovereignty of God with a powerful and fruitful soul-winning ministry. He fought against the hyper-Calvinists on the one side, and the Arminians on the other in a way I consider exemplary.

18. See also Matthew 10:39 and 16:24-26, Luke 9:24-25 and 17:33, John 12:25, and Revelation 12:11.

19. Sermon 368, *Migne Patrologia Latina* 39, 1652.

20. Jonathan Edwards, ed., *The Life and Diary of David Brainerd* (Chicago: Moody Press, 1949, original, 1749), p. 149. By "self-interest" I take Brainerd to mean "worldly, self-interest that does not have the glory of God for its pleasure." He goes on to say that "love is a pleasing passion; it affords pleasure to the mind where it is." But the object of love is never that pleasure. The object is God and the love is pleasurable. This is why it is confusing at times when we speak of seeking pleasure. It sounds as though pleasure has taken the place of God. But this is not the case. As Brainerd says, God's glory and our happiness become one common interest. We seek pleasure in God. Not from God.

21. Cited in Samuel Zwemer, "The Glory of the Impossible" in *Perspectives on the World Christian Movement*, Ralph Winter and Stephen Hawthorne, eds. (Pasadena: William Carey Library, 1981), p. 259. Emphasis added.

22. On this last text Adolf Schlatter comments powerfully, "Paul cannot look at his position as a Christian in isolation, separated from his work in the service of Jesus, as though the way he performed his ministry had no significant connection with his salvation. Since it was the Lord who gave him his ministry Paul stays bound to Him only if he carries it out faithfully. And the Gospel would no longer be valid in his own life, if he forsook his ministry. That gives Paul's love its purity. He enters into community with all, that he might win them. But his will remains free from the presumption that says to others that only they are in danger and need salvation. Rather the question of salvation retains for him, as also for them its full seriousness. He takes pains therefore that he save others for his own salvation." *Die Korintherbriefe*, vol. 6, *Erlaeuterungen zum Neuen Testament* (Stuttgart: Calwer Verlag, 1974), p. 118.

23. Colin Grant, "Europe's Moravians: A Pioneer Missionary Church" in *Perspectives on the World Christian Movement*, p. 206.

24. Andrew Murray, *Key to the Missionary Problem* (Fort Washington: Christian Literature Crusade, 1979, original 1905), p. 127.

25. Cited in Ruth Tucker, *From Jerusalem to Irian Jaya* (Grand Rapids: Zondervan, 1983), p. 237. Charlotte Diggs (Lottie) Moon was born in 1840 in Virginia and sailed for China as a Baptist missionary in 1873. She is known not only for her pioneering work in China, but also for her mobilizing the women of the Southern Baptist Church for the missionary cause.

26. Cited in *From Jerusalem to Irian Jaya*, p. 239.
27. E. G. Carre, *Praying Hyde* (South Plainfield: Bridge Publishing Co., n.d.), p. 66.
28. Cited in *From Jerusalem to Irian Jaya*, p. 277.
29. Daniel Fuller, *Gospel and Law: Contrast or Continuum?* (Grand Rapids: Eerdmans, 1980), pp. 117-19.
30. From a letter to Father Perez in Francis M. DuBose, ed., *Classics of Christian Missions* (Nashville: Broadman Press, 1979), pp. 221 ff.
31. Mary Drewery, *William Carey, A Biography* (Grand Rapids: Zondervan, 1978), p. 157.
32. Dr. and Mrs. Howard Taylor, *Hudson Taylor's Spiritual Secret* (Chicago: Moody Press, n.d., original 1932), p. 209. Consistently, he once answered an admirer's praise with these words: "I often think that God must have been looking for someone small enough and weak enough for Him to use, and that He found me" (pp. 201ff.). His son comments that he would have been fully in accord with Andrew Murray who wrote, "Take time to read His Word as in His presence, that from it you may know what He asks of you and what He promises you. Let the Word create around you, create within you a holy atmosphere, a holy heavenly light, in which your soul will be refreshed and strengthened for the work of daily life" (p. 236).
33. Jeremiah Burroughs, *The Rare Jewel of Christian Contentment* (Edinburgh: Banner of Truth, 1964, original 1648), p. 83.
34. Elisabeth Elliot, *Shadow of the Almighty: The Life and Testament of Jim Elliot* (New York: Harper and Brothers, 1958), p. 19.

Notes, Chapter 10 (pages 213-238)

1. Richard Wurmbrand, *Reaching toward the Heights* (Bartlesville, OK: Living Sacrifice Books, 1992), back cover.
2. Quoted by Philip Yancey in "Frozen Fire," *Christianity Today*, October 5, 1984, p. 109.
3. Marvin Vincent, I. C. C., *Epistle to the Philippians and to Philemon* (Edinburgh: T. & T. Clark, 1897), p. 78.
4. Joseph Tson, "A Theology of Martyrdom," an undated booklet of The Romanian Missionary Society, P. O. Box 527, Wheaton, IL, 60189-057, p. 4.
5. Stephen Neil, *A History of Christian Missions* (Harmondsworth, Middlesex: Penguin Books Ltd., 1964), pp. 43-44.
6. Quoted in "The Martyrdom of Polycarp," in *Documents of the Christian Church*, Henry Bettenson, ed., (London: Oxford University Press, 1967), p. 10.
7. "The Martyrdom of Polycarp," pp. 9-10.
8. "The Martyrdom of Polycarp," p. 11.
9. "The Martyrdom of Polycarp," p. 12.
10. George Otis, Jr., *The Last of the Giants: Lifting the Veil on Islam and the End Times* (Grand Rapids: Chosen Books, 1991), pp. 261, 263.
11. Quoted in Joseph Tson, "A Theology of Martyrdom," p. 1.
12. See the examples in John Piper's *Let the Nations Be Glad: The Supremacy of God in Missions* (Grand Rapids: The Baker Book House, 1993), pp. 94-96. See almost any of the books by Richard Wurmbrand, for example, *Tortured for Christ* or *If That Were Christ, Would You Give Him Your Blanket?* or *Victorious Faith*. Other sources include *Called to Suffer, Called to Triumph* by Herbert Schlossberg, and *God Reigns in China* by Leslie Lyall.
13. Joseph Tson, "A Theology of Martyrdom," p. 2.
14. "A Theology of Martyrdom," p. 3.
15. Richard Wurmbrand, "Preparing for the Underground Church," in *Epiphany Journal*, Vol. 5, No. 4, Summer, 1985, p. 50.
16. Brother Andrew, "God's Smuggler Confesses," an interview with Michael Maudlin in *Christianity Today*, December 11, 1995, p. 46.

Notes, Epilogue (pages 239-254)

1. Karl Barth, *Church Dogmatics*, III, 4 (Edinburgh: T. and T. Clark, 1961), pp. 379-80.
2. C. S. Lewis, *A Mind Awake: An Anthology of C. S. Lewis*, ed. Clyde Kilby (New York: Harcourt Brace and World, 1968), p. 22.
3. *A Mind Awake*, p. 25.
4. *A Mind Awake*, pp. 22-23.
5. George Bush, *Notes on Exodus*, vol. 2 (Minneapolis: James and Klock, 1976, original 1852), p. 225.
6. Henry Alford, *The Greek New Testament*, vol. 2 (Chicago: Moody Press, 1958, orig. 1873), p. 403.
7. *The Treatise Concerning the Religious Affections*, in *The Works of Jonathan Edwards* (Edinburgh: Banner of Truth Trust, 1974), p. 236. See the discussion of the meaning of the affections in chapter three, note 1.
8. John Murray, *Principles of Conduct* (Grand Rapids: Eerdmans, 1957), pp. 38-39.
9. Howard and Geraldine Taylor, *Hudson Taylor's Spiritual Secret* (Chicago: Moody Press, n.d., original 1932), p. 30.

Note, Appendix 1 (pages 255-266)

1. For a larger development of this understanding of God's righteousness, see John Piper's *The Justification of God*, 2d ed., (Grand Rapids: Baker Book House, 1993).

Notes, Appendix 2 (pages 267-276)

1. For example, B. B. Warfield, *The Inspiration and Authority of the Bible* (London: Marshall Morgan and Scott, 1959); F. F. Bruce, *The New Testament Documents: Are They Reliable?* (Grand Rapids: Wm. B. Eerdmans Publishing Co., 1943); J. Norval Geldenhuys, *Supreme Authority* (Grand Rapids: Wm. B. Eerdmans Publishing Co., 1953); J. I. Packer, *Fundamentalism and the Word of God* (London: InterVarsity Press, 1958); Edward J. Young, *Thy Word Is Truth* (Grand Rapids: Wm. B. Eerdmans Publishing Co., 1957); J. B. Phillips, *The Ring of Truth* (New York: The Macmillan Co., 1967); John W. Wenham, *Christ and the Bible* (London: Tyndale Press, 1972); James Boice, ed., *The Foundation of Biblical Authority* (Grand Rapids: Zondervan Publishing House, 1978); D. A. Carson and John D. Woodbridge, *Scripture and Truth* (Grand Rapids: Zondervan Publishing House, 1983).
2. The Apocrypha is a group of ancient books written during the time between the Old and New Testaments. They are included in Catholic editions of the Old Testament, but Protestants have generally rejected them as part of the authoritative inspired canon of Scripture. For the texts, see *The Oxford Annotated Apocrypha of the Old Testament*, ed. Bruce Metzger (New York: Oxford University Press, 1965).
3. Norman Anderson, *God's Word for God's World* (London: Hodder and Stoughton, 1981), p. 112. The Jewish Scriptures include all our Old Testament but in a different order.
4. For pursuing such a study, I recommend Daniel Fuller, *Easter Faith and History* (Grand Rapids: Eerdmans, 1965) and John W. Wenham, *Christ and the Bible* (London: Tyndale, 1972).
5. After translating the Gospels into "racy modern English," J. B. Philips wrote the following in *The Ring of Truth* (London: Hodder and Stoughton, 1967), pp. 57-58: "I felt, and feel, without any shadow of doubt that close contact with the text of the Gospels builds up in the heart and mind a character of awe-inspiring stature and quality. I have read, in Greek and Latin, scores of myths but I did not find the slightest flavor of myth here. There is no hysteria, no careful working for effect and no attempt at collusion. These are not embroidered tales: the material is cut to the bone. One sensed again and again that understatement

which we have been taught to think is more 'British' than Oriental. There is an almost child-like candor and simplicity, and the total effect is tremendous. No man could ever have invented such a character as Jesus. No man could have set down such artless and vulnerable accounts as these unless some real Event lay behind them."

6. *The Baptist Catechism*, commonly called *Keach's Catechism*, revised and edited by Paul Jewett (Grand Rapids: Baker Book House, 1952), p. 16.

Notes, Appendix 3 (pages 277-286)

1. Part of this appendix is adapted from an article that first appeared in *Christianity Today* (August 12, 1977), pp. 6-9.

Notes, Appendix 4 (pages 287-290)

1. J. C. Ryle, *Holiness* (Grand Rapids: Baker Book House, 1979, original 1883), p. XXIX.
2. *The Encyclopedia of Philosophy*, 1967 ed. s.v. "Hedonism," vol. 3, p. 433 .
3. C. S. Lewis, *Letters to Malcolm: Chiefly on Prayer* (New York: Harcourt Brace Jovanovich, 1963), p. 90.
4. V. Eller, *The Simple Life* (Grand Rapids: Eerdmans, 1973), p. 12.
5. *The Simple Life*, p. 12.
6. *The Simple Life*, p. 109.
7. *The Simple Life*, pp. 121-22.
8. C. H. Pinnock, *Reason Enough* (Downers Grove: InterVarsity Press, 1980), p. 54.
9. Quoted in C. S. Lewis, *George MacDonald: An Anthology* (London: Geoffrey Bles: The Centenary Press: 1946), p. 19.

SCRIPTURE INDEX

Genesis
1:3 296
1:26-27 255
1:28 256
1:31 256
2 179-81
2:18 179
2:19-20 179
2:21 179
2:23-24 180
2:23 179
2:24 179,181,275
4:8 274
11:1-4 256,257
12:1-2 257
15:6 257
50:20 38

Exodus
14:4,18 258
19:5 297
20:3-5 259
20:17 247
32 245
32:11-14 260
32:31-32 245
32:32 245

Leviticus
19:17-18 248
19:18 178,278

Numbers
14:13-16 260
14:21 256

Deuteronomy
8:3 125
8:17-18 168
9:27-29 260
28:47 293
28:47-48 242-43,289
30:6 63
32:46-47 124
32:47 125

Joshua
24:12-14 260-61

Judges
10:18 182
11:8-9 182

1 Samuel
12:19-23 261

2 Samuel
7:23 261
12:10 57
22:44 182

1 Kings
1-22 261
4:29 128
8 261
8:29 262
8:41-45 262

2 Kings
1-25 261
6:24-7:20 239
7:9 239

16:31,33 293
19:34 262
20:6 262

2 Chronicles
16:9 146
24:21 274

Ezra
6:22 37
7:9,10 131-32

Nehemiah
8:10 10,293

Job
2:7 36
2:10 36
22:25 20
42:2 36

Psalms
1:1-2 130
4:7 93
5:7 80
5:11 93
9:2 93
16:11 19,81,97,166,284
17:15 93
18:19 128
18:43 182
19:1 44,94
19:7-8 129
19:7 123,124
19:8,10-11 122
19:8 130
23:2-3 123
23:3 261
25:11 261
27:4 81,142,240
30:11-12 80
32:11 84,293

33:1 293
33:6 125
33:8 80
33:10-11 34
33:20-22 146
34:8 19
35:9 293
36:8 19
37:4 9,19,20,55,81,84,
                87,97,242,244,289
40:3 207
40:8 93
40:8,16 293
42:1-2 19,80,293
42:5 80,86,248
43:4 19
46:10 80
50:12,15 144
50:12 85
50:15 140,144
50:23 56
51:10,12 93
51:17 80,248
63:1 19,34,80
63:1,11 293
63:1-3 94
63:3 112
63:5 85
64:10 293
73:22 86
73:25-26 80,94,142
73:25 144
76:10 79
78:5,7 128
78:65 290
84:10 251
95:1,12 293
96:6-8 78
98:4 293
100:2 248
104:31 42
104:34 293
105:3 293

106:6-8 258
106:13 146
110:1 269,275
115:3 32,34,35,50
119:9 128
119:11 128
119:16 130
119:18 153
119:45 128
119:50,52 129
119:97 130,132
119:98 129
119:103 19
119:105 128
119:111 130
123:2 147
130:5 80
135:5-7 38
147:11 54
148:7,9 78

Proverbs
3:13 129
3:11-12 217
13:14 74
16:33 35,39,293
21:1 37
31:10 174

Ecclesiastes
3:11 214

Isaiah
1:11 253
6:1-3 240
7:8 182
8:13 80
8:17 146
29:13 76,78
30:15,16 146
30:18 146
41:16 293

42:1 44
43:6-7 55
43:7 256
46:1 145
46:9-10 35
48:9-11 263
48:11 45,54
49:3 257
53:4,10 41
54:2-3 208
57:15 79,80
58:11 236
58:13-14 253
64:4 145,149

Jeremiah
2:11-13 87
9:24 100
10:5 145
15:16 130
24:7 63
32:40-41 54
32:41 300

Lamentations
2:11 36
3:37-38 36

Ezekiel
11:19-20 63
11:19 57,62
18:32 40
20:5-9 258
20:13-14 259
20:21-22 259
36:22-32 277
36:22-23,32 263
36:26-27 63
36:26 57,62,298

Daniel
4:34-35 35-36

Hosea
11:8-9 300

Joel
2:23 293

Amos
3:6 36
3:15 171
5:21-24 253
8:11-12 92

Micah
6:8 21,98,99,103,251

Habakkuk
2:20 80

Haggai
1:8 263

Zechariah
2:5 263
2:10 293
10:7 293

Malachi
2:2 264

Matthew
1:21 207
3:17 44
4:4,7,10 275
4:4 125
5:3-9 268
5:10 210
5:11-12 234,250
5:16 231,265
5:17-18 275
5:22 57
6:3-4 166,252
6:4 252

6:6 136
6:10 140
6:19-20 110
6:19-21 165
6:24 148
6:33 288
7:12 281
7:14 53
7:15-27 302
7:21 52
7:29 269
8:12 58
9:9-13 268
9:38 152
10:29 39
10:32-33 270
10:37 65
10:39 304
11:29 262
12:32 58
12:39-40 271
12:41-42 270
13:15 296
13:38 297
13:42-43 153
13:44 20,52,66,297
13:47-50 302
15:8-9 78
15:8 79,81,268
16:4 271
16:24-26 304
18:3 65,296
18:9 58
18:35 248
19:4-5 275
19:28 296
21:42 271
22:11-14 302
22:13 58
22:15-22 269
22:18 269
22:29 275
22:39 178

22:41-46 269
23:15 207
24:14 195,196
24:43-44 290
24:51 58
25:2 54
25:21,23 20
25:30 58
25:32 54
25:41,46 58
26:54,56 275
26:61 269,271
28:11-15 271

Mark

1:27 270
2:5 270
2:17 147,207
3:4-5 268
4:12 296
6:31-34 268
7:9 275
7:24-30 268
8:34-35 65,202
8:35 244
8:36 171
9:24 153
9:32 272
9:47-48 58
10:13-16 268
10:17-22 270
10:17-31 196-97,201
10:21 269,297
10:23 168
10:25-27 197
10:27 199,201,210
10:28-30 201
10:28 202
10:29-30 206,210
10:30 209
10:45 144,269
10:46-52 268

11:15-17 268
12:14 269
12:36 275
14:58 271

Luke

3:11 169,172
6:22-23 234
6:35 118,166,234
6:46 248
7:36-50 268
9:23-24 221
9:24-25 304
9:58 169,202
10:3 221
10:25 278
10:27 . .277,278,279-80,284
10:29-37 278-86
11:13 153
12:1 268
12:5 248
12:29 168-69
12:32-34 165
12:33 110,158,166,168,
252
12:35-37 144-45
12:57 273
14:13-14 165,166
14:14 166,235
14:18 297
14:26-33 270
14:33 65,112
15:1,2,7 300
15:7 106
16:1-13 166
16:8 290
16:9 158,166
16:17 275
17:11-19 268
17:24 95
17:33 304
19:8 169

21:12,16,18-19 209
21:16 221
21:34-36 152
22:3 217
22:15 269
22:26 184
22:32 153,269,296
23:11 37
23:21 37
23:24 37
23:34 126,269
23:36 37
24:11 272
24:21 272
24:25 275
24:44 274

John

1:1 44
1:12 65
1:14 242
2:19 269,271
3:6 77
3:18-20 68
3:20 75
3:21 296
3:36 65
4 268
4:4-6 73
4:7-38 73-74
4:9-10 139
4:23 79,90
4:23-24 72
4:34 115,264
5:35 91
6:44,65 198
6:63 74
7:18 264,169
7:37-39 74
7:46 269
8:32 90,128
8:34 128

8:46 269
10:3-4,14 198
10:16 199,200,201
10:18 213
10:35 275
11:43 198
11:52 153,199
12:25 176,203,304
12:27-28 264
12:40 296
13:1-17 268
14:13 137,138,149
14:26 74,276
15:3 128
15:5 138,199
15:7-8 138,151
15:7 129,150
15:11 130
15:13 101
15:15 138,151
15:16-17 151
15:20 221
16:13 276
16:20-22 149
16:24 136,137,149,155,
156
17:4 264
17:17 90,128,153
17:20 200
17:24-26 44
17:24 266
17:26 119
19:30 223
20:8-9,25 272
20:19 272
20:31 125

Acts

1:14 153
2:23 37
2:24 272
2:32 272

2:36 273
3:15 272
3:19 61,65,296
4:2 272
4:12 192
4:23-31 153
4:27-28 37
5:31 62
5:40-41 111
5:41 235
6:4 153
7:58 189
9:15-16 220
10:9 153
10:38 268
11:18 61,62
12:5 153
13:3 153
13:46 192
13:48 200
14:22 10,209,221
14:23 153
14:27 61,62
15:3 61
16:14 62,198
16:30 65
16:31 54,55,61,65
17:24-25 144
17:25 47,300
18:9-10 199
18:27 297
20 107
20:35 107,108,153,293
20:37 107
26:15-18 273
26:16-18 191-92
28:27 296

Romans
1:14-16 193
1:20-21 56,192
1:23 56

3:10 57
3:23 56
3:25-26 41,60
3:25 264
4:4-5 147
4:17 198
4:20-21 257
4:20 56
4:25 59
5:1 198,248
5:2,11 68
5:3-4 127,215,235
5:9 223
5:19 223
6:5 60
7:18 138
8:3 60
8:5 127
8:7-8 57,62
8:13 147
8:18 205,234
8:28 53,54,126
8:29 118
8:30 302
8:38-39 246
9 297
9:1-23 292,293,297
9:3-6 297
9:3 245-46
9:16 64
10:1 100
10:2 90
10:17 126
11:20 248
11:25-26 38
11:31 28
11:36 47,199,253
12:8 20,21,248,253
12:10 248
12:11 247,248
12:12 215,248
12:15 248
13:9 278

14:17-18 149
14:23 102
15 190
15:1-3 98,100
15:3 300
15:4 128
15:13 67,69,126,127
15:18 149,199
15:19-21 190
15:23-24 190
15:23 190
15:26 102
15:30-31 152
16:18 147

1 Corinthians

1:18 54
1:23-24 60,296
1:28-29 249
2:13 127,276
2:14 127
3:6 191
3:7 199
4:10 220
4:11-13 220
4:16 222
9:22 192
9:23 205
10:24 98,100
10:31 15,55,265
10:33 98,100
13 102
13:3 99,101,102
13:4-7 101
13:5 45,47,98,100
15:6 272
15:19 231
15:10 149,189
15:19 212,214,218,219
15:29-31 220
15:31 221
15:32 218,219

15:49 118
16:1-4 102
16:22 65

2 Corinthians

1:5 220
1:6 10
1:8-9 222
1:23-2:4 104-5
1:24 105,123
2 106
2:2 105
2:3 21,105,239
2:4 105,106
3:5 199
4:4 44,57,62
4:6 94
4:10-12 225
4:16-18 234
4:17 205
5:6 299
5:21 60
6:8-10 126
6:10 10
8 106
8-9 102
8:1 102
8:1-3 105
8:1-4,8 102
8:1-8 102-4,112
8:2 103
8:3-4 103
8:4 107
8:8 102
8:16-17 102-3
9:6-7 104
9:7 21,96,248,253,293
9:8 172
11:2 180
11:23-29 219
11:24-29 190
11:25,27 218

12:7-10 217
12:8 216
12:9-10 223
12:15 170

Galatians
1:11-17 273
3:2-3 147
3:2 127
3:28 180
5:6 153
5:14 278
5:22 127,153
6:17 225

Ephesians
1:5-6 46,249
1:12 46
1:14 46
1:18 153
1:20-22 180-81
1:22 182
1:23 180
2:1 192
2:1,5 57,62
2:3 57,62
2:5-8 296
2:5 198,296
2:5,8 64
2:7 145,249
2:9 249
2:18 68
4:18 192
4:28 172
4:32 248
5:18 127
5:20 248
5:21-33 186,187
5:21 184
5:22-24 181-82
5:22 186
5:23 182,183,184

5:25-30 175
5:25 184
5:27 181
5:28 174,178
5:28-29 286
5:29-30 176,183
5:29 183,280
5:31 178,179
5:32 179,181
6:12 152
6:17-18 152
6:17 129
6:19 152

Philippians
1:9 153
1:21 232
1:23 232,299
1:25 67,126,233
1:29 221
2:3 248
2:8 223
2:13 149
2:17 10,232
2:27 224
2:29 224
2:30 224
3:1 293
3:7-10 205
3:7-11 220
3:8 232
3:10-11 232
3:21 118
4:1 233
4:3 245
4:4 244,248,293

Colossians
1:4-5 153
1:24 212,223,224,225,
          228,230,234,236
1:27 236

2:9 44
3:5 20
3:15 248
3:17 248
4:3 152

1 Thessalonians
1:6-7 234
2:19-20 233
2:20 100
3:3 222
3:4-5 216
3:8-9 236
5:16 248
5:17 147

2 Thessalonians
1:7 145
1:9 57
1:9-10 265
1:10 46
3:1 152

1 Timothy
1:15 59,125
4:2-5 168
4:8 160
6:5-10 159-60
6:5 160
6:6-10 164
6:6 160,173
6:7-10 161
6:7 161
6:8 162,170
6:9-10 163,173
6:9 159,163,164
6:10 159
6:12 167
6:17-19 164-65
6:17 167,168
6:18 171
6:18,19 159

6:19 165,167,173

2 Timothy
1:9 167
2:10 10,230
2:24-26 64
2:25 106
3:12 222,237

Titus
3:5 296

Hebrews
1:3 44,125
2:10 41,67,115
3:6 67
4:15 216,223
5:8 223
5:9 65
9:12 223
10 112
10-12 111-13
10:14 223
10:32-35 111-12
10:34 . . .21,67,112,117,293
11 115
11:1 127
11:3 125
11:6 67,90
11:24-26 112
11:25 115,244
11:25-26 238
11:26 67,117,245
12 217
12:1-2 113,300
12:2 9,113,115,117,
175,189
12:14 128
12:15-17 244
12:22-24 67
13:5-6 162
13:5 67,247

13:17 10,21,252,293
13:20 302
13:21 200

James
1:18 125
2:8 278
2:16 101
2:19 61
4:3-5 141
4:9 248
5:19-20 296

1 Peter
1:8 . . . .
1:13 248
1:17 248
1:22 248
1:23 125
2:2 248
2:24 60
3:1-6 186
3:1 186
3:7 179
3:10 203
3:18 60,68
4:11 148,265
4:13 111,236
4:19 215
5:1-2 108
5:2 21,293
5:7 146

2 Peter
1:4 128
1:21 276
3:16 276

1 John
1:3,4 150
1:4 107,239
2:14 129
2:29 64
3:2-3 118
3:9 64
3:18 101
4:2-3 64
4:7 64
5:1 63
5:2-4 251,252
5:13 129

3 John
4 109

Revelation
2:10 177
3:16 289
5:5-6 300
5:9-13 41
5:9 153,199,232
6:11 227,231
7:9 153,193
12:11 177,227
13:8 245
14:11 58
17 37
17:8 245
17:13-14 37
17:17 37
20:15 245
21:23 265
21:27 245
22:17 95

Subject and Person Index

Accountability
    and moral inability, 296
    for what you know, 56
Affections. *See also* Emotions,
        Feelings
    definition, 298
    essential to Christian life, 247-
        49
    God the center of his own, 33
Affliction. *See also* Suffering,
        Persecution
    completing Christ's, 223-25
    joy in it, 215
    Love weeps, 106-7
Agape and Eros, 300
Alford, Henry, 246
Anderson, Norman, 274,306
Apocrypha, 274,306
Aristotle, 182
Art for art's sake, 243-44
Assurance, 129, 235
Augustine, Saint, 142-43,203,241,
        301
Awe
    as an end in itself, 82
    in worship, 80

Barth, Karl, 177-78,240,302
Barrett, David, 303
Baxter, Richard, 11,293
Bedale, Stephen, 302
Belief. *See also* Faith
    inadequacy of saying "Believe,"
        54-55
Benefactor of God? 85,97
Benevolence toward God? 97

Bethel College, 233
Bethlehem Baptist Church, 9,10,291
Bible. *See* Scripture
Bilney, "Little," 125
Blessedness of giving, 107-8
Bloom, Jon, 11
Boasting vs. self-pity, 249-50
Boice, James, 306
Books by John Piper
    available to order, 291
Bounds, E. M, 299
Brainerd, David, 86,203-4,304
Broadus, John, 92,300
Brooks, Phillips, 109-10,301
Bromiley, Geoffrey, 181,302
Brother Andrew, 236,305
Bruce, F. F., 306
Bryant, David, 196,301-2,304
Buhlmann, Walbert, 191
Burroughs, Jeremiah, 305
Bush, George, 245,306,306
Bush, Luis, 303

Call of God. *See also* Regeneration
    creation of new life, 63,296
    two kinds, 296
Calvin, John, 297-98
Calvinistic incentives for missions,
        196-202
Camaraderie of Christian Hedonism,
        12
Cancer
    as suffering for Christ, 215-218
Canon, extent and authority, 274
Carey, William, 200,205,208-9
Carmichael, Amy Wilson, 206

Carnell, Edward John, 83,86,177, 295-96,299,302
Carson, D. A., 306
Celibacy, 168
Chauncy, Charles, 90
Cheerful giver loved of God, 104
Chief end of man, 15,83-84,97,254,290
Clairvaux, Bernard of, 92
Condemnation by God, 57
Conditions of salvation. See Salvation
Contentment with godliness, 160,164. See also Happiness, Joy, Pleasure
Contrition in worship, 80
Conversion
    condition of salvation, 65
    definition, 61
    gift of God, 62. See also Faith
Creation of male and female,179-80
Crusoe, Robinson, 139-40,142,144

Damnation. See also Hell, Condemnation
    willingness to be damned for glory of God, 244-47
Dansa, 228-29
Day, Dorothy, 114-17
Darwin, Charles, 88-89
Decision. See also Conversion
    born of delight, 67-68
    not sufficient for salvation, 248
Decrees of God. See Sovereignty of God
Delight. See Joy, Happiness, Pleasure
Desire. See also Affections
    end in itself, 82
    honors God, 86
    stage in worship, 86
    too weak, 16-17
Desiring God Ministries, 291
Disease
    as suffering for Christ, 215-218

Disinterestedness, 19
    in doing good, 97-98
    in loving, 99,100,101
    two kinds of "self-interest," 304
Dissatisfied contentment, 107
Doctor. See Physician
Dread in worship, 80
Drewery, Mary, 208-9
Dürer, Albrecht, 131
Duty
    better without joy than not at all, 248
    indirect fulfillment, 86
    its inadequacy, 82-84

Eastman, Dick, 301-2
Eddy, Sherwood, 206
Edwards, Jonathan, 9,32,39-40, 58-59,90-91,96,98-99,137, 150,177,247,293,294,295, 296,298-99,300-1,302,304, 306
Eller, Vernard, 288,307
Elliot, Elisabeth, 210-11,305
Elliot, Jim, 210-11
Emmanuelle, Sister, 191
Emotion. See also Affections, Feelings
    commanded, 247-48
    end in itself, 81-82,84
    vigor required in religion, 91
    in worship, 76,78-60
Epaphroditus, 224
Epicureanism, 218
Eros vs. agape, 300
Eternal security, 166,302
Evil and the sovereignty of God, 35-42

Faith. See also Belief
    begets joy, 125
    comes through Scripture, 125-26
    effect of regeneration, 61-63
    glorifies God, 56

God's creation, 198
  involves deep change, 61
  part of conversion, 61
  receives benefits of the cross, 61
  receives Holy Spirit, 127
  rooted in a new joy in God, 66
  spiral of joy, 69
  transforms all of life, 66
Fall
  effect of on marriage, 186-87,
    302
Fasting, 168
Fear as an end in itself, 82
Feelings. See also Affections, Emotion
  necessary to love, 101-2
Fellowship with God as heaven's
    treasure, 66
Fellowship with Jesus in prayer, 149-
    50
First Commandment
  ground of second, 283-85
Franck, Johann, 92-93
Freedom through Scripture, 128
Frontier Missions. See Missions
Fuller, Daniel P., 11,207,239,295,
    301,306

Geldenhuys, J. Norval, 306
Giving satisfies, not getting, 152
Glory of God
  author's experience, 94-95
  belittled by bad service, 144-49
  created us for, 55,256
  Christian Hedonism glorifies
    God, 253-54
  definition, 42-43,255
  goal in all he does, 33,43,255-66
  God's delight in it, 42-43
  God's pursuit of it our joy, 44-50
  our duty to live for it, 55-56,265
  our happiness not above it, 137
  pursuit of it and pursuit of joy,
    137-38,253

reflected in his work, 44-45
  reflected in Jesus, 44
  shown by needing him, 137-49
  sin as falling short of, 56-57
God
  breathtaking, 240-42
  decrees of, see Sovereignty of
    God
  faith in, see Faith
  God's word, see Scripture
  his grace, see Grace of God
  happiness of, 33-50, see also
    Happiness of God
  heart's only satisfaction, 17,19
  his chief end to glorify himself,
    33,42-43,255-66
  his effectual call, see Call of God
  his judgment, see Hell,
    Condemnation
  his love, see Love of God
  his Son, see Jesus Christ
  his Spirit, see Holy Spirit
  holiness of, see Holiness of God
  how not to serve God, 144-49
  no one's beneficiary, 85,97
  our glorious servant, 149
  prayer to, see Prayer
  righteousness of, see
    Righteousness of God
  sovereignty, see Sovereignty
    of God
  waiting for, 145-49
  why I believe in God, 267-68
  works for us, 144-49
  worship of, see Worship, Glory
    of God
Godliness
  as means of gain, 160-65
Gospel
  God's joy and ours coincide, 50
  Jesus sent to die for sinners, 59-
    60
  not a "help wanted" ad, 146

Gospel Recordings, 195
Grace of God
    cause of love, 102
Grace
    increasing addiction to, 120
    love longs for power of, 119-21
Grant, Colin, 205,304
Gratitude
    an end in itself, 82,84
    in worship, 80
Gregory the Great, 228
Grief
    an end in itself, 81-82
Greed. *See also* Desire, Money
    beware desire to be rich, 160-64
    for joy in God, 119
Grudem, Wayne, 303

Halliday, Steve, 11
Happiness. *See also* Happiness of
        God, Joy, Pleasure
    all men seek, 16,177-78
    Edwards's resolution to pursue,
        137
    fruit of faith, 67
    George Mueller's quest each day,
        132
    in God, 20,23,66,69-70,80-81,
        85,92-94,97,101-4,137,
        243-44,253-54,268,289
    in worship, 80-81
    ours not above God's glory, 137
    seriousness of, 9
    spiral of faith, 69
Happiness of God
    foundation for Christian
        Hedonism, 33-50
    in fellowship of Trinity, 45
    in his glory, 42-43
    in making us happy, 50,53-54
Harrer, Heinrich, 120
Hate your own life? 176-77
Hawthorne, Steven, 301

Head in worship, 90-92
Headship of the husband, 181-87
Health, wealth, and prosperity
        doctrine, 168-71
Heart in worship, 78-90
Hedonism, Christian
    channel for holy joy, 178
    combats pride, self-pity, 249-51
    creating a Christian Hedonist,
        54-70
    definition, 22-23,287
    glorifies God, 253-54
    honors God, 85,253-54
    horizontal, 97
    is humble, 85,249-51
    its ultimate ground, 33
    not a theory of moral
        justification, 20
    others' use of term, 287-89
    promotes genuine love for
        people, 251-53
    what is it? (poem), 25-31
    why be a Christian Hedonist?
        239-254
    why call it that? 287-90
Heidelberg Catechism, 21-22
Hell
    all people deserve it, 57-58
    popular argument against, 295
Henry, Matthew, 11,293
Herbert, George, 241
Holiness of God discovered in
        conversion, 67
Holy Spirit
    comes through hearing with
        faith, 127
    God's joy and ours in God, 298
    living water, 74
    in regeneration, 62-63
    relationship in Trinity, 294
Homosexuality not created, 180
Hope
    begotten by Scripture, 127-28

synonym of faith, 127-28
Hopkins, Samuel, 296
Humility
    in worship, 80
    promoted by Christian
        Hedonism, 249-51
Hyde, John "Praying," 206,305
Hymns, hedonistic, 92
Hyper-Calvinism, 304
Hypocrisy in worship, 19,81

Ichii, Tokichi, 126-27
Idolatry and joy in things, 141-44
Inability, moral, 62,65,198,296
Indirect fulfillment of duty, 86
Islam
    and martyrdom, 228

Jesus Christ
    a portrait, 267-271
    evidence for his resurrection,
        271-74
    God's delight in him, 44
    his hope of joy, 112-17
    his pursuit of joy, 112-17
    his view of Scripture, 274-75
    opposites meet in him, 94
    sent to save sinners, 59-60
    our treasure chest of holy joy, 66
Jewett, Paul, 307
Joy. See also Happiness, Pleasure
    choosing against it, 236
    fruit of knowing Spirit through
        the word, 128
    how love and joy relate, 20-21
    in God, 19,23,66,69,80-81,85,
        92-94,97,101-4,137,243-
        44,253-54,268,289-90
    in deed and reward, 117-19
    in suffering, 234
    its consummation, 153
    love as overflow of joy in God,
        102-4

love comes from joy in God,
    119-21
love rejoices in joy of beloved,
    104-6
obedience in spite of, 248-49
our joy and God's glory become
    one, 254
Paul's converts his joy, 233
pursuit of commanded, 234,
    242-47
work of our lives, 11
Judicial sentiment, 59,267,295-96

Kant, Immanuel, 17,88,89,92
Kierkegaard, Søren, 288
Kittle, Gerhard, 302

Lake Avenue Church, 233
Lanphier, Jeremiah, 154-55
Law of God revives the soul, 123
Lewis, C. S., 9,16-18,19,43,48-49,
    84,88,108,119,143,242,
    287,293,294,299,301,306,
    307
Leadership of husband servantlike,
    182-85
Legalism, opposite of love, 106
Livingstone, David, 201,203-4, 231
Longing of human heart for God,
    241-42
    See also Desire
Love. See also Self-love, Love of God
    compared to high and low
        pressure zones, 121
    condition of final salvation, 65
    draft from high to low pressure
        zone, 121
    delights to contemplate joy in
        others, 106
    empowered by prayer, 151-55
    enjoys ministry, 108-10
    four marks of genuine, 102-3
    for God is love for me, 284

for God is satisfaction in him, 284
harsh and dreadful thing, 114-17
how it comes from joy in God, 119-20
how love and joy relate, 20-21
longs for the power of grace, 119-20
love poem, 25-31
loving others with love for God, 284-85
more than deeds, 101-21
motivated by rewards, 98-99
of mercy, 98-99
of money, 159,162-63
overflow of joy in God, 102-4
promoted by Christian Hedonism, 251-53
pursuit of our joy in the beloved's joy, 175-76
rejoices in joy of beloved, 104-6
suffers for joy, 111-17
the way God loves, 100
weeps, 106-7
Love of God
is he for us or for himself? 45-49
must seek men's praise, 49
seeks its own, 47. See also Grace of God
Luther, Martin, 112,130-31
Lyall, Leslie, 305

MacDonald, George, 295
McDonald, Miss, 126
Manson, T. W., 302
Marriage
Christian pattern, 178-87
effects of Fall, 186-87,302
great mystery, 180-81
husband's servantlike leadership, 182-87
John Piper's, 10
seek joy in joy of other, 175

submission of wife, 181-84,185-86
Martyrdom
a full number planned, 227, 231
blood is seed, 226
Islamic impact, 228
of Polycarp, 226-27,305
Maudlin, Michael, 305
Memorizing Scripture, 131-32
Mercenary
how not to be one, 108
pursuing money through art, 243
Mercy. See also Love
loving mercy, 98-99
Mickelsen, Alvera and Berkeley, 302
Mind
use of in worship, 90-92
Ministry
enjoyed by love, 108-10
Missionaries. See Missions
Missions
and prayer, 153
biblical basis, 196-211
closure, 194
dramatic growth, 195
"expect great things," 208
"Frontier Missions," 189-91
God's spiritual health regimen, 207
incentives for commitment, 197-202
needed? 191-92
Paul as frontier missionary, 190-91
people groups, 193-94
sacrifice, 9,203-11
suffering but not ultimate sacrifice, 9,203-11
Ten-Forty Window, 194,303
unreached peoples, 194
unreached peoples, definition, 303

what are people groups? 193-96
what is a "world Christian"? 196
Money
    desire to be rich, 160-65
    how we serve it, 148
    investment, 165
    love of, 159,162-63
    pride, 168
    pursuit of heavenly reward, 165-66
    reasons not to pursue wealth, 161-65
    reasons to live simply, 162-63
    wartime lifestyle, 169-71
    wealth and prosperity doctrine, 168-69
    what should the rich do? 162-73
    why God gives us so much, 172-73
Moon, Lottie, 188,206,304
Motivation. See Desire, Joy, Happiness
Mountain climbing for dreadful joy, 116
Mouw, Richard, 21
Mueller, George, 122,132-34,301
Murray, Andrew, 205,304
Murray, Iain H., 301,304
Murray, John, 249,306
Muslims. See Islam

Neil, Stephen, 226,305
New Covenant, 63

Obedience
    suffering in its path, 216
    when cheerfulness is not there, 248-49
Objections, 19-23,46-50,85,97-98, 243-47
O'Connor, Flannery, 89-90
Organic relationship between deed and reward, 117-19

Orr, J. Edwin, 302
Ortlund, Ray, 233
Otis, George, 227-28,305
Owens, Virginia Stem, 299

Packer, J. I., 11,293,295,306
Pain. See Suffering, Affliction, Persecution
Pascal, Blaise, 16,17-18,177,293,302
Pastor to work cheerfully, 108-10
People groups. See Missions
Perez, Father, 305
Persecution
    pain of God's therapy, 209-10
    rejoice in it, 234
    relation to sickness, 215-218
    with and for Christ, 215-218
Perseverance. See also Eternal Security
    of Paul in ministry, 304
Philips, J. B., 306-7
Philo, 182
Physician
    God as ours, 207
Pigott, Jean Sophia, 93
Pinnock, Clark, 289,307
Piper, Abraham, 9
Piper, Barnabas, 9
Piper, Benjamin, 9
Piper, John, 293,297,302,303,305, 306
    books available, 291
    hardest years, 10
    marriage, 10,12
    pastorate, 10,233
Piper, Karsten, 9
Piper, Noël, 9, 25-31
Piper, Talitha, 9
Plato, 182
Pleasure. See also Happiness, Joy, Pursuit of Pleasure
    not the god of Christian Hedonism, 20

pursuit of essential for good
deeds, 97
we are too easily pleased, 110-11
Poem
lessons from a love poem, 25-31
Praise. *See also* Worship
commands to praise God, 46
consummation of joy, 48-49
echo of God's excellence, 50,53
highest calling of humanity, 19
overflow of all enjoyment, 19
Prayer
and spiritual warfare, 151-53
as pursuit of God's glory, 138-49
as pursuit of our joy, 149
empowers for love, 151-55
fellowship with Jesus, 149-50
for things, 142-44
heart of Christian Hedonism,
140
hedonistic prayers in Psalms,
93-94
key to Frontier Missions, 153
plan to, 155-56
prayer life of George Mueller,
132-34
self-centered? 140-48
unifies pursuit of joy and God's
glory, 138-56
wartime walkie-talkie, 152
wrong prayer, 141-44
Preaching
appeal to desire, 92
enjoy ministry, 108-10
with heat and light, 91
Pride
and money, 167
combatted by Christian
Hedonism, 249-51
root of sin, 285-86
Propitiation
definition, 60,296
Prosperity teachings, 168-71

Pursuit of pleasure. *See also*
Happiness, Joy, Desire,
Pleasure
essential to genuine love, 97-
121,104
essential to good deeds, 97
eternal not fleeting, 112-13
in Scripture, 130
mandatory, 97,242-47

Rand, Ayn, 46-47,89
Redemptive history, 42,50
definition, 41,255-66,294
Reformed Catechisms, 20-22
Regeneration
a divine work, 62-64
definition, 296
Repentance
effect of regeneration, 62-64
part of conversion, 61
receives the benefits of the cross,
61
Resurrection
evidence for Jesus', 271-73
suffering for it, 232
Retirement not a blessing, 189-90
Reverence in worship, 80
Revival. *See also* Conversion of the
soul, 123
through prayer, 153-55
Riches. *See* Money
Rewards
and genuine love, 167
and the use of money, 165-67
motivating love, 98-99,107-8
organic relation of deed and
reward, 117-19
Righteousness of God
demonstrated in death of Jesus,
41
Robinson Crusoe's text, 139-40
Ryle, Bishop, 287,307
Sabbath a day for joy in God, 254

Sacrifice. *See also* Suffering, Affliction, Persecution
  beware of sacrificial spirit, 202-11
  how beautiful? 213
  in another world, 246
  is there any? 231-32
  no ultimate sacrifice in obedience, 203-11
Salvation. *See also* Conversion
  how it is conditional, 64-66
  past and future, 64-65
  a miracle of God, 64-66
Sanctification by the Scripture, 128
Satan
  has no saving faith, 61
  his aim in suffering, 216-18
  overcome by the Word, 129
Schlatter, Adolf, 304
Schlier, Heinrich, 182
Schlossberg, Herbert, 305
Scott, Peter Cameron, 200-01
Scripture
  begets assurance, 129
  begets faith, 125-27
  begets hope, 127-28
  begets freedom, 128
  begets sanctification, 128
  begets wisdom, 128-29
  defeats Satan, 129
  Holy Spirit comes through hearing, 127
  kindling for Christian Hedonism, 123-34
  memorization of, 132
  pursuit of pleasure in, 130
  role in prayer, 131-34
  source of strength and light, 305
  why I believe it is true, 267-76
  your life, 124-25
Scriven, Joseph, 136
Self-confidence will never satisfy, 120
Self-consciousness kills joy, 243,299

Self-denial
  and God's good gifts, 168
  condition of salvation, 65
  good in proper place, 168
  hate your own life? 176-77
  in missions, 202-11
  may dishonor God, 84-85
  not an end in itself, 17
  objection to Christian Hedonism, 244
  when it is bad, 202
Self-esteem, 277-86
Self-interest, two kinds, 304
Self-justification, 278-79,286
Self-love
  all have it, 178
  Brainerd's wrestling, 203
  love neighbor as self, 277-86
  not self-esteem, 178,277-86
  of Christ, 176
  regular and irregular, 203
Self-pity
  form of pride, 250
  combatted by Christian Hedonism, 249-51
  wrong view of sacrifice, 206,209-10
Self-reliance
  escaping it, 222
Self-sufficiency of God, 45,47
Selfishness not same as self-interest, 176
Seriousness and happiness, 9
Service of God
  beware of it, 144-49
  proper service, 147-49
Shame for Christ, 235
Sickness
  as suffering for Christ, 215-218
Silence in worship, 80
Simple lifestyle
  wartime lifestyle, 170
  why it is good, 162-63

Sin
    all have sinned, 56
    failure to glorify God, 56-57
    grieves God, 40
    renouncing greater good for
        lesser, 89-90
Singer, Charles, 182
Sorrow in worship, 86-87
Sovereignty of God
    and moral evil, 36-42
    biblical basis, 36-39
    definition, 34
    foundation of his happiness, 34-
        42
    his decrees beyond hindrance,
        37-38
    he sees the world through two
        lenses, 40
    personal struggle of Jonathan
        Edwards, 39-40
    two kinds of divine will, 293-94
Spurgeon, Charles, 139-40,301,304
Steinbach, Carol, 12
Stewart, James, 169,302
Stoics, 17,88
Submission of wife to husband, 181-
    84,185-87
Suffering. *See also* Affliction,
        Persecution
    a choice for joy, 232
    choosing it, 213,214-15,219-20,
        231,237
    Christ's propitiate, 230
    completing Christ's, 223-25
    deep thing learned, 223
    for sake of gain, 232
    in love, 111-17
    joy in it, 231-38
    of missionaries without ultimate
        sacrifice, 203-11
    ours propagate, 230
    Satan's design in, 216-218
    sickness for Christ, 215-218
    thorn in flesh, 217-18
    with and for Christ, 215-218

Taste for God, 68
Taylor, Hudson, 129-30,209,250,
    252,301,306
Taylor, Dr. and Mrs. Howard,129-
    30,305
Taylor, Jeremy, 9,289
Ten-Forty Window. *See* Missions
Thorn in flesh, 217-18
Threats if we will not be happy, 242-
    43,289-90
Torture, 235
Traherne, Thomas, 142,301
Trier, Archbishop of, 130
Trinity, Edwards's view, 294
Trust. *See* Faith
Tson, Joseph, 225, 230,305
Tucker, Ruth, 304,305

Universalism not true, 191-93
Unreached peoples. *See* Missions
Unselfishness not highest virtue, 17

Vanauken, Sheldon, 299
Vincent, Marvin, 305
Virtue
    can oppose worship, 87

Wagner, C. Peter, 303
Warfare
    spiritual, 152
Waiting for God, 145-49
Warfield, B. B., 306
Wartime lifestyle, 169-71
Watts, Isaac, 277
Wealth. *See* Money
Wealth and prosperity doctrines,
    168-71
Weeping of love, 106-7
Wenham, John W., 306
West, Miss, 126

Westminster Catechism, 20-22
White, J. Campbell, 188
Willpower when joy is missing, 248-49
Williams, Charles, 14
Winter, Ralph, 170,189,194-95,301, 302,303,304
Wisdom
    from Scripture, 128-29
Wonder. See Awe
Wood, Rick, 194,303
Woodbridge, John D., 306
Work
    for God? 144-49
World Christians. See Missions
Worship
    affair of the heart, 79-80
    affair of the mind, 90-92
    awe, 80
    balance of head and heart, 91
    contrition, 80
    discovering its meaning, 18
    disinterested duty, 87
    dread, 80
    end in itself, 81-85
    feast of Christian Hedonism, 60-95
    forms, 92-94

    feelings essential, 81
    gladly, 78-79
    gratitude, 80
    humility, 80
    hypocrisy, 81
    "in spirit," 77
    in vain, 79
    inadequacy of duty, 83-84
    its fuel, 77-78
    joy, 80-81
    killed by revolt against hedonism, 87-90
    reflection of God's radiance, 79, 83,84,87
    silence in, 80
    three stages, 85-87
    with emotions and thought, 76
Wurmbrand, Richard, 213,218,219, 235,305
Wycliffe Bible Translators, 194

Xavier, Francis, 208

Yancey, Philip, 305
Young, Edward J., 306

Zwemer, Samuel, 206,304
Zylstra, Carl, 299-300

STUDY GUIDE

DESIRING GOD

I prepared this Study Guide for my own teaching of these chapters to a Wednesday evening class of about 100 people. The questions are intended to help people think about what they read. They include not merely "what" questions, but much more, "why" and "how" questions. The assumption is that thinking hard about important things is good for our faith and obedience. I say with the apostle Paul, "Think over what I say, for the Lord will grant you understanding in everything" (2 Timothy 2:7). Notice that *thinking* and *receiving* do not exclude each other. They go together. God ordains that we receive understanding from him *through* our mental effort to deal with his Word. Of course, my word is not his Word. I am fallible. He is not. Test all things by God's infallible Scripture. Hold fast to what is good.

INTRODUCTION
How I Became a Christian Hedonist

1. What does the author say is the aim of this book? (p. 15)

2. What text of Scripture does the author cite to prove that the issue of glorifying God relates to every area of life, including how you drink your orange juice at breakfast?

3. Evidently the author does not think that the Biblical meaning of "glorifying God" is obvious to everyone, since he writes a whole book about it. What do you think the word "glorify" might be taken to mean that the author would think is unbiblical? Hint: What if you took "glorify" in the same sense as "beautify" or "fortify" or "purify"?

4. The author thinks that by enjoying God we glorify him. To get on the author's wavelength you might try to think of some examples in your life where you "glorify" something or someone or some activity by enjoying it.

5. As the author describes the emerging of Christian Hedonism in his college days, two things seemed in conflict in his experience. One was an inherited moral principle and the other was an inescapable reality of the heart. What were this principle and this reality? (p.15)

6. Pascal's quote on page 16 says that even people who commit suicide do it because they are driven by a longing for happiness. Can you state that fact in a way that overcomes the objection that it can't be true because some people commit suicide without any knowledge of what lies beyond death?

7. In the quote from C. S. Lewis on pages 16-17, where does he think the notion has come from that it is a bad thing to desire our own good and to earnestly hope for the enjoyment of it?

8. What evidence does Lewis cite that the human problem is not that we are all seeking pleasure but that we are seeking it in a half-hearted way?

9. How is the point which the author learned from Lewis an advance on the first point learned from Pascal?

10. What was the third insight the author gained in his emerging Christian Hedonism?

11. From the quote by Lewis on page 18 what is the relationship between delight in the countryside and praise of the countryside?

12. In view of the preceding answer, explain why Lewis's early idea about God was wrong — the idea that when God commanded praise from his people in the Psalms he was "like a vain woman wanting compliments." In other words, if God is not vain to demand our praise, what is he in view of the preceding answer?

13. Would it be virtuous for you to imitate God and seek praise for yourself the way God seeks it for himself?

14. On page 19 the author refers to "the most liberating discovery" he ever made. What was the discovery and why do you think the author calls it "liberating"?

15. Are we actually commanded to pursue our pleasure? Where?

16. On page 20 the author distances himself from the health, wealth, and prosperity gospel. How?

17. Why doesn't Christian Hedonism make a God out of pleasure?

18. If I am living for pleasure, why am I not putting pleasure above God?

19. The author is eager not to have his book seen as "another spin-off from modern man's enslavement to the centrality of himself." From what we have seen so far, why shouldn't it be?

20. What point in the definition of Christian Hedonism on page 23 has not been touched on in the introduction?

21. What is the source that the author claims for his insight?

1

The Happiness of God: Foundation for Christian Hedonism

(With Appendix 1)

1.1. The ultimate ground or basis of Christian Hedonism is the fact that God is uppermost in his own affections. Can you take the words, "God is uppermost in his own affections," and say that in another way? Try several other statements that mean the same thing.

1.2. We will discuss below why it is that God's happiness in himself (rooted in his sovereignty) is indispensable for our pursuit of joy, that is, why God's happiness in himself is the foundation of Christian Hedonism. (See questions 7, 10, 11.) But at this point we need to establish two things: one is that God is indeed uppermost in his own affections (questions 2-13), and the other is that he is indeed sovereign (questions 14-20).

On page 43 there is an effort to get at a definition of God's glory. Write out in your own words how you would try to communicate the glory of God to someone who knows nothing about the Bible.

1.3. Appendix 1 (p. 255) gives the biblical basis for the claim that God delights in his glory above all things, in other words, that he is uppermost in his own affections. From this appendix, what other biblical phrase means virtually the same as God's doing something "for his glory"?

1.4. Explain how God's creating man and woman in his own image was the same as creating them for his glory. (pp. 255-256)

1.5. At the Tower of Babel, people said they aimed to "make a name for ourselves" (Genesis 11:4). God was very displeased with this. But when God called Abram he said, "I will make your name great" (Genesis 12:2). Basing your answer on God's pursuit of his own glory, explain why God is displeased with the people at the Tower of Babel having a great name, but he was not displeased with Abram having a great name.

1.6. Exodus 20:5 says that God is jealous. (a) Define legitimate, healthy jealousy in ordinary human relationships. (b) Then explain how God's jealousy relates to his glory and his people.

1.7. Explain how it is that God's all-surpassing passion for his own glory is the foundation of the gospel — that God has mercy on sinners who look to him for mercy. The key to this explanation is found in texts like Ezekiel 20:5-9; Psalm 106:6-8 (p. 258); 1 Samuel 12:19-23 (p. 261); Isaiah 48:9-11; Ezekiel 36:22-33 (p. 263); Psalm 25:11. See question 1.10 for a similar issue.

1.8. One important text not included on pages 264f concerning the reason Jesus came and died, is Romans 15:8-9. After reading this text, (a) state the three reasons that Jesus came and (b) put in your own words what it is that unites these three reasons.

1.9. After reading Appendix 1, what then is the goal of all God does in history?

1.10. A big question that rises after we decide that God is pursuing his own glory in all that he does is this: Is this a loving thing for God to do? Paul said in 1 Corinthians 13:5 that "love seeks not its own." Yet it appears that God seeks "his own" praise in all that he does. Why is it loving for God to exalt himself in this way, but not for us to exalt ourselves like this? (See pp. 45-48)

1.11. A very closely related question is, Why is God's happiness in himself (his glory) indispensable for our pursuit of joy? Or, Why is God's happiness in himself the foundation of Christian Hedonism?

1.12. Another way to get at this same point is to recognize that you can't delight fully in an unrighteous God, and then to recognize that God would indeed be unrighteous if he were unhappy. Why would God be unrighteous if he were not fully happy in his own glory? (See pp. 43 and 47f)

1.13. The author maintains that God can delight in his people and his works without contradicting the full delight that he has in himself, that is, in his own glory. State briefly why this is so. (pp. 44-45)

1.14. Saying that God is uppermost in his own affections means that God's happiness is based on himself. His own glory is what makes God glad. But for God to be infinitely happy in himself and what he does, something must be true about God's ability. (a) What is that? (b) And why is this necessary for God's happiness? (pp. 35f)

1.15. If we are expected to "rejoice always," (1 Thessalonians 5:16; Philippians 4:4) even though we are not sovereign, why must God be sovereign in order to always be happy? (This question is not explicitly answered in the book. Think about it.)

Now we must return to the Biblical foundation of God's sovereignty. We have spoken about the necessity of God's sovereignty as the basis of his happiness. But we must now look at the Biblical basis of the doctrine of God's sovereignty.

Some texts are cited on pp. 35-39. The theological problem is addressed on pp. 38-40. I will assume you have read these pages as I ask the following questions.

1.16. What text from the Bible do you think shows most plainly that, even in the sinful acts of men, God's plan is not thwarted but is fulfilled?

1.17. But surely Satan must be reckoned with as a significant cause in the evil and pain of the world. Using Satan's involvement with Job in Job 1 and 2, describe how the will of God and the will of Satan interrelate in bringing about misery like Job's.

1.18. If God's sovereignty means that in some sense he wills all things, then it seems as though he wills things that he disapproves of. This creates a major problem that we need to try to solve. One way to state the problem is to say God seems to be inconsistent, willing something that in Scripture he says he does not will. Another way to say it is that it seems to make God the author of sin. What is one way to solve this problem of God's apparent inconsistency in seeming to will some things which he says he does not will? (See especially p. 40 and p. 293 note 4.)

1.19. This kind of problem inevitably raises the problem of why God saw fit to permit or ordain the existence of sin and evil. It is not adequate to say that all evil is owing to "free will." If God knew what was going to happen and still chose to allow men to choose sin, then we must answer why. Some solve this problem today by saying that God did not know what was going to happen when he created man with a will. The author regards this "solution" as very wide of the biblical mark. Others have said that God was willing to allow all the sin and misery in the world because there was no other way that he could make men free; and he values the freely chosen love of people so much that it was worth the sin and misery of the world to get it. That may be part of the answer, if "freely chosen" does not mean "chosen without God's decisive enabling grace." But it is not the whole answer.

We have seen that God created all things and does all things for his glory. Therefore somehow the existence of sin and misery has to relate to this great overarching goal of God. Reflect for a moment on how the existence of sin and misery might serve to glorify aspects of God's nature that otherwise could not have been displayed. What attributes of God might shine forth with greater glory because sin and misery exist?

1.20. As we become more and more confident that God sovereignly controls all things, we need to become more and more confident of two or three other attributes of God in order to maintain joy and peace. What would these other attributes be and why must we be sure of them?

2

Conversion: Creation of a Christian Hedonist

2.1. If you put Jeremiah 32:40-41 (pp. 53-54) beside Romans 8:28 (p. 54) what emerges as the answer to this question: Who are the people in Jeremiah 32:40-41 whom God is going to do good to with all his heart? Or, to ask the question another way, how can you know that you are one of those whom God is rejoicing over to do them good? What would be the answer if, instead of Romans 8:28, you use Psalm 147:11 or Isaiah 64:4 or 2 Chronicles 16:9?

2.2. What are the two reasons the author gives (pp. 54-55) for using the new terminology of Christian Hedonism in relation to conversion instead of simply saying the Biblical sentence, "Believe on the Lord Jesus Christ, and you shall be saved" (Acts 16:31)?

2.3. The first answer to question 2.2 (cf. third from last paragraph, p. 54) is based on an unstated assumption. What is it? It has to do with the relationship between faith and works. When you think you know what the assumption is, list some Bible verses that might support it.

2.4. On pages 55-62 the author unfolds one way of summing up the need for conversion and the way of conversion in six steps. Most Christians agree that in order to put saving faith in Jesus, a person has to admit that he is a sinner and in need of forgiveness and change. But that means people need to have some understanding of what sin is. Sin is discussed in step 3 (pp. 56-57). What is the essence of sin that makes steps 1 and 2 so important to make plain first? Or: how do steps 1 and 2 help get people ready to grasp what sin really is?

2.5. One popular notion about how the gospel should be presented is that most people today already feel so bad about themselves and about life that you don't need to tell them the bad news that they are sinners as part of a gospel presentation. All you need to do is present Jesus as the solution to the misery they already feel. In view of the answer to 2.4, why is this mistaken?

2.6. Turning now to step 4 (pp. 57-59), the consequences of sin must be addressed. It is not a loving thing to keep silent about impending calamity if a person can escape it. The calamity impending for sinners is hell (according to the texts gathered on these pages). Two objections to the historic view of hell as eternal punishment are raised. Let's ponder them one at a time. One is this: it cannot be just to punish eternally a sin or series of sins that took only seventy years to commit. Hell is an unjust overreaction to finite evil. In your own words, what answer is given to this?

2.7. The other objection to hell is found in note 4 on page 58. It is given by the popular novelist of the nineteenth century, George MacDonald. He says that God is bound by his justice to destroy sin in his creation — that is, get rid of it, not just punish it. In fact, ongoing punishment of sin gives a home in the universe to "victorious evil." "God is triumphantly defeated" if there is a hell. What is the problem with this?

2.8. The foundation of the gospel is found in Romans 3:25-26 (p. 60). Answer the following questions on this text. (a) What had happened that made it necessary for God's righteousness to be demonstrated? (b) Taking your cue from the nearby verse 23, state the answer to "a" in terms of the glory of God. (c) In view of your answer to "b" how would you define God's righteousness so as to make clear why it needed to be vindicated? (d) Why does the blood (i.e. death) of Christ vindicate the righteousness of God? (For a hint see John 17:4; 12:27f. Keep thinking in the terms of Romans 3:23.) (e) Why does your own hope depend on God's vindicating his righteousness?

2.9. After we see all that God has done to accomplish redemption through the death and resurrection of Jesus we have to ask: What must we do to benefit from what Jesus did? The answer is that we must be "converted." What is the author's argument that true conversion involves faith and repentance? (p. 61)

2.10. What is true about us as human beings that requires the event of conversion to be brought about by a miracle of divine grace rather than human achievement? (p. 62)

2.11. Cite some texts that show that conversion (repentance and faith) is a gift of God. (p. 63)

2.12. "Regeneration" is a technical word for being born again. Does the author think that we are born again (regenerated) by faith or that we are enabled to have faith by being born again? What verses would he use to show this?

2.13. The author believes that regeneration is the same thing as God's "effectual calling" or what some call "irresistible grace." What passage of Scripture would he use to argue that there is an internal and effectual call of God that is different from the general call that all people hear when someone preaches the gospel? What would he mean by saying that this call or this work of grace is irresistible since the Bible says very plainly that we can quench (1 Thessalonians 5:19) or grieve (Ephesians 4:30) or resist (Acts 7:51) the Holy Spirit? (p. 296)

2.14. What are two reason mentioned in 1 Corinthians 1:26-31 why God would call people in this sovereign way?

2.15. In pages 66-68 the author tries to show that what really happens in regeneration or in effectual calling (by irresistible grace) is the "creation of a Christian Hedonist." In other words, behind and before the act of saving faith and repentance something happens to the human heart by the grace of God that gives it the inclination to embrace Christ as all-sufficient for my needs and my longings. Where once there was no sense at all that Christ is beautiful and desirable, suddenly there is a sense that he is all of that and true. This change is the creation of a Christian Hedonist — a person who now finds joy and peace in the beauty of Christ's perfections. Use Hebrews 11:6 and John 3:18-20, and argue in your own words that a new taste for Christ must be created before there can be saving faith.

3

Worship: The Feast of Christian Hedonism

3.1. The introduction to this chapter (pp. 73-78) is a kind of exposition of John 4:1-38, the story of "the woman at the well." Jesus has been alone with the Samaritan woman while his disciples are in the town getting food. After they return they offer him something to eat (v. 31) and he responds, "I have food to eat of which you do not know." (a) What is the food that Jesus was eating while they were away? (v. 34) (b) More specifically, what is God's purpose (stated earlier in this chapter) that Jesus has been up to while the disciples were away?

3.2. Jesus offers the Samaritan woman a kind of water that enables a person never to thirst again! And even more amazing, he says this water actually becomes a spring of water welling up to eternal life (v. 14)! Evidently this is the sort of "bait" you use when you are hunting worshipers for the living God (v. 23). If so, what would be one of the simplest definitions of worship?

3.3. What is the water that Jesus gives? The author suggests two possibilities from other passages in the Bible and then shows that these two possibilities really fit together to give one answer. (a) What are the two possible things that "water" is? And (b) how do these fit together to give a full answer to what the "water" is?

3.4. In view of what you have just answered in 3.3b, what kind of worship does the Father want in John 4:23 where it says, "True worshipers will worship Him *in spirit and truth*, for such the Father seeks to worship him"? That is, what does worship in "spirit and truth" mean?

3.5. Changing the metaphor on page 77, the author suggests that we can get a picture of worship with the following images. Put the reality beside the image.

    The fuel of worship =

    The fire of worship =

    The furnace of worship =

    The heat of worship =

3.6. Why does the author say that worship is "*gladly* reflecting back to God the radiance of his worth"? Why not just say it is a reflecting back to God the radiance of his worth? Why add "gladly"?

3.7. But if worship can include the emotions of contrition and brokenness, how can we include "gladly" as a necessary part of the definition of true worship?

3.8. List the sequence of emotions (pp. 79-81) that are included in worship and give at least one verse to illustrate each one.

3.9. The author argues (pp. 81-85) that worship is "an end in itself." Strictly he means that worship cannot be performed as a means to anything else. Like fund-raising or missions or education or church growth. (a) Does the author mean that worship will not have good effects in these areas? (b) What does he mean? Illustrate from your experience.

3.10. Why does insisting that the emotions of worship are ends in themselves guard the God-centeredness of worship?

3.11. (a) How does the author show the inadequacy of duty as a motive for true worship, and (b) how does he recover duty as a noble and helpful Christian concept?

3.12. It appears then that the pursuit of joy is an essential part of the duty to worship God. Or to put it another way, to the degree that we strive against our passion for happiness we will hinder our capacity for genuine worship. If the pursuit of my happiness is at the heart of worship, how can this be thought of as humble?

3.13. What are the "three stages of worship" and why do they all honor God?

3.14. What is the "moral enemy of worship"?

3.15. Define evil from Jeremiah 2:11-13. (p. 87)

3.16. A great danger of stressing the emotional essence of worship as the author has is that it might lead some people to try to manufacture the emotion in artificial ways (e.g. with music or lighting or incense or other rituals). What counsel from Jonathan Edwards will guard us from this mistake?

3.17. What two things are the "forms" of worship supposed to do in relation to the true emotional experience of worship?

4

Love: The Labor of Christian Hedonism

4.1. The author distinguishes between "vertical" Christian Hedonism and "horizontal" Christian Hedonism. What is vertical Christian Hedonism?

4.2. What is the thesis of this chapter? (p. 97)

4.3. What is one common view of how genuine love (or morality) and the pursuit of happiness relate to each other — the view that the author is striving against?

4.4. Pages 97-100 deal with some passages of Scripture that seem to contradict the thesis of this chapter. For example 1 Corinthians 13:5; 10:24,33; Romans 15:1-3. Take 1 Corinthians 13:5 ("Love seeks not its own.") and point out two clues in the nearer context that show Paul does *not* mean it is wrong to pursue joy in the obedience of love. Do you see any other clues besides the ones the author found?

4.5. Look at the last sentence (in parentheses) in the quote by atheist Ayn Rand on page 89. Now find the sentence on page 100 that says almost exactly the same thing. It is a tragedy that Ayn Rand rejected Christianity, thinking that the view of morality she was attacking was truly Christian. What should we have said to Ayn Rand from what you have seen so far in this chapter? Another way to ask the question would be to say, What would Jonathan Edwards have said to Ayn Rand about the distortion of 1 Corinthians 13:5 that she was scorning?

4.6. What text would you cite to show that God not only does acts of love but that he loves to do acts of love? Should we try to be like him in this way?

4.7. If Jesus said, "Greater love has no man than this, that he lay down his life for his friends," (John 15:13), how can Paul say that it is possible to "give your life to be burned and have not love" (1 Corinthians 13:3)?

4.8. It is amazingly common to hear people say, "Love is not a feeling. Love is an act of will. Love is a deed of helpfulness." The author concedes that there are at least two good intentions behind these statements. What are they?

4.9. But the author thinks it is misleading and inaccurate to talk this way, as though love does not have to have any component of feeling. What are some evidences in the context of 1 Corinthians 13 itself that love does involve feel-ings, including some and excluding others?

4.10. How feelings relate to love can be seen if we look at a living example of genuine love described by Paul in 2 Corinthians 8:1-8. According to this ex-ample of love in the lives of the Macedonian Christians, (a) what is the ultimate source of genuine love? (b) How does this produce love? (c) What does love look like practically? (d) What definition of love emerges from this text?

4.11. The definition of love on page 103 is not quite satisfying to explain the impulse of love. Something is missing. But that "something" is implied two paragraphs later when it says, Love "is first a deeply satisfying experience of the fullness of God's grace, and then a *doubly satisfying experience of sharing* that grace with another person." What impulse is implied in these words that is not explicit in calling love an "overflow"?

4.12. How does 2 Corinthians 9:7 confirm the point that mere acts of help-fulness are not necessarily genuine love?

4.13. Can you state in a few sentences now why the thesis of this chapter included the statement that if you forsake the pursuit of your joy, you cannot love people or please God?

4.14. Another text that gives a real life example of love is 2 Corinthians 1:23-2:4. Show from these verses that when love is abounding between two people, each is not merely seeking the joy of the other but, more than that, is seeking *his own joy* in the joy of the other.

4.15. What does the author mean when he says that if love is the *labor* of Christian Hedonism, it must also be the *leisure* of Christian Hedonism? What passage of Scripture illustrates each of these?

4.16. If love is the overflow of JOY that seeks to expand itself in the joy of others, how can there be weeping and "anguish of heart" in the life of a consis-tently loving person?

4.17. Compare the middle paragraph on page 99 ("Someone no doubt...") and the first indented paragraph on page 108. What words in 1 Corinthians 13:3 and Acts 20:35 make it very hard to accept the common notion that reward is a good *result* of love but a bad *motive*?

4.18. Explain from 1 Peter 5:1-2 and Hebrews 13:17 why it is unloving for a pastor to abandon the pursuit of his joy in the ministry.

4.19. What radical element of Christian Hedonism does Luke 12:33 make explicit?

4.20. In each of the three texts from Hebrews (pp. 111-113) what is the key power of love? If we today want to be as radically loving as were the early Christians and Moses and Jesus, what must we labor to cultivate in our hearts?

4.21. How does the author show in his letter to Ronn (pp. 114ff) that Jesus' pursuit of joy in the cross was not mercenary but was, in fact, infinitely caring of us?

4.22. Is there joy in the conquests of mountain climbing that cost you to lose toes and fingers to frostbite? What might be the counterpart to this strange experience in the moral life? A fuller explanation of this powerful impulse to see our weaknesses overcome is given on pages 119-121. Use this to describe the real dynamic of how love is driven the way a mountain climber is driven.

4.23. One way of making the imaginary dialogue on pages 116-117 real in your own life is to ask, "Do you feel more loved when you are visited in the hospital by someone who comes cheerfully (because they anticipate joy in your encouragement and healing) or by someone who comes dutifully (because it is part of their pastoral job and God's expectation)?

4.24. What do I mean that the nature of a loving act and the hoped for reward must be "organically related"? How is this illustrated in the reward we hope for in Romans 8:29 and Luke 6:35?

5

Scripture: Kindling for Christian Hedonism

5.1. What are several biblical evidences that every day with Jesus is not (in this life) sweeter than the day before?

5.2. If the life of joy in God is not one of steady, unremitting improvement, how would you describe the normal (biblical) Christian life of joy in God?

5.3. If you describe this normal Christian life of joy in God with two or three different metaphors, what role does the Bible play for the Christian in each of these metaphors? For example, if the Christian life is a "journey," you might say the Bible plays the role of road map.

5.4. How would you answer someone who lived by another "holy book" contrary to the Bible and said that its teachings brought them joy and satisfaction?

5.5. Describe four different ways that "the Word of God is your life."

5.6. On pages 125-127 we see that the reformer, "Little Bilney," and the criminal Tokichi Ichii each pointed to a specific word of Scripture that God used to awaken spiritual life. Which texts were these? Did God use a specific verse to do this for you? Can you think of other historical persons who point to one specific word that caused them to be born again?

5.7. If someone comes to you in distress that their faith has wavered and they are full of doubts about the love of God and the reality of Christ and heaven and forgiveness, what might be one of the most helpful things you could do for them? Show from Scripture the basis of your answer.

5.8. What are two verses that show that the link between joy and the word of God is believing that word?

5.9. Since the fruit of the Holy Spirit is joy, we will surely want the fullness of the Spirit's effects in our lives. Develop two different Biblical lines of evidence that filling ourselves with the word is a crucial way to have the fullness of the Spirit and thus the fullness of joy.

5.10. At Bethlehem Baptist Church one of the signs says, "Hope in God." Suppose someone read that sign and said, "How can you obey a command like that? I can't just turn hope on and off in my heart." What might you respond to that person to help him see how to obey that command?

5.11. The Word of God frees. This can be thought about in two ways: 1) we may need freedom from confusion and ignorance about what way to go in life or what to think about an idea; or 2) we may need freedom from some bondage to a pleasure that is wrong and harmful. Explain how the Bible functions in those two different needs to give freedom.

5.12. What are three passages of Scripture that make explicit the link between the Word of God and victory over Satan's power?

5.13. If the Word of God gives and sustains life, if it begets and sustains faith, if it brings the Spirit of God, if it gives and sustains hope, if it makes us free and wiser than our teachers, if it gives assurance of salvation, if it conquers the great enemy Satan, and if it "*rejoices* the heart" (Psalm 19:8), why is it that so many professing Christians give it so little time in their lives? List (if you can!) some things that are more important to do than be in the Word for an extended time each day.

5.14. What helpful insights for prayer and Bible reading did you find in the testimony of George Mueller?

6

Prayer: The Power of Christian Hedonism

6.1. What is the author's answer to the criticism that pursuing pleasure in all of life puts pleasure above God or puts the interests of man above the interests of God? (p.137)

6.2. It is very close to the heart of this book to say, "Our interest and his glory are one" (p. 137). Be sure you can give an account of why this is so.

6.3. Explain from John 14:13 and John 16:24 how Jesus' view of prayer helps support the sentence in question 6.2 that "our interest and God's glory are one." (pp. 137f)

6.4. Why is it that when we pray the way Jesus taught us to we shift glory from ourselves to God? (pp. 137-139)

6.5. In answering the question, "Is prayer self-centered?" the author admits that in all prayer we are seeking our joy, but he says that this is implied in the prayer, "Thy will be done on earth, as it is in heaven." How does that prayer support his claim? (pp. 140f)

6.6. How can prayer be used to make a cuckold out of God and adulteresses out of those who pray? (A "cuckold" is a man whose wife is unfaithful.)

6.7. Express in your own words the explanation why delighting in and praying for things that are not God, does not dishonor God as the all-satisfying source of joy. Let Saint Augustine and C. S. Lewis help you. (pp. 142f)

6.8. In view of his endorsement of desiring things other than God, how does the author interpret the words "There is nothing upon earth that I desire besides thee" from Psalm 73:25? (pp. 143f)

6.9. Prayer calls attention to the surprising fact that it may not honor God to "serve" him. Describe the kind of serving that would dishonor God and cite two or three texts that warn us not to serve God in this way. (p. 144)

6.10. How is God very unlike the gods Bel and Nebo? (p. 145)

6.11. Show from 2 Chronicles 16:9 that God's call into radical discipleship is not a "Help Wanted" ad. (p. 146)

6.12. What would be one example of something you can give to God that won't belittle him as needy? (p. 146)

6.13. How then shall we serve God, if it is so belittling to him to treat him as needing us? Use Matthew 6:24 and 1 Peter 4:11 to justify your answer. (pp. 148f)

6.14. Now get your bearings in the flow of the chapter by reading the paragraph on page 149. Restate what two goals prayer holds together.

6.15. What is the first reason given why prayer leads to fullness of joy? Show how this is based on John 16:20-22.

6.16. "Prayer is a fountain of joy because it is the source of the power to love" (and love is the capstone of joy). The author argues for this by unpacking the logic of John 15:16-17. Be sure you get this (p. 151) and then put the logic in your own words.

6:17. What conception of prayer does the author think is missing from many prayer meetings that make it malfunction? (p. 152)

6.18. Give several Bible verses to show that prayer is designed for advancing the mission of the gospel in the world. (p. 152)

6.19. What will be the final joy of God's people? And how does prayer relate to that? (p. 153)

6.20. One last time, state how prayer holds these two great goals together: your quest for joy and God's zeal for his glory.

7

Money: The Currency of Christian Hedonism

7.1. People often stumble over the statement in 1 Timothy 6:10, "The love of money is the root of all evils." The NIV even paraphrases it very loosely to try to avoid the problem, "The love of money is the root of all *kinds* of evil." There is another way of understanding this sentence that really does take the phrase "all evil" more literally. How does the author state this understanding? How does the love of money relate to "all evil"?

7.2. Paul deplores the "depraved mind" that treats godliness as a means of gain" (1 Timothy 6:5). In opposing this depravity does he attack the motive of gain? What does he do?

7.3. "There is great gain in godliness." That sentence is subject to great misuse. What is the misuse, and how does adding the words "with contentment" protect against that misuse?

7.4. What biblical sentence proves that it is "very profitable not to pursue riches"?

7.5. What similar activities should we *not* confuse with the wrong pursuit of riches? What precisely *is* Paul warning against when he points out the danger of wanting to be rich?

7.6. The first argument (from 1 Timothy 6:7) given on pages 161f (to support the claim that there is great gain in godliness *with contentment*) is that "we brought nothing into the world and we cannot take anything out of the world." But there is an assumption behind this argument without which it would not be compelling. What is the assumption? (Hint: why couldn't someone argue just the opposite: "since 'you can't take it with you,' get as much as you can now and live it up"?)

7.7. A second argument (from 1 Timothy 6:8) to support the claim that there is great gain in godliness *with contentment* is that we can and ought to be happy with the simple necessities of life. In a sentence for each, state the three reasons why it is possible and good for a Christian to be content with the simple necessities of life without needing luxuries?

7.8. Explain from 1 Timothy 6:9-10 why no Christian Hedonist wants to be rich.

7.9. It may sound like the author does not believe in the free market system of economics. But he says he does. In your own words what is the reason he gives?

7.10. From Matthew 6 and Luke 12 explain what Jesus' investment strategy is.

7.11. How practically and specifically do you lay up treasures in heaven by using your money on earth? Give at least two specific biblical supports.

7.12. One scholar objects on page 166 that "You do not live this way for the sake of reward." What are two texts that seem to state exactly the opposite? If you wanted to make this objection be valid, what meaning would you have to give to the word "reward"?

7.13. Why is almsgiving or an act of mercy which is motivated by a desire for the promised reward not unloving or uncaring?

7.14. Explain how the way we use our money can lay hold on eternal life without this being a salvation by works. If we can forfeit our life by the way we use our money, then how is the use of money *not* a way of earning eternal life?

7.15. Explain why there is such a close connection between riches and pride that Paul has to warn the rich "not to be haughty."

7.16. What emotion (according to 1 Timothy 6:17) do riches tend to direct away from God to themselves? Why, according to Psalm 147:11, would this be a great mistake?

7.17. If God promises to "richly furnish us with everything to enjoy" (1 Timothy 6:17), and if he promises to "prosper all that we do" (Psalm 1:3), then why does this not lead to a prosperity teaching which attempts to glorify God by displaying the tokens of the wealth that he has so graciously and powerfully given?

7.18. Why is "wartime lifestyle" a better term than "simple lifestyle"?

7.19. How does the author counsel a person who owns or is thinking of owning an extra "lake home" which sits empty part of the year?

7.20. Why has God given his people in America so much? (Use Ephesians 4:28 and 2 Corinthians 9:8.)

8

Marriage: The Matrix of Christian Hedonism

Ephesians 5:25-30

Husbands, love your wives, as Christ loved the church and gave himself up for her, (26) that he might sanctify her, having cleansed her by the washing of water with the word, (27) that he might present the church to himself in splendor, without spot or wrinkle or any such thing, but that she might be holy and without blemish. (28) Even so husbands should love their wives as their own bodies. He who loves his wife loves himself. (29) For no man ever hates his own flesh, but nourishes and cherishes it, as Christ does the church, (30) because we are members of his body.

8.1. What does the word "matrix" mean?

8.2. Using the text above (Ephesians 5:25-30) express what the aim of Christ's loving self-sacrifice for the Church was. It is stated in two stages. Verse 26 gives one stage and verse 27 gives the next stage. In your own words state why this is an example of Christian Hedonism.

8.3. In verses 29-30 what reason is given why Christ nourishes and cherishes the church? Explain why this is an example of Christian Hedonism.

8.4. How do we know we should call this kind of nourishing and cherishing "love"?

8.5. What is the meaning of love between a husband and a wife in view of these verses and the observations you have just made? How can something that is so driven by the desire for joy be loving toward others?

8.6. How does this definition of love relate to the one given on page 103? Is there any disagreement or tension?

8.7. Why is there no contradiction between Ephesians 5:29 ("No man ever hates his own flesh") and John 12:25 ("He who loves his life loses it, and he who hates his life in this world will keep it for eternal life")? Is Revelation 12:11 ("They loved not their lives even unto death") a contradiction of Ephesians 5:29?

8.8. When Paul says in verse 28, "Husbands should love their wives as they love themselves," he is applying which command of Jesus?

8.9. What is the common modern understanding of this text about self-love which the author thinks is a misunderstanding? What is the proper meaning of self-love according to the author, and its relation to love for others?

8.10. This understanding of self-love implies a rule for the way a husband should love his wife. What is this rule? (pp. 178f)

8.11. Is there an argument in Ephesians 5:25 that would make you think we are on the right track here in thinking about the motivation of love between husbands and wives who are "one flesh"?

8.12. When God said in Genesis 2:18 that it is not good for man to be alone, did he imply that God's own fellowship was insufficient to satisfy Adam? What was it that was not good?

8.13. In Ephesians 5:31 Paul quotes Genesis 2:24, "For this reason a man shall leave his father and mother and be joined to his wife and the two shall become one flesh." Then in verse 32 he says, "This is a great mystery, and I am speaking with reference to Christ and the church." In what sense is marriage a mystery?

8.14. What specific distinct roles for husband and wife does Paul choose to focus on which are implied in the mystery of marriage?

8.15. What do each of these roles correspond to in the relationship between Christ and the church?

8.16. Give two or three reasons why "leadership" is implied in the idea of headship.

8.17. Why does the author define Biblical submission as "disposition to yield and an inclination to follow"?

8.18. Why does the overarching principle of "mutual submission" not rule out the role distinction of the husband as head and the wife as the supporter of that headship?

8.19. The author thinks that in Ephesians 5:22-33 the effect of Christ's redemption is applied to the effects of the Fall on the marriage relationship. These effects are reversed. State the results of the Fall that emerge between men and women in Genesis 3, and how Christ reverses these sinful effects of the Fall.

9

Missions: The Battle Cry of Christian Hedonism

9.1. Many today believe that all people will be saved regardless of what they believe or what they do. Many others believe that any sincere religious faith, whether Christianity or any other, is a sure road to eternal life. But the author argues that people are cut off from eternal life unless the gospel reaches them and they believe. Write a sentence or two in your own words to explain how the following passages of Scripture show that what is at stake in the Christian missionary enterprise is eternal life: Acts 26:16-18; 1 Corinthians 9:22; Acts 13:46; Acts 4:12

9.2. If people cannot be saved without hearing and believing the gospel of Jesus Christ, how can God be just to condemn people who have no access to the gospel because they live among peoples who have never been reached with the gospel?

9.3. Why, in general, do liberal churches and denominations put *little emphasis on frontier missions*?

9.4. Would the author approve of the statement, "We are all missionaries?" Why or why not?

9.5. In Romans 15:23 Paul said, "I no longer have any room for work in these regions." He was referring to the part of the world from Jerusalem northward and westward to the northern part of Greece called Illyricum (Romans 15:19). He even said that in this region he had "fulfilled the gospel of Christ." How can Paul say that there is no more room for work and that he has fulfilled the gospel in an area where there are still thousands of unbelievers who could be converted to Christ and saved from judgment?

9.6. How then would you define "frontier missions"?

9.7. (a) What new insight and emphasis in missions thinking would explain this statement: "The remaining task of Frontier Missions is no longer conceived mainly in geographic terms"? (b) Another way to ask the question would be to ask, When Jesus said, "This gospel will be preached throughout the whole world as a testimony to all nations," why might the English word "nations" be misleading?

9.8. Why, according to Ralph Winter, is World Missions a finishable task, but evangelism is not?

9.9. Even though there is widespread consensus about the identity of the 12,000 people groups in the world and the fact that in the mid 1990s about 10,000 of them are at least penetrated with the gospel, why does Ralph Winter suggest that there may be many more "people groups" than this estimate of 12,000?

9.10. Read over the table on page 195 and then jot down in your own words why this is very good news for Great Commission Christians.

9.11. In a sentence, what, according to David Bryant, is a "World Christian"?

9.12. The story of the Rich Young Ruler from Mark 10:17-31 teaches two powerful incentives for engaging in frontier mission work. The first one is described on pages 197-200. (a) What's the verse in Mark 10 that contains this incentive? (b) But if you read carefully you will see that this incentive really has two distinct parts. Can you put each of these parts in a sentence?

9.13. In what sense does Jesus mean that it is impossible for the Rich Young Ruler to be saved (Mark 10:25-27)?

9.14. The first part of this first incentive is contained also in John 10:16, "I have other sheep that are not of this fold; I must bring them also, and they will heed my voice." There are three clauses in that verse. Take each one and paraphrase it in your own words to make clear how it is a great incentive for hopeful frontier missions.

9.15. How did God use this text to create the Africa Inland Mission?

9.16. The second part of the first incentive found in the story of the Rich Young Ruler is expressed in texts mentioned at the bottom of page 198 and the top of page 199. How do passages like these keep a faithful missionary from boasting in his own heroic courage?

9.17. The second incentive found in the story of the Rich Young Ruler is unfolded on pages 201ff. What *displeased* Jesus about Peter's readiness to sacrifice for Christ when Peter said, "Lo, we have left everything and followed you"?

9.18. What clue is there *in the text* (Mark 10:28-30) that we should *not* take the promise for 100 houses to mean that Christ will make all his obedient disciples wealthy real estate magnates?

9.19. In Mark 10:28-30, is Jesus contradicting the teaching on self-denial in Mark 8:34-35? Peter seemed ready to deny himself to follow Jesus, and Jesus seems to correct him with the promise of reward. What then does he mean by self-denial?

9.20. Read the quote from the missionary David Brainerd on page 203. He shows that there is a good kind of self-love and a bad kind. Put in your own words what the difference is. Then in the very last line of this quote he says "hope of self-interest" is bad. How can hope of self-interest be bad in view of the definition he has just given for the good (regular) self-love?

9.21. What did David Livingstone mean when he said, "I never made a sacrifice" (p. 204)? Chapter ten is written to make sure this question gets answered correctly.

9.22. If our trusted doctor says that we need to spend a week in the hospital for special treatments, we may have to deny ourselves some previously made appointments. We may have to be away from our family. We may have to tolerate some unpleasant smells. But one thing is for sure, we are in the hospital to get well — and to let the doctor show his wisdom and skill. We are *not* there to pay back a debt to the doctor. Daniel Fuller (p. 207) applies this analogy to the missionary (patient) going to the mission field (hospital). What's the point of this analogy? Why do "people who regard themselves as invalids make excellent missionaries"?

9.23. Does William Carey's motto, "Expect great things from God; attempt great things for God," contradict Daniel Fuller's statement above about invalids? Why or why not?

9.24. Why did Elisabeth Elliot not regard the murder of her husband Jim as "a nightmare of tragedy"?

10

Suffering: The Sacrifice of Christian Hedonism

10.1. What is the difference between Paul's answer and the abbot's answer to the question: "Is the Christian life a good life even if it proves to be based on a falsehood in the end?" (pp. 213-215)

10.2. Why does Paul think his life of joy would be pitiable if there were no resurrection from the dead? (p. 215)

10.3. How are persecution and sickness different kinds of suffering? But give an example of how one's obedience to a Christian ministry can result in suffering without persecution. (p. 215)

10.4. What is the common threat in all suffering? (p. 216)

10.5. When we speak of suffering "with Christ" and "for Christ" we usually think of the persecution that was similar to Christ's. But the author says that all suffering in the path of our Christian calling is "with Christ" and "for Christ." Describe two ways that our sufferings can be "with Christ" and two ways our sufferings can be "for Christ" even if it is not from persecution. (p. 216)

10.6. What is Satan's design in all our suffering? (pp. 216-218)

10.7. Give one or two illustrations that show how the suffering of sickness and the suffering of persecution are not always distinguishable. (p. 218)

10.8. When Paul says in 1 Corinthians 15:32, "Let us eat and drink," what does he mean? (pp. 218-219) In view of this, what are we called to in the Christian life?

10.9. When Paul calls suffering a gift (Philippians 1:29), what did he have in mind? How can something so painful be a "gift"? (p. 221)

10.10. What evidence is there that the promises of Jesus that his disciples would suffer also apply to later Christians and not just the original twelve? (pp. 221-222)

10.11. What is God's universal purpose in all the suffering of his children? (p. 222)

10.12. Explain from 2 Corinthians 12:9-10 how suffering can serve to magnify the grace of Christ. (pp. 222-223)

10.13. Show how the illustration of Epaphroditus in Philippians 2:27-30 explains the meaning of Paul's words in Colossians 1:24, "complete what is lacking in the afflictions of Christ." (pp. 224-225)

10.14. Be sure you see *how* Paul intended to "complete what was lacking in the afflictions of Christ." (p. 225)

10.15. Show from Revelation 6:11 that God's intention is to complete the Great Commission through the suffering of his people. (p. 227)

10.16. How does Joseph Tson sum up one key difference between our suffering and Christ's suffering? (p. 230)

10.17. Why does the author think that calling suffering a "sacrifice" in this chapter is *not* a contradiction of the quote from David Livingstone on page 199 where he says, "I never made a sacrifice"? (p. 231)

10.18. From Philippians 3:8 and 1:21,23 explain why Paul's choosing to suffer was still Christian Hedonism. (p. 232)

10.19. Why does cherishing the glory of Christ above all things not allow a person to be indifferent to whether perishing sinners are converted? (p. 232)

10.20. Explain how Christ can be Paul's joy and yet he can also call his converts his joy. (p. 233)

10.21. Why does the author think that it is all but blasphemy to say that the obedience of suffering for Christ may be pursued but not the joy of suffering? (p. 234)

10.22. What is the basis of the joy that Christ commands in suffering according to Matthew 5:11-12? (pp. 234-235)

10.23. What is the reason Paul rejoices in suffering according to Romans 5:3-4? Don't just quote the text. Explain the connections between the parts. (p. 235)

10.24. Show how the logical connection between the two halves of 1 Peter 4:13 teaches that joy in suffering now is the way of attaining joy in the presence of Christ when he comes. (pp. 235-236)

10.25. Explain from Hebrews 11:25-26 why choosing to suffer *the way Moses did* does not glorify our courage, but God's worth. (p. 237)

10.26. If the essence of Christian Hedonism is the truth that "God is most glorified in us when we are most satisfied in him," explain why Christian Hedonism is most vividly expressed when God's people rejoice in suffering for the sake of the Name. (p. 238)

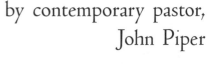